Prince—Is Back On Top, The Man, The Artist

Prince—Is Back On Top, The Man, The Artist

IN HIS OWN WORDS

Jel D. Lewis (Jones)

Copyright © 2006 by Jel D. Lewis (Jones)

ISBN 10:	Hardcover	1-4257-3214-3
	Softcover	1-4257-3213-5
ISBN 13:	Hardcover	978-1-4257-3214-1
	Softcover	978-1-4257-3213-4

All rights reserved. No part of this book may be reproduced or transmitted in any form or by any means, electronic or mechanical, including photocopying, recording, or by any information storage and retrieval system, without permission in writing from the copyright owner.

This book was printed in the United States of America.

To order additional copies of this book, contact:
Xlibris Corporation
1-888-795-4274
www.Xlibris.com
Orders@Xlibris.com
35961

Contents

Chapter One	About Prince	9
Chapter Two	Vanity 6	17
Chapter Three	Apollonia 6	22
Chapter Four	Morris Day	25
Chapter Five	Prince and the Revolution Band	31
Chapter Six	Behind The Name Change	34
Chapter Seven	The Movie—Purple Rain—1984	43
Chapter Eight	The Movie—Under The Cherry Moon—1986	49
Chapter Nine	The Movie—Graffiti Bridge—1990	58
Chapter Ten	Prince First Interview Central High School February 16, 1976	64
Chapter Eleven	News Chain of Events	66
Chapter Twelve	Rolling Stone Interview Prince By Bill Adler February 19, 1981	81
Chapter Thirteen	The Secret Life of America's Sexiest One-man band Rolling Stone Magazine By Debbie Miller—1983	84
Chapter Fourteen	Prince, The Pauper Rolling Stone Magazine By Debbie Miller—1983	87
Chapter Fifteen	Black Lace Bikini Underwear Rolling Stone Magazine By Debbie Miller—1983	91
Chapter Sixteen	What Time Is It? Rolling Stone Magazine By Debbie Miller—1983	94
Chapter Seventeen	Rolling Stone—April 26, 1985 Prince Talks By Neal Karlen	97
Chapter Eighteen	MTV Interview Prince By Michael Shore—1985	105
Chapter Nineteen	Prince Interview	113

Chapter Twenty	Prince In The News Prince's Resurrection Rolling Stone Magazine By David Wild August 25, 1988	124
Chapter Twenty-One	Rolling Stone Magazine Interview Prince By Neal Karlen—1990	127
Chapter Twenty-Two	Prince In The News Prince Previews European Show By David Fricke June 14, 1990	139
Chapter Twenty-Three	ACT I—San Francisco April 10, 1993	141
Chapter Twenty-Four	ACT II—Chanhassen, Minnesota July 12, 1993	144
Chapter Twenty-Five	Prince In The News The Elusive Prince Returns Triumphant Rolling Stone Magazine By Alan Light—1993	147
Chapter Twenty-Six	Prince Retires—Maybe Rolling Stone Magazine By Michael Goldberg—1993	150
Chapter Twenty-Seven	Vibe Magazine Interview Prince Monte Carlo May 2, 1994	153
Chapter Twenty-Eight	Time Out Interview Prince By Peter Paphides March 1995	159
Chapter Twenty-Nine	Prince In The News Stories from Saint Paul Pioneer Press By Bruce Orwall—1995	165
Chapter Thirty	Esquire Gentleman Interview Prince By Julie Baumgold Fall, 1995	177
Chapter Thirty-One	Forbes Magazine Interview Prince By Joshua Levine—1996	183
Chapter Thirty-Two	USA Today Interview Prince By Edna Gundersen November 12, 1996	186
Chapter Thirty-Three	New York Times Interview Prince By Jon Pareles November 17, 1996	190
Chapter Thirty-Four	MSN Music Centeral Interview Prince By Edna Gunderson—1996	196
Chapter Thirty-Five	Hello Magazine Interview Prince (UK) By Solange Plamondon December 1996 Issue	202
Chapter Thirty-Six	Minneapolis Associated Press Stories— March 1997	206

Chapter Thirty-Seven	Spike Lee Interview Prince The Artist—1997 208
Chapter Thirty-Eight	About Spike Lee 216
Chapter Thirty-Nine	Harper's Bazaar By Eve Mac Sweeney May 1997 223
Chapter Forty	AOL Live Interview Prince July 22, 1997 227
Chapter Forty-One	Vegetarian Times Interview Prince October 1997 236
Chapter Forty-Two	Yahoo Internet Life Interview Prince By Ben Greenman October 1997 240
Chapter Forty-Three	El Pais Spain Interview Prince By Bruno Galindo December 15, 1997 245
Chapter Forty-Four	ABC Good Morning America Interview Prince By Kevin Newman 251
Chapter Forty-Five	Guitar World Interview Prince By Serge Simonart October 1998 257
Chapter Forty-Six	Bass Player Interview Prince By Karl Coryat November 1999 264
Chapter Forty-Seven	New York Times Interview Prince By Anthony De Curtis—1999 272
Chapter Forty-Eight	Minneapolis Star Tribune Interview Prince By Vickie Gilmer—1999 276
Chapter Forty-Nine	USA Today Interview Prince By Steve Jones April 13, 1999 280
Chapter Fifty	Entertainment Weekly Interview Prince By Tom Sinclair May 28, 1999 283
Chapter Fifty-One	Reviews Of 3121 285
Chapter Fifty-Two	The Y-life Interview Prince Yahoo! Internet Life—June 2001 By Bilge Ebiri 292
Chapter Fifty-Three	Rolling Stone Interview Prince By Anthony Decurtis—2004 301
Chapter Fifty-Four	CBS Interview Prince By Co-anchor Rene Syler New York—July 20, 2004 305
Chapter Fifty-Five	Ebony Interview Prince By Lynn Norment September 2004 308

Chapter Fifty-Six	Entertainment Weekly Interview Prince By Jeff Jensen April 23, 2004 313
Chapter Fifty-Seven	Newsweek Interview Prince By Lorraine Ali Party Like It's 2004 320
Chapter Fifty-Eight	The Observer Interview Prince February 19, 2006... 323
Chapter Fifty-Nine	Lyrics To Some Of Prince's Song 329

Chapter One

ABOUT PRINCE

PRINCE ROGERS NELSON was born in Minneapolis, Minnesota at Mount Sinai Hospital on June 7, 1958 to John L. Nelson and Mattie Shaw. John L. Nelson played in a jazz trio The Prince Rogers Trio, hence Prince's birth name. There are a number of myths regarding Prince's ethnicity and gender, some spread by Prince himself. The most pervasive is that he is the child of a black father and white mother, a myth later bolstered by the cult film *Purple Rain* starring Prince and fellow artists Morris Day of The Time, and Apollonia. In more recent years, it has been noted in numerous publications, including "The Chiq Files", published by Gwendolyn Kelly Boyer, that Prince's parents are in fact African-American. His mother had Italian ancestry. After the birth of his sister, Tika Evene in 1960, Prince saw his parents gradually drift apart. Prince's parents formally separated and he had a troubled relationship with his stepfather causing him to run away from home. He lived briefly with his father, who bought him his first guitar. Later, Prince moved in with a neighborhood family, the Andersons, and became friends with their son, Andre Anderson (later called André Cymone).

Prince and Anderson joined Prince's cousin Charles Smith in a band called Grand Central, formed in junior high school. Initially his involvement was just part of a mainly instrumental band that played clubs and parties in the Minneapolis area. As time went by and Prince's musical knowledge broadened he found himself dictating the arrangements to the rest of the band. Before long he had become the band's frontman. By the time Prince had entered high school, Grand Central evolved into Champagne and started playing original music already drawing on a range of influences including Sly Stone, James Brown, Jimmy Page and Jimi Hendrix.

In 1976, he started working on a demo tape with producer Chris Moon in a Minneapolis studio. He also had the patronage of Owen Husney, to whom Moon introduced him, allowing him to produce a quality demo. Husney started contacting major labels and ran a campaign promoting Prince as a star of the future, resulting in a bidding war eventually won by Warner Brothers Records. They were the only label to give Prince creative control of his songs and offered him a contract.

Pepe Willie, husband of Prince's cousin, was an influential presence in Prince's early career. Willie acted as mentor and manager, along with Husney, for Prince in the Grand Central days, and employed Prince in the studio for his own recordings. In 1977, Willie formed 94 East, a band with Marcy Ingvoldstad and Kristie Lazenberry. Willie enlisted the talents of Prince and Andre Cymone as session musicians for their studio recordings and in 1986 released the re-recorded tracks (except for Prince and Cymone's parts) from 1975-1977 as *Minneapolis Genius*. In 1995, the original recordings with Prince and Cymone were released by Willie as *94 East featuring Prince, Symbolic Beginning*.

Prince's first album for Warner Bros, released in 1978, was titled *For You*. The majority of the album was written and performed by Prince, except for the song *Soft and Wet* (Music by Prince; Lyrics by Prince and C. Moon). Tommy Vicari was the Executive Producer in *For You*. Starting with *For You*, one can read in all of Prince's albums the now ubiquitous legend: Produced, Arranged, Composed and Performed by Prince. Prince spent twice his initial advance recording the first album, which sold modestly, making the bottom reaches of the Billboard 200, while the single "Soft and Wet" performed well on the R&B charts. In the album *For You*, Prince used *Prince's Music Co.* for publishing his songs.

By 1979, Prince had recruited his first backing band with Cymone on bass, Gayle Chapman and Matt Fink on keyboards, Bobby Z on drums and Dez Dickerson on guitar. Prince intentionally enlisted a multi-racial, mixed-gender group, much like the backing band of one of Prince's most salient influences, Sly Stone. He recorded his second, self-titled album still mostly on his own, which made the Billboard 200 and contained two R&B hits in "Why You Wanna Treat Me So Bad?" and "I Wanna Be Your Lover." These two R&B hits were performed on January 26, 1980 on the TV show *American Bandstand* with his first backing band. For his second album, Prince used *Ecnirp Music—BMI* for publishing his songs, which he would also use for the album *Dirty Mind*.

Prince first attracted attention for the colorful clothes he put on his 5 foot, 2 inch frame. He wore high-heeled shoes and boots, and when questioned by the press he remarked he liked the way he looked in them. In his early years, he liked to dress provocatively. He also was known to strongly flaunt and express his sexuality while on stage and in his music, which had people questioning his sexual orientation early on. This bought him some trouble as an opening act for The Rolling Stones' two Los Angeles Coliseum shows in 1981, where he was infamously pelted with garbage whilst wearing underwear and a trenchcoat. Prince was actually booed off the stage that night, a clip of which was later used by Prince for his "Pop Life" single in 1985 (if you listen, you can actually hear one member of the audience yell, "Throw the bum out!")

In 1980, Prince released *Dirty Mind*, a solo effort released using the original demos. On stage, Lisa Coleman replaced Chapman in the band, who felt the sexually explicit lyrics and stage antics of Prince's concerts conflicted with her religious beliefs. *Dirty Mind* was particularly notable for its sexually explicit material.

Prince supported Rick James in a 1980 tour with the label "punk funk" being applied to both artists, although it didn't sit comfortably with Prince. He recorded the album *Controversy*, released in 1981, with the single of the same name making international charts for the first time. In October of 1981, Prince perfomed "Partyup" on Saturday Night Live. Starting with the album *Controversy*, Prince used *Controversy Music—ASCAP* for publishing his songs, which he would use for his following sixteen records until *Emancipation* came out in 1996.

Prince also wrote, produced, and in some instances performed on, the debut album for The Time, containing former members of Flyte Tyme, including frontman Morris Day. In the coming decade, Prince would also collaborate with Vanity (of Vanity 6), Apollonia (of Apollonia 6) and Sheila E. He also composed material, using former bandmates as another outlet for his prolific output. He also wrote hits for artists such as Sheena Easton and The Bangles and his songs would be covered in hit versions by artists as diverse as Chaka Khan, Tom Jones with The Art of

Noise, and Sinéad O'Connor. O'Connor's cover of a song Prince initially wrote for The Family, "Nothing Compares 2 U," was a huge commercial success in 1990.

Prince was backed in the 80s by The Revolution, and in the 90s by the New Power Generation. He also worked on different occasions with famous jazz and funk musicians, such as Miles Davis, Larry Graham, George Clinton, and Maceo Parker. Throughout his career, Prince has also recorded with Ani DiFranco, Madonna, Kate Bush, Rosie Gaines, Carmen Electra, Gwen Stefani, Chuck D, Angie Stone, Chaka Khan, and Sheryl Crow.

In 1982 Prince released the *1999* double-album which proved to be a breakthrough album both in the U.S. and internationally, selling over three million copies. The title track was a protest about nuclear proliferation and become his first top ten hit internationally. With "Little Red Corvette" he joined Michael Jackson and Lionel Richie as part of the first wave of black artists on MTV and "Delirious" also went top ten on the Billboard Hot 100. The album was placed at number six in The Village Voice's annual Pazz & Jop critics poll. Stevie Nicks related a story in a television interview that she had come up with her 1983 song "Stand Back" after being inspired by the synthesizer part in "Little Red Corvette." When it was time to record the song, it happened that Prince was in Los Angeles near her recording studio. She called his people and soon afterwards Prince came by the studio, sat down at the synthesizer, and played the song-opening riff.

"Purple Rain" is a power ballad by Prince and the The Revolution. It was his third US single (second UK) and title track from the legendary 1984 album *Purple Rain*. The song is quite emotional and combines elements of rock and roll, pop and gospel music. It won the Oscar for Best Original Score in 1984.

The song was recorded live at the Minneapolis club First Avenue in 1983. The performance was the live debut of Wendy Melvoin, and also netted the final three songs of the *Purple Rain* album, although the songs would undergo studio overdubs later. Interestingly, "Purple Rain" contained an extra verse about money that was wisely edited out, as it diluted the emotional impact of the song.

"Purple Rain" opens with a lone guitar quickly followed by live drumming and a prominent organ, evoking images of church gospel music. Three verses are followed by a singalong chorus, with a building emotional delivery. After the final chorus, a searing guitar-solo takes over the song, delivering just as much impact as the lyrics. The song ends with a gentle piano solo and orchestral strings.

The emotional lyrics have multiple meanings; on the surface, they seem to be an apology from one lover to another, though on a deeper level, they become more of a spiritual allegory. It is a theory that "Purple Rain" is a metaphor for heaven, inspired by the testimonies of a woman who died on the operating table that the afterlife is full of falling purple rain.

The song is a staple of Prince's live performances. He has played it on nearly every tour since 1984, except for a period after his name change when he avoided his older hits for a few years. The song reached #2 in the U.S., and is Prince's signature song.

This song has been covered by dozens of other artists ranging from popular artists of various genres such as Tori Amos, LeAnn Rimes and The Waterboys to jazz and orchestral versions.

The B-Side, "God" is much more overtly religious number (Prince's most religious to date), recalling the book of Genesis. The song also features extensive vocal experimentation. Towards the end, Prince mentions "The Dance Electric", which was a song given to former band member André Cymone. In the UK, the 12" Single also included an instrumental of "God", from which an edited portion appears in the *Purple Rain* film.

Purple Rain (in conjunction with the film of the same name) sold over thirteen million copies in the U.S. and spent twenty-four consecutive weeks at the top of the Billboard 200. The film, while dismissed by humorist-critic Joe Queenan as "sexist, juvenile, and moronic," grossed over $80 million in the United States alone. However, *Purple Rain* would prove to be Prince's only cinematic success. Although Prince would later direct and star in *Under The Cherry Moon* (1986) and *Graffiti Bridge* (1990), both films were met with public indifference and critical derision. Two songs from *Purple Rain*, "When Doves Cry" and "Let's Go Crazy" would both top the U.S. singles charts and were hits around the world, while the title track would go to number two on the Billboard Hot 100. Simultaneously, Prince held the spot of number one film, number one single, and number one album in the U.S. Prince won the Academy Award for Best Original Score for Purple Rain, and the album ranks in the top 100 of *Rolling Stone's* 500 Greatest Albums of All Time, released in late 2003. When she overheard her twelve-year-old daughter, Karenna, playing "Darling Nikki" Tipper Gore founded the Parents Music Resource Center, which has spurred the use of "explicit lyric" stickers and imprints on album covers.

In 1985, after the U.S. *Purple Rain* Tour, Prince gave up live performances and making videos on the release of *Around the World in a Day*, which went to the top of the U.S. album charts for three weeks. Prince's ban on videos ended as the album stalled in the charts with a video for "Raspberry Beret" which reached number two on the Billboard Hot 100.

In 1986, Prince released the album *Parade* as a soundtrack to the film *Under The Cherry Moon*. The album went to number three on the Billboard 200 album chart and number two on the R&B album charts. The first single, "Kiss," would top the Billboard Hot 100. At the same time, "Manic Monday" by The Bangles reached number two on the Hot 100, which Prince had written under the pseudonym "Christopher." Following the film and album, Prince returned to touring with a stripped-down show.

Some of Prince's music mixes spirituality and sensuality. "I Would Die 4 U," refers to Jesus. "The Cross," from *Sign "☮" the Times*, is a stronger reference to Prince's Christian beliefs. *Sign "☮" the Times*, released in 1987 as a double album, reached the top 10 of the Billboard 200 and achieved perhaps the greatest critical acclaim of his career, topping the annual Pazz & Jop critics poll, and reaching the top 100 of *Rolling Stone's* 500 Greatest Albums of All Time list.

Following the album, Prince launched the *Sign "☮" the Times* Tour in Europe. At the end of the last tour Prince disbanded his long-time performance band, known since the release of the movie and album *Purple Rain* as The Revolution, and parted ways with Wendy Melvoin, Lisa Coleman, Bobby "Z" Rivkin, and Mark Brown (Brown Mark). His follow-up live performance band retained Matt Fink on keyboards, and added Boni Boyer on keyboards, Sheila E on drums, Levi Seacer, Jr. on bass, and Miko Weaver on guitar. In 1987, a live concert film was shot of the *Sign "☮" the Times* Tour in Rotterdam and Antwerp. Portions were re-recorded and the performances mimed in the soundstage of his newly-opened Paisley Park Studios complex in Chanhassen, Minnesota. Housing three complete recording studios, and a complete soundstage for performances and video production, the studios have been Prince's playground since their opening. Situated near his home in Minnesota, Paisley Park has allowed Prince to record at the drop of a hat.

1987 saw the potential for two of pop's biggest stars coming together to perform a duet. Michael Jackson talked with Prince about performing a duet together for the title track of his new album *Bad*. Prince liked the idea, seeing as Jackson was his main rival in pop stardom, so he agreed to it. However, Jackson and Prince ended up having creative differences in the lyrics and beats for the song. Finally, Prince left the project when he thought Jackson wasn't making the song dark enough. Jackson ended up cutting the title track for the album on his own, and it went to number one on the charts.

Also In 1987, Prince recorded *The Black Album*, a funk-oriented album whose erotically-charged lyrics were considered so blatant that it was not officially released. The album circulated through the bootleg underground music world until it was finally given an official release in 1994. The 1988 album *Lovesexy* was Prince's spiritual answer to the dark message of *The Black Album*. *Lovesexy* was a disappointment in its chart performance, only reaching number eleven on the Billboard 200. The *Lovesexy* Tour in the

U.S. also proved to be commercial disappointment. Prince lost money as dates failed to sell out. Prince recouped his losses with the European and Japanese legs of the tour.

In 1989, Prince would record the soundtrack for *Batman*, which would return him to the top of the U.S. album charts, with the single and worldwide hit "Batdance" reaching the top of the Billboard Hot 100. Prince next released the film sequel to *Purple Rain*, titled *Graffiti Bridge*, which performed poorly at the box office. The soundtrack featured Prince and other artists such as Tevin Campbell, Mavis Staples of the Staple Singers, and Morris Day and The Time. It would reach a chart peak of number six in the U.S. and number one in the UK.

The *Diamonds and Pearls* album in 1991 gave Prince album charts success with the song "Cream" giving him his fifth U.S. number one single. *Diamonds and Pearls* also marked the debut of the New Power Generation featuring rapper Tony M, Rosie Gaines on vocals, Michael Bland on drums, Levi Seacer and Kirk Johnson on guitar, Sonny T on bass, and Tommy Barbarella on keyboards.

Having mysteriously thanked Kate Bush in the credits of his Diamonds And Pearls album, Prince worked on Bush's 1993 album, *The Red Shoes*. Collaborating chiefly on the song "Why Should I Love You," Prince added bass, guitar, keyboards, his vocals and other arrangements to the mix. This would be the final "Prince" credit, until 2000. Kate Bush reciprocated in 1996 and is featured on background vocals on the *Emancipation* track, "My Computer."

Prince's twelfth album was titled "Symbol," dubbed by critics as *The Love Symbol Album*. It reached the top ten of the U.S. album charts. In 1993, he would change his name to Symbol (often represented in ASCII text as O(+>. The symbol is said to be a melding of the symbols for male and female. Due to Prince's (Symbol) being unpronounceable, he was often referred to as "The artist formerly known as Prince," "TAFKAP," or simply "The Artist." In 1993, at the request of Warner Bros., Prince released a 3-CD greatest hits compilation entitled *The Hits/The B-Sides*. The first two discs were also sold separately as *The Hits 1* and *The Hits 2*. In addition to featuring the majority of Prince's hit singles (with the exception of "Batdance," which was strangely omitted), *The Hits* includes an array of previously hard-to-find recordings, notably B-sides spanning the majority of Prince's career, as well as a handful of previously unreleased tracks, such as the Revolution-recorded "Power Fantastic." A new song, "Peach," was chosen as a promotional single to accompany the album. Unfortunately, neither the album nor single performed as well on the charts as Prince and Warner Bros. would have hoped. To this day, however, *The Hits* remains the closest thing to a definitive overview of Prince's musical output from 1978 to 1993.

Prince Controlled Corporations

Paisley Park Enterprises:
Prince's main business, it owns Paisley Park Studios in Chanhassen. Paisley Park Enterprises also handles Prince's recording contract with Warner Bros. Records, his publishing royalties and his work producing records for other artists. Recently acquired the Los Angeles version of the Glam Slam nightclub.

PRN Productions:
The company that handles transactions related to Prince's touring.

NPG Records:
The independent record label that Prince has recently launched in opposition to his contract with Warner Bros. Records. It has two releases so far: the single "The Most Beautiful Girl in the World" by Prince and "1-800-New-Funk," a compilation of artists on the NPG roster.

Paisley Park Retail:
The Company that owns and operates the New Power Generation stores in Uptown Minneapolis and at the Mall of America. Also sells Prince-related merchandise via an 800-phone line.

Heaven and Earth:
The Minnesota Corporation that owns and operates the 4-year-old Glam Slam nightclub in downtown Minneapolis. Gilbert Davison, a former Prince bodyguard who is also the former president of Paisley Park Enterprises, controls the corporation. Most of the start-up funding was paid for or arranged by Paisley Park Enterprises, which has no ownership interest in Heaven & Earth.

Chapter Two

VANITY 6

VANITY 6 WAS A female vocal trio assembled by Prince in the early 1980s. They released one album, which blended the sounds of pop, New Wave, dance music, R&B and funk.

In 1981, Prince presented his high school girlfriend Susan Moonsie, his wardrobe mistress and Boston native Brenda Bennett and his personal assistant Jamie Shoop with an idea: Prince, himself a rising musical star, suggested that his three female friends form a girl group that would be called "The Hookers."

Ideally to Prince, the three women would perform in lingerie and sing sensual songs with lyrics about sex and fantasy. The original trio recorded a few demos before Prince met Denise Matthews, a nude model and Canadian B-movie actress, in January of 1982. Prince was so taken by Matthews' charisma that he decided that she would be the perfect front-woman for his "Hookers" project. Around this time, Prince and Matthews began a romantic relationship. With Matthews' arrival, Shoop bowed out of the group. Prince suggested that Matthews use the stage name "Vagina." She refused this idea, and instead took up the name "Vanity."

With the new trio finalised, Prince renamed the group Vanity 6 (the 6 represented the group's breast count). Keeping with Prince's initial "Hooker" concept, the women were photographed wearing lingerie and high heels, and were written provocative songs to sing (although within the album credits, group members were sometimes given sole writing credits). Their first single, "He's So Dull," did not do much on the charts, but did appear in the film *National Lampoon's Vacation*.

The second single "Nasty Girl" was a hit on both the US R&B chart and US Dance chart (where it hit number one), and it also made an appearance on the Bubbling Under Hot 100 Singles chart.

"Nasty Girl" still has lasting significance to this day, having been recently covered in a house music style by Inaya Day. The third single "Drive Me Wild" was another minor hit. Videos were shot for all three singles. The one and only released Vanity 6 album was eventually certified gold. The group opened up on the Triple Threat Tour, between 1982 and 1983, which also featured The Time and Prince, as the headliner.

To the other group members' dismay, Prince chose Vanity to pose with him for a Richard Avedon photograph used on the cover of an issue of *Rolling Stone* magazine. The magazine issue with Prince and Vanity on the cover also contained a two-page Avedon photo of Vanity 6.

In 1983, Vanity recorded a demo for a new song, "Sex Shooter," and started training for her lead role in *Purple Rain* opposite Prince. Prior to the shooting of the movie, Vanity decided to leave the Prince camp later in 1983. Many reasons were given for her sudden split with him, including money, the end of their romantic relationship, and most importantly, having been offered a lucrative solo offer from Motown Records.

Vanity was replaced in *Purple Rain* by Patty Kotero, who would later use the stage name Apollonia. She also inherited the lead role in Vanity 6, which was renamed Apollonia 6, alongside Bennett and Moonsie. The new trio recorded one album in 1984 that went on to outsell the Vanity 6 album, mainly on the strength of Apollonia's newfound fame, thanks to her movie role and its popularity.

In the years since the group's breakup, Matthews renounced her Vanity persona and music and became a born again Christian. Susan Moonsie married actor David Garfield on December 29, 1988. David died on November 24, 1994. Source: Wikipedia, the free encyclopedia

Album Credits

Vanity 6 released one self-titled album in 1982. Music was provided by The Time and it was produced by "The Starr Company," one of many Prince pseudonyms. All three women shared lead and background vocal duties. The album was released by Warner Brothers Records and is long out-of-print.

1. "Nasty Girl" (lead vocal: Vanity, writer: Vanity)
2. "Wet Dream" (lead vocal: Vanity, writers: Vanity 6)
3. "Drive Me Wild" (lead vocal: Susan, writer: Susan)
4. "He's So Dull" (lead vocal: Vanity, writers: Dez Dickerson and Vanity)
5. "If a Girl Answers (Don't Hang Up)" (lead vocal: Vanity and Brenda, writers: Vanity 6 and Terry Lewis. The "other woman" rap is speculated to be performed by either Lewis or Prince.)
6. "Make-Up" (lead vocal: Susan, writer: Susan)
7. "Bite the Beat" (lead vocal: Brenda, writers: Brenda and Jesse Johnson)
8. "3 X 2 = 6" (lead vocal: Vanity, writer: Vanity)

Music Videos

- Nasty Girl
- He's So Dull
- Drive Me Wild

Trivia

- Vinyl copies of the album were pressed with "Side 1" and "Side 6" on the label.
- Members of the group (Bennett in particular) also provided backing vocals on Prince albums.
- "17 Days," the B-side to Prince's "When Doves Cry," was originally to be recorded by Vanity 6 for their second album. The demo version of the song ended up being released by Prince, and Bennett's background vocals are still on the recording.
- "Sex Shooter," also planned for the second album, was released by Apollonia 6.
- Ironically, in 1982, Vanity 6's "Nasty Girl" was knocked out of number one on the Hot Dance Music/Club Play chart by Prince's "1999."

Vanity 6: Denise Katrina Matthews:

Denise Katrina Matthews was born January 4, 1959 in Niagara Falls, Ontario, Canada and is also known as Denise Smith. Denise had a troubled childhood: her mother left the family when she was just a little girl, and Denise says she was raised by an abusive father who would beat her. When Denise met Prince in the early '80s, he was a rising star and she was an unknown actress and model. They met after Denise had given some lyrics to Prince's manager, who passed her work on to Prince. Prince and Denise began an intense love affair soon after they met. Prince decided to put together an all-girl singing group, with Denise as the star of the group. Prince toyed with idea of calling the group Hookers. It was also rumored that Prince originally wanted Denise's stage name to be Vagina. But realizing those names would be too controversial, Denise was given the name Vanity and her group was called Vanity 6.

The group was all about sex appeal. Vanity 6's biggest hit was a song called "Nasty Girl." Vanity 6's first and only album was a modest success and it wasn't long before Vanity decided she wanted a solo career. Prince and Vanity split up. After breaking up with Prince, Vanity released two solo albums, which were minor hits. She also starred in some movies, including "The Last Dragon" and "Action Jackson," none of which were major box office hits. In the late '80s, Vanity started dating Nikki Sixx, bass player for Motley Crue. In the Motley Crue tell-all book "The Dirt," Nikki said he and Vanity often freebased cocaine together and that Vanity would play mind games with him. Although it was reported in the media that Nikki and Vanity were engaged, Nikki now claims they were never officially engaged and that Vanity would only say they were engaged when she was high on cocaine. Vanity cheekily said in interviews that after she married Nikki, she would be Vanity Sixx. But the relationship didn't last and except for the occasional acting role, Vanity's career as an entertainer slowed down significantly.

In the mid 90s, Vanity became a born-again Christian and said she no longer wanted to be known as Vanity but as Denise. But, Denise gave interviews to the media about herself, and in many of the interviews she said she was disgusted by her past in the entertainment business. According to Nikki Sixx in the book "The Dirt," Vanity lost a kidney and had hearing and eyesight problems because of her drug abuse. In a documented TV interview, Denise admitted that she had abused cocaine when she was Vanity and after becoming a born-again Christian, she said she burned or threw away many of her possessions that reminded her of Vanity. In 1995, Denise married pro football player Anthony Smith after a month-long courtship. Denise said in a Jet magazine interview that as soon as she met

Anthony, God told her that Anthony was destined to be her husband. But the marriage didn't last and it ended in divorce. She has reportedly vowed to never work in the entertainment industry again, and according to the Internet Movie Database, one of Denise's recent occupations has been as a public relations director for the Genesis Technology Group. Denise, who is now an evangelist who gives sermons around the U.S., has written an autobiography called "Blame It On Vanity," and it will reportedly be published sometime in 2002/3. Her decision to publish her autobiography indicates that Denise hasn't retired from the public eye. Today, Denise remains devoted to Christianity and spends a lot of time in church. *Source: TV.com*

Vanity 6—Brenda Bennett:

Brenda Bennett is an American singer from Boston, Massachusetts, USA who married Prince's set-designer Roy Bennett, and then became Prince's "wardrobe mistress". Prince gave her a "tough-girl, cigarette-smoking" persona and enlisted her in a girlgroup that he was attempting to create, Vanity 6 in 1982.

That group broke up a year later due to the departure of its lead singer Vanity, after only minor success. But Bennett stuck around for its reincarnation, with a new lead singer, as Apollonia 6 in 1984. Bennett's image in both of the groups was that of the bad girl: she smoked and had the most attitude. She also had a part in the film *Purple Rain* alongside the group's lead singer Apollonia.

Vanity 6—Susan Moonsie:

Susan Moonsie from Minneapolis was Prince's High School girlfriend. She became a member of Vanity 6 in 1982. Susan was given a "teenage Lolita" image by Prince and he knocked her age back to 16 for shock value. Susan and Brenda joined Patty Kotero as Apollonia 6 in 1984 while filming *Purple Rain*. In addition to 'Private Joy', Prince's hit "When Doves Cry" was inspired by his relationship with Susan. She married actor David Garfield on December 29, 1988. David passed away November 24, 1994

Chapter Three

APOLLONIA 6

APOLLONIA 6 WAS A Prince-created 1980s trio of female singers that was a continuation of the previous group, Vanity 6. After a number of disputes with Prince, Denise Matthews, also known as Vanity, the lead singer of Prince-created Vanity 6, fled the Prince entourage in 1983 to pursue solo endeavors recording with Motown Records and acting in films. She left open an acting position for the role written for her by Prince in the film *Purple Rain*.

After a frantic casting call, the film's director met actress and model Patricia Kotero. Renamed by Prince as "Apollonia", Kotero stepped into Vanity's role in the film *Purple Rain*, as well as in the fragmented group, Vanity 6. The other two members of Vanity 6, Brenda Bennett and Susan Moonsie, joined Apollonia and reformed the group as Apollonia 6 for the film and one album. During this time it was rumored that Apollonia and

Prince were romantically involved with one another, but it was later revealed that Apollonia was actually married. Her "relationship" with Prince had been more of a PR stunt for the film than anything serious.

Apollonia 6 only had one hit with "Sex Shooter" in 1984, but their album outsold its Vanity 6 predecessor and went platinum on the strength of the film and Apollonia's newfound popularity.

Prince had originally intended his classic tracks "Manic Monday" (later recorded by The Bangles), "17 Days" (later used as the B-side to "When Doves Cry"), and "The Glamorous Life" (recorded by Sheila E. in 1984) for the *Apollonia 6* album but he soon lost interest in the project when he became convinced that Apollonia was only there to fulfill her job's obligations and would not be continuing with his group after her contractual obligations to completing the film and one album were fulfilled. Apollonia 6 were slated to open the *Purple Rain* tour with Prince and Sheila E., but that idea was scrapped after the group returned from a promotional tour of Europe.

After the group's demise, Apollonia continued working on TV shows such as *Falcon Crest* and in B-movies for the next decade. She even released a solo album to lackluster success in 1988. The main speculation for the album's failure was that Apollonia tried too hard to give the impression of change; she adopted a more pop/California sound in place of her signature R&B/funk sound that had been successfully established for her formerly by Prince.

Vanity 6—Patricia Kotero—Lead Singer, Matthews Replacement

Patricia Kotero was born on August 2, 1959 in Santa Monica, California, Apollonia Kotero is a swimsuit model, actress and singer. She joined Prince's entourage after the departure of Vanity, Denise Matthews, as lead in the film *Purple Rain* and as lead-singer of recording group Vanity 6.

Kotero had taken part in nationwide audition to find a replacement for Vanity before being cast by Prince in the role that had originally been given to Vanity. It was at this time that Prince gave Kotero the stagename Apollonia and she also inherited Vanity's former lead role in Prince's girl group, with original members Brenda Bennett and Susan Moonsie. *Purple Rain* eventually became a huge success and Apollonia attained overnight stardom.

The newly renamed Apollonia 6 released one album in October, 1984 and released the hit single "Sex Shooter". The band became famous for appearing on stage in lingerie only. Although the album is credited to a producer named Jamie Starr, it has always been obvious that the album was completely produced by Prince himself.

Apollonia had originally recorded a version of the song "Manic Monday" for the 1984 Apollonia 6 album. Written by Prince as well, the song would later become a worldwide hit single for the girl group The Bangles. It was rumored that Prince had lost interest in the Apollonia 6 project and therefore removed several hit singles from their album (shortly before its release): namely "Manic Monday," "The Glamorous Life" (which instead ended up on the debut album of drummer Sheila E, and "Take Me With U" (the duet Apollonia performed with Prince, which ended up on the *Purple Rain* soundtrack album instead). "Take Me With U" is Apollonia's highest charting single, reaching #25 on the Top-40 chart in the U.S.

Apollonia left the Prince camp in 1985 to pursue a role on television in *Falcon Crest* (1986). She was allowed to appear under her own stage name "Apollonia" on the show and also performed several solo songs, none of which would later be released (one of the songs, which was often played and referred to on the show was a title called "Red Light Romeo," which was written by US songwriter Jon Lind who had penned the US No 1 hit "Crazy For You" for Madonna). Kotero stayed on the show for 10 consecutive weeks, playing the girlfriend of teenage heartthrob Lorenzo Lamas.

In 1988 she released her first (and so far only) solo album, simply titled "Apollonia" on Warner Bros. Records. Containing high energy dance music, three singles were released from the album: "Since I Fell For You", "The Same Dream", and "Mismatch". It was produced by several hit producers, such as Ric Wake (Taylor Dayne, Diana Ross), Terry Lupton (Michael Learns To Rock, Jamie Stevens), or songwriter Andy Goldmark (Jennifer Rush).

She also starred in 3 straight-to-video movies: "Back To Back," "Black Magic Woman" and "Ministry of Vengeance," which can all be referred to as classic B-movies.

Shortly after these films and the release of her debut album, she disappeared out of the spotlight for nearly five years. She married General Hospital actor Kevin Bernhardt but divorced him a few years later.

In the mid-90's she slowly returned into the show business and did guest appearances on the US TV shows "Sliders" (with Jerry O'Connell) and "Air America" (starring Lorenzo Lamas with whom she had previously starred together in "Falcon Crest" in 1986). She can often be seen on film premieres and media events in California.

Chapter Four

MORRIS DAY

MORRIS DAY (BORN December 13, 1957, in Minneapolis, Minnesota) is an American musician and composer. He is best known as the charismatic lead singer of The Time, a band that also launched the careers of famous producers Jimmy Jam & Terry Lewis.

Jam & Lewis, founders of The Time, selected Day as their band's frontman because of his professional association with Prince, in the hopes that he would broaden their group's appeal. He stayed on in this role until the breakup of the band in the 1990s.

Their most prolific and visible period came during the 1980s when Day played the antagonist to Prince in his film musicals, which helped establish Day's playboy stage presence. Typically escorted by his manservant, "Jerome" (Jerome Benton), Day won fans with his exaggerated vanity ("Jerome bring me my mirror!") and strutting bravado, acting as a comic foil to Prince's romantic, sensitive lead. This persona was further exploited for comic effect on The Time's records, on songs such as "Chili Sauce" and "If The Kid Can't Make You Come" from the album Ice Cream Castle.

That album, the group's most popular, is best remembered for the infectious singles "Jungle Love" and "The Bird". With their palpable pop energy and catchy choruses, both songs were huge hits on both Urban and Pop radio. From that high point, Day's success began to wane in the 1990s. With the breakup of his band, the mediocre sales of his solo records, and the general decline of Prince's popularity, Day's public visibility and creative output waned considerablity.

In 1990, he formed his own girl band (not unlike Prince's Vanity/Apollonia 6) called The Day Zs.

Today, he remains a popular concert draw, fronting a revamped lineup of The Time. Though few original members of the group remain, Day continues to employ "Jerome" in his stage shows and the comic scenes the two act out together are typically the highlight of a Time performance.

Though he had continued to act in films from time to time in small parts (Richard Pryor's *Moving* being a brief but memorable turn), Day's presence on the screen decreased until, in 2001, he returned to film in Kevin Smith's Jay and Silent Bob Strike Back, performing "Jungle Love" and dancing with the movie's stars in the movie's coda.

Metroactive.com Interview Morris Day
Time and Time Again
By Nicky Baxter

"What time is it?" was once the rallying cry for fans who couldn't get enough of a certain funky but sleek Minneapolis group whose pop-eyed front man was by turns cool as a cucumber and kooky as a loon. The Time was reportedly Prince's more commercial musical mouthpiece in the early 1980s before he became a symbol of his former self. Even if that's true—and the Time vehemently argued otherwise—the group quickly assumed a character all its own.

First, there was lead singer Morris Day, whose "Little Richard as Don Juan" persona was a scream. In concert (and the Time really was a show band), Day was a sight for bored eyes. Watching the conk-haired, razzle-dazzle singer primp and preen like a peacock was a Kodak moment not soon forgotten.

But if Day was a jive-time joker, in guitarist Jesse Johnson, keyboardist Jimmy Jam and bassist Terry Lewis (aided and abetted by drummer Jellybean Johnson and keyboardist Monte Clair), the Time boasted some serious musicianship. Produced by Prince (alias Jamie Starr), the Time's eponymous 1981 debut did solid business on the black front.

Three singles—"Get It Up," "Cool" and the irresistibly twitchy of "777-9311"—swaggered their way into the black pop charts' Top 10. The follow-up, *What Time Is It?*, however, was the real hit, exploding all over Soulsville. Soon, preb-girls and—boys all over wanted to know what time it was.

Unhappily, that album proved to be the band's artistic peak. *Ice Cream Castles* (1984) may have shipped platinum, but it was a soppy affair without Jam and Lewis, both of whom had been forced to walk the plank by tiny taskmaster Prince prior to the recording. The Minneapolisians reformed for *Pandemonium* (1990), a surprisingly credible effort. Six years later, and the "Time" has returned. Any clocks in the house?

The Wave Interview Morris Day
By David Farley

Morris Day wouldn't make a very good subject for VH1's *Behind the Music*. Though his band, The Time, are on-again, off-again, and his short-lived solo career stumbled as soon as it left the gate, Day didn't snort a gazillion dollars up his nose, nor was he almost killed in a car accident after a night of partying. Instead, he has quietly been retired to stud in the American pop-culture stable. Constantly on tour, Day hasn't put out an album in over a decade. The million-dollar swagger, the flashy suits, the blue-blood attitude are all still there. So is his very own stage-side butler, Jerome "bring-me-the-mirror" Benton. When we caught up with Day in Atlanta, where he now lives, he was just about to hop on a plane to his former haunt, Minneapolis, to play an afternoon set for the meat-loving crowd at this year's Rib Fest. Who says slowly fading away isn't cool?

The Wave: What time is it?
Morris Day: It's time to be cool.

TW: Are you checking yourself out in a mirror right now?
MD: [Laughs] Actually that's what I was doing when I put you on hold a few seconds ago.

TW: Is Jerome standing there holding it up for you?
MD: Actually, right now, I don't look exactly as you'd picture. I just got in from a nice morning jog and I'm just chillin'.

TW: What's it like going back to Minneapolis?
MD: It's always really cool. People come out in nice numbers to see us. It's a special occasion to play there. We're homegrown talent, so people there really enjoy us, not to mention the fact that we rip it up on stage.

TW: In addition to constantly touring, what else is going on with The Time?
MD: We're just about to ink a deal with Hollywood Records, so look for a new album in the first part of 2004. It's gonna be off the chain. We've been beating the pavement, but we've always wanted to do another album—we just weren't sure if we were going to go the independent route or hook up with a major label.

TW: Is there anything you regret about the '80s?
MD: Not really. The music scene was totally different. I was living what I had learned up until that point. So I understood what was going on with the music. But right now, I'm standing on the outside looking in when it comes to what the kids are doing on the radio these days. While we'll probably come into contact with some of the younger artists out there, we're putting stuff down that they don't know how to do anymore: real drums, real bass, and so on.

TW: What was the worst thing about the '80s?
MD: It's hard for me to say there was anything bad about that decade. My band was on fire and I was loving the club and music scene.

TW: Some historians credit American pop culture in the '80s for playing a crucial part in the erosion of the Soviet Union. How much did Morris Day and the Time help in bringing down the Iron Curtain?
MD: [Laughs] I've never really looked at it on that level. I tend not to be so in depth to world issues. But if our music did help, I'm glad.

TW: Of the very, very few good things critics said about Prince's last movie, *Graffiti Bridge*, the most common was that you and Jerome stole the movie. Why haven't you acted more?
MD: There was a time when I thought that might be attractive, and I was hanging out in Hollywood and doing that whole thing. I quickly found out that sort of thing doesn't work well with my aura. Some people liked what I did in *Purple Rain* and *Graffiti Bridge*, and those are the people who call with acting offers, but to actively be on the block in Hollywood and go to readings is not my thing. I'm a musician and I can earn my keep very well. That's not to say that if someone comes along and offers me $20 million to do a movie . . .

TW: Do you still talk to Prince?
MD: Not as much as I used to. We pretty much grew up together from the time we were 13. We were always hanging out. But times have changed, and I'm here in Atlanta and he's in Minneapolis. We talk every once in a while.

TW: Didn't you ever want to punch him in the face? Wait!—Didn't you guys get into a fistfight on the set of *Purple Rain*?
MD: No. That was misreported.
TW: Do you think you could take him?
MD: Yeah! [Laughs]

TW: But really, didn't you ever want to bitch-slap him?
MD: He likes to be in control sometimes—to the point where it got to be . . . Well, there were times when . . . I'll just leave it at that. You've got to take the good with the bad, you know?

TW: What's the meanest thing Prince ever did to you?
MD: One time when we were touring with him, he and his band threw eggs at us while we were on stage. Then when he went on, we threw eggs back. But I thought that was kind of low. I know it was meant in fun, but when you're trying to do your show in front of a bunch of people, throwing eggs is not too cool.

TW: Did you have any animosity because The Time was Prince's band? He even had the power to fire people, like when Jimmy Jam and Terry Lewis were late for a gig because their plane was delayed and Prince sacked them.
MD: Yeah, that was fucked up. For me, it was like being the president, but having to answer to the CEO. I had a fair amount of control and power within the organization, but the bottom line was always his. There were moments, like when he fired Jimmy Jam and Terry Lewis, that were tough. One thing I always hated about my favorite bands was when they changed members a lot, so the reality of that happening to my band was hard to take. That's when I started thinking about a solo career.

TW: What kind of car do you drive? Let me guess: a Bentley? A Rolls Royce?
MD: [Pause] Um . . . yeah, I've got all that. I don't discriminate with my cars.

TW: What's the key to being sexy?
MD: I ain't no Prince, you know what I'm saying? I think he might not say it, but he has some really cut and dry ways of considering that question. But I just think that being cool makes me a sexy man.

TW: What can you not live without?
MD: Money.

TW: If you were to take out a personal ad in a paper, what would yours say?
MD: [Long pause] Cute, pretty fine, handsome whatever with money looking for like-minded and like-assetted female.

TW: Was this the best interview ever, or what?
MD: [Loud laugh] It was absolutely the best interview ever, my man!

Chapter Five

PRINCE AND THE REVOLUTION BAND

THE REVOLUTION WAS Prince's backing band from the late 1970s through 1986. It is unknown when the band was actually dubbed "The Revolution," but the name was indicated (in reverse lettering) on Prince's *1999* album, released in 1982. The band was prominently identified and provided more input on the next three albums: *Purple Rain, Around the World in a Day* and *Parade*. In the film *Purple Rain*, Prince (as "The Kid") *and* the band are identified as "The Revolution".

When Prince formed his backing band after the release of his first album, he followed in the footsteps of one of his idols, Sly Stone by creating a multi-racial, multi-gendered musical ensemble. The band initially consisted of:

- Dez Dickerson on guitar
- André Cymone on bass

- Bobby "Z" Rivkin on drums
- Gayle Chapman and Matt Fink on keyboards

Though officially unnamed, Prince experimented with the band acting as a side project known as *The Rebels*, recording material in 1979. The recordings were a group effort with lead vocals by Cymone, Dickerson or Chapman. The project was shelved for unknown reasons, however two of the tracks would later be re-recorded and given away by Prince. "You", became "U", and was released on Paula Abdul's *Spellbound* album while "If I Love You Tonight" was released by both Mica Paris and Prince's later wife, Mayte Garcia.

Gayle Chapman quit the band in 1980 due to religious conflicts and was replaced by Lisa Coleman. Coleman was usually only identified by her first name, while Fink started wearing surgical scrubs on stage and became known as "Doctor" Fink. Wanting more creative control, André Cymone left the next year and was replaced by Mark Brown, renamed Brownmark by Prince.

In 1982, when the band was actually identified, it consisted of:

- Dez Dickerson on guitar
- Brownmark on bass
- Bobby Z. on drums
- Lisa Coleman and Doctor Fink on keyboards

When the *1999* tour ended, Dez Dickerson left the band for religious reasons and was replaced by Lisa's childhood friend Wendy Melvoin. Wendy and Lisa shortly thereafter formed a special bond with Prince and greatly influenced his output during the rest of their tenure in the band. Prince's former mostly R&B/funk offerings would be more diversified with rock, pop and classical music elements.

In 1986, for the *Parade* Tour, Prince augmented The Revolution with several new members to perform the complex and jazzy arrangements from the album. The horn section from the album joined him on tour, as well as a new guitarist, backing vocalist and dance group. The new members were:

- Mico Weaver on guitar
- Eric Leeds on saxophone
- Atlanta Bliss (Matt Blistan) on trumpet
- Jerome Benton, Wally Safford and Greg Brooks as dancers/vocalists
- Susannah Melvoin on backing vocals

Weaver was pulled from Sheila E.'s band. Leeds, Benton, and Melvoin were remnants of the disbanded The Family. Susannah was Wendy's twin sister, and also Prince's love interest at the time. Blistan was a friend and former bandmate of Eric Leeds. Brooks and Safford were former bodyguards for Prince.

Despite the steller performance of the band on tour, discontent in The Revolution had been brewing and was about to reach a boiling point. Wendy and Lisa were unhappy with their lack of credit and creativity and left the band shortly after the *Parade* tour in 1986 to perform as a duo. With the nucleus of the band gone, Prince decided to make several changes. Susannah left, following a hurtful breakup with Prince. Bobby Z. was replaced by the more versatile Sheila E. Brownmark was asked to stay, but decided to pursue a solo career. Dr. Fink decided to remain with Prince.

The fragmented Revolution retained many of the newer members (Weaver, Brooks, Safford, Bliss and Leeds) while Prince added Sheila E. associates Levi Seacer, Jr. on bass and Boni Boyer on keyboards/vocals. The new incarnation of the band was unnamed, though some members of the new band referred to the group as the "Counter-Revolution", and fans came to dub it as "The Lovesexy Band". Prince may have been toying with a new band name in 1988, when on the album *Lovesexy*, Prince states, "Welcome to the New Power."

Chapter Six

BEHIND THE NAME CHANGE

IN 1994, DURING NEGOTIATIONS regarding the release of Prince's album *The Gold Experience*, a battle between Warner Bros. and Prince's ensued, struggling over the artistic and financial control of Prince's output. During that time, Prince's appeared in public only with the word "Slave" written on his cheek. Prince explained his name change as follows:

"The first step I have taken towards the ultimate goal of emancipation from the chains that bind me to Warner Brothers was to change my name from Prince to Symbol. Prince is the name that my Mother gave me at birth. Warner Bros. took the name, trademarked it, and used it as the main marketing tool to promote all of the music that I wrote. The company owns the name Prince and all related music marketed under Prince. I became merely a pawn used to produce more money for Warner Bros . . . . I was born Prince and did not want to adopt another conventional name. The only acceptable replacement for my name, and my identity, was a symbol with no pronunciation, that is a representation of me and what my music is about. This symbol is present in my work over the years; it is a concept that has evolved from my frustration; it is who I am. It is my name."

Prince's strategy behind the name change seems to have been to reinvent himself, going back to a smaller audience to redevelop his style. One commentator noted:

Prince started his career as a big R&B star with limited mainstream success. At that point, he left the middle of the road and headed for the ditch. In 1980, it was risky to record new wave songs with lusty lyrics that assured no radio airplay (the classic Dirty Mind), but it paid off. Critics took notice and he became an underground favorite. This paved the way for his huge success with 1999 and Purple Rain. Certainly that was the pinnacle of his career, as far as worldwide earnings and universal adulation are concerned. But by heading for the ditch again, by changing his name and experimenting with his style, by lowering his stock value and escaping his record contract, Prince has become an underground artist again. In late 1996, the first collection of Prince's music since his break with Warner Bros. appeared in record stores, a sprawling three-hour extravaganza integrating great dance grooves and slow-burning ballads. Critical response has been overwhelmingly positive, and sales have been brisk despite the high price of a 3-CD set. It's no coincidence that he titled this album "Emancipation."

In 1994 Prince's attitude towards his artistic output underwent a notable shift. He began to view releasing albums in quick succession as a means of ejecting himself from his contractual obligations to Warner Bros. The label, he believed, was intent on limiting his artistic freedom by insisting he release albums on a more sporadic basis. He also blamed it for the poor commercial performance of his latest work (namely *The Love Symbol Album*), feeling it had failed to market the album effectively. Out of this state of affairs a proposal came about to subject the aborted *Black Album* to an official release, approximately seven years after its initial creation. This new release, which was already in wide circulation as bootlegs, also sold relatively poorly.

Following that disappointing venture, Warner Bros. succumbed to Prince's wishes to release an album of new material, to be entitled *Come*. The label had refused to grant the album a release in the past, believing the music on it to be dreadfully mediocre and lacking a potential hit single. When *Come* was eventually released, it confirmed all of Warner's worst fears. It became Prince's poorest-selling album to date, struggling to even shift 500,000 copies. Even more frustrating was the fact that Prince insisted on crediting the album to "Prince 1958-1993."

Prince pushed to have his next album *The Gold Experience* released simultaneously as "Prince's" material. As a test case, Warner Bros. allowed the single "The Most Beautiful Girl In The World" to be released via a small, independent distributor, Bellmark, in February 1994. The release was successful, reaching #3 on the U.S. Billboard Hot 100 and #1 in many other countries, but this was not to be a forerunner of what was to come. Warner Bros. still resisted releasing *The Gold Experience*, fearing poor sales and citing "market saturation" as a defense. When eventually released in September 1995, *The Gold Experience* failed to sell well, despite reaching the top 10 of the Billboard 200 initially.

The *Chaos And Disorder* album of 1996 was his final album of new material for Warner Bros., and was one of his least successful. Prince attempted a major comeback later that year, when, free of any further contractual obligations to Warner Bros., he released *Emancipation*. The album was released via his own NPG Records with distribution through EMI. To publish his songs, in *Emancipation*, Prince for the first time did not use *Controversy Music—ASCAP*, which he had used in all his records since 1981, rather he used *Emancipated Music Inc.—ASCAP*. While certified Platinum by the RIAA, some critics felt that the sprawling 36-song, 3-CD set (each disk was exactly 60 minutes long) lacked focus. *Emancipation* would be Prince's first album in which he would include covers of songs of other artists; for example, CD number three includes Joan Osborne's top 10 hit song of 1995 "One of Us". Other covers on the album include "Betcha By Golly Wow!" (written by Thomas Randolf Bell and Linda Creed), "I Can't Make You Love Me" (written by James Allen Shamblin II and Michael Barry Reid) and "La-La Means I Love You" (written by Thomas Randolf Bell and William Hart).

Prince married Mayte Garcia, backup singer and dancer, on Valentine's Day of 1996. *Emancipation* was largely dedicated to their union and their then-unborn child. The child, rumored to have been named Gregory, was born with Pfeiffer syndrome, a rare skull disease and died shortly after birth. This tragic event may have contributed to marital troubles, leading to an eventual annulment of their marriage in 1998.

Prince released *Crystal Ball*, a 4-CD collection of unreleased material, in 1998. The distribution of this album was shambolic, with some fans pre-ordering the album on his website up to a year before it was eventually shipped to them, and months after the record had gone on sale in retail stores. The *Newpower Soul* album released three months later failed to make much of an impression on the charts.

In 1999, Prince once again teamed up with a major record label, this time Arista Records, for a new album, *Rave Un2 The Joy Fantastic*. In an attempt to make his new album a success, Prince gave more interviews than he'd ever done in his career. However, *Rave Un2 The Joy Fantastic* failed to make much of a commercial impression. A few months earlier, Warner Bros. had also released *The Vault: Old Friends 4 Sale*, a collection of unreleased material recorded by Prince throughout his career, and his final recording commitment on his contract with Warner Bros. The greatest success he had during the year was with the single "1999: The New Master," released in time for Prince to collect a small portion of the sales dollars Warner Bros. had been seeing for the album and singles of the original *1999*. Both critics and fans panned "The New Master", declaring it unimaginative.

A pay-per-view concert, "Rave Un2 The Year 2000", was held on December 31, 1999 and had appearance by many guest stars such as Lenny Kravitz, George Clinton and The Time. It was released to home video the following year. Also, a remix album, *Rave In2 The Joy Fantastic*, was released exclusively through Prince's NPG Music Club in April 2000.

On May 16th of 2000, he ceased using the name "Symbol" and started to use the name "Prince" again after his publishing contract with Warner-Chappell expired. In a press conference stating that he was now free from undesirable relationships associated with the name "Prince," he formally reverted to his original name and opened the door to endless "The Artist Formerly Known As The Artist Formerly Known As Prince" digs. However, Prince still uses the symbol as a logo occasionally, and continues to play a "Symbol" shaped guitar.

On December 31st of 2001, Prince married his former Paisley Park employee Manuela Testolini in Hawaii and supposedly became a Jehovah's Witness.

For the next three years, Prince primarily released new music through his Internet subscription services, first NPGOnlineLtd.com, and now NPGMusicClub.com. However, two albums which showcased the substantial influence of jazz music on Prince did surface at record stores for the general public: *The Rainbow Children* in 2001, and the all-instrumental *N.E.W.S* in 2003. The latter received a Grammy nomination for Best Pop Instrumental Album. In 2002, he released his first-ever live album, *One Nite Alone . . . Live!*, which features recordings of performances from the *One Nite Alone* tour. The costly 3-CD box set, which also includes a disc of "aftershow" music called *It Ain't Over!*, failed to make an impact on the charts. During this time Prince sought to engage more effectively with his fan base via the NPG Music Club, pre-concert sound checks, and at yearly "celebrations" at Paisley Park. Fans were invited into Prince's studios for tours, interviews, discussions and music-listening sessions. Some of these fan discussions were filmed for an unreleased documentary, directed by Kevin Smith. Smith discusses what happened during those days at length in his *An Evening with Kevin Smith* DVD—more information here and here. Performances were also arranged to showcase Prince himself, as well as related artists and guests (including Alicia Keys, The Time, Erykah Badu, Nikka Costa, George Clinton, Norah Jones and others).

On February 8, 2004, Prince made a significant leap out of obscurity by appearing at the Grammy awards with Beyoncé Knowles. The duo were allegedly selected as a last-minute replacement for Janet Jackson, whose controversial incident at Super Bowl XXXVIII the week before had made her an undesirable choice to appear at the awards ceremony. In a performance that opened the show, Prince and Beyoncé ripped through a medley of classic *Purple Rain* songs, namely the title track, "Let's Go Crazy" and "Baby I'm a Star." The performance also featured a rendition of Beyoncé's "Crazy in Love."

The following month Prince was inducted into the Rock and Roll Hall of Fame. The award was presented to him by Alicia Keys, along with Big Boi and André 3000 of OutKast. As well as performing a trio of his own hits during the ceremony, Prince also participated in a tribute to fellow inductee George Harrison in a rendition of the deceased artist's "While My Guitar Gently Weeps." The performance was mostly led by Tom Petty, but also featured Jeff Lynne and Harrison's son, Dhani. The tribute shed notable light on Prince, who concluded the performance with a lengthy guitar solo (*video*).

In April 2004, Prince released *Musicology* through a unique one-album agreement with Columbia Records. This deal, which meant that Columbia was obliged to distribute and promote the album, was constructed in such a way that ensured Prince himself still garnered the majority of the royalties (as he had been accustomed to through his own independent music service). The album, which rose to the top 5 in the album charts of several countries (including the United States, United Kingdom, Germany and Australia), featured some of the artist's most economical and commercially appealing music in years. That same year, Pollstar named Prince the top concert draw among musicians in America. Grossing an estimated $87.4 million, Prince's *Musicology* tour was the most profitable tour in the industry during 2004. The artist played an impressive run of 96 concerts, the average ticket price for each being $61. Further highlighting the success of the album, Prince's *Musicology* went on to receive two Grammy wins, for Best Male R&B Vocal Performance for "Call My Name" and Best Traditional R&B Vocal Performance for the title track. It was also nominated for Best R&B Song, Best R&B Album, and Best Male Pop Vocal Performance for "Cinnamon Girl." The album became the artist's most commercially lucrative since *Diamonds and Pearls*, partly due to a radical scheme devised on his part which enabled copies of the album presented to those who purchased tickets on the *Musicology* tour to be included in the album's overall sales as compiled by *Billboard*.

Prince has worked with PETA to promote a compassionate and healthy vegetarian lifestyle.

In December 2004, Prince was chosen by Rolling Stone magazine's readers as the best male performer and most welcome comeback. During that same month, Prince was named number five on the Top Pop Artists of the Past 25 Years chart.

In February 2005, Rolling Stone magazine published the list of top money makers of 2004; Prince was on top with estimated net earnings of $56.5 million

In March 2005, Prince won an NAACP Image Award for Outstanding Album (*Musicology*) and a Vanguard Award.

In April 2005, Prince played guitar (along with En Vogue singing backing vocals) on Stevie Wonder's first new single in six years, "So What The Fuss." The single debuted at number thirteen on the Billboard Adult R&B chart. Despite rumours of an appearance or duet with Stevie Wonder at Live 8 in Philadelphia, Prince did not perform at the concert.

In the aftermath of Hurricane Katrina, which devastated the city of New Orleans on August 29, 2005, Prince offered a personal response by recording two new songs, "S.S.T." and the instrumental "Brand New Orleans," at Paisley Park in the early hours of September 2. The artist, in a typical moment of inspiration, played all instrumental and vocal parts without collaboration. These recordings were quickly dispersed to the public via Prince's NPG Music Club, and "S.S.T." was later picked up by iTunes, where it reached number one on the R&B chart. On October 25, Sony Records released a version of the single on CD.

On December 9, 2005, it was reported that Prince had determined an agreement with Universal Records to release his next album, *3121*. This deal is believed to be similar to that which the artist struck with Columbia Records for *Musicology*. The debut single put forward from the album was the Latin-tinged "Te Amo Corazon," the video for which debuted on VH1 on December 13, and was directed by actress Salma Hayek. The piece was filmed in Marrakesh, and showed Prince accompanied on-screen by Mía Maestro. She was also present at a brief press conference which Prince made in promotion of the new single and video. The video for "Black Sweat," the second single from *3121*, premiered on February 2, 2006, demonstrating a rather more minimalistic approach both in the sound of the song and the style of the video. Prince is also believed to have a concert tour in the works to promote the new album.

On February 4, 2006, Prince was the musical guest on Saturday Night Live, where he performed two new songs, the guitar-driven "Fury" and "Beautiful, Loved & Blessed," with up-and-coming R&B singer Támar. Both are featured on Prince's own *3121*, with "Beautiful, Loved & Blessed" also appearing on Tamar's album, titled *Beautiful Loved & Blessed* (due for release on May 2, 2006).

On February 15, 2006, Prince performed at the Brit awards alongside Wendy, Lisa and Sheila E. He played "Te Amo Corazon" and "Fury" from *3121*, and "Purple Rain" and "Let's Go Crazy" from *Purple Rain*, in a performance which was generally regarded as the best of the night.

Ultimate is the title of Prince's latest greatest hits compilation album. Originally slated to be released in North America on 14 March 2006, the album was cancelled just days prior to its release. However, copies were already available in some retailers and have been sold.

The double disc set is slated to consist of one CD of hits, while the second disc will contain extended versions and mixes that, for the most part were previously unavailable on CD. Artwork for a promo copy revealed that the selection included these tracks: "Let's Go Crazy (Special Dance Mix)," "Little Red Corvette (Dance Remix)," "Let's Work (Dance Remix)," "Pop Life (Fresh Dance Mix)," "She's Always In My Hair (12" Version)," "Raspberry Beret (12" Version)," "Kiss (Extended Version)," "U Got The Look (Long Look)," "Hot Thing (Extended Remix)," "Thieves In The Temple (Remix)," and "Cream (N.P.G. Mix)."

3121 was leaked to the internet on March 6, 2006. Prince achieved his first career number-one debut on the Billboard 200 (in the issue dated April 8, 2006) with *3121*. The set sold 183,000 copies in the United States in its first week, according to Nielsen SoundScan. It also debuted at number one on Billboard's Top R&B/Hip-Hop Albums tally. *3121* also took over the number one spot on Billboard's European Top 100 Albums chart the following week, giving the legendary artist his highest charting international album of the decade.

On May 24, 2006, Prince performed "Lolita" and "Satisfied" from his album *3121* on the last results show of the fifth season of *American Idol*. He was the only artist to perform without any contestant in the episode. The infamous judge on the show, Simon Cowell, has recently turned his barbed comments toward the artist saying, "It just tells you how selfish he is. He comes on, not a word—'I'm not gonna sing with anybody else, I'm not gonna say goodbye.' Thank you for your generosity, Prince." in regard to Prince's late arrival and abrupt departure.

On June 12, 2006, Prince was honored with a Webby Lifetime Achievement Award in recognition of his "visionary" use of the Internet that included becoming the first major artist to release an entire album—1997's "Crystal Ball"—exclusively on the Web. "Everything you think is true," Prince said, coming in under the five-word limit and leaving everyone wondering what he meant as he launched into a solo number. The performance ended abruptly as he suddenly chucked his guitar back over his head with a crash and raced off to a waiting limousine.

PRINCE—IS BACK ON TOP, THE MAN, THE ARTIST

On June 27, 2006, Prince appeared at the BET awards. He was awarded Best Male R&B artist. In his acceptance speech he told the crowd that he was surprised but honored to receive the award. He also thanked Jehovah, Chaka Khan, Stevie Wonder, India.Arie, and Yolanda Adams. Later in the evening Prince participated in a tribute to Chaka Khan with the other artists he had named in his speech. The tribute was part of Chaka Khan's lifetime acheievement award given to her that evening. Prince also closed the show, alongside Támar, with his song "3121" from his album of the same name. He was joined onstage by musician will.i.am from The Black Eyed Peas.

At 12:00 AM on July 4, 2006, to the dismay of his fans, Prince abruptly shut down his official NPGMC website citing the following:

> Greetings Family,
>
> The NPG Music Club has been in xistence 4 more than 5 years. In that time we've learned a great deal from each other and about this brave new online world we have all chosen 2 b part of. The members we have been 4tunate enough 2 have join r family have truly made this the best music club any artist could ever dream of. And all the things we have been a part of 2gether—the concerts, the celebrations, the soundchecks, the discussions and the un4gettable music—have shown us what a New Power Generation can truly b. We thank u from r hearts 4 sharing urselves and ur love of the music with all of us. It has been a blessing.
>
> Once the NPG Music Club won the 2006 Webby Award, discussions within the NPG began 2 center on what was next. What's the next step in this ever-changing xperiment? The achievements of the past cannot be questioned and we are truly grateful 4 everything that has been accomplished. But in its current 4m there is a feeling that the NPGMC gone as far as it can go. In a world without limitations and infinite possibilities, has the time come 2 once again make a leap of faith and begin anew? These r ?s we in the NPG need 2 answer. In doing so, we have decided 2 put the club on hiatus until further notice.
>
> The NPG Music Club was a first step; the lessons learned will last 4ever. Now comes a time of great reflection and restructuring. The future holds nothing but endless opportunity and we plan on seizing it wholeheartedly. Don't u want 2 come?
>
> Love4oneanother,
NPG Music Club 4ever

R.I.P. NPG: Prince Pulls The Plug On His Music Club
By: ChartAttack.com Staff

Prince launched NPG (named after his backing band, New Power Generation) on Valentine's Day in 2001 as an attempt to bring his fans together in an online community. He planned to use it as an outlet for the release of non-LP music as well as a venue where fans could interact, get choice seats for concerts, and find invitations to sound-checks and after-parties.

The site had two options for membership: $7.75 U.S. for basic monthly access or $100 for a premium annual membership. The basic membership promised fans three new songs a month, a one-hour radio show hosted by Prince or other NPG members, and exclusive multimedia content such as a make-your-own-mix program.

The premium membership offered preferred seating to all Prince concerts, VIP passes to after-parties, more music and videos, and exclusive merchandise.

Though an ambitious project, NPG started out on a rocky road. A lot of members complained in various online forums that they felt they weren't getting their money's worth. During the club's first year, Prince's song quota was infrequently reached and releases were most often remixes.

In the second year, Prince promised members that they would receive four albums before the year concluded. At the last minute, subscribers were shipped a four-CD box set titled One Nite Alone . . . Live. Though the four-disc promise was fulfilled, fans were still disgruntled because they received little else that year, and because the One Nite set was available in stores for $50.

One continuing complaint that NPG faced was that the tickets section of the site was too bogged down with traffic to be usable.

In a reaction to fan complaints, Prince eventually lowered NPG's membership price to $2.50 a month or $25 for a lifetime membership.

There were other fans however, who spoke out about their satisfaction with the Music Club, citing their once-in-a-lifetime opportunities to see Prince at sound-checks and after-parties for his concerts. NPGMC won a Webby Award, the online equivalent of an Oscar, earlier this year.

It's unclear at this time whether or not NPGMC will return, or what form it might take if it does reappear.

"The NPG Music Club was a first step; the lessons learned will last 4ever," concludes the statement. "Now comes a time of great reflection and restructuring.

"The future holds nothing but endless opportunity and we plan on seizing it wholeheartedly. Don't u want 2 come?"—Scott Bryson

Chapter Seven

THE MOVIE—PURPLE RAIN—1984

PURPLE RAIN IS a 1984 movie directed by Albert Magnoli and written by Prince and William Blinn. Prince stars in this semi-autobiographical movie, which was clearly developed around him and his particular talents.

The movie is tied in to the album of the same name, which spawned three chart-topping singles: the opening number "Let's Go Crazy", "Purple Rain", and "When Doves Cry." Much of the movie's cinematography, by Donald Thorin, is closer to that of 1980s music videos than conventional film.

Prince plays "The Kid", an aspiring Minneapolis musician with a difficult home life. He runs into singer Apollonia Kotero and they become involved in an untidy relationship. The plot centers on Prince trying not to repeat the pattern of his abusive father (Clarence Williams III) and keep his group, The Revolution, and his relationship with his girlfriend, together. His main antagonist is fellow musician Morris Day and his group The Time. Oddly, excluding Prince, almost every actor in the movie uses their actual name for their character.

The movie idea was apparently developed by Prince during his Triple Threat tour. Initially with a rather darker and more coherent script, Prince had intended to play opposite girlfriend Vanity, until they fell out. Her role was offered to Jennifer Beals before going to Apollonia. The movie won an Academy Award for Original Music Score.

Purple Rain Profile:

Directed by:	Albert Magnoli
Produced by:	Robert Calvallo, Steven Fargnoli, Joseph Ruffalo
Written by:	Albert Magnoli and william Blinn
Starring:	Prince, Morris Day and Apollonia Kotero
Music by:	Prince, Michael Colombier and John L. Nelson
Distributed by:	Warner Bros.
Release Date:	July 27, 1984
Running Time:	111
Minutes Awards:	Academy Award, Best Original Score, 1984
Language:	English
Budget:	$7,000,000

Amazon Customers Reviews for Purple Rain Movie

5-Stars: Elmwood Park, NJ, April 2005: For the 20th anniversary of it's release, Warner Brothers re-released the classic "Purple Rain" on DVD in two-disc form. It was a breath of fresh air compared to the previous and more boring DVD that had almost no features. "Purple Rain" is a semi-autobiographical tale about Prince's journey to fame. It is almost identical to Eminem's "8 Mile" and still holds it's own today as one of the greatest rock films ever. This DVD was packed with featurettes, music videos, the trailer and the ultra rare 1984 MTV premiere party. The film was also re-mastered and takes you back to 1984 to re-live the magic. "Purple Rain" is a must see!

5-Stars: Austria, March 2005: Just have seen "Purple Rain" for the first time in my life today. I am born in 1985, so I haven't experienced any of the hype for the film back then. What should I say? I enjoyed the film and the especially the music all the way through. I didn't know that so many classic Prince songs actually just came off this film. The plot of the film is good, although the main eye lays on the rivalry of the two bands and for this matter on their music. Still I didn't feel that the acting of this "non-actors" was cheesy! They played themselves so why should it?

For me the real winner of this film is Morris Day. I have been a lover of his pimp-funk for several years now and always assumed that he was the baddest around. This film gives proof. He's acting (or is it "acting"?) is just funny and you have to listen to his voice and especially to his laugh. I ended up skipping back to his laughing scenes all the time. Never seen such a laughable, funny guy yet—who plays such great funky music. Morris Day & The Time's performances & scenes are worth the money alone!!! The special features are cool too. The producer even begins to cry when talking about a certain scene & music in the film. It was touching. Still, I missed Prince and Morris Day being interviewed and some cut out scenes of the film. Prince is a genius! I loved that film!

4-Stars: UK, March 2005: After reading a 5-star review of this album in a music magazine discussing all-time classic albums, I thought I'd buy it out of sheer curiosity (and it was on sale in the music shop). I listened with inquisitive ears . . . and was completely compelled and hooked by the music from start to end . . . so the next logical step was to see the film they came from. I'm now officially a secret prince fan! (Let's face it; it's not cool to admit this in modern times!) Not because of his acting (which he did try his hardest) nor the plot of the film (if there is one) or anything like that, but simply for those mesmerizing performances that blow you away! I can't get enough of seeing him prancing around with all that energy doing those great songs and guitar solos.

Being a fan of modern music, I can't help but feel there's something raw and edgy missing out of it that was present in those songs and performances . . . oh well! Just buy the DVD for the kicking performances.

3-Stars: Japan, February 2005: What can I say? Prince's first movie was a big hit. The music was outstanding in every way. Prince is a true musical genius and gifted performer. I remember seeing this as a teen. Now watching it with more mature eyes, I can see some of its shortcomings. Sadly, the acting it less than stellar. Ok at best. The story is thin and un-inspiring. At the time, I thought it was one of the most compelling pieces of drama put on film. Now I see it as basically two rival bands dueling it out in the clubs. Actually Morris Day (Prices real life cousin) turns in the best acting job of all the non-professional actors. Ok, enough harping on the story and acting. The real star was the music and stage choreographs. This movies energy comes charging though full force when each band struts their stuff. When Prince has his guitar and a mic in front of him, he is on fire. When he is just acting, he should be set on fire. (Sorry Prince, I love your music, but you're not an actor). Of the 3 movies Prince has done, this is by far the best. I give this movie 3 stars for its music. Don't look too hard at the acting or story.

5-Stars: December 2004: Saw this for the second time in almost 20 years, and it brought back some great memories. Playing this movie makes you want to go back 20 plus years and party all over again "Like it's 1999." The 80s, when life was simple, long before the 'net, cell phones, IPOD, XBOX and other modern day distractions. Ah, the memories, the days of big hair and big parties, where nothing else mattered, and you only had to worry about which party to go to.

In the Movie, Prince endures a turbulent home life and an abusive father, animosity with his band members, a tug of war within his inner being, a rivalry with his nemesis, Morris Day, and the roller coaster relationship with his illegally and sinfully beautiful girlfriend, Apollonia Kotero. Despite all of these obstacles, Prince, or "the kid" comes out on top at the end with "Purple Rain", the title of the album that would alter the music landscape forever.

While the acting was a little cheesy, nonetheless, it is a must have for any Prince fan, let alone any pop music lover. Even if you are not a prince fan, you will appreciate him after watching this film. After finishing, I have re-gained a newfound respect for Prince, not only as an artist, but also as a person. In fact, the more I watch it, the more powerful and ingratiating it becomes, at least to me. While I don't have every single Prince album, Purple Rain, 1999, and Around The World in a Day are my favorites. If you don't have this or haven't seen this, do so!

5-Stars: October 2004: So I was watching "Purple Rain" the other day, just the ending actually, and I've never seen the beginning or middle so I really have no idea what the thing is all about. I gather from Prince's other movie it's more "Soul mate" kinda stuff but I'm not really sure. Anyway, so I was watching it and Morris Day and the time, who play the antagonists in the movie, they're on stage doing this upbeat funk style song "The Bird," right? And the audience is into it. Because not only is it a song—it's also a dance. The dance. According to them anyway. I mean they're really into it. So they really get the audience into it, and I guess it's some sort of best-band contest or something. So you start thinking, "I feel sorry for whoever has to follow that." Wouldn't you know it . . . it's Prince. Yep. Prince is the one who has to follow it. And as Morris Day and the Time exit the stage . . . they pass Prince's dressing room. The door is open. There is tension in the air. They walk down the hallway laughing, celebrating, all the while knowing how great they just did and what an obstacle Prince has to overcome if he's going to win. It seems impossible. And as Morris Day passes Prince's locker room, he says something cruel. Something I don't remember. But I know it was something hurtful, I know it was. SO . . . our man Prince prepares to take the stage and even though he has the backing of The Revolution, he still somehow feels all alone. He walks out. Somber. Sorrowful. Sad. A chill comes over the audience. After all, they'd just done "The Bird" . . . they were so excited about it too. And now this sorrowful, somber purple guy is coming out and breaking up the vibe. One would have expected him to try and top "The Bird" with some upbeat funk of his own. That's where Prince's strategy comes into play. There is a hush. A silence. A nervous tension. Prince steps up to the microphone. He casually yet emotionally dedicates the next song to his dad. The crowd is in awe. What is this man doing? Prince starts playing his guitar. A slow, reflective, sorrowful melody. This is what he's doing to top "The Bird"? He's got to be out of his mind. But somehow, as he starts into "Purple Rain" the audience becomes sad too. "I only wanted just one time to see you laughing. I only wanted to see you laughing in the Purple Rain . . ." By this point . . . the audience is his. They too wanted to see Prince's dad laughing in the Purple Rain. Or maybe their own dads. Does it matter? Is there even a difference? Not now. They're so enveloped in the melancholy mood that they're even willing to pardon the next verse, "I never wanted to be your weekend lover . . ." Now, really . . . who does want to be their own dad's weekend lover? Maybe someone else's dad, but . . . ya know. The audience doesn't even care. Because they've forgotten about Prince's dad. They've forgotten about everything that brought them to this point. They're living completely in this moment. This sad, powerful, sorrowful moment. A request by Prince for "everybody over here to come on wave your hands" is answered by the entire audience in unison engaging in the act of hand waving. And the lighters . . . oh the lighters. They're out in full force. Not that "Full Force" is in this movie . . . they're in the original House Party, not Purple Rain. It's just an expression though. And so . . . "The Bird" is forgotten. Prince's dad lives on. Prince knows times are changing and it's time we all reach out for something new, that means you too. And Prince wins over the crowd with the power of sadness. Later he goes on to tell us that he would die for us, he's not our lover, he's not our friend, he's something that we'll never comprehend. All true statements continuing the theme of sadness and its power. Did he win the contest? I don't think we ever truly find out. But he won the movie. That's for sure. It certainly wasn't Morris Day and/or The Time. It was Prince. And it was all due to the power of sadness.

4-Stars: August 2004: "Purple Rain" was a phenomenon that successfully merged music and film like no other movie since its release. It was a solid box office hit, and the soundtrack spent 24 consecutive weeks at Number One, going multiplatinum, winning Grammys and even snatching up an Academy Award. In this movie, Prince is the Kid; a struggling musician who leads a band called the Revolution and is trying to keep his gig at the First Avenue, the same club where rival Morris Day (and the Time) also performs. Meanwhile, he crosses paths with 19-year-old Apollonia, who also has dreams of making it big. Let it be immediately known that the Kid is not a pleasant dude at all. In fact, he's a bit of an arrogant jerk. Throughout the movie, he slaps Apollonia, dupes her into jumping into a lake, and treats her as little more than a sex object. On top of that, the Kid has some pretty major control issues as well. He insists that the band performs only the Kid's own material, and he snubs any contribution from members Wendy and Lisa. And when we're introduced to his parents, we immediately understand why the Kid treats women so badly. His father (played by Clarence Williams III) routinely abuses his mother, and watching this constant abuse drives the Kid to the brink. So can the Kid rise above his violent past, mend his fraying band, keep his gig at the club, and ultimately find peace within himself and Apollonia? You'll have to see the movie to find out. The plot in "Purple Rain" covers very familiar ground, but what really makes the movie watchable are the musical performances. Prince rips through classics like "Let's Go Crazy," "Baby I'm a Star," the salacious "Darling Nikki," and the title song, while the Time also holds its own with hits like "The Bird" and "Jungle Love." Even Apollonia made an amusing impression in "Sex Shooter," one of the "so-bad-it's-good" songs of the 1980s. The acting, a term I use fairly liberally in this review, is a different matter. Clarence Williams seems to be the only professional of the bunch, while Morris Day and Jerome Benton are true naturals in front of the camera, giving the movie a much needed comic uplift and counterbalancing some of the more wooden performances by Apollonia and Prince himself. The DVD presents "Purple Rain" for the first time in wide screen format, with re-mastered sound and a bevy of features on the second disc. These include music videos for every single released from this soundtrack, including an 18 minute performance of "I Would Die 4 U/Baby I'm a Star." We also get a handful of retrospective documentaries featuring interviews with cast and crewmembers such as members of the Revolution, Jellybean Johnson, Jimmy Jam and Terry Lewis (who weren't even in "Purple Rain"), director Albert Magnoli, and MTV journalist Kurt Loder. (Prince, Day, Apollonia, Williams are all MIA.) While these clips are interesting, they don't do much more than praise Prince to high heaven. But the real treat is the original MTV Premiere Party, featuring then VJ Mark Goodman, as well as guests Eddie Murphy, Sheila E, Wendy, Lisa, and Lionel Richie among others. "Purple Rain" is no masterpiece, and it has its awkward moments, but it's still a fun movie to watch for both Prince fans and non-Prince fans. 20 years later, the rain still falls.

Chapter Eight

THE MOVIE—UNDER THE CHERRY MOON—1986

UNDER THE CHERRY Moon is a 1986 movie directed by and starring Prince and Time member Jerome Benton as gigolos who swindle beautiful French women. The situation gets complicated when Christopher Tracy (Prince) falls in love with Mary (Kristin Scott Thomas). Mary's father (Steven Berkoff) also disapproves of the romance and provides an excellent adversary for Tracy.

The movie was released in black-and-white and was filmed on location in Nice, France, partly to ensure that there was good weather for filming and also to ensure that Prince was free of American film unions. The movie attempts to combine different styles and themes, including a musical, romantic comedy and drama. The film's soundtrack features the hit single "Kiss".

At the time of its release in 1986, many critics were expecting, in one form or another, a direct sequel to *Purple Rain*. However, barring a performance of "Girls & Boys" by Prince in a French restaurant, most of the soundtrack remains as background music, thus shaving much commercial potential off the film. The majority of critics were unimpressed, citing Prince as a self-indulgent egomaniac, although there was praise for the film's cinematography. The film was originally slated to be directed by Mary Lambert, the director behind some of Madonna's most famous music videos, but after disagreements about the film's direction, she was made a creative consultant instead. Much of her input was disregarded and numerous drafts of the screenplay exist to show the revisions the story went through.

The cast was also changed during pre-production. Isaac Sharon (Mary's father) was originally slated to be played by Terrance Stamp, although he didn't like the direction the film was going and eventually quit, replaced by Steven Berkoff. Susannah Melvoin (twin sister of Revolution guitarist Wendy, and Prince's then-girlfriend) was to play the part of Mary Sharon, but quit before filming started as she and Prince were nearing the end of their relationship. Emmanuelle Sallet who played Katie in the final version was originally included in a much smaller role, but had her part expanded after she met with Prince over dinner. Allegedly, the part of Mary's mother was also much larger, but was cut down in the final draft of the screenplay.

Filmed with a budget of about $12 million, *Under the Cherry Moon* failed to gain any breakout audience, despite much pre-publicity (including a special MTV premiere in Sheridan, Wyoming). It only just managed to make back $10 million in worldwide ticket receipts, and current figures (if VHS/DVD rentals and sales are included) stand at about $12.5 million. It was this commercial failure that saw the beginnings of Warner Brothers' long-running feud with Prince.

Under The Cherry Moon Profile:

The Movie:	Under The Cherry Moon
Directed by:	Prince
Produced by:	Cavallo, Ruffullo and Farginoli
Written by:	Becky Johnston
Starring:	Prince, Jerome Benton, Kristin Scott Thomas, ... Steven Berkoff
Music by:	Prince and The Revolution
Distributed by:	Warner Bros.
Release Date:	1986
Running Time:	98 Minutes
Language:	English
Budget:	$12,000,000

Amazon Customers Reviews for Under The Cherry Moon

4-Stars: USA, October 2004: As popular as Prince was in the 80's, it's hard to believe it has taken 18 years for Under The Cherry Moon to find it's way to DVD. Critics largely considered the film a stinker, especially considering it was only two years behind Purple Rain, but Under The Cherry Moon was a very good film, although very different than Purple Rain. Shot in black and white, Under The Cherry Moon starred Prince as Christopher Tracey, him and his buddy Tricky (Jerome Benton from The Time) are living it up in Europe. They wine and dine the rich and upper class and take their money, basically they are gigolos. They swear it never gets personal until Mary Sharon comes into the picture. Christopher falls for Mary in a big way, but her father Issac Sharon isn't having it. Drama ensues. The soundtrack is awesome and includes the songs "U Need Another Lover Like You Need a Whole In Your Head," "Mountain," and "Kiss" and the DVD includes the videos for the songs shot for the film. A must have for Prince fans.

4-Stars: Houston, Texas, August 2004: I shouldn't like this movie, but I kind of do. It's a total vanity project for Prince, but it's charming and funny so I enjoyed watching it. Prince plays Christopher, a gigolo who plays piano in the French Riviera. He sets his sights on a rich heiress, and then finds himself falling in love. Meanwhile the father does not approve, and wants him hurt or dead. The movie is photographed extremely well by a legendary lensman called Michael Ballhaus. It looks phenomenal! And Kristin Scott Thomas seems to breathe some real life and class to her role as Mary. Jerome Benton is just fun to watch as he goofs on everyone. And Prince is Prince—mysterious and fully decked out in stack heels and full make-up. Filmed on location in South of France.

5-Stars: March 2006: I guess I understand why this movie was so savagely criticized during it's year of release, 1986. Prince was still enjoying huge popularity based largely on the success of "Purple Rain," both the film and the soundtrack. And critics love to knock someone off a pedestal, which is what they did to Prince in those days. Many claimed that the movie was nothing more than an ego trip. They couldn't believe Prince had the nerve to fire the director and then assume that role himself. It was all way too harsh criticism for a movie that isn't trying to be anything more than a fun romantic comedy.

   Of course, poor critical response alone doesn't usually keep the public from making a movie popular. Yet "Under the Cherry Moon" was a bomb at he box office. Probably the main reason for this is that the movie, although shot in color, was released in black-and-white. For some unfathomable reason, the general movie-going public is more often than not horrified at the prospect of seeing a black-and-white movie. Now don't get me wrong, I'm not claiming that had the movie been released in color that people would have flocked to it in droves. I'm only saying that it would have attracted more of an audience if it had been in color. I will acknowledge that this movie's target audience is Prince fans. Since I am one myself, and have been most of my life, I'm not the most entirely objective viewer.

But I make no apologies for my love of this movie. It's not a "guilty pleasure" for me, because I proudly hold this as one of my favorites. I had only seen it a couple times before the DVD release—and unfortunately I missed it in theaters (I couldn't get anyone to take me, I was only 12 and none of my friends were into P and certainly not my parents—though my dad went with me a few years later to see "Graffiti Bridge" on opening night, but that's for another review). But since it's DVD release in 2004, this has become one of my most-watched discs in my collection.

The soundtrack is killer. The tunes make up one of the best Prince albums ever. There's even some great stuff heard in the movie that didn't make the album (some of which was issued on 12" vinyl). Plus, I think the movie looks great—the cinematographer was Michael Ballhaus, who has multiple Academy Award nominations to his credit (and was the DP on numerous Martin Scorsese classics). I wonder how the movie would feel in color, but I do think black-and-white was the right way to go. Even though the movie is set in then-contemporary times, it has the feel of something from the '30s.

There are so many classic moments in this movie; I won't try to list them all. But here are a few . . . Christopher Tracy (Prince) giving his "Bela Lugosi eyes" . . . Tricky (Jerome Benton) tossing rose petals into the tub while Christopher takes a bath . . . Christopher freaking out when he sees bats at the eatery . . . the "Wreka Stow" scene . . . the car race between Christopher and Mary Sharon (Kristen Scott Thomas).

As for the acting, I've heard a lot of people saying that Prince's performance was no good. I don't see much truth in that claim. After being so serious in "Purple Rain," it was a nice contrast to see him so loose and funny in this. Jerome Benton proved he could do just fine even without Morris Day at his side (as in "Purple Rain")—I'm surprised Jerome hasn't done much additional acting outside of Prince movies. And obviously Kristen Scott Thomas moved on from this, her first major role, to become an Oscar-nominated, highly respected leading lady.

How is the DVD presentation? Pretty good, for such a largely overlooked movie. The wide screen transfer and 2.0 stereo mix aren't anything phenomenal, but get the job done nonetheless; the movie looks and sounds fine. As for features, anyone expecting a full-blown Special Edition like the 2-disc "Purple Rain" will be disappointed. But at least it's not a completely bare-bones release—four music videos are included, though unfortunately not presented in optimal audio/visual quality (though they are passable, I would've preferred 5.1 mixes). The highlight is the live performance of "another lover" which was taken from a never-released (at least not domestically, not sure if it saw the light of day anywhere outside the U.S.) concert video documenting the Parade tour.

MTV held an interesting (i.e.—very weird) contest to determine where "Under the Cherry Moon" would have its world premiere. The ten-thousandth caller to an MTV hotline would accompany Prince to the premiere, which would be held in their hometown. MTV ran a special that covered the premiere party—and unlike the premiere of "Purple Rain" unfortunately this program is not to be found on "Under the Cherry Moon"'s DVD release. Lisa Barber was the contest winner, and the movie did indeed premiere in her hometown of Sheridan, Wyoming—a very unusual place for a big movie to premiere. When asked what he thought of the town of Sheridan, Prince summed it up with a single word: "Purple."

4-Stars: Elmwood Park, NJ April 2005: Prince's 1986 romantic comedy "Under the Cherry Moon" finally received the DVD treatment it deserved in the Summer of 2004. When the film was released, it was bombarded with bad reviews but this film is actually decent. Of course the music stands out but it actually succeeds as a comedy. The acting may be full of flaws but it's the 80's, what do you expect? Prince and Jerome Benton, from The Time, are gigolos living it up in South France and they come across a beautiful heiress (Kristin Scott Thomas) who happens to get her trust fund on her 21st birthday. They both woo her for the money but Prince ends up catching feelings for her. With a beautifully filmed movie and an incredible soundtrack, "Under the Cherry Moon" fails to disappoint.

Under The Cherry Moon News—People Weekly—July 21, 1986

First you win a contest, then you win friends. That's how it happened for Lisa Barber, 20, a Sheridan, Wyo. motel chambermaid who last month dialed an MTV contest number and, by being the 10,000th caller, won a date with Prince and the opportunity to have his much-hyped new movie, Under the Cherry Moon, premiered in her hometown. Barber, a veteran contest entrant who had never won more than "a couple of Big Macs and a curling iron," was ecstatic. So were her friends, many of whom she had never met. Moments after her name was announced, callers from California to the Carolinas began ringing up to ask for one or two or 10 of the 200 tickets she'd been allotted for Prince's frontier fandango. Her mother, Elena Holwegner, fielded the endless requests with humor, if not compromise. *Ring!* "No, Lisa's not here," she fibbed to one caller. "You say you're calling from Maine? Sorry." *Ring!* "You say you want to come over and take pictures of me doing housework? I've got a better idea. You come over and do housework, and I'll take pictures of *you*." *Ring!* "Sorry, no more tickets. What? You say you have six days to live? Well, sorry to break the news, honey, but you'll be long gone before Prince gets here. What? You say you can hold on an extra day? Well, I can't. Sorry!" *Click*.

For Prince—who, when it comes to publicity, is usually about as visible as a microbe and only slightly more talkative—the sojourn to Sheridan seemed to serve two purposes. After years of performing in bikini underwear and a raincoat and singing such single-entendre hits as "Head" and the incest-themed "Sister," he is, say pals, concerned that the public hasn't seen enough of the happy-go-lucky, Little House on the Prairie side of his personality. "He's perceived by the media as a bad boy, a rude boy," says his friend and protégé, singer Sheila E. "He is very conscious of his reputation, and I think he's making an effort to turn it around. Basically, he's an easy-going guy." Says Lisa Coleman, keyboardist with Prince's band, the Revolution, "He's so consumed by what he's doing that sometimes he has not noticed what is happening to his public image. He realizes it now."

The other reason Prince is courting publicity is that as Cherry Moon goes, so may go his movie career. If Moon succeeds, he'll be seen as a screen phenomenon; if it fails, his first movie, the $80 million-grossing Purple Rain, may be seen as a fluke. Adding to the tension is the fact that the new film, a black-and-white fantasy romance set in the South of France, is pure Prince: He stars in the movies, conceived the plot, handpicked the cast and took over for the original director, Mary Lambert, after she left because of "artistic differences." He also reportedly refused Warner Bros.' entreaties to inject conflict into the script, saying that atmosphere and music would keep the audience entertained.

Sheridan hadn't hosted such a dramatic event since 1865, when locals took on Arapaho Indians in a skirmish that preceded the Little Big Horn. By the time Prince pulled into town—11 days after Barber made her call—Sheridan was ready. The pro-Prince contingent gathered at the airport, carrying signs *(Welcome to Sheridan. We're proud of our town. Got any extra tickets?)* and hoping for a glimpse of the would-be minimogul. Others, less enthralled, could be found at the coffee counter in Ritz Sporting Goods, where rancher Dugan Wragge noted, "This town's known for fishing lures. We don't care about no boy who wears tight pants and struts around like a woman." Ventured another customer: "I'm going to paint a fence. If Prince wants to help me, that's fine." A third recalled that when he first learned of Prince's impending arrival, it set him to thinking about a visit Queen Elizabeth made to Sheridan in 1984 to look at equestrian stock: "I told my wife, 'This is real nice. First his mother, and now him.'"

The airport crowd let out a hoot when Prince's Learjet appeared as a dot in the Western sky. It landed and sat on the strip for a few minutes, the passenger door open. Then one tiny, high-heeled boot appeared. Then all 5'3" of Prince Rogers Nelson, decked out in a purple paisley silk suit, emerged smiling. He walked down a red carpet and threw his jacket over a fence to the crowd, then politely exchanged pleased-to-meet-you's with Sheridan's mayor, Max DeBolt, and other dignitaries. DeBolt, who takes every opportunity to plug Sheridan's tourist attractions (hunting and fishing), and neighborly life-style ("I think we had a thief here—once"), was delighted with the hoopla. As Prince climbed into a gray-and-black limo, he said, to no one in particular, "I'm going to buy a house here."

Meanwhile, back at the small cottage behind her mother's trailer home, Lisa Barber fretted like a prom queen should. Prince's staff had cured one headache by providing a black-and-white outfit that would match the evening's decor. "I was real worried about what I was going to wear," says Barber. "I usually shop at K Mart." Prince also sent over a hair stylist and a makeup artist. After that, Lisa has nothing to do except sit perfectly still until date time, 6 p.m.

Her guy pulled up, 15 minutes late, at the wheel of a white Buick convertible with personalized license plates that read LOVE. Eschewing the gravel driveway, he vaulted the chain-link fence and knocked on the door. "Hello," he said, kissing her hand. "My name is Prince. Ready to have a good time?" Unfazed by the fact that her date was wearing more makeup and—thanks to a midriff-baring shirt—showing more skin than she was, Barber answered in the affirmative and took her seat in the car. Preceded by Sheridan's female riding troupe, the Equestri-Annettes, and trailed by a posse of costumed cowboys, the couple cruised to the Centennial Twin theater, where 800 enthusiastic but inexpert stargazers waited. Singer Joni Mitchell entered unnoticed; crooner Ray Parker, Jr., a newspaper reported, was misidentified by some as Lionel Richie. "We cheered for anyone who was dressed weird or who was black," says one Sheridan.

Inside, Prince sat with Barber in a back row. He did not buy her any Raisinets or popcorn but otherwise behaved like a perfect gentleman. "Well, there was one time during the movie when he played with my hair and he put his arm around me," says Barber. "But that's all he did. Honest." And did Prince, rock's reigning purple enigma, actually engage in conversation sometime in the evening? "Oh, yeah," says Barber. "I asked him how he liked it here. He said it was real pretty and that I was lucky to live here. In the car he asked me what the best radio station was, and when he turned to it, the deejay was talking about him. He said, 'If I had a phone in here, I'd call him.'" At Cherry Moon, she says, "I told him I liked the movie. [Prince's co-star and sidekick] Jerome Benton asked me if I liked to fish but I told him 'No way.'"

And how did the all-important Sheridan critics react to Under the Cherry Moon? The first review came from a young woman who, when Prince's tightly suited form first appeared on the screen, yelled out "Nice butt!" After that things got a little less precise. "I liked it, but I didn't get it," said one local, whose opinion was echoed by others throughout the evening. "It was great!" offered another. "Like one long rock video! But I didn't really figure out what was going on." The next day, when Cherry Moon opened at 941 theaters around the country, paid critics began weighing in with reviews that made the townfolk seem kind. The New York Times called Prince's character a "self-caressing twerp of dubious provenance." The Washington Post said that in black-and-white, "Prince begins to remind you of something your biology teacher asked you to dissect." USA Today, at least, pointed out that Prince's principal draw isn't his dramatic skill: "Fewer people saw [Purple] Rain for the acting than saw Old Yeller for the sex." In its first weekend, the film grossed $3.1 million—about the same as Walt Disney's new movie The Great Mouse Detective.

That was in the future, however, and there was still joy in Sheridan as the movie crowd spilled out of the theater and into a party at the Holiday Inn. At 10 p.m. Prince climbed onto a specially built stage and unleashed 45 minutes of radioactive funk. "He's incredible," said a surprised Lillie Belle Johnson, 66. "I never realized what we were missing." With uncharacteristic informality, he and his band members mingled with the locals and made small talk about movies and trout. Cherry Moon might have gone over like wheat rust, but you couldn't tell that from the crowd's mood or from the mouths of Prince's entourage, who were hard-pressed to find fault with their mentor. "I thought it was the perfect thing for him to do," said bandmate Lisa Coleman. "Purple Rain was a heavier film; this is lighter." Casey Terry, lead singer in the Prince spin-off group Mazarati, pronounced him "scintillating to work with. If you can't handle his energy, you're up a creek." Said Cherry Moon co-star Kristin Scott-Thomas: "He was a joy to work with." Seconded Jerome Benton, who has worked with Prince as a roadie, backup singer and actor: "He's a genius. I won't ever leave, unless he couldn't use me. I like being under that protective wing."

Lisa Barber also enjoyed her time under the protective wing. When the party ended, her date made sure she had a ride home in a limousine. "I'll have lots of memories, but I know he'll probably never see him again," she said of her beau, who gave her earrings and a gold necklace as keepsakes. "I'll never take them off," she vowed. Looking back, she says the only good flaw in a perfect evening involved a misunderstanding over some costume jewelry Prince had impulsively asked to borrow. "He was a dream date," says Lisa, "even if he didn't give me back my pearls." *Written by Culter Durkee, Reported by Cathy Free & Jeff Yarbrough*

Chapter Nine

THE MOVIE—GRAFFITI BRIDGE—1990

GRAFFITI BRIDGE IS a film written, directed and starring Prince. It is a sequel to his highly successful first film, *Purple Rain*, though notorious for its relatively low quality and poor performance at the box-office. However, like *Purple Rain*, it was accompanied by a hit soundtrack.

The plot re-joins *Purple Rain*'s lead character The Kid, in his future life as a performer and club co-owner. Morris Day, his rival from *Purple Rain*, returns as co-owner of The Kid's club Glam Slam as well as several others in the area, including his mainstay Pandemonium. Prince is forced into paying Morris $10,000 so Morris can pay off the mayor; Prince in turn can keep co-ownership of his club. Losing clientelle, The Kid challenges Morris to a music battle for ownership of Glam Slam.

The film was panned universally for having a wealth of filler; indeed, the film seems to be a collection of music videos strung together with a loose plotline. The film's screenplay was even rejected by Madonna, who turned down the role of the mysterious angel-like figure, Aura, stating that the writing was awful.

While Prince's earlier movies have become cult classics, *Graffiti Bridge* has yet to achieve any status outside it's initial box-office flop. Most fans regard it as a low-point in his career.

The critical response for the film was far from favourable, with many reviewers arguing that Prince was attempting to position himself as a "Christ-like" figure, particularly during the sequence for the songs "Still Would Stand All Time" and "Graffiti Bridge". It seemed that The Kid was a far different character from the one in *Purple Rain*. Indeed, the only characters who remained unchanged were Morris Day and his sidekick Jerome Benton. Cameos included gospel singer Mavis Staples, up-and-coming teen star Tevin Campbell and funk icon George Clinton, although each were confined to roughly one song in the film. The music of the film was seen as the highlight, though "Thieves In The Temple" was the only song to really make an impact on the charts.

Graffiti Bridge got its title from an actual railroad bridge in northern Eden Prairie, Minnesota that crossed over Valley View Road. It was legal to spray graffiti on the bridge, and when the movie came out, a large mural of Prince was featured on the bridge. The bridge was torn down in the early 90's when Valley View Road needed to be widened (the road narrowed to one lane under the bridge, with each direction of traffic taking turns to pass under). When the bridge was torn down, pieces of the bridge were sold as mementos along with a miniature newspaper article about the

Graffiti Bridge Profile:

Directed by:	Prince
Produced by:	Randy Phillips and Craig Rice
Written by:	Prince
Starring:	Prince, Morris Day and Ingrid Chavez
Music by:	Prince
Distributed by:	Warner Bros.
Release Date:	November 2, 1990
Running Time:	95 Minutes
Awards:	None
Language:	English
Budget:	Unknown

Amazon Customers Reviews for Graffiti Bridge

3-Stars: June 2005: Graffiti Bridge was largely ignored on its release in the fall of 1990. And it's not hard to see why: It's horribly edited, rather horribly acted, and it doesn't make a whole lot of sense. Even die-hard Prince fans—myself among them—had a hard time supporting this one.

The main problem is probably that Warner Bros. wanted a sequel to the mega-hit Purple Rain. Prince apparently didn't want to make a sequel, but a fifties-style true musical. Unfortunately, a linear sequel to Purple Rain and a fifties-style musical just can't co-exist in the same film. Sure, it's got Prince as the Kid, Morris Day & Co., and a handful of references to the previous film. But people break into song whether or not they're on stage, and (in the aforementioned horrible editing) the sounds don't always match the performers' movements. The worst example of this is in Clinton's Club, when funky ol' George Clinton is singing "We Can Funk" . . . the song is a duet with Prince on the soundtrack album, and you can HEAR Prince singing in the scene, but he's nowhere to be found. And speaking of the soundtrack, some of the best cuts on the disc (released a good 6 months prior to the film's release) don't even appear in the film.

So why do I even give it a generous 3 stars? Well, I guess the thing kind of grows on ya after awhile. It's all pretty lightweight stuff, despite Prince's patented pseudo-Christian imagery. And the music that did make the cut is quite good, though Purple Rain fanatics will balk at the "new jack" sound that was all the rage in 1990.

In short, this isn't going to win Prince any new fans. But for those of us who still believe the Purple Wonder is about the best thing out there, Graffiti Bridge is a playful little curiosity that, in the end, really isn't so bad.

Oh, and it's nice to have the 4 music videos, especially a rare live version of "The Question of U."

3-Stars: April 2005: Speaking as a Prince fan, he took himself too seriously with this one. 1990's "Graffiti Bridge" was slammed when it was released and it all falls on Prince. When promoting the film, he should've never presented it as a drama. "Graffiti Bridge" is a musical and that's it. It may not have a big setting like "Moulin Rouge" but it is similar to a 60's beach musical. The point of it is to enjoy the music, and on that part "Graffiti Bridge" delivers. It played like one long music video and that's the point. Prince knows that but he wanted to be a serious director and actor, something he is not. "Graffiti Bridge" is for an acquired taste, you either love it or hate it.

5-Stars: September 2004: First off I will say that I am not a prince fan. I have nothing bad to say about him or his music or his movies, I am just not into it. However I love this movie. I've read a lot of horrible reviews about it, and all I can say to them is that most of them are due to the fact that you are trying to compare movies. On its own this movie is beautiful, the schematics of it, the scenary and set design, and the use of music to tell the story. To watch this movie on its own without a mind bias of assuming that because you liked and understood the previous movies, you will like and understand this one . . . you find many elements of it that do appeal. The fact that there was very little speaking and more body language is beautiful, The total distinction between all of the characters is beautiful. The total distinction in each and every song being unique is beautiful. When I first saw this movie the one thing that outright attracted me was "Aura". Ingrid Chavez's use of body language, in particular her facial expressions throughout this film are amazing. Each character had a very clear role and very clearly expressed what that role is. The set designs are both nostalgic and creative without being too overly artistic, there is no exact time and place for this film, sometimes you think you're in the 1920's in a back alley of a speakeasy, sometimes you think you're in the 1980's dreaming about the 1990's. I believe the main thing that causes people to dislike this movie so much is a misunderstanding of the roles and the purposes in it. Yes it is a battle between good and evil in a sense, but good (the kid) and evil(Morris day) are NOT the focus points of it. The focus is Aura. In a chess game it is necessary to protect the king, however the queen is the most powerful player on the board and it is very difficult to win a game if she is lost unless her sacrifice is so that the king or the other players are in position to check mate. She can move in any direct and any amount of spaces. Ingrid Chavez did that very well. Aura was quiet yet not silenced, she only spoke when necessary and all the rest was expressed in her face. She did just what anyone else would do in her situation, knowing what the outcome would be, she still attempted to get there in other ways. Along side of the character of Aura, is the music. People are forgetting that this is NOT just a movie but a musical. Musicals are meant to be expressive and theatrical, they are not meant to WOW you like other films by visuals and plots. They are meant to open your mind and make you think and possibly find answers to things you don't know. Does anyone know if angels exist? Would you know an angel if you saw one? Could someone's heart really truly be bad? Can people change? Is all music good or just the kind that makes us dance? Do actions speak louder than words? Do sinners have souls? All these questions can be pondered by watching this movie. But most people don't see that, all they see is that this movie isn't like Purple Rain, or Under the Cherry Moon, all they can see is that they have to think a little bit in order to enjoy it and since it isn't spelled out for them or so overly artistic that it must have reason then it must be the "worst prince movie ever". For Prince fans they don't see that, all they see is that Prince is not the main point, he is not as involved in it as he was in the other films, there are even less scenes with him even in it, and to them the music doesn't compare to the outright served up on a silver platter music of the others. It must be the "worst prince movie ever". Loose all of your biases, and this movie becomes one of the classic good movies. The main bias to loose is that this is not a Prince Movie . . . It's a Movie/Musical from the mind of Prince.

5-Stars: August 1999: Prince allows us a peek into a colorful world he has created, in "Grafitti Bridge". This film takes a visionary look at the lives of musicians and the "crooked" business they are in. Prince operates on a higher plane here, as he asks us "are there really angels?, or are they just in our minds?." The surreal landscape of "Graffiti Bridge" is a magical place. It is a place of dreams. It is a place where love once lived. But because of the dark forces of greed and corruption, the city has been tainted. Its dwellers have nearly succumbs to the evil advances of Morris Day and his entourage. Who will save their souls? Like a bat out of—Prince breaks them off some, and kicks some royal—with vengeance.

All set to a mystical soundtrack, check out Prince as he schools us with "Elephants and Flowers". All the while he wanders the lonely streets of this Erotic City crooning the Question of U, dedicated 2 Aura. Back at the ranch, Jill Jones remains under Morris's evil spell. Their next conquest . . . . Aura. It all plays out like a comic book. Will The Thieves In The Temple be dealt with? It all comes out in the wash in time.

2-Stars: August 2001: This is almost not a movie. What I mean is, it plays like a bunch of music videos with tidbits of plot thrown in between. If you're reading this, I take it you have an interest in Prince . . . or at least Morris Day and the Time. The soundtrack CD is really great, and if you really spend enough time listening to it, it kind of paints it's own picture in your mind. I don't know if that sounds crazy, but I bought the CD when it came out—a couple months before the release of the movie. The music is so detailed and vivid, I imagined what the movie would be like. Ultimately I was disappointed with how it actually turned out. "Purple Rain" towers above this movie, and I think a lot of it has to do with the fact that it (purple rain) had a screenwriter and director separate from Prince. With "Graffiti Bridge", Prince bit off more than he could chew by writing/directing/starring. I think there were some good ideas here that definitely needed some shaping.

Morris Day is the scene-stealer, as he was in "Purple Rain", though again I'm not so sure Prince wrote him as strong a part as he deserved. This movie is a semi-sequel to "Purple Rain"—which was a bad idea. "Purple Rain" had a realistic feel to it. "Graffiti Bridge" has a slightly surreal feel. Plus, unlike "Purple Rain", it was shot almost entirely on soundstages—resulting in a very set-bound, manufactured atmosphere.

Chapter Ten

PRINCE FIRST INTERVIEW
CENTRAL HIGH SCHOOL
FEBRUARY 16, 1976

NELSON FINDS IT "Hard To Become Known" "I play with Grand Central Corporation. I've been playing with them for two years," Prince Nelson, senior at Central, said. Prince started playing piano at age seven and guitar when he got out of eighth grade.

Prince was born in Minneapolis. When asked, he said, "I was born here, unfortunately." Why? "I think it is very hard for a band to make it in this state, even if they're good. Mainly because there aren't any big record companies or studios in this state. I really feel that if we would have lived in Los Angeles or New York or some other big city, we would have gotten over by now."

He likes Central a great deal, because his music teachers let him work on his own. He now is working with Mr. Bickham, a music teacher at Central, but has been working with Mrs. Doepkes.

He plays several instruments, such as guitar, bass, all keyboards, and drums. He also sings sometimes, which he picked up recently. He played saxophone in seventh grade but gave it up. He regrets he did. He quit playing sax when school ended one summer. He never had time to practice sax anymore when he went back to school. He does not play in the school band. Why? "I really don't have time to make the concerts."

Prince has a brother that goes to Central whose name is Duane Nelson, who is more athletically enthusiastic. He plays on the basketball team and played on the football team. Duane is also a senior.

Prince plays by ear. "I've had about two lessons, but they didn't help much. I think you'll always be able to do what your ear tells you, so just think how great you'd be with lessons also," he said.

"I advise anyone who wants to learn guitar to get a teacher unless they are very musically inclined. One should learn all their scales too. That is very important," he continued.

Prince would also like to say that his band is in the process of recording an album containing songs they have composed. It should be released during the early part of the summer.

"Eventually I would like to go to college and start lessons again when I'm much older."

Chapter Eleven

NEWS CHAIN OF EVENTS

1977

- Prince Rogers Nelson, 19, signs a three-record, $1 million contract with Warner Bros. Records.

1978

- Prince self-produced debut, "For You," is released to critical acclaim. He played all the instruments on the LP. The hit "Soft And Wet" is the only track on the LP not written exclusively by Prince. Its U.S. sales of 150,000 make it the only Prince album to date—not certified as at least gold (sales of 500,000 or more).

1979

- Signs a contract with the Los Angeles management firm of Cavallo Ruffalo and Fargnoli. Steve Fargnoli, a partner in the firm, takes control of building his career. Second album "Prince" goes platinum (1 million U.S. sales).

1980

- The landmark LP "Dirty Mind" establishes Prince's taste for controversial subject matter and goes gold.
- **104** Singles Artist of the Year
- Prince hit the Top 10 with "I Wanna Be Your Lover."
- Prince was certified platinum.
- The single "I Wanna Be Your Lover" was certified gold.
- Dirty Mind was released and received great reviews by critics (ranking **18** on Rolling Stone's "100 Best Albums of the 80s."

1981

New album "Controversy" sells 1 million copies in the United States. The strong reaction Prince evokes is highlighted when he is booed off the stage opening for the Rolling Stones in Los Angeles.

1982

- Controversy was certified gold.
- Prince's commercial breakthrough arrives with "1999," a 3 million seller in the United States. The 2-LP set, *1999*, introduced Prince more to pop audiences the following year. The set included the hits "1999," "Little Red Corvette," "Delirious," and "Let's Pretend We're Married."

1983

- After the successful "1999" tour, shooting begins around Minneapolis for Prince's first film, "Purple Rain." The $7 million film is partially funded by Prince himself, who puts up about $2 million.
- January of 1983 "1999" was certified gold.
- Prince's appeal on the pop charts didn't occur until "Little Red Corvette" became a hit in 1983. *1999*, was Prince's first major crossover hit and prepared him for super stardom. Prince received

even more notoriety with his radio and video hits, "1999" and "Delirious." The LP was later ranked at #16 on Rolling Stone's "100 Best Albums of the 80s."
- May of 1983 "1999" was certified platinum.

1984

- Release of the "Purple Rain" film and soundtrack puts him in the commercial stratosphere. U.S. sales of 11 million and $70 million in domestic ticket grosses, followed by a world tour that plays to 1.7 million people.
- January 1984, Prince was nominated for 2 **American Music Awards** for Favorite Soul/R&B Male Artist and Favorite Soul/R&B Album (1999).
- February 1984, Prince was nominated for a **Grammy Award** for Best R&B Vocal Performance—Male ("International Lover").
- June 1984, it might be said that 1984 was the year of Prince. He starred in the movie Purple Rain, which found sound success with the critics, but more importantly created a soundtrack to the movie that exemplified the musical genius of Prince. The LP sold over 13 million copies and produced the #1 hits: "When Doves Cry," "Let's Go Crazy," and "Purple Rain." The LP also contained the hits "I Would Die 4 U" and "Take Me With You," the controversial track, "Darling Nikki" and the haunting "The Beautiful Ones." Prince went on to win an Academy Award for the film's music. When Rolling Stone ranked the "100 Best Albums of the 80s," Purple Rain came in at # 2.
- Dirty Mind was certified gold and the single "When Doves Cry" was certified platinum.
- August 1984, the *Purple Rain* soundtrack was certified platinum.
- October 1984, "1999" was certified 2x platinum.
- September 1984, Prince hit the Top 10 with "Let's Go Crazy."
- November 1984, the Purple Rain soundtrack was certified 8x platinum and the single "Let's Go Crazy" was certified gold.
- December 1984, the single "Purple Rain" was certified gold.

1985

- "I'm going to find the ladder," Prince says in announcing that he will not perform live for a period of years. Album "Around the World in a Day" takes creative risks and sales slip to 2 million. Prince's new Warners-affiliated record label, Paisley Park Records, is formed.

- January 1985, *"Controversy"* was certified platinum and the *Purple Rain* soundtrack was certified 9x platinum.
- Prince won 3 **American Music Awards** for Favorite Pop/Rock Album and Favorite Soul/R&B Album (*Purple Rain*) and Favorite Soul/R&B Single ("When Doves Cry"), and was nominated for Favorite Pop/Rock Male Artist, Favorite Pop/Rock Male Video Artist, Favorite Pop/Rock Single, Favorite Soul/R&B Male Artist, Favorite Soul/R&B Male Video Artist, and Favorite Pop/Rock Video and Favorite Soul/R&B Video ("When Doves Cry").
- February 1985, Prince won 3 **Grammy Awards** for Best Rock Vocal Performance by a Duo or Group, Best Album of Original Score Written for a Motion Picture or TV Special (*Purple Rain*) and Best R&B Song (songwriter) (**Chaka Khan**'s "I Feel For You") and was nominated for Album of the Year (*Purple Rain*).
- The *Purple Rain* soundtrack was certified 10x platinum.
- April 1985, Prince's much anticipated follow-up LP came in 1985 with *Around The World In A Day*. The LP was described as a more pop-friendly Prince with less sexual overtones in his music. Prince topped the charts with "Raspberry Beret" and had success with "Pop Life" and "America."
- June 1985, Prince & The Revolution hit the Top 10 with "Raspberry Beret."
- July 1985, *"1999"* was certified 3x platinum and *Around The World In A Day* was certified 2x platinum.
- September 1985, the video for "When Doves Cry" was nominated for a **MTV Video Music Award** for Best Choreography.

1986

- Construction begins on Paisley Park Studios in a Chanhassen cornfield. Release of "Parade," soundtrack to Prince's directorial debut, "Under the Cherry Moon." Album sells 1.8 million domestically; film bombs.
- January 1986, Prince was nominated for 3 **American Music Awards** for Favorite Pop/Rock Male Artist, Favorite Soul/R&B Male Artist, and Favorite Soul/R&B Male Video Artist.
- March 1986, Prince tried his hand at the movie/soundtrack combination again with *Parade*, the soundtrack to *Under The Cherry Moon*. Critical praise was very hard to find for the film, but Prince's music did continue his success with the #1 track "Kiss" and hits "Anotherloverholenyohead" and "Mountains."
- May 1986, the single "Kiss" was certified gold.

- June 1986, "Parade" was certified platinum.
- Prince & The Revolution hit the Top 40 with "Mountains."
- September 1986, the video for "Raspberry Beret" won a **MTV Video Music Award** for Best Choreography.

1987

- "Sign 'O' the Times," an ambitious double album that many call his best, is released and sells about 1.8 million copies U.S. copies. Price had to be dissuaded from releasing it as a triple album, which would have further diminished its commercial prospects. European tour is filmed and released as a movie. At the last minute, Prince halts release of "The Black Album," a dark and daring dance record that is h
- January 1987, Prince was nominated for an **American Music Award** for Favorite Soul/R&B Single ("Kiss").
- February 1987, Prince won anther **Grammy Award** for Best R&B Vocal Performance by a Duo or Group ("Kiss") and was nominated for Best R&B Song (songwriter) ("Kiss").
- March 1987, the release of *Sign O' The Times* returned Prince to the top of the critic's choices lists and earned him a Grammy nomination for Album Of The Year. The 2-CD set contained the hits "U Got The Look," "I Could Never Take The Place Of Your Man," "Housequake," "If I Was Your Girlfriend," "Hot Thing," and the #1 title track. The LP was ranked as the 74th "Greatest Album of the 80s" by *Rolling Stone*.
- A bootleg Prince LP, *The Black Album* was "released." The LP was later officially released to the public in 1994 in limited amounts.
- April 1987, Prince hit #1 with "Sign 'O' The Times."
- July 1987, *Sign O' The Times* was certified platinum.
- October 1987, Prince hit #1 with "U Got The Look." eavily bootlegged. Paisley Park Studios opens in the fall.

1988

- "Lovesexy," a more positive replacement for "The Black Album." U.S. sales stall at about 1 million copies. The subsequent tour is hailed as one of the best rock shows ever, but American audiences stay away in droves. It is Prince's last U.S. arena tour.
- March 1988, Prince was nominated for 3 **Grammy Awards** for Album of the Year (*Sign O' The Times*), Best R&B Song (awarded to songwriter) Best R&B Vocal Performance by a Duo or Group ("U Got The Look") with **Sheena Easton**).

- May 1988, Prince released *Lovesexy* and hit the Top 10 with "Alphabet St." The LP was Prince first non-Platinum LP since becoming a superstar.
- September 1988, the video for "U Got The Look" won 2 **MTV Video Music Awards** for Best Male Video and Best Stage Performance Video and was nominated for Best Choreography and Best Editing.
- December 1988, *Lovesexy* was certified gold.

1989

- Prince fires Fargnoli as manager and dumps his Los Angeles attorney. Al Magnoli, director of "Purple Rain," takes over as his manager. Another L.A. attorney, Gary Stiffelman, takes over. New business manager Nancy Chapman later discloses that despite Prince's commercial success, he is in financial trouble. Prince soundtrack to "Batman" movie marks a commercial revival: 2 million sold domestically. Magnoli fired as manager, replaced by film producers Randy Phillips and Arnold Stiefel.
- June 1989, Prince performed music for the *Batman* soundtrack and returned to the spotlight for a bit after a poor response for, *Lovesexy*. The "all-Prince" soundtrack to the hit movie gave Prince another #1 hit with "Batdance" and the additional hits "Partyman," "The Arms Of Orion" (with **Sheena Easton**), and "Scandalous."
- July 1989, Prince hit the Top 40 and Top 10 with "Batdance."
- August 1989, Prince #1 for a week with "Batdance."
- The *Batman* soundtrack was certified 2x platinum and the single "Batdance" was certified platinum.
- September 1989, Prince hit the Top 40 and Top 10 with "Partyman."
- The video for "I Wish U Heaven" was nominated for a **MTV Video Music Award** for Best Special Effects.
- November 1989, the single "Partyman" was certified gold.
- Prince hit the Top 40 with **Sheena Easton** with "The Arms Of Orion."

1990

- Prince's fourth film, "Graffiti Bridge," stiffs at the box office, and sales of the soundtrack do not reach a million in the United States. Prince provides most of the financing for Glam Slam, a new nightclub in downtown Minneapolis owned by his bodyguard, Gilbert Davison. In December, Stiefel and Phillips are fired as manager and Prince goes without a formal manager. Davison is appointed president of Paisley Park Enterprises and Prince's publicist, Jill Willis, as executive vice president.

- January 1990, Prince was nominated for an **American Music Award** for Favorite Soul/R&B Male Artist and was honored with the Award of Achievement.
- February 1990, Prince was nominated for 4 **Grammy Awards** for Best Pop Vocal Performance—Male (*Batman* soundtrack), Best R&B Vocal Performance—Male ("Batdance"), Best Song Written for a Motion Picture, Television or Other Visual Media (songwriter) ("Partyman"), and Producer of the Year.
- August 1990, Prince embarked on another movie/soundtrack combination with *Graffiti Bridge* and found failure with both. Although the soundtrack did contain the Top 10 "Thieves In The Temple," more attention was paid to the soundtrack contributions of **Tevin Campbell** and **Mavis Staples**.
- Prince hit the Top 40 with "Thieves In The Temple."
- September 1990, Prince hit the Top 10 with "Thieves In The Temple."
- The video for "Batdance" was nominated for a **MTV Video Music Award** for Best Video from a Film.
- October 1990, the single "Thieves In The Temple" was certified gold.
- November 1990, *Graffiti Bridge* was certified gold.

1991

- "Diamonds and Pearls" provides a commercial boost with 5 million sold worldwide. Prince and his former manager, Fargnoli, trade lawsuits that are eventually resolved out of court.
- **18** Singles Artist of the Year.
- February 1991, Prince was nominated for a **Grammy Award** for Song of the Year (songwriter) ("Nothing Compares 2 U").
- September 1991, Prince & The N.P.G. hit the Top 40 with "Gett Off."
- October 1991, Prince re-emerged with another commercial success: "*Diamonds And Pearls*." The LP found audiences in the emerging hip-hop arena as well as the VH-1 crowd. Songs on the LP ranged from the sexy funk of "Gett Off" and to the more vocal focused title track. Prince hit #1 with the title track and "Cream" and found success with "Money Don't Matter 2 Night" and "Insatiable."

- The single "Gett Off" was certified gold.
- Prince hit the Top 40 and Top 10 with "Cream."
- November 1991, Prince hit #1 for 3 weeks with "Cream."
- December 1991, Prince hit the Top 40 with "Diamonds And Pearls"
- Diamonds And Pearls was certified platinum.

1992

- Prince announces that he has signed a new deal with Warner Bros. that is worth $100 million—a figure delicately downplayed by Warners. The new contract calls for Warner Bros. to become a partner in the operation of Prince's Paisley Park Enterprises.
- **13** Singles Artist of the Year
- January 1992, *Diamonds And Pearls* was certified 2x platinum and the single "Cream" was certified gold.
- Prince hit the Top 10 with "Diamonds And Pearls."
- Prince was nominated for an **American Music Award** for Favorite Soul/R&B Male Artist.
- February 1992, Prince & the NPG hit #1 for a week with "Diamonds And Pearls."
- Prince & the NPG were nominated for a **Grammy Award** for Best R&B Vocal Performance by a Duo or Group ("Gett Off").
- March 1992, Prince & the NPG topped the Billboard R&B Singles chart for 1 week with "Diamonds And Pearls."
- April 1992, Prince hit the Top 40 with "Money Don't Matter 2 Night."
- September 1992, the video for "Cream" won a **MTV Video Music Award** for Best Dance Video.
- October 1992, the release of *Prince & The New Power Generation* continued Prince's success with hits such as "Sexy MF' and Top 10 "7."
- Prince hit the Top 40 with "My Name Is Prince."
- November 1992, Prince hit the Top 40 with "7."
- December 1992, the LP *Prince & The New Power Generation* was certified platinum.

1993

- Prince announces in April that he is retiring from studio recording and will instead focus on "alternative media"—live theater, interactive media, nightclubs and motion pictures.
- **21** Singles Artist of the Year
- January 1993, Prince hit the Top 10 with "7."

- February 1993, Prince & the NPG were nominated for a **Grammy Award** for Best Pop Vocal Performance by a Duo or Group ("Diamonds And Pearls").
- March 1993, the single "7" was certified gold.
- April 1993, Prince hit the Top 40 with "The Morning Papers."
- June 1993, he celebrates his 35th birthday.
- September 1993, Prince changed his name to a combination of the male and female symbol. His name pronunciation since then has ranged from "The Artist Formerly Known As Prince," "TAFKAP," The Artist," and "Victor." Yet, most people, Rock On The Net included, have their own pronunciation of the symbol: "Prince." Prince also implied that he might never release a studio LP again.
- As fans pondered what to call Prince, they were rewarded with a 3-CD release of his hits.
- *The Hits—The B-Sides.* The video for "7" was nominated for a **MTV Video Music Award** for Best R&B Video.
- October 1993, Prince hit the Top 40 with "Pink Cashmere."
- **Rolling Stone: "The 100 Top Music Videos"** included "Kiss" at # **18**, "Gett Off" at # **21** and "Little Red Corvette" at # **85**.
- December 1993, *The Hits* was certified gold.

1994

- Warner Bros. and Prince announce the collapse of their joint venture, and the Paisley Park Records label is disbanded. Prince forms a new record label—NPG Records—and releases the single "The Most Beautiful Girl in the World." Paisley Park Enterprises acquires Glam Slam clubs in L.A. and Miami, but the company—increasingly hounded by creditors—also begins a dramatic downsizing of its staff, firing many key staffers. Two albums—"Come" and "1987's "The Black Album"—are released. Prince begins campaigning for release from his Warners contract, calling it "institutionalized slavery." In club dates, he promotes another new album, "The Gold Experience," which he says will never be released.
- **16** Singles Artist of the Year
- March 1994, Prince hit the Top 40 with "The Most Beautiful Girl In The World"—a single he released independently as *The Beautiful Experience* (7 remixes of "The Most Beautiful Girl In The World").
- April 1994, Prince hit the Top 10 with "The Most Beautiful Girl In The World" and hit #1 for 3 weeks by the end of the month.

- May 1994, the single "The Most Beautiful Girl In The World" was certified gold.
- July 1994, the *Purple Rain* soundtrack was certified 11x platinum.
- August 1994, "Old Prince" material was released as *Come 1958-1993*—an attempt to put "Prince" to rest.
- Prince hit the Top 40 with "Letitgo."
- October 1994, *Come 1958-1993* was certified gold.

1995

- January 1995, "The 22nd Annual American Music Awards" will present Prince with an award of merit for "outstanding contributions to the musical entertainment of the American public." He is also being honored for being "an entertainment entrepreneur."
- **62** Singles Artist of the Year
- Prince was honored at the **American Music Awards** with a nominated for Favorite Soul/R&B Male Artist.
- March 1995, Prince was nominated for a **Grammy Award** for Best R&B Vocal Performance—Male ("The Most Beautiful Girl In The World").
- August 1995, *The Hits* was certified platinum.
- Septembe1995, Prince released *The Gold Experience* which contained his #1 hit "The Most Beautiful Girl In The World" as well as "Gold" and "Billy Jack Bitch." The LP received great reviews with many stating it was Prince best work since *Sign O' The Times*.
- Prince hit the Top 40 with "I Hate U."
- December 1995, *The Gold Experience* was certified gold.
- Prince hit the Top 40 with "Gold."

1996

- **105** Singles Artist of the Year

February 1996, Prince was nominated for a few **Grammy Awards** including Best R&B Album (*The Gold Experience*) and Best R&B Vocal Performance—Male ("I Hate U").

March 1996, Prince could be heard on the *Girl 6* soundtrack—including the hit "Pink Cashmere."

May 1996, the *Purple Rain* soundtrack was certified 13x platinum.

July 1996, Prince released his final offering from Warner Brothers, *Chaos And Disorder* with the moderate hit, "Dinner With Delores."

Prince's dissatisfaction with fulfilling his record company's obligations were evident when he appeared on the *Today Show* performing tracks from the LP with the word "slave" written on his face.

August 1996, Prince released an ambitious 3-CD set called *Emancipation* and hit the Top 40 with the remake "Betcha By Golly Wow!." His marriage and media support for *Emancipation* had appeared to reduce Prince's aloof image and his music was once again appreciated.

December 1996, Prince hit the Top 40 with "Betcha By Golly Wow!"

1997

- **56** Singles Artist of the Year

January
Emancipation was certified platinum.
Rock 'N Roll Hall Of Fame's 500 Songs That Shaped Rock And Roll includes "Little Red Corvette" and "When Doves Cry."
Prince hit the Top 10 with "Betcha By Golly Wow!"

February
Emancipation was certified 2x platinum.
Prince hit the Top 40 with "The Holy River."
Prince released a 3-CD set of unreleased material available by mail-order from Prince's website. With Prince no longer associated with EMI Records, the artist felt a greater sense of musical freedom: "My success is no longer defined by others . . ." Internet sales of *Crystal Ball* have shown to be brisk. Although total sales are less than a typical release would initiate, the direct profit for the musicians is more substantial. Prince stated that ". . . charts, awards and grades at school R sociopsychotic illusion."

March
Crystal Ball was later sold exclusively at Best Buy stores followed by Musicland and Blockbuster stores. The CD set—a collection of older, unreleased Prince material—included the acoustic tracks on *The Truth* (a CD free when the *Crystal Ball* was also purchased).

1998

- January 1998, when the nominations for the 12th annual Soul Train Awards were announced, Prince got a nomination for Best R&B/Soul Album—Male for *Emancipation*.
- May 1998, Ranked # **18** on **VH1: Greatest Artists of Rock & Roll** (and # **27** on Rock On The Net's Poll).
- June 1998, Prince released *Newpower Soul* with the single "The One." The LP was distributed through NPG Records.
- Prince allowed fans to download his 26-minute single, "The War" for free off his website, love4oneanother, and talked with *SonicNet Music News*: "It's our music . . . go tape it and give it to friends . . . spread it around." Prince is also encouraging fans who download the song make a donation to a children's charity.
- September 1998, Prince had to postpone several dates of his current tour with **Chaka Khan** after he sprained his ankle while performing in Atlantic City. The accident was believed to be due to a slick stage caused by a fog machine.
- December 1998, Prince announced that he have annulled his marriage to Mayte and the 2 will remain apart until next year's Valentine's Day when they will be re-married.

1999

- **102** Singles Artist of the Year.
- February 1999, Prince released *1999—The New Masters*—a collection of "1999" remixes.
- March 1999, "*1999*" was certified 4x platinum.
- August 1999, Warner Bros. Records released older, unreleased Prince music in the form of *Vault—Old Friends 4 Sale*. The LP contains music recorded between 1985 and 1994 and includes the first single "Extraordinary."
- November 1999, Prince hit the record shelves with new material entitled *Rave Un2 The Joy Fantastic* after allowing a record label (Arista Records) to release the music. The first single was "The Greatest Romance Ever Sold" and the LP features appearances by **Ani DiFranco**, **Sheryl Crow**, Chuck D of **Public Enemy**, and **Gwen Stefani** of **No Doubt**.
- Prince hit the Top 40 with "The Greatest Romance Ever Sold."
- December 1999, *Rave Un2 The Joy Fantastic* was certified gold.
- Prince ended the year with a pay-per-view concert on New Year's Eve and officially retired his hit "1999" stating on *The Early Show*

"This is going to be the last time we play it. We're going to retire it after this, and there won't be no need to play it in the 00s."

- **MTV: 100 Greatest Videos Ever Made** includes "1999" at # **91**.

2000

- January 2000, **VH1: 100 Greatest Rock Songs** includes "When Doves Cry" at # **92**.
- March 2000, Prince was honored with the "Artist of the Decade" award at the Soul Train Music Awards.
- The same month Prince disputed with his new label Arista and refused to release a remix of his latest LP stating that his label did not promote his LP adequately enough for a hit single.
- May 2000, Prince asked that he be called 'Prince' again instead of ♀—a symbol he used as his name "to free myself from all undesirable relationships"—Prince also broke with Arista Records.
- June 2000, Prince celebrated the reinstitution of his name with a 6-day open house and tour of his Paisley Park studios ending with a 3+ hour concert.
- October 2000,
- **VH1: 100 Greatest Dance Songs** includes Prince's "1999" at # **66**.
- November 2000, Prince kicked off his "Hit N' Run" tour in Massachusetts.
- **Rolling Stone & MTV: 100 Greatest Pop Songs** includes "When Doves Cry" at # **27** and "Little Red Corvette" at # **50**.

2001

- January 2001, **VH1: 100 Greatest Albums** includes *Purple Rain* at # **18**, *Sign O' The Times* at # **35**, and *1999* at # **49**.
- May 2001, **VH1: 100 Greatest Videos** includes: # **17**—"When Doves Cry" and # **81**—"1999."
- June 2001, Prince kicked off a 7-week North America tour—but the tour was cancelled for unknown reasons in July.
- July 2001, Prince released another hits compilation—*The Very Best Of Prince.*
- November 2001, Prince released *The Rainbow Children.*

2002

- Septmeber 2002, Prince ranked # **5** on **VH1: 100 Sexiest Artists**.
- November 2002, *The Very Best Of Prince* was certified gold.

- December 2002, Prince released the 3-CD live set—*One Nite Alone Live.*

2003

- June 2003, **VH1: 100 Best Songs of the Past 25 Years** includes "When Doves Cry" at # **7** and "Little Red Corvette" at # **23**.
- July 2003, Prince released the EP *N.E.W.S.*
- August 2003, Prince released the DVD *Live At The Aladdin Las Vegas.*
- December 2003, **Rolling Stone: The 500 Greatest Albums of All Time**: # **72**: *Purple Rain*, # **93**: *Sign O' The Times*, # **163**: *1999*, # **204**: *Dirty Mind.*

2004

- **139** Singles Artist of the Year
- February 2004, Prince was nominated for a **Grammy Award** for Best Pop Instrumental Album (*N.E.W.S.*). Prince opened the ceremony with a performance with **Beyoncé Knowles**.
- March 2004, Prince was inducted into the Rock & Roll Hall of Fame and said at the ceremony "When I first started out in this music industry, I was most concerned with freedom. I wish you all the best on this fascinating journey. It ain't over."
- April 2004, Prince released his next LP *Musicology*—released by Columbia Records instead of the Internet.
- May 2004, Prince appeared on the cover of *Rolling Stone.*
- *Musicology* was certified gold.
- June 2004, *Musicology* was certified platinum.
- August 2004, the video for "Musicology" was nominated for a **MTV Video Music Award** including Best Male Video.
- September 2004, *The Very Best Of Prince* was certified platinum.
- November 2004, Prince was nominated for 2 **American Music Awards** for Favorite Soul/R&B Male Artist and Favorite Soul/R&B Album.
- December 2004, Prince was chosen by *Rolling Stone* magazine's readers as the best male performer and most welcome comeback.
- **5** on the **Top Pop Artists of the Past 25 Years** chart.

2005

- January 2005, *Musicology* was certified 2x platinum.
- February 2005, Prince won 2 **Grammy Awards** for Best Traditional R&B Vocal Performance ("Musicology") and Best R&B Vocal

Performance—Male ("Call My Name"), and was nominated for Best Pop Vocal Performance—Male ("Cinnamon Girl"), Best R&B Song (awarded to the songwriter) ("Call My Name"), and Best R&B Album (*Musicology*).
- March 2005, Prince won a NAACP Image Award for Outstanding Album (*Musicology*). Prince was also honored with the Vanguard Award at the ceremony.
- September 2005, Prince released the charity single "S.S.T." on-line with proceeds going to help those impacted by Hurricane Katrina.

2006

- February 2006, Prince performed on *Saturday Night Live*.
- March 2006, Prince released *3121*.
- Prince topped the Billboard Hot Singles Sales chart with "Black Sweat."
- April 2006, Prince topped the Billboard 200 LP chart for the first time in 17 years and Top R&B/Hip-Hop Albums chart with *3121*—the LP sold over 183,000 copies in the US its first week of release.
- June 2006, Prince won a BET Award for Best Male R&B Artist. *Source: Rockonthenet.com*

Chapter Twelve

ROLLING STONE INTERVIEW PRINCE
BY BILL ADLER
FEBRUARY 19, 1981

SNAKING OUT FROM the wings toward center stage at the Ritz, prancing like a pony with his hands on his hips and then flinging a clorine kick with a coquettish toss of his head, Prince is androgyny personified. Slender and doe-eyed, with a faint pubescent mustache, he is bare-chested beneath a gray, hip-length Edwardian jacket. There's a raffish red scarf at this neck, and he's wearing tight black bikini briefs, thigh-high black leg warmers and black-fringed go-go boots. With his racially and sexually mixed five-piece band churning out the terse rhythms of "Sexy Dancer" behind him, the effect is at once truly sexy and more than a little disorienting, and his breathy falsetto only adds to his ambiguity—for sheer girlish vulnerability, there's no one around to touch him: not Michael Jackson, not even fourteen-year-old soul songbird Stacy Lattisaw. At age twenty, Prince may be the unlikeliest rock star, black or white, in recent memory—but a star he definitely is.

As quickly becomes apparent, Prince's lyrics bear little relation to standard AM radio floss. In addition to bald sexual come-ons and twisted love plaints, he champions the need for independence and self-expression. And one song, "Uptown," is, among other things, an antiwar chant. Further complicating the proceedings are the heavy-metal moans Prince wrenches out of his guitar and the punchy dance-rock rhythms of his band (bassist Andre Cymone, guitarist Dez Dickerson, keyboardists Lisa Coleman and Dr. Fink and drummer Bobby Z.), all of whom are longtime cohorts from Prince's hometown—Minneapolis, of all places.

"I grew up on the borderline," Prince says after the show. "I had a bunch of white friends, and I had a bunch of black friends. I never grew up in any one particular culture." The son of a half-black father and an Italian mother who divorced when he was seven, Prince pretty much raised himself from the age of twelve, when he formed his first band. Oddly, he claims that the normalcy and remoteness of Minneapolis provided just artistic nourishment he needed.

"We basically got all the new music and dances three months late, so I just decided that I was gonna do my own thing. Otherwise, when we did split Minneapolis, we were gonna be way behind and dated. The white radio stations were mostly country, and the one black radio station was really boring to me. For that matter, I didn't really have a record player when I was growing up, and I never got a chance to check out Hendrix and the rest of them because they were dead by the time I was really getting serious. I didn't even start playing guitar until 1974."

With his taste for outlandish clothes and his "lunatic" friends, Prince says he "took a lot of heat all the time. People would say something about our clothes or the way we looked or who we were with, and we'd end up fighting. I was a very good fighter," he says with a soft, shy laugh. "I never lost. I don't know if I fight fair, but I go for it. That's what 'Uptown' is about—we do whatever we want, and those who cannot deal with it have a problem within themselves."

Prince has written, arranged, performed and produced three albums to date (*For You, Prince and Dirty Mind*), all presenting the same unique persona. Appearances to the contrary, though, he says he's not gay, and he has a standard rebuff for overenthusiastic male fans: "I'm not about that; we can be friends, but that's as far as it goes. My sexual preferences really aren't any of their business." A *Penthouse* "Pet of the Month" centerfold laid out on a nearby table silently underscores his point.

It took Prince six months alone in the studio to concoct his 1978 debut album, because, he says, "I was younger then." *Prince* required six weeks. He controlled the making of both records, but notes that they were "overseen" by record company and management representatives. *Dirty Mind*, however, was made in isolation in Minneapolis. "Nobody knew what was going on, and I became totally engulfed in it," he says. "It really felt like me for once."

The result of this increased freedom was a collection of songs celebrating incest ("Sister") and oral sex ("Head") in language raw enough to merit a warning sticker on the album's cover. "When I brought it to the record company it shocked a lot of people," he says. "But they didn't ask me to go back and change anything, and I'm real grateful. Anyway, I wasn't being deliberately provocative. I was being deliberately *me*."

Obviously, judging by the polished eclecticism of *Dirty Mind*, being himself is the best course. "I ran away from home when I was twelve," Prince says. "I've changed address in Minneapolis thirty-two times, and there was a great deal of loneliness. But when I think about it, I know I'm here for a purpose, and I don't worry about it so much."

Chapter Thirteen

THE SECRET LIFE OF AMERICA'S SEXIEST ONE-MAN BAND ROLLING STONE MAGAZINE BY DEBBIE MILLER—1983

"GOOD EVENING, THIS is your pilot, Prince, speaking" comes out of the loudspeakers, all softness and breath, full of welcome. It's a flight you may not have taken before. Brace yourself, he ought to say. This is "International Lover," something the globe-conquering Prince claims to be. And this is his live act, which takes place on a grand, two-tiered stage hung with gigantic Venetian blinds. In high-heeled boots, a flouncy ruffled blouse and a purple quasi-Edwardian suit, Prince begins to climb to the higher level, taking long strides that end in a hip-locking sway, a Rita Hayworth sort of walk. "You are flying aboard the Seduction 747," he rasps. "To activate the flow of excitement, extinguish all clothing materials." Standing alone on the upper riser, Prince simply points a finger, and—you imagine this happens every time Prince extends his long index finger—a brass bed materializes. Stripping off his jacket, his shirt, unbuckling his belt so that a long strap hangs between his legs, Prince climbs onto the mattress and begins to undulate over the bed. "We are now making our final approach to satisfaction. Please bring your lips, your arms, your hips into the up and locked position for landing," he says, panting, and lets out a piercing scream that seems to announce the sudden fall from the sky of the flight of Seduction 747—and Prince and the bed disappear.

All cocky, teasing talk about sex, that's Prince. Forget Mr. Look So Good; meet the original Mr. Big Stuff. He's afraid of nothing onstage: ready to take on all the desires of a stadium full of his lusty fans, ready to marry funky black dance music and punky white rock music after their stormy separation through the Seventies, ready to sell his Sex Can Save Us message to anybody who'll give his falsetto a listen. Nor does anything scare him when he's at home alone, composing.

Out comes a paean to incest called "Sister," a song called "Head" about a bride who meets Prince on her way to be wed and says, "I must confess, I wanna get undressed and go to bed," and a song called "Jack U Off." He even advised the president, "Ronnie Talk to Russia." So bold that half of his material is radio-censored, Prince is wailing, "Guess I should have closed my eyes when you drove me to the place where your horses run free/Cuz I felt a little ill when I saw all the pictures of the jockeys that were there before me" (in "Little Red Corvette"), while Lionel Richie is everywhere on the radio with "Truly, I love you truly."

His music, a technofunk and rock blend that many have started to call "the Minneapolis sound" because of the way the Minnesota native's influence is spreading, is the freshest thing around. So Kraftwerk made *The Man Machine*? This is the Man Sex Machine. He usually plays every instrument on his albums, even sings his own backup most of the time. His upper register can give you goose flesh when he's singing gospel style, and he can turn around and hiccup his way through rockabilly like a perfect descendant of Elvis. There just don't seem to be any bounds to Prince's nerve or talent—each album is better than the last (he's made five), each stage show more outrageous.

A tour begun in November of last year had grossed almost $7 million before the end of March. Prince's new double album, *1999*, has sold almost 750,000 copies, with its hottest single, "Little Red Corvette," closing in on the Top Twenty on *Billboard*'s Hot 100 chart. And two groups he helped form made the black chart's Top Ten this winter: Vanity 6, a coquettish trio that performs in lingerie and whose "Nasty Girls" was a disco smash, and the Time, the tightest, funkiest live band in America.

Prince, just twenty-two, is the father of it all. But just try checking out the lineage. There isn't just a private side to Prince, there's an almost mysterious aspect. While the art of self-promotion has never been alien to rock & roll, it seems only to frustrate Prince. He was fairly outspoken until last fall, when, after his first interview to promote *1999*, he walked out of the room and announced that he would never talk to the press again. "He's afraid he might say something wrong or say too much," says a former aide-de-camp.

When he did talk, he often contradicted himself. Rumors started to spread, and now his silence feeds them. Is Prince his real name? Is he black or white, straight or gay (questions he himself raised on his 1981 hit-cum-Lord's Prayer recitation, "Controversy")? Is he the Jamie Starr who produced albums by the Time and Vanity 6? Is he a shy little Prince or a despotic king?

"Prince controls the whole scene in Minneapolis," says a local musician who has worked with him. Others who've lived with him or worked alongside him say he loves to surround himself with an air of mystery, to create false identities to tangle the clues that lead to him. Cutting off all but a few close friends, Prince tends to hole up at his huge home, with its modern basement studio, on a lake twenty miles west of Minneapolis. One member of his band says he's had just one personal conversation with Prince in all the years he's known him. "He's a real 'to himself' kind of person," says Morris Day, the Time's frontman and a longtime friend.

"He doesn't like to talk," says Vanity, the awesomely beautiful leader of Vanity 6, who accompanied Prince to the Grammys in February.

"Sir Highness," says another friend, "has a way of secluding himself."

Chapter Fourteen

**PRINCE, THE PAUPER
ROLLING STONE MAGAZINE
BY DEBBIE MILLER—1983**

PIECE TOGETHER PRINCE'S story from his own partial accounts, and you come up with sort of a musical Wild Child, an untamed loner who raised himself and taught himself how to survive among the wolves. Patch together the history told by the people close to him, and you get a version like this:

The first notes of the Minneapolis sound were heard in a big brick house in North Minneapolis, an aging, primarily black section of town that draws outsiders only to the Terrace Theater, a movie house designed to look like a suburban backyard patio, and the Riverview Supper Club, the nightspot a black act turns to after it has polished its performance on the local chitlin circuit. North Minneapolis is a poor area by local standards, but a family with not too much money can still afford the rent on a whole house. It was there that Bernadette Anderson, who was already raising six kids of her own by herself; decided to take in a doe-eyed kid named Prince, a pal of her youngest son, Andre.

The thirteen-year-old Prince had landed on the Anderson doorstep after having been passed from his stepfather and mother's home to his dad's apartment to his aunt's house. "I was constantly running from family to family," Prince has said. "It was nice on one hand, because I always had a new family, but I didn't like being shuffled around. I was bitter for a while, but I adjusted."

His father, John Nelson, was a musician himself—a piano player in a jazz band by night, a worker at Honeywell, the electronics company, by day. Nelson is black and Italian; his ex-wife, says Prince of his mother, "is a mixture of a bunch of things." Onstage, the father was called Prince Rogers, and that is what he named his son, Prince Rogers Nelson.

John Nelson moved out of the family home when Prince was seven. But he left behind his piano, and it became the first instrument Prince learned to play. The songs he practiced were TV themes—*Batman* and *The Man From U.N.C.L.E.* "My first drum set was a box full of newspapers," he has said, explaining how he came to play a whole range of instruments. "At thirteen, I went to live with my aunt. She didn't have room for a piano, so my father bought me an electric guitar, and I learned how to play." But the aunt wasn't keen on the noise, and she threw him out. It was then that Prince turned up at Andre's.

Hardly into their teens, Prince and Andre (who uses the surname Cymone) had already formed their first group. Prince recalled, "I got my first band. I wanted to hear more instruments, so I started Champagne, a twelve-piece band. Only four of us played. Eight were faking. Andre and I played saxophone. I also played piano. I wrote all the music. The songs were all instrumentals. No one ever sang. When I got into high school, I started to write lyrics. I'd write the really, really vulgar stuff."

Andre, on the other hand, claims the first band had Prince playing lead guitar, Andre himself on bass guitar, his sister Linda on keyboards and the Time's Morris Day on drums. The group was called Grand Central, later renamed Champagne. The musicians all wore suede-cloth suits with their zodiac signs sewn on the back (Prince, born on June 7th, 1960, had Gemini, the twins, on his). For a time, they were managed by Morris' mother, which didn't make Prince very happy. "She wasn't fast enough for Prince," says Mrs. Anderson. "He wanted her to get them a contract right away."

The band practiced in Andre's basement, where Prince had established a bedroom of his own. "It sounded like a lot of noise" says Bernadette Anderson. "But after the first couple of years, I realized the seriousness of it. They were good kids. Girls were crazy about them."

Andre—whose father had played bass in the Prince Rogers Band—says that although the family was poor, Prince "dug the atmosphere. It was freedom for him." There wasn't enough money to buy records, but there was a family friend—a reclusive black millionaire, says one source—who gave the kids the money to go to a local studio to record a few songs. The studio they picked was called Moon Sound.

Moon Sound was an eight-track studio that charged about thirty-five dollars an hour back in 1976, when Prince and Andre and the rest of Champagne walked in the door. The owner, Chris Moon, was a lyricist looking for a collaborator. "Prince always used to show up at the studio with a chocolate shake in his hand, sipping out of a straw," Moon remembers. "He looked pretty tame. Then he'd pick up an instrument and that was it. It was all over."

Prince soon agreed to work with Moon, and the studio owner handed the seventeen year-old a set of keys to the studio. "He'd stay the weekend, sleep on the studio floor," Moon says. "I wrote down directions on how to operate the equipment, so he'd just follow the little chart—you know, press this button to record and this button to play back. That's when he learned to operate studio equipment. Pretty soon, I could sit back and do the listening."

One person who heard Prince's early recordings was Owen Husney, who became his first manager. Husney put together an expensive package that included a demo tape of three twelve-minute songs on which Prince sang and played all the instruments, and he went off to L.A. to make a pitch to the record companies. Three labels—CBS, Warner Bros. and A&M—eventually made offers. Prince finally signed with Warner Bros., where, says an executive, they "were taken with the simplicity of his music and a future that looked wide open," and where he was offered a firm three-LP contract, unheard of for a new artist.

Lenny Waronker, then head of A&R and now president of the label, was impressed enough to allow Prince to act as producer of his debut album. "I met him when we first signed him," Waronker recalls. "[Producer] Russ Titelman and I took him into the studio one day, much to his chagrin. So we said, 'Play the drums,' and he played the drums and put a bass part on, a guitar part. And we just said, 'Yeah, fine, that's good enough.'"

Sales of the first Prince album, *For You*, released in 1978, weren't so hot, but the fact that the kid was a one-man band—and his own producer—got a lot of attention. Then, in 1979, the single "I Wanna Be Your Lover" from his eponymous second LP went to Number One on the soul charts. But the age of innocence was almost over. Prince was back in Minneapolis putting together a band a straggly mix of blacks and whites, all recruited locally. His old friend Andre Cymone was among them, playing bass.

There was a lot of pressure from my ex-buddies in other bands not to have white members in the band," Prince has said. "But I always wanted a band that was black and white. Half the musicians I knew only listened to one type of music. That wasn't good enough for me."

The band, with its double keyboards, learned to reproduce the music Prince had been creating alone in the studio. The synthesizers, often playing horn lines, are a hallmark of the Minneapolis sound. The guitar signature is edgy rock, but the beat reins in any long guitar solos. "Around here, if it's not synthesizers, it's nothing," says a local Minneapolis musician. "This is a keyboard town. It's *simplicity*. If you listen to a lot of Prince or the Time, it's simple. It's direct and straight to the point. And it feels so good."

With a band to spread the word on the road, Prince was ready, in 1980, to unleash *Dirty Mind*, his bawdy third album. *1999* wasn't very far away.

Chapter Fifteen

BLACK LACE BIKINI UNDERWEAR
ROLLING STONE MAGAZINE
BY DEBBIE MILLER—1983

PRINCE DOES NOT dress like your average rock star. Not for him the futuristic, stretchy costumes of the Commodores, or the raggedy jeans of the Bruce Springsteen types. He wears bright eye makeup, and his hair seems a cross between Little Richard and neorockabilly styles. He dresses in his own rococo street-kid fashion. Last year, when Prince won an award from a Minneapolis weekly newspaper for Minnesota Musician of the Year, he showed up in his most formal clothes—black trench coat and white go-go boots (his acceptance speech: "When do they give the award for the best ass?").

And he's been known to perform in nothing but boots and a pair of bikini underpants. It's quite an act—that lean, almost nude body singing no-holds-barred lyrics. "How come you don't call me?" he wails in gospel falsetto in one song. "Don't you wanna play with my tootsie roll?" And he entreats his audiences into the singalong to "Head—"I'll give you head, love you till you're dead."

It's sex sure—girls screech whenever he tosses black lace bikini underwear into the audience—but it's also very funny. Teddy Pendergrass, Marvin Gaye and Richard "Dimples" Fields are all out of the same school of seduction, but Prince seems to have been off studying with Mae West, learning high camp and low-rent vamping. He's developed a great sense of humor, even if he takes his sex-is-liberation politics very seriously. And from the giddy "Gotta Stop Messin' About" to "Let's Work," nobody has so well expressed the exhilarating freedom of adolescent sexual energy since Michael Jackson yelped "I Want You Back."

"Prince has brought a boldness out of black entertainers again," says Alexander (O'Neil—there's a penchant for first names only in this crowd), a Minneapolis singer who fronted an early version of the Time. "Jimi Hendrix and Little Richard—they *always* dressed bizarre. Now Prince is doing it in a new era. He's making a lot of entertainers wake up to things. You're making a statement in life. It's all about being your own self. Like Prince says, 'It's all about being free."

Why so much sex? someone asked him once. "My songs are more about love than they are about sex," he answered. "I don't consider myself a great poet, or interpreter a la Moses. I just know I'm here to say what's on my mind, and I'm in a position where I can do that. It would be foolish for me to make up stories about going to Paris, knocking off the queen and things of that nature."

Prince was just seventeen when he co-wrote, with studio owner Chris Moon, the single from his first LP, a song called "Soft and Wet." Already, they had considered the commercial potential of an innocent sexuality. "That was the original concept," says Moon, "and it's stayed true to that. I had a conversation with him on the phone about a year ago, and I said, 'I see you're still staying with the "Soft and Wet" theme. But you're making it a little more blatant. What is this I hear about "Head"?' And he goes, 'Yeah, well, I decided to make it a little more straightforward so that everyone would get it."

Everyone does seem to be getting it these days, including Prince's dad. "When I first played the *Dirty Mind* album for him," Prince has said of his father, "he said, 'You're swearing on the record. Why do you have to do that?' And I said, 'Because I swear.'"

Prince, apparently, is not a character played out in the music. "His persona is Prince, onstage and offstage," says his friend and personal manager, Steve Fargnoli. "He's just as outspoken and outrageous offstage, in his business dealings." But he *is* shy, Fargnoli adds, and he says what he has to say about his politics and music on his records, not in conversation. And soon, he'll be saying it all in a movie: Prince has written the film treatment and most of the score for a musical that he'll also act in. "He is demanding of himself and of everyone who works around him," says Fargnoli. "You always have to be on your toes. He doesn't play by the rules."

The rules he plays by, instead, are *his* rules. He comes on strong. Is he—with his androgynous look, his royal name and his sex-mad lyrics—scarier to white audiences than Mr. T? Album-oriented radio is certainly skittish about playing Prince, saying that funk doesn't cut it with their heavy-metal-loving listeners. On the other hand, his videos are popular with MTV viewers. Prince's audience actually seems to be as integrated as that of the old soul stars (Prince's management company estimates his concert audiences to be forty percent white). People who like, say, James Brown have found Prince, and they like the way he uses elements of rock & roll while keeping an R&B backbone in the music.

And although armchair sociologists might suggest that a really outrageous performer has a better chance of succeeding in conservative times like these and may cite Little Richard's reign in the Fifties as an example, neither Little Richard nor Prince would have made a dent in the music market without talent. Prince, whose refusal to speak to the press has made him less visible than other musicians, probably is popular in spite of not because of, his image. After all, he has a following of people caught up in the visceral charge of his music, not an audience of voyeurs.

He can count among his fans John Cougar, who was so impressed on hearing Prince's "Little Red Corvette" that he started touting Prince to his own concert audiences. Before 20,000 fans in Tulsa, he ran backstage to get his cassette deck, then played a tape of Prince's hit single into his microphone. For the LP Cougar is producing for Mitch Ryder, the first 45 is likely to be Ryder's recording of Prince's "When You Were Mine." And Cougar has—unsuccessfully, so far—been trying to get a message to Prince: would he sing on Cougar's new album?

Chapter Sixteen

WHAT TIME IS IT?
ROLLING STONE MAGAZINE
BY DEBBIE MILLER—1983

JONI MITCHELL SONGS blare out of the PA between the sets of Prince's road show, at his request. Vanity 6, three women in lacy camisoles, open the concert. "I love lingerie," explains Vanity, the leader of the group. "I used to sneak into my mother's closet and try to wear her lingerie to school." She picked her nickname because "a girl's best friend is her pride," she says. Like her cohorts, Brenda and Susan, Vanity gave a demo tape of her songs to Prince a year ago. "He said there were a couple other girls whose minds seemed to run alongside mine," she says. Prince then arranged to bring Vanity, a twenty-two-year-old former model from Toronto, to Minneapolis to meet the other two, flying Brenda in from Boston. Soon, the three were writing songs like "Drive Me Wild" and "Nasty Girls" in which Vanity coos, "I can't control it/I need seven inches or more."

It all seems a figment of Prince's imagination, a living fantasy. "Prince and I happen to think alike," says Vanity.

On their record, Vanity 6 is backed by the Time; onstage, they're followed by the Time (who, in turn, are followed by Prince). At one point in the Time's set, frontman Morris Day, a terrific dancer, calls out his valet. The valet—who often follows Morris' own dance steps like a shadow—brings out a table, sets it with a white cloth and a vase of flowers, and uncorks a bottle of champagne. Morris, meanwhile, in his trademark two-tone Stacy Adams shoes, waltzes with a girl chosen from the audience. This sort of classy deportment was the starting point for the Time, as organized by Morris. "The image was *cool*. That's the key word," he says. "That's what we built the Time around. Cool is an attitude, a self-respect thing."

Morris didn't exactly put the group together—all but guitarist Jesse Johnson had been playing around Minneapolis in a band called Flyte Tyme (known familiarly as the Tyme even then). But it is Morris who has led the band to the point where it now often steals the show from the scantily clad Vanity 6 and even from Prince. Morris, the former drummer, has stayed closer to traditional R&B but, by injecting his good humor, has developed one of the best live acts in the country.

Prince, says Morris, helped the band get its Warner Bros. contract in 1981. Asked why the Time shares the same teenage-sex themes as Prince, Morris says, "Sex is present in everybody's life. I don't think anybody owns the rights to that." Asked if Prince influenced their sound, Morris says what Vanity says: "We believe in the same things." Asked about Jamie Starr, an icy tension descends. Although Morris Day and one Jamie Starr are credited as producers on the Time's first record, there is reason to believe that the record was, in fact, produced by Prince. One source very close to the situation says that not only is all the material written by Prince (mysteriously, there are no writing credits on the LP), but that the instruments are played by Prince and the voice is Prince's doubled with Morris Day's. This insider claims that the record—a more commercial, more straightforward R&B album—is a project Prince offered Warner Bros. because his own bolder stuff wasn't selling impressively. So, goes this theory, Prince set the Time in motion—and created a pseudonym, Jamie Starr, for his new project.

Prince did tell a reporter in an early interview with the *Minnesota Daily*, when he was just seventeen, that someday he would make jazz recordings under an alias. (In that same interview, Prince claimed not to be averse to choreography, but he drew the line at spins—"I get nauseated.") So the idea of working with a fictitious name had occurred to him at the beginning of his career.

And although Morris says that he and the band wrote the songs on their first LP, *The Time*, a call to the American Society of Composers, Authors and Publishers (ASCAP), with whom the songs are registered, casts some doubt. The composer of the hits "Get It Up" and "Cool" is Prince Rogers Nelson (with Dez Dickerson on "Cool"), says an ASCAP spokesman. Prince's manager says that the fact that Prince's name is registered for the Time's record is "a filing mistake."

"Let me clear up a few rumors while I have the chance," Prince told the *Los Angeles Times*. "One, my real name is Prince. Two, I'm not gay. And three, I'm not Jamie Starr."

"Jamie Starr is an engineer, the coproducer of our record. Of course he's real," says Morris Day, whose band now outplays whoever it was on the first Time record.

But if there is a Jamie Starr, why can't he be reached? Manager Steve Fargnoli says it's because he's "in and out of Minneapolis," because he's "a reclusive maniac" like Prince) and because "it could be months before I see him." Can he be reached by phone? "No." Well, you wouldn't need to call him over to Prince's home studio if he's already there. "Prince is Jamie Starr" says former Warner Bros. artist and fellow Minneapolitan Sue Ann (Carwell), who has been a friend of Prince's for years—ever since he wrote and produced her first demo tape. Others who are close to Prince also say that he is Jamie Starr, but they refuse to be quoted in print. But, says one, "everybody knows who's the main man behind everything."

Chapter Seventeen

**ROLLING STONE—APRIL 26, 1985
PRINCE TALKS
BY NEAL KARLEN**

JOHN NELSON TURNS sixty-nine today, and all the semiretired piano man wants for his birthday is to shoot some pool with his firstborn son. "He's real handy with a cue," says Prince, laughing, as he threads his old white T-bird through his old black neighborhood toward his old man's house. "He's so cool. The old man knows what time it is."

Hard time is how life has traditionally been clocked in North Minneapolis; this is the place 'Time' forgot twelve years ago when the magazine's cover trumpeted "The Good Life in Minnesota," alongside a picture of Governor Wendell Anderson holding up a walleye. Though tame and middle-class by Watts and Roxbury standards, the North Side offers some of the few mean streets in town.

The old sights bring out more Babbitt than Badass is Prince as he leads a leisurely tour down the main streets of his inner city Gopher Prairie. He cruises slowly, respectfully: stopping completely at red lights, flicking on his turn signal even when no one's at an intersection. Gone is the wary Kung Fu Grasshopper voice with which Prince whispers when meeting strangers or accepting Academy Awards. Cruising peacefully with the window down, he's proof in a paisley jump suit that you can always go home again, especially if you never really left town.

Tooling through the neighborhood, Prince speaks matter-of-factly of why he toyed with early interviewers about his father and mother, their divorce and his adolescent wanderings between the homes of his parents, friends and relatives. "I used to tease a lot of journalists early on," he says, "because I wanted them to concentrate on the music and not so much on me coming from a broken home. I really didn't think that was important. What was important was what came out of my system that particular day. I don't live in the past. I don't play my old records for that reason. I make a statement, then move on to the next."

The early facts, for the neo-Freudians: John Nelson, leader of the Prince Rogers jazz trio, knew Mattie Shaw from North Side community dances. A singer sixteen years John's junior, Mattie bore traces of Billie Holiday in her pipes and more than a trace of Indian and Caucasian in her blood. She joined the Prince Rogers trio, sang for a few years around town, married John Nelson and dropped out of the group. She nicknamed her husband after the band; the son who came in 1958 got the nickname on his birth certificate. At home and on the street, the kid was "Skipper." Mattie and John broke up ten years later, and Prince began his domestic shuttle.

"That's where my mom lives," he says nonchalantly, nodding toward a neatly trimmed house and lawn. "My parents live very close by each other, but they don't talk. My mom's the wild side of me; she's like that all the time. My dad's real serene; it takes the music to get him going. My father and me, we're one and the same." A wry laugh. "He's a little sick, just like I am."

Most of North Minneapolis has gone outside this Sunday afternoon to feel summer, that two-week season, locals joke, between winter and road construction. During this scenic tour through the neighborhood, the memories start popping faster. The T-Bird turns left at a wooden two-story church whose steps are lined with bridesmaids in bonnets and ushers in tuxedos hurling rice up at a beaming couple framed in the door. "That was the church I went to growing up," says Prince. "I wonder who's getting married." A fat little kid waves, and Prince waves back.

"Just all kinds of things here," he goes on, turning right. "There was a school right there, John Hay. That's where I went to elementary school," he says, pointing out a field of black tar sprouting a handful of bent metal basketball rims. "And that's where my cousin lives. I used to play there every day when I was twelve, on these streets, football up and down this block. That's his father out there on the lawn."

These lawns are where Prince the adolescent would also amuse his friends with expert imitations of pro wrestlers Mad Dog Vachon and the Crusher. To amuse himself, he learned how to play a couple dozen instruments. At thirteen, he formed Grand Central, his first band, with some high school friends. Grand Central often traveled to local hotels and gyms to band-battle with their black competition: Cohesion, from the derided "bourgeois" South Side, and Flyte Time, which, with the addition of Morris Day, would later evolve into the Time.

Prince is fiddling with the tape deck inside the T-Bird. On low volume comes his unreleased "Old Friends 4 Sale," an arrow-to-the-heart rock ballad about trust and loss. Unlike "Positively 4th Street"—which Bob Dylan reputedly named after a nearby Minneapolis block—the lyrics are sad, not bitter. "I don't know too much about Dylan," says Prince, "but I respect him a lot. 'All Along the Watchtower' is my favorite of his. I heard it first from Jimi Hendrix."

"Old Friends 4 Sale" ends, and on comes "Strange Relationships," and as-yet-unreleased dance tune. "Is it too much?" asks Prince about playing his own songs in his own car. "Not long ago I was driving around L.A. with [a well-known rock star], and all he did was play his own stuff over and over. If it gets too much, just tell me."

He turns onto Plymouth, the North Side's main strip. When Martin Luther King got shot, it was Plymouth Avenue that burned. "We used to go to that McDonald's there," he says. "I didn't have any money, so I'd just stand outside there and smell stuff. Poverty makes people angry, brings out their worst side. I was very bitter when I was young. I was insecure and I'd attack anybody. I couldn't keep a girlfriend for two weeks. We'd argue about anything."

Across the street from McDonald's, Prince spies a smaller landmark. He points to a vacant corner phone booth and remembers a teenage fight with a strict and unforgiving father. "That's where I called my dad and begged him to take me back after he kicked me out," he begins softly. "He said no, so I called my sister and asked her to ask him. So she did, and afterward told me that all I had to do was call him back, tell him I was sorry, and he's take me back. So I did, and he still said no. I sat crying at that phone booth for two hours. That's the last time I cried."

In the years between that phone-booth breakdown and today's pool game came forgiveness. Says Prince, "Once I made it, got my first record contract, got my name on a piece of paper and a little money in my pocket, I was able to forgive. Once I was eating every day, I became a much nicer person." But it took many more years for the son to understand what a jazzman father needed to survive. Prince figured it out when he moved into his purple house.

"I can be upstairs at the piano, and Rande [his cook] can come in," he says. "Her footsteps will be in a different time, and it's real weird when you hear something that's a totally different rhythm than what you're playing. A lot of times that's mistaken for conceit or not having a heart. But it's not. And my dad's the same way, and that's why it was hard for him to live with anybody. I didn't realize that until recently. When he was working or thinking, he had a private pulse going constantly inside him. I don't know, your bloodstream beats differently."

Prince pulls the T-Bird into an alley behind a street of neat frame houses, stops behind a wooden one-car garage and rolls down the window. Relaxing against a tree is a man who looks like Cab Calloway. Dressed in a crisp white suit, collar and tie, a trim and smiling John Nelson adjusts his best cuff links and waves. "Happy birthday," says the son. "Thanks," says the father, laughing. Nelson says he's not even allowing himself a piece of cake on his birthday. "No, not this year," he says with a shake of the head. Pointing at his son, Nelson continues, "I'm trying to take off ten pounds I put on while visiting him in Los Angeles. He eats like I want to eat, but exercises, which I certainly don't."

Father then asks son if maybe he should drive himself to the pool game so he won't have to be hauled all the way back afterward. Prince says okay, and Nelson, chuckling, says to the stranger, "Hey, let me show you what I got for my birthday two years ago." He goes over to the garage and gives a tug on the door handle. Squeezed inside is a customized deep-purple BMW. On the rear seat is a copy of Prince's latest LP, Around the World in a Day. While the old man gingerly back the car out, Prince smiles. "He never drives that thing. He's afraid it's going to get dented." Looking at his own white T-Bird, Prince goes on: "He's always been that way. My father gave me this a few years ago. He bought it new in 1966. There were only 22,000 miles on it when I got it."

An ignition turns. "Wait," calls Prince, remembering something. He grabs a tape off the T-Bird seat and yells to his father, "I got something for you to listen to. Lisa [Coleman] and Wendy [Melvoin] have been working on these in L.A." Prince throws the tape, which the two female members of his band have mixed, and his father catches it with one hand. Nelson nods okay and pulls his car behind his son's in the alley. Closely tailing Prince through North Minneapolis, he waves and smiles whenever we look back. It's impossible to believe that the gun-toting geezer in Purple Rain was modeled after John Nelson.

"That stuff about my dad was part of [director-cowriter] Al Magnoli's story," Prince explains. "We used parts of my past and present to make the story pop more, but it was a *story*. My dad wouldn't have nothing to do with guns. He never swore, still doesn't, and never drinks." Prince looks in his rearview mirror at the car tailing him. "He don't look sixty-nine, do he? He's so cool. He's got girlfriends, lots of 'em." Prince drives alongside two black kids walking their bikes. "Hey, Prince," says one casually. "Hey," says the driver with a nod, "how you doing?"

Passing by old neighbors watering their lawns and shooting hoops, the North Side's favorite son talks about his hometown. "I wouldn't move, just cuz I like it here so much. I can go out and not get jumped on. It feels good not to be hassled when I dance, which I do a lot. It's not a think of everybody saying, 'Whoa, who's out with who here?' while photographers flash their bulbs in your face."

Nearing the turnoff that leads from Minneapolis to suburban Eden Prairie, Prince flips in another tape and peeks in the rearview mirror. John Nelson is still right behind. "It's real hard for my father to show emotion," says Prince, heading onto the highway. "He never says, 'I love you,' and when we hug or something, we bang our heads together like in some Charlie Chaplin movie. But a while ago, he was telling me how I always had to be careful. My father told me, 'If anything happens to you, I'm gone.' All I thought at first was that it was a real nice thing to say. But then I thought about it for a while and realized something. That was my father's way of saying 'I love you.'"

A few minutes later, Prince and his father pull in front of the Warehouse, a concrete barn in an Eden Prairie industrial park. Inside, the Family, a rock-funk band that Prince has been working with, is pounding out new songs and dance routines. The group is as tight as ace drummer Jellybean Johnson's pants. At the end of one hot number, Family members fall on their backs, twitching like fried eggs.

Prince and his father enter to hellos from the still-gyrating band. Prince goes over to a pool table by the soundboard, racks the balls and shimmies to the beat of the Family's next song. Taking everything in, John Nelson gives a professional nod to the band, his son's rack job and his own just-chalked cue. He hitches his shoulders, takes aim and breaks like Minnesota Fats. A few minutes later, the band is still playing and the father is still shooting. Prince, son to this father and father to this band, is smiling.

The night before, in the Warehouse, Prince is about to break his three-year public silence. Wearing a jump suit, powder-blue boots and a little crucifix on a chain, he dances with the Family for a little while, plays guitar for a minute, sings lead for a second, then noodles four-handed keyboard with Susannah Melvoin, Wendy's identical-twin sister.

Seeing me at the door, Prince comes over. "Hi," he whispers, offering a hand, "want something to eat or drink?" On the table in front of the band are piles of fruit and a couple bags of Doritos. Six different kinds of tea sit on a shelf by the wall. No drugs, no booze, no coffee. Prince plays another lick or two and watches for a few more minutes, then waves goodbye to the band and heads for his car outside the concrete barn.

"I'm not used to this," mumbles Prince, staring straight ahead through the windshield of his parked car. "I really thought I'd never do interviews again." we drive for twenty minutes, talking about Minnesota's skies, air and cops. Gradually, his voice comes up, bringing with it inflections, hand gestures and laughs.

Soon after driving past a field that will house a state-of-the-art recording studio named Paisley Park, we pull down a quiet suburban street and up to the famous purple house. Prince waves to a lone, unarmed guard in front of a chain-link fence. The unremarkable split-level house, just a few yards back from the minimum security, is quiet. No fountains out front, no swimming pools in back, no black-faced icons of Yahweh or Lucifer. "We're here," says Prince, grinning. "Come on in."

One look inside tells the undramatic story. Yes, it seems the National Enquirer—whose Minneapolis exposé of Prince was excerpted in numerous other newspapers this spring—was exaggerating. No, the man does not live in an armed fortress with only a food taster and wall-to-wall, life-size murals of Marilyn Monroe to talk to. Indeed, if a real-estate agent led a tour through Prince's house, one would guess that the resident was, at most, a hip suburban surgeon who likes deep-pile carpeting.

"Hi," says Rande, from the kitchen, "you got a couple of messages." Prince thanks her and offers up some homemade chocolate-chip cookies. He takes a drink from a water cooler emblazoned with a Minnesota North Stars sticker and continues the tour. "This place," he says, "is not a prison. And the only things it's a shrine to are Jesus, love and peace."

Off the kitchen is a living room that holds nothing your aunt wouldn't have in her house. On the mantel are framed pictures of family and friends, including one of John Nelson playing a guitar. There's a color TV and VCR, a long coffee table supporting a dish of jellybeans, and a small silver unicorn by the mantel. Atop the large mahogany piano sits an oversize white Bible.

The only unusual thing in either of the two guest bedrooms is a two-foot statue of a smiling yellow gnome covered by a swarm of butterflies. One of the monarchs is flying out of a heart-shaped hole in the gnome's chest. "A friend gave that to me, and I put it in the living room," says Prince. "But some people said it scared them, so I took it out and put it in here."

Downstairs from the living room is a narrow little workroom with recording equipment and a table holding several notebooks. "Here's where I recorded all of 1999," says Prince, "all right in this room." On a low table in the corner are three Grammys. "Wendy," says Prince, "has got the Academy Award."

The work space leads into the master bedroom. It's nice. And . . . normal. No torture devices or questionable appliances, not even a cigarette butt, beer tab or tea bag in sight. A four-poster bed above plush white carpeting, some framed pictures, one of Marilyn Monroe. A small lounging area off the bedroom provides a stereo, a lake-shore view and a comfortable place to stretch out on the floor and talk. And talk he did—his first interview in three years.

A few hours later, Prince is kneeling in front of the VCR, showing his "Raspberry Beret" video. He explains why he started the clip with a prolonged clearing of the throat. "I just did it to be sick, to do something no one else would do." He pauses and contemplates. "I turned on MTV to see the premiere of 'Raspberry Beret' and Mark Goodman was talking to the guy who discovered the backward message on 'Darling Nikki.' They were trying to figure out what the cough meant too, and it was sort of funny." He pauses again. "But I'm *not* getting down on him for trying. I like that. I've always had little hidden messages, and I always will."

He then plugs in a videocassette of "4 the Tears in Your Eyes," which he's just sent to the Live Aid folks for the big show. "I hope they like it," he said, shrugging his shoulders.

The phone rings, and Prince picks it up in the kitchen. "We'll be there in twenty minutes," he says, hanging up. Heading downstairs, Prince swivels his head and smiles. "Just gonna change clothes." He comes back a couple minutes later wearing another paisley jump suit, "the only kind of clothes I own." And the boots? "People say I'm wearing heels because I'm short," he says, laughing. "I wear heels because the women like 'em."

A few minutes later, driving toward the First Avenue club, Prince is talking about the fate of the most famous landmark in Minneapolis. "Before Purple Rain," he says, "all the kids who came to First Avenue knew us, and it was just like a big, fun fashion show. The kids would dress for themselves and just try to took really cool. Once you got your thing right, you'd stop looking at someone else. You'd be yourself, and you'd feel comfortable."

Then Hollywood arrived. "When the film first came out," Prince remembers, "a lot of tourists started coming. That was kind of weird, to be in the club and get a lot of 'Oh! There *he* is!' It felt a little strange. I'd be in there thinking, 'Wow, this sure is different than it used to be.'"

Now, however, the Gray Line Hip Tour swarm has slackened. According to Prince—who goes there twice a week to dance when he's not working on a big project—the old First Avenue feeling is coming back. "There was a lot of us hanging around the club in the old days," he says, "and the new army, so to speak, is getting ready to come back to Minneapolis. The Family's already here, Mazarati's back now too, and Sheila E. and her band will be coming soon. The club'll be the same thing that it was."

As we pull up in front of First Avenue, a Saturday-night crowd is milling around outside, combing their hair, smoking cigarettes, holding hands. They stare with more interest than awe as Prince gets out of the car. "You want to go to the [VIP] booth?" asks the bouncer. "Naah," says Prince. "I feel like dancing."

A few feet off the packed dance floor stands the Family, taking a night off from rehearsing. Prince joins the band and laughs, kisses, soul shakes. Prince and three of Family members wade through a floor of Teddy-and-Eleanor-Mondale-brand funkettes and start moving. Many of the kids Prince passes either don't see him or pretend they don't care. Most of the rest turn their heads slightly to see the man go by, then simply continue their own motions.

An hour later, he's on the road again, roaring out of downtown. Just as he's asked if there's anything in the world that he wants but doesn't have, two blondes driving daddy's Porsche speed past. "I don't," Prince says with a giggle, "have them."

He catches up to the girls, rolls down the window and throws a ping-pong ball that was on the floor at them. They turn their heads to see what kind of geek is heaving ping-pong balls at them on the highway at two in the morning. When they see who it is, mouths drop, hands wave, the horn blares. Prince rolls up his window, smiles silently and speeds by.

Off the main highway, Prince veers around the late-night stillness of Cedar Lake, right past the spot where Mary Tyler Moore gamboled during her TV show's credits. This town, he says, is his freedom. "The only time I feel like a prisoner," he continues, "is when I think too much and can't sleep from just having so many things on my mind. You know, stuff like, 'I could do this, I could do that. I could work with this band. When am I going to do this show or that show?' There's so many things. There's women. Do I have to eat? I wish I didn't have to eat."

A few minutes later, he drops me off at my house. Half a block ahead, he stops at a Lake Street red light. A left up lake leads back to late-night Minneapolis; a right is the way home to the suburban purple house and solitude. Prince turns left, back toward the few still burning night-lights of the city he's never left.

Chapter Eighteen

MTV INTERVIEW PRINCE
BY MICHAEL SHORE—1985

PRINCE'S NEXT FEATURE film, Under the Cherry Moon—and the much-anticipated followup to his smash debut, Purple Rain—should be out in theaters in three or four months. It's even more eagerly awaited because it's also Prince's feature-film *directing* debut.

Originally, the film was to be directed by Mary Lambert, a premier music-video director who has overseen Madonna's "Borderline" and "Material Girl," Sheila E.'s "The Glamorous Life," and the Go-Go's "Yes Or No." But in mid-September, about a month or so into the movie's two-month shooting schedule, Lambert abruptly walked off the set and handed the directing reins to His Royal Badness.

Lambert issued a statement, which read, in part, "I'm leaving under totally amicable circumstances. It's just become quite apparent that Prince has such a strong vision of what this movie should be, a vision that extends to so many areas of the film, that it makes no sense for me to stand between him and the film anymore. So I'm going off to work on my own feature and letting him finish his."

Lambert's was not the first departure from the set of Under the Cherry Moon. Just days into filming, veteran British actor Terrance Stamp walked off the set, allegedly due to "scheduling conflicts," which may or may not be public relations' diplomacy. In any case, Stamp was replaced in short order by Steven Berkoff, who played the heavies in both Beverly Hills Cop and Rambo. He'll be seen as the father of Prince's love interest in the film.

Under the Cherry Moon is a love story, set in the 1940s and shot in black and white. Word from the set has it that the plot is more or less spelled out in the lyrics to "Condition of the Heart" on Around the World in a Day, which appears to be about a musician falling in love with a woman too rich and worldly for his own lifestyle.

In Under the Cherry Moon, Prince's love interest is a rich girl named Mary Sharon who, according to one cast member, "wears miniskirts and pigtails." Prince plays Christopher, a piano player in a casino-style lounge in a place similar to the French Riviera, where the film was shot. One unconfirmed story was that Prince wanted to shoot some scenes in Monte Carlo but Prince Rainier wouldn't grant permission. Guess he felt one prince on the premises was enough.

While the plot may come from a Prince song, don't expect much Prince music in Under the Cherry Moon. Another unidentified crew member says the Revolution was on the set only to shoot the video for "America," that there's no band music in the film at all, and that the only Prince music in the film is His Royal Badness at the acoustic piano. So there may or may not be soundtrack album. Another crew member confirmed, though, that there is one actual "song," and it's called something like "Snowing in July." You'll recall that when Prince announced he would stop touring late in the Purple Rain tour, one of his cryptic reasons was, "Sometimes it snows in July."

The rest of the cast includes little-known British actress Kristen Scott-Thomas as Mary Sharon; Jerome Benton, Morris Day's former valet in the Time and now a member of the Family, as Prince's "partner"; veteran British actress Francesca Annis as an older woman with whom Prince's character reportedly has an affair; and Victor Spinetti, whose career as a supporting player in rock movies goes all the way back to the Beatles' A Hard Day's Night and Help!

So what'll the movie be like? Your guess is as good as ours or anyone else's at this point. But consider another hot report from one crew member. In order to complete the film on time after he took over from Lambert, Prince shot the remaining scenes in one take.

Maybe that's a good sign. After all, His Royal Badness did all right making records by himself for a long time, and surprised a lot of supposed experts with the success of Purple Rain. Somehow, it's hard to believe Prince is finished surprising us.

Late in 1985, Prince broke his self-imposed silence and spoke to the public for the first time in almost four years. First came an interview for Rolling Stone Magazine. Later came an interview for MTV. Prince's agreement to be interviewed took MTV so suddenly that the staff at the cable network were unable to arrange to conduct the interview in person. Consequently, the Music News staff resorted to simply providing a list of questions to be read to Prince by his manager and answered by Prince on videotape. MTV elected to broadcast only parts of the interview. The full interview was then offered to other broadcasters.

The videotaped interview was conducted in France, where Prince was shooting his forthcoming motion picture, Under the Cherry Moon. He first took a break to film the video for America, the third single from the Around the World in a Day LP, before 2,000 kids at the Theatre de la Verdure (translation: Greenery Theatre), which is a huge tent on the Promenade des Anglais in Nice. Once the video shoot was completed, Prince & the Revolution treated the audience to a 90-minute concert. Afterwards, Prince sat with a few of the young people in attendance and answered the questions prepared by the MTV Music News staff. It marked the first time in his career that Prince had said more than two sentences on TV. Unfortunately, in many cases, he didn't answer the questions posed, as you'll see. Although Prince is very good at many things, his inexperience with interviews shows greatly.

The first and most obvious question is, why have you decided to drop your media guard with the recent Rolling Stone interview and this one for MTV? And why were you so secretive prior to this?

Well, as you can see, I've made a lot of friends here, but I was homesick and I missed America. I guess I just wanted to talk to somebody.

A lot of observers have remarked on your apparent need for control, and only with your two most recent albums, you gave credit to your band for composing, arranging and performing. It seems to us, from what we know of your personal background, that the need for control arose from your childhood and early teen years when you had a total lack of control over your life and were shuttled from home to home. Is this the case? If not, how does the need for control and/or your current, more open stance relate to your music?

I was horrible. To be perfectly honest, I was surrounded by my friends, but nevertheless, we had a difference of opinion in a lot of situations—musically speaking, that is. A lot had to do with me not being quite sure exactly which direction I wanted to go in. Later on toward the Controversy period, I got a better grip on that. That's when we started to see more and more people participating in recording activities. Boom.

Someone in Minneapolis recently told us that several months ago they were in a studio there when David Rifkin, your sound engineer, walked in. They asked him what he thought of the new Prince album, Around The World In A Day. He said, "It's great, but wait 'til you hear the new album." Apparently, he meant you're already working on a new LP, and that this one would be a strong return to your funk roots. Is this true? Can you elaborate? What will it be called? When will it be due out, and what's the music like?

Don't you like surprises? Guess not. Ah, it is true I record very fast. It goes even quicker now that the girls help me—the girls, meaning Wendy and Lisa. I don't really think I left my funk roots anywhere along the line. Around The World In A Day is a funky album. Live it's even funkier.

Why did you make the announcement that there'd be no singles or videos from that LP, and then start issuing singles and making videos anyway?

Because I wanted this album to be listened to, judged, critiqued as a whole. It's hard to take a trip and go around the block, and stop when the trip is 400 miles. Dig?

Speaking of singles and videos, your latest is "America." This is one of the most political songs you've ever done. Could you tell us what the song is supposed to say to people? For example, is it straightforwardly patriotic or more complicated than that?

Straightforwardly patriotic.

We understand you directed the "America" video, and that you also directed "Raspberry Beret." How do you approach directing a video? Do you consult others in order to keep a certain perspective when directing yourself?

Yes, definitely. When directing myself, I consult Steve (Fargnoli), my manager. On directing other Paisley Park artists, I consult the artists first and foremost. One of the things I try to do with the things I direct—namely for our acts—is go for the different, the out-of-the-norm, the avant purple, so to speak. And the thing that's unique about the situation I'm in now with these people is that they all know who they are, and they agree with me when we say the one thing we produce is the alternative. If someone wants to go along for that ride, then cool.

Would you ever like to direct your own movie?

Yes, (very enthusiastically) yes, yes.

Speaking of movies, tell us as much as you can about Under The Cherry Moon.

Ooooh.

What's the plot, what kind of characters, what kind of music, how many songs, what can we expect?

It's a French film. It's a black-and-white French film, and ah, she's in it (girlish giggles can be heard). And her name's Emanuelle.

A lot of people were offended by what they saw as sexism in Purple Rain.

Now, wait, wait. I didn't write Purple Rain. Someone else did. And it was a story, a fictional story, and should be perceived that way. Violence is something that happens in everyday life, and we were only telling a story. I wish it was looked at that way, because I don't think anything we did was unnecessary. Sometimes, for the sake of humor, we may've gone overboard. And if that was the case, then I'm sorry, but it was not the intention.

When and how did you first get the idea for Purple Rain? Did you really spend a year or so taking notes in a purple notebook, like some people have said?

Yes.

Did you ever think Purple Rain, the movie and the album, would be as big as they were?

See this cuff link? Give a brother a break. I don't know.

Speaking of brothers, some have criticized you for selling out to the white rock audience with Purple Rain, and leaving your black listeners behind. How do you respond to that?

Oh, come on, come on! Okay, let's be frank. Can we be frank? If we can't do nothing else, we might as well be frank. Seriously, I was brought up in a black-and-white world and, yes, black and white, night and day, rich and poor. I listened to all kinds of music when I was young, and when I was younger, I always said that one day I would play all kinds of music and not be judged for the color of my skin but the quality of my work, and hopefully I will continue. There are a lot of people out there that understand this, 'cause they support me and my habits, and I support them and theirs.

How do you feel about Jesse Johnson leaving the Time? Have you heard his album, and if so, what do you think of it?

Jesse and Morris and Jerome and Jimmy and Terry had the makings of one of the greatest R&B bands in history. I could be a little pretentious in saying that, but it's truly the way I feel. There's no one that could wreck a house like they could. I was a bit troubled by their demise, but like I said before, it's important that one's happy first and foremost. And, as far as Jesse's record goes, chocolate. You know.

It was obvious from the Purple Rain tour that, with the extended jams on some of these songs, you were paying tribute to James Brown. Would you agree? Who, besides James Brown, were your major musical inspirations and influences? Obviously you were thinking of Hendrix, Clinton and Sly Stone.

James Brown played a big influence in my style. When I was about 10 years old, my stepdad put me on stage with him, and I danced a little bit until the bodyguard took me off. The reason I liked James Brown so much is that, on my way out, I saw some of the finest dancing girls I ever seen in my life. And I think, in that respect, he influenced me by his control over his group. Another big influence was Joni Mitchell. She taught me a lot about color and sound, and to her, I'm very grateful.

In your Rolling Stone interview, you said you were surprised by so many people comparing you to Hendrix because you've always been more into Santana than Hendrix as a guitarist.

A lot has to do with the color of my skin, and that's not where it's at. It really isn't. Hendrix is very good. Fact. There will never be another one like him, and it would be a pity to try. I strive for originality in my work, and hopefully, it'll be perceived that way.

Your father is a musician too. Have you ever, or would you ever, try to get your father's music released on an album?

I did. He co-wrote "Computer Blue," "The Ladder" and several tunes on the new album. He's full of ideas. It'd be wonderful to put out an album on him, but he's a little bit crazier than I am.

You gave Andre Cymone the song, "Dance Electric," for his new album, and we know that you two had some kind of falling out a few years back. When and how did you patch things up?

I saw him in a discotheque one night and grabbed him by his shirt and said, [at this point, Prince reenacts the scene down to the last facial gesture], "Come on, I got this hit. You know I got this hit, don't you? "Dance Electric"? Yeah, it's great. You need it, you need it. no . . . Hey, come here, don't you play, hey, no, no, no you're not crazy, I'm crazy. I'm the one that's crazy, K? What chu gonna do? You gonna come by? For real? You ain't mad or nothing? So what? Yeah tomorrow. Noon. Cool."

We hear rumors that the Revolution may record an album of its own.

I don't know. It'd be too strange. They're very talented people, but they're (motions with his hands like a spastic hula girl), and together we're (motions with his hands, making them neatly parallel). I'd rather stay here (parallel), than (spastic).

Can you tell us about Paisley Park?

Paisley Park is an alternative. I'm not saying it's greater or better. It's just something else. It's multicolored, and it's very fun.

Can you comment on the incident that occurred after the American Music Awards in January 1985?

We had talked to the people that were doing USA for Africa, and they said it was cool that I gave them a song for the album. It was the best thing for both of us, I think. I'm strongest in a situation where I'm surrounded by people I know. So it's better that I did the music with my friends than going down and participating there. I probably would have just clammed up with so many great people in a room. I'm an admirer of all of the people who participated in that particular outing, and I don't want there to be any hard feelings. As far as the incident concerning the photographer goes, it's on the flip side of "Pop Life." The main thing it says is that we're against hungry children, and our record stands tall. There is just as much hunger back here at home, and we'll do everything we can, but y'all got to understand that a flower that has water will grow and the man misunderstood will go.

Have you changed your mind about touring since you announced the Purple Rain tour would be your last?

No. I don't plan on touring for a while. There are so many other things to do.

Now that Purple Rain has made you such a huge superstar, do you worry about the possibility of a backlash against you?

One thing I'd like to say is that I don't live in a prison. I am not afraid of anything. I haven't built any walls around myself, and I am just like anyone else. I need love and water, and I'm not afraid of a backlash because, like I say, there are people who will support my habits as I have supported theirs. I don't really consider myself a superstar. I live in a small town, and I always will. I can walk around and be me. That's all I want to be, that's all I ever tried to be. I didn't know what was gonna happen. I'm just trying to do my best and if somebody dug it then (kiss, kiss to the camera).

What are your religious beliefs?

I believe in God. There is only one God. And I believe in an afterworld. Hopefully we'll all see it. I have been accused of a lot of things contrary to this, and I just want people to know that I'm very sincere in my beliefs. I pray every night, and I don't ask for much. I just say, "Thank you" all the time.

Chapter Nineteen

PRINCE INTERVIEW

Why have you decided that now is the time to talk?

There have been a lot of things said about me, and a lot of them are wrong. There have been a lot of contradictions. I don't mind criticism, I just don't like lies. I feel I've been very honest in my work and my life, and it's hard to tolerate people telling such barefaced lies.

Do you read most of what's been written about you?

A little, not much. Sometimes someone will pass along a funny one. I just wrote a song called "Hello," which is going to be on the flip side of "Pop Life." It says at the end, "Life is cruel enough without cruel words." I get a lot of cruel words. A lot of people do.

I saw critics be so critical of Stevie Wonder when he made Journey through the Secret World of Plants. Stevie has done so many great songs, and for people to say, "You missed, don't do that, go back"—well, I would never say, "Stevie Wonder, you missed." *[Prince puts the Wonder album on the turntable, plays a cut, then puts on Miles Davis' new album.]* Or Miles. Critics are going to say, "Ah, Miles done went off." Why say that? Why even tell Miles he went off? You know, if you don't like it, don't talk about it. Go buy another record!

Not long ago I talked too George Clinton, a man who knows and has done so much for funk. George told me how much he liked Around the World in a Day. You know how much more his words meant than those from some mamma-jamma wearing glasses and an alligator shirt behind a typewriter?

Do you hate rock critics? Do you think they're afraid of you?

[Laughs] No, it's no big deal. Hey, I'm afraid of *them!* One time early in my career, I got into a fight with a New York writer, this real skinny cat, a real sidewinder. He said, "I'll tell you a secret, Prince. Writers write for other writers, and a lot of time it's more fun to be nasty." I just looked at him. But when I really thought about it and put myself in his shoes, I realized that's what he had to do. I could see his point. They can do whatever they want. And me, too. I can paint whatever picture I want with my albums. And I can try to instill that in every act I've ever worked with.

What picture were you painting with 'Around the World in a Day'?

[Laughs] I've heard some people say that I'm not talking about anything on this record. And what a lot of other people get wrong about the record is that I'm *not* trying to be this great visionary wizard. Paisley Park is in everybody's heart. It's not just something that I have the keys to. I was trying to say something about looking inside oneself to find perfection. Perfection is in everyone. Nobody's perfect, but they can be. We may never reach that, but it's better to strive than not.

Sounds religious.

As far as that goes, let me tell you a story about Wendy. We had to fly somewhere at the beginning of the tour, and Wendy is deathly afraid of flying. She got on the plane and really freaked. I was scared for *her*. I tried to calm her down with jokes, but it didn't work. I thought about it and said, "Do you believe in God?" She said yes. I said, "Do you trust him?" and she said she did. Then I asked, "So why are you afraid to fly?" She started laughing and said, "Okay, okay, okay." Flying still bothers her a bit, but she knows where it is and she doesn't get freaked.

It's just so nice to know that there is someone and someplace else. And if we're wrong, and I'm wrong, and there is nothing, then big deal! But the whole life I just spent, I at least had some reason to spend it.

When you talk about God, which God are you talking about? The Christian God? Jewish? Buddhist? Is there any God in particular you have in mind?

Yes, very much so. A while back, I had an experience that changed me and made me feel differently about how and what and how I acted toward people. I'm going to make a film about it—not the next one, but the one after that. I've wanted to make it for three years now. Don't get me wrong—I'm still as wild as I was. I'm just funneling it in a different direction. And now I analyze things so much that sometimes I can't shut off my brain and it hurts. That's what the movie will be about.

What was the experience that changed you?

I don't really want to get into it specifically. During the Dirty Mind period, I would go into fits of depression and get physically ill. I would have to call people to help get me out of it. I don't do that anymore.

What were you depressed about?

A lot had to do with the band's situation, the fact that I couldn't make people in the band understand how great we could all be together if we all played our part. A lot had to do with being in love with someone and not getting any love back. And there was the fact that I didn't talk much with my father and sister. Anyway, a lot of things happened in this two-day period, but I don't want to get into it right now.

How'd you get over it?

That's what the movie's going to be about. Paisley Park is the only way I can say I got over it now. Paisley Park is the place one should find in oneself, where one can go when one is alone.

You say you've now found the place where you can go to be alone. Is it your house? Within the family you've built around yourself? With God?

It's a combination of things. I think when one discovers himself, he discovers God. Or maybe it's the other way around. I'm not sure . . . It's hard to put into words. It's a feeling—someone knows when they get it. That's all I can really say.

Do you believe in heaven?

I think there is an afterworld. For some reason, I think it's going to be just like here, put that's part . . . I don't really like talking about this stuff. It's so personal.

Does it bother you when people say you're going back in time with 'Around the World in a Day'?

No. What they say is that the Beatles are the influence. The influence wasn't the Beatles. They were great for what they did, but I don't know how that would hang today. The cover art came about because I thought people were tired of looking at *me*. Who wants another picture of him? I would only want so many pictures of my woman, then I would want the real thing. What would be a little more happening than just another picture *[laughs]* would be if there was some way I could materialize in people's cribs when they play the record.

How do you feel about people calling the record "psychedelic"?

I don't mind that, because that was the only period in recent history that delivered songs and colors. Led Zeppelin, for example, would make you feel differently on each song.

Does you fame affect your work?

A lot of people think it does, but it doesn't at all. I think the smartest thing I ever did was record Around the World in a Day right after I finished Purple Rain. I didn't wait to see what would happen with Purple Rain. That's why the two albums sound completely different. People think, "Oh, the new album isn't half as powerful as Purple Rain or 1999." You know how easy it would have been to open Around the World in a Day with the guitar solo that's on the end of "Let's Go Crazy"? You know how easy it would have been to just put it in a different key? That would have shut everybody up who said an album wasn't half as powerful. I don't *want* to make an album like the earlier ones. Wouldn't it be cool to be able to put your albums back to back and not get bored, you dig? I don't know how many people can play all their albums back to back with each one going to different cities.

What do you think about the comparisons between you and Jimi Hendrix?

It's only because he's black. That's really the only thing we have in common. He plays different guitar than I do. If they really listened to my stuff, they'd hear more of a Santana influence than Jimi Hendrix. Hendrix played more blues; Santana played prettier. You can't compare people, you really can't, unless someone is blatantly trying to rip somebody off. And you really can't tell that unless you play the songs.

You've got to understand that there's only so much you can do on an electric guitar. I don't know what these people are thinking—they're usually non-guitar-playing mamma-jammas saying this kind of stuff. There are only so many sounds a guitar can make. Lord knows I've tried to make a guitar sound like something new to myself.

Are there any current groups you listen to a lot or learn from?

Naah. The last album I loved all the way through was [Joni Mitchell's] The Hissing of Summer Lawns. I respect people's success, but I don't like a lot of popular music. I never did. I like more of the things I heard when I was little. Today, people don't write songs; they're a lot of sounds, a lot of repetition. That happened when producers took over, and that's why there are no more [live] acts. There's no box office anymore. The producers took over, and now no one wants to see these bands.

People seem to think you live in an armed monastery that you've built in honor of yourself.

First off, I don't live in a prison with armed guards around me. The reason I have a guy outside is that after the movie, all kinds of people started coming over and hanging out. That wasn't so bad, but the neighbors got upset that people were driving by blasting their boxes or standing outside and singing. I happen to dig that. That's one reason I'm going to move to more land. There, if people want to come by, it will be fine. Sometimes it gets lonely here. To be perfectly honest, I wish more of my friends would come by.

Friends?

Musicians, people I know. A lot of the time they think I don't want to be bothered. When I told Susannah [Melvoin] that you were coming over, she said, "Is there something I can do? Do you want me to come by to make it seem like you have friends coming by?" I said no, that would be lying. And she just put her head down, because she knew she doesn't come by to see me as much as she wants to, or as much as she thinks I want her to. It was interesting. See, you did something good, and you didn't even know it.

Are you afraid to ask your friends to come by?

I'm kind of afraid. That's because sometimes everybody in the band comes over, and we have very long talks. They're few and far between, and I do a lot of the talking. Whenever we're done, one of them will come up to me and say, "Take care of yourself. You know I really love you." I think they love me so much, and I love them so much, that if they came over all the time I wouldn't be able to be to them what I am, and they wouldn't be able to do for me as what they do. I think we all need our individual spaces, and when we come together with what we've concocted in our heads, it's cool.

Does it bother you that strangers make pilgrimages to your house?

No, not at all. But there's a time and a place for everything. A lot of people have the idea that I'm a wild sexual person. It can be two o'clock in the afternoon, and someone will make a really strange request from the call box outside. One girl just kept pressing the buzzer. She kept pressing it, and then she started crying. I had no idea why. I thought she might had fallen down. I started talking to her, and she just kept saying, "I can't believe it's you." I said, "Big deal. I'm no special person. I'm no different than anyone." She said, "Will you come out?" I said, "Nope, I don't have much on." And she said, "That's okay."

I've lectured quite a few people out there. I'll say, "Think about what you're saying. How would you react if you were me?" I ask that question a lot. "How would you react if you were me?" They say, "Okay, okay."

It's not just people outside your door who think you're a wild sexual person.

To some degree I am, but not twenty-four hours a day. Nobody can be what they are twenty-four hours a day, no matter what that is. You have to eat, you have to sleep, you have to think, and you have to work. I work a lot, and there's not to much time for anything else when I'm doing that.

Does it make you angry when people dig into your background, when they want to know about your sexuality and things like that?

Everyone thinks I have a really mean temper and I don't like people to do this or do that. I have a sense of humor. I thought that the Saturday Night Live skit with Billy Crystal as me was the funniest thing I ever saw. His imitation of me was hysterical! He was singing, "I am the world, I am the children!" Then Bruce Springsteen came to the mike, and the boys would push him away. It was hilarious. We put it on when we want to laugh. It was great. Of course, that's not what it is.

And I thought the Prince Spaghetti commercial was the cutest thing in the world. My lawyers and management are the ones who felt it should be stopped. I didn't even see the commercial until after someone had tried to have it stopped. A lot of things get done without my knowledge because I'm in Minneapolis and they're where they are.

It's a good and a bad thing that I live here. It's bad in the sense that I can't be a primo "rock star" and do everything absolutely right. I can't go to the parties and benefits, be at all the awards shows, get this and get that. But I like it here. It's really mellow.

How do feel when you go to New York or L.A. and see the life you could be leading?

L.A. is a good place to work. And I liked New York more when I wasn't known, when I wasn't bothered when I went out. You'd be surprised. There are guys who will literally chase you through a discotheque! I don't mind my picture being taken if it's done in a proper fashion. It's very easy to say, "Prince, may I take your picture?" I don't know why people can't be more humane about a lot of the things they do. Now when I'm visiting, I like to sneak around and try stuff. I like to sneak to people's gigs and see if I can get away without getting my picture taken. That's fun. That's like cops and robbers.

You've taken a lot of heat for your bodyguards, especially the incident in Los Angeles in which your bodyguard Chick Huntsberry reportedly beat up a reporter.

A lot of times I've been accused of sicking bodyguards on people. You know what happened in L.A.? My man the photographer tried to get in the car! I don't have any problem with somebody I *know* trying to get in the car with me and my woman in it. But someone like that? Just to get a picture?

Why isn't Chick working for you anymore?

Chick has more pride than anybody I know. I think that after the L.A. incident, he feared for his job. So if I said something, he'd say, "What are you jumping on *me* for? What's wrong? Why all of sudden are you changing?" And I'd say, "I'm *not* changing." Finally, he just said, "I'm tired. I've had enough." I said fine, and he went home. I waited a few weeks and called him. I told him that his job was still there and that I was alone. So he said that he'd see me when I was in New York. He didn't show up. I miss him.

Is it true that Chick is still on the payroll?

Yes.

What about the exposé he wrote about you in the 'National Enquirer'?

I never believe anything in the Enquirer. I remember reading stories when I was ten years old, saying, "I was f—by a flying saucer, and here's my baby to prove it." I think they just took everything he said and blew it up. It makes for a better story. They're just doing their thing. Right on for them. The only thing that bothers me is when my fans think I live in a prison. This is not a prison.

You came in for double heat over the L.A. incident because it happened on the night of the "We Are the World" recording. In retrospect, do you wish you would have shown up?

No, I think I did my part in giving my song [to the album]. I *hope* I did my part. I think I did the best thing I could do.

You've done food-drive concerts for poor people in various cities, given free concerts for handicapped kids and donated lots of money to the Marva Collins inner-city school in Chicago. Didn't you want to stand up after you were attacked for "We Are the World" and say, "Hey, I do my part."

Nah, I was never rich, so I have very little regard for money now. I only have respect for it inasmuch as it can feed somebody. I can give a lot of things away, a lot of presents and money. Money is best spent on somebody who needs it. That's all I'm going to say. I don't like to make a big deal about the things I do that way.

People think that you're a dictator in the studio that you want to control everything. In L.A., however, I saw Wendy and Lisa mixing singles while you were in Paris. How do you feel about your reputation?

My first album I did completely alone. On the second I used André [Cymone], my bass player, on "Why You Wanna Treat Me So Bad?" He sang a small harmony part that you really couldn't hear. There was a typo on the record, and André didn't get any credit. That's how the whole thing started. I tried to explain that to him, but when you're on the way up, there's no explaining too much of anything. People will think what they want to.

The reason I don't use musicians a lot of the time had to do with the hours that I worked. I swear to God it's not out of boldness when I say this, but there's not a person around who can stay awake as long as I can. Music is what keeps me awake. There will be times when I've been working in the studio for twenty hours and I'll be falling asleep in the chair, but I'll still be able to tell the engineer what cut I want to make. I use engineers in shifts a lot of the time because when I start something, I like to go all the way through. There are very few musicians who will stay awake that long.

Do you feel others recognize how hard you work?

Well, no. A lot of my peers make remarks about us doing silly things onstage and on records. Morris [Day, former lead singer of the Time] was criticized a lot for that.

What kind of silliness, exactly?

Everything—the music, the dances, the lyrics. What they fail to realize is that is exactly what we want to do. It's no silliness, it's sickness. Sickness I just slang for doing things somebody else wouldn't do. If we are down on the floor doing a step, that's something somebody else wouldn't do. That's what I'm looking for all the time. We don't look for whether something's cool or not, that's not what time it is. It's not just wanting to be out. It's just if I do something that I think belongs to someone else or sounds like someone else, I do something else.

Why did Morris say such negative things about you after he left the band?

People who leave usually do so out of a need to express something they can't do here. It's really that simple. Morris, for example, always wanted to be a solo act, period. But when you're broke and selling shoes someplace, you don't think about asking such a thing. Now, I think Morris is trying to create his own identity. One of the ways of doing that is trying to pretend that you don't have a past.

Jesse [Johnson, former guitarist for the Time] is the only one who went away who told what happened, what really went down with the band. He said there was friction, because he was in a situation that didn't quite suit him. Jesse wanted to be in front all the time. And I just don't think God puts everybody in that particular bag. And sometimes I was blunt enough to say that to people: "I don't think you should be in the frontman. I think Morris should."

Wendy, for example, says, "I don't want that. I want to be right where I am. I can be strongest to this band right where I am." I personally love this band more than any other group I've every played with for that reason. Everybody knows what they have to do. I know there's something I have to do.

What sound do you get from different members of the Revolution?

Bobby Z was the first one to join. He's my best friend. Though he's not such a spectacular drummer, he watches me like no other drummer would. Sometimes, a real great drummer, like Morris, will be more concerned with the lick he is doing as opposed to how I am going to break it down.

Mark Brown's just the best bass player I know, period. I wouldn't have anybody else. If he didn't play with me, I,d eliminate bass from my music. Same goes for Matt [Fink, the keyboard player]. He's more or less a technician. He can read and write like a whiz, and is one of the fastest in the world. And Wendy makes me seem all right in the eyes of people Watching.

How so?

She keeps a smile on her face. When I sneer, she smiles. It's not premeditated, she just does it. It's a good contrast. Lisa is like my sister. She'll play what the average person won't. She'll press two notes with one finger so the chord is a lot larger, things like that. She's more abstract. She's into Joni Mitchell, too.

What about the other bands? Apollonia, Vanity, Mazarati, the Family? What are you trying to express through them?

A lot has to do with them. They come to me with an idea, and I try to bring that forth. I don't give them anything. I don't say, "Okay, you're going to do this, and you're going to do that." I mean, it was Morris' idea to be as sick as he was. That was his personality. We both like Don King and get a lot of stuff off him.

Why?

Because he's outrageous and thinks everything's so exciting—even when it isn't.

People think you control those bands, that it's similar to Rick James, relationship with the Mary Jane Girls. A lot of people think he's turning all the knobs.

I don't know their situation. But you look at Sheila E. performing, and you can just tell she's holding her own. The same goes for the Family. You and I were playing Ping-Pong, and they were doing just fine.

After all these years, does the music give you as much of a rush as it used to?

I increases more and more. One of my friends worries that I'll short-circuit. We always say I'll make the final fade on a song one time and [Laughs, dropping his head in a dead slump]. It just gets more and more interesting every day. More than anything else, I try not to repeat myself. It's the hardest thing in the world to do—there's only so many notes one human being can muster. I write a lot more than people think I do, and I try not to copy that.

I think that's the problem with the music industry today. When a person does get a hit, they try to do it again the same way. I don't think I've ever done that. I write all the time and cut all the time. I want to show you the archives, where all my old stuff is. There's tons of music I've recorded there. I have the follow-up album to 1999. I could put it all together and play it for you, and you would go "Yeah!" And I could put it out, and it would probably sell what 1999 did. But I always try to do something different and conquer new ground.

In people's minds, it all boils down to "Is Prince getting too big for his breeches?" I wish people would understand that I always thought I was bad. I wouldn't have got into the business if I didn't think I was bad.

Chapter Twenty

PRINCE IN THE NEWS PRINCE'S RESURRECTION ROLLING STONE MAGAZINE BY DAVID WILD AUGUST 25, 1988

PRINCE OPENS HIS Lovesexy '88 Tour in Paris and proves he can still rock hard. But is His Purple Highness hearing the call of a higher consciousness?

"I dig you, and you dig me," Prince told a cheering crowd of 17,000 Parisians at the Palais Omnisport Bercy toward the end of one of the extraordinary shows that opened his Lovesexy '88 Tour. "And together we'll dig him to death. Thank you, Jesus." Pointing his guitar meaningfully toward the heavens, or at least toward the painted clouds that hung overhead, Prince then ripped into "Purple Rain," offering one of his most divinely inspired solos of the evening.

Prince has long featured a tantalizing mix of the sacred and the secular—even the sleazy—in his musical sermons on the mount. But in Paris he gave every indication of having gone trough a genuine spiritual conversion. In a characteristically veiled autobiographical essay included in the Lovesexy '88 Tour program, Prince offers a parable that apparently explains his decision to release Lovesexy instead of the X-rated Black Album. Prince writes of "a boy named Camille" who lets his dark side, Spooky Electric, create "something evil"—the Black Album. Spooky Electric, Prince explains, must die in those who desire "Lovesexy—the feeling you get when u fall in love, not with a girl or boy but with the heavens above."

Whether or not it is meant as a religious revival show, the Lovesexy '88 Tour is hardly your average tent show. Prince has spent nearly $2 million mounting the world tour, which is scheduled to hit the States this fall. It will be Prince's first American tour since 1985.

Always a master of the grand gesture, Prince makes a dramatic entrance for the show in a white 1967 Thunderbird rigged up to take a quick spin around the tri-level, seventy-by-eighty-foot stage—complete with swing set and basketball hoop—set up in the center of the hall. Prince and his eight-piece band—drummer extraordinaire Sheila E., longtime keyboardist Dr. Fink, guitarist Miko Weaver, bassist Levi Seacer, Jr., singer and sensual presence Cat, keyboardist and singer Boni Boyer and horn players Eric Leeds and Atlanta Bliss—are in constant motion during the show, which is presented in the round under a complex light show.

Nearly three hours long, the show is equally ambitious musically. In the first half, Prince openly confronts his past in what at times seems like the summer's *real* dirty-dancing tour: starting with "Erotic City," Prince runs through a set heavy with some of is most wonderfully purple material: "Sister;" "I Wanna Be Your Lover;" "Jack U Off;" the Black Album's funky immorality play, "Bob George;" and even "Head" (with Cat gamely performing said act on a microphone held between Prince's legs).

The most inspired moments of the first half of the Paris shows came during Dirty Mind's "When You Were Mine," which Prince has brilliantly reworked as a rambling midtempo rocker that would sound out of place on a John Cougar Mellencamp album. And the set-closing "Anna Stesia" was given a powerful treatment, with Prince passionately singing the "Love is God/God is love/Boys and girls love God above" riff as a hydraulic lift took him and his piano toward the rafters.

The second set—which was played out on a less cluttered stage decorated with giant fake flowers—featured a number of songs with a higher calling, including "The Cross" and "I Wish U Heaven," as well as "Kiss," "1999," "Purple Rain" and a silkily soulful "When 2 R in Love." In a few shows, Prince also added two fascinating new numbers, titled "God Is Alive" and "Blues in C."

As the shows went on, Prince became increasingly direct about his intentions. "The first half, I gave it to you because you were expecting it," he said during the third night in Paris. "The second half is what it's all about. It's about how we all dig each other and him."

Seemingly in good spirits, the normally reclusive rocker attended a private party after the first show, where he shyly expressed satisfaction with the performance and said this tour would definitely make it to America. "I'm coming," he said, "I'm looking forward to that." And at 4:20 a.m.—more than four hours after the first show ended—Prince and his band took over the tiny stage of Bains Douches, a chic Paris club, for a brilliant hour-long show that featured riveting versions of "Forever in My Life" and "Strange Relationship" and a medley of "Housequake" and James Brown's "Cold Sweat." Midway through the set, Mavis Staples (who recently completed a record for Prince's Paisley Park label) joined Prince and the band for a soulful version of "I'll Take You There."

God knows, Prince has had his disappointments at the box office and on the charts since Purple Rain. But if the Paris shows are any indication, all Prince has to do to turn things around is hit the road over here. After all, a Prince concert has always been a religious experience.

Chapter Twenty-One

**ROLLING STONE MAGAINE
INTERVIEW PRINCE
BY NEAL KARLEN—1990**

THE PHONE RINGS at 4:48 in the morning.

"Hi, it's Prince," says the wide-awake voice calling from a room several yards down the hallway of this London hotel. "Did I wake you up?"

Though it's assumed that Prince does in fact sleep, no one on his summer European Nude Tour can pinpoint precisely when. Prince seems to relish the aura of night stalker; his vampire hours have been part of his mad-genius myth ever since he was waging junior-high-school battles on Minneapolis's mostly black North Side.

"Anyone who was around back then knew what was happening," Prince had said two days earlier, reminiscing, "I was *working*. When they were sleeping, I was *jamming*. When they woke up, I had another groove. I'm as insane that way now as I was back then."

For proof, he'd produced a crinkled dime-store notebook that he carries with him like Linus's blanket. Empty when his tour started in May, the book is nearly full, with twenty-one new songs scripted in perfect grammar-school penmanship. He has also been laboring over his movie musical Graffiti Bridge, which was supposed to be out this past summer and is now set for release in November. Overseeing the dubbing and editing of the film by way of dressing-room VCRs and hotel telephones, Prince said, has given him an idea. "One of these day," he said, "I'm going to work on just one project, and take my time."

Despite his all-hours intensity, the man still has his manners. He wouldn't have called this late, Prince says apologetically, if he didn't have some interesting news. He'd already provided some news earlier in the week, detailing, among other things, a late-night crisis of conscience a few years back that led him not only to shelve the infamous Black Album but also to try and change the way he wrote his songs—and led his life.

The crisis didn't involve a leap or a loss of faith, Prince has said, but simply the realization that it was time to stop acting like such and angry soul. "I was an expert at cutting off people in my life and disappearing without a glance back, never to return," he'd said. "Half the things people were writing about me were true."

But what's never been true, he felt, was what people have written about his music. Until, that is, just this minute. It seems that a fresh batch of reviews of the soundtrack of Graffiti Bridge were faxed from Minneapolis to the hotel while Prince was performing one of his fifteen sold-out concerts in England.

What Prince has read in the New York Times has astounded him. "They're starting to *get* it," he says from his phone in the Wellington Suite, which he has turned into a homey workplace with the addition of some bolts of sheer rainbow-colored cloth, film equipment, a stereo and tacked-up museum-shop posters of Billie Holiday and Judy Garland. "I don't believe it," he says again, "but they're getting it!"

They, in this case, are members of the rock intelligentsia who have alternately canonized and defrocked Prince. In the past, he has derided his professional interpreters as "mamma jammas" and "skinny sidewinders." Two days ago, it became obvious that his epithets, but now his feelings, had tempered concerning those who would judge him.

"There's nothing a critic can tell me that I can learn from," Prince had said earlier. "If they were musicians, maybe. But I hate reading about what some guy sitting at a desk *thinks* about me. You know, 'he's back, and he's black,' or 'He's back, and he's bad.' Whew! Now, on Graffiti Bridge, they're saying I'm back and more traditional. Well, 'Thieves in the Temple' and 'Tick, Tick, Bang' don't sound like *nothing* I've ever done before."

But hadn't he been cheered by the album's almost uniformly rave notices? "That's not what it's about," Prince had said. "No one's mentioning the lyrics. Maybe I should have put in a lyric sheet."

Now, in predawn London, he's called to say he was wrong. "They're starting to get it," he says one last time, unbothered by the fact that the Times article *trashes* his lyrics. That's okay, he says, because "they're paying attention." Sounding more amazed than pleased, Prince hangs up the phone and goes back to his dime-store notebook.

Five years have passed since Prince opened the passenger door to his 1966 Thunderbird and took me on a three-day schlep around the hometown he has never left. When I finally got out, I felt like Melvin Dummar, the doofus milkman who claimed to have driven through the Nevada desert with a surprisingly human Howard Hughes. No one had believed Melvin, and no one, I thought, would believe Prince was a being orbiting so close to planet Earth.

Not that Prince hadn't shown some signs of unease with his still-new superstardom. Alone, he's been animated, funny and self-aware. But out in public, even walking into places as hospitable as Minneapolis's First Avenue club, he would palpably stiffen at the first sign of a gawk, his face set in granite, his voice reduced to a mumble.

Now Prince seems more open and comfortable, less likely to slip into stridency. "You have a few choices when you're in that position," he says, remembering the first year after Purple Rain. "You can get all jacked up on yourself and curse everybody, or you can say this is the way life is and try to enjoy it. I'm still learning that lesson. I think I'll always be learning that lesson. I think I'm a much nicer person now."

This isn't to say that Prince has turned into Dale Carnegie—he still has the hauteur of a star. But something has changed; his philosophy no longer seems to hinge on things like the size of one's boot heels. "Cool means being able to hang with yourself," he says. "All you have to ask yourself is 'Is there anybody I'm afraid of? Is there anybody who if I walked into a room and saw, I'd get nervous?' If not, then you're cool."

Many things, however, have stayed the same. Prince is still very funny. ("You can always renegotiate a record contract. You just go in and say, 'You know, I think my next project will be a country & western album.'")

He can still play the cocky rocker. "I don't go to awards shows anymore," he says. "I'm not saying I'm better than anybody else. But you'll be sitting there at the Grammys, and U2 will beat you. And you say to yourself, 'Wait a minute. I can play that kind of music, too. I played La Crosse [Wisconsin] growing up, I *know* how to do that, you dig? But *you* will not do 'Housequake.'"

His grasp of history and current events remains quirky. Prince can cite chapter and verse from biographies of Little Richard and Jerry Lee Lewis, but he seems genuinely unaware that his own life story was turned into a book by an English rock critic. He knows, blow by blow, the events in the Mideast, relating the crisis to everything from the predictions of Nostradamus to the drug-interdiction policy of George Bush. But he hasn't yet heard of 2 Live Crew.

There is still some residue of emotional pain. "What if everybody around me split?" he asks. "Then I'd be left with only me, and I'd have to fend for me. That's why I have to protect me."

Prince's detractors might diagnose these words as the classic pathology of a control freak. His high-minded supporters might say those are normal protective feelings for somebody who was kicked onto the streets by his beloved father at age fourteen. Prince himself, however, echoes Popeye more than Freud as he analyzes just who he is. "I am what I am," he says. "I feel if I can please myself musically, then I can please others, too."

Finally, there is one more philosophy unchanged with the years. "I play music," Prince has said. "I make records. I make movies. I *don't* do interviews."

So what are we doing? "We're just talking," he says. Hence, his decision not to be taped or allow notes to be taken or even a pad of questions to be brought out. That would inhibit him, he says; that would mean doing the thing that he just doesn't do.

No, Prince vows, he isn't trying to be a purposeful pain. What he says he simply wants to avoid is "that big Q followed by that big A, followed by line after line of me either defending myself or cleaning up stories that people have told about me."

No matter what he might say in a traditional interview, Prince continues, he'd only end up looking ridiculous. "Some magazine a little while ago promised me their cover if I answered five written questions," he says. "The first one was 'What are your exact beliefs about God?' Now how can I answer that without sounding like a fool?"

True. But isn't he afraid of being misquoted? No, he says softly, staring at the holstered tape recorder on the table before him. When Prince says no, with pursed lips and a slight shake of the head, it carries a certain *finality*.

Still, in the coming days he addresses just about everything short of Kim Basinger ("I really don't know her that well") or anybody else he's dating ("I never publicize that. My friends around town are surprised when I introduce them to someone I'm seeing").

"And you really would feel better having your words taken down the second you say them?"

"No."

Okay.

A couple of nights later, Prince is dealing with the painstaking minutiae of piecing together his almost-finished movie. "People are going, 'Oh, this is Prince's big gamble,'" he says, sitting on the floor of his London hotel room, fast-forwarding a video version of his most recent cut. "What gamble? I made a $7 million movie with somebody else's money, and I'm sitting here finishing it."

Prince stops the tape at a point when gospel queen Mavis Staples is leaning out of a window in Minneapolis's Seven Corners, waxing wise on the night action down the street. The movie appears to be set in the 1950s, when Seven Corners was a Midwestern hotbed of clubs and hipsters. The Seven Corners set, raised on the Paisley Park sound stage, resembles the kind of backdrop used in Gene Kelly musicals. "Yeah, cheap!" says Prince with a laugh. "Actually, that's okay. It's like how we did Dirty Mind. But man, what I'd do with a $25 million budget. I'll need a big success to get that, but I'll get it, I *will* get it."

Film-speak is now part of his vocabulary; the first director Prince mentions he admires is Woody Allen, "because I like anyone who gets final cut." Movies have also worked their way into his philosophical references. "If you're making your moves in life because of money or pride," he says, "then you'll end up like that dude who got beat up on the grass at the end of Wall Street. He'd been wheeling and dealing, then *oomph!* That's what time it was."

He's been studying, he says, and learning from his own film failures. "I don't regret anything about Under the Cherry Moon," he says. "I learned that I can't direct what I didn't write." Participating in Batman, meantime, allowed him to spy on the making of a megaton hit. Composing songs on locations, Prince mostly stayed on the sidelines and just watched. "There was so much pressure on [director] Tim [Burton]," he says, "that for the whole picture, I just said, 'Yes, Mr. Burton, what would you like?"

Burton had hired him on the recommendation of Jack Nicholson, a longtime Prince fan. Prince, who'd never met Nicholson before, found the inspiration for "Partyman" when he first saw the actor on the set. "He just walked over, sat down and put his foot up on a table, real cool," Prince says. "He had this attitude that reminded me of Morris [Day]—and there was that song."

Prince says he'll survive if Graffiti Bridge is less than a blockbuster. "I can't please everybody," he says. "I didn't want to make Die Hard 4. But I'm also not looking to be Francis Ford Coppola. I see this more like those 1950s rock & roll movies."

Unfortunately, rumors have swirled for months that better comparison might be the 1959 howler Plan 9 From Outer Space. "I don't mind," says Prince. "Some might not get it. But people also said Purple Rain was unreleasable. And now I drive to work each morning to my own big studio."

Originally, Graffiti Bridge was going to be a vehicle for the reborn Time, with Prince staying behind the camera. But Warner Bros. wouldn't go for it, so Prince wrote himself into a new movie. Later, visitors to Paisley Park saw a version of a script that was allegedly obtuse to the point of near gibberish. "That was just a real rough thirty-page treatment I wrote with Kim," Prince says. "Graffiti Bridge is an entirely different movie."

As in Purple Rain, the plot features Prince as a musician named the Kid. Willed half-ownership of a Seven Corners club named Glam Slam, the Kid must share control with Morris Day, once again playing a comic satyr combining Superfly smoothness and Buddy Love sincerity. It's a fight of good versus evil, and band versus band, for the soul of Glam Slam.

Then there's the unknown Ingrid Chavez, Prince's first female movie lead who doesn't look like she was ordered out of a catalog. Throw in the talents of Staples, the reborn Time, George Clinton, and the thirteen-year-old Quincy Jones protégé Tevin Campbell, and you've got, Prince says, "a different kind of movie. It's not violent. Nobody gets laid."

It's impossible to judge Graffiti Bridge from just a few selected scenes. Still, they *were* very good scenes. Prince fast-forwards to a sequence in which Day tries to seduce Chavez on the fairy-tale-looking Graffiti Bridge.

When Prince is amused, which is almost every time Morris Day comes on the screen, he slaps his hands, shakes his head and throws himself back in his seat. "I *hope* Morris steals this movie," he says, recalling the charge made after Purple Rain. "The man *still* thinks he can whup me!"

Prince pushes rewind, searching for a scene with the Time. Waiting, he reminisces about the old days, when he oversaw the band. For a tutorial on the proper onstage attitude, Prince remembers, he showed the Time videos of Muhammed Ali trouncing, and then taunting, the old champ Sonny Liston. "To this day," he says, "they're the only band I've ever been afraid of."

At first it seems strange for to hear Prince talking in such fond and nostalgic terms about Day and the band. Day left the Minneapolis fold right after Purple Rain, with some nasty words about the boss's supposedly dictatorial ways. Now, Prince says, "I honestly don't remember how we got it together again."

Day's old charge of overbossing, however, brings a quirkier and crosser memory. "That whole thing came from my early days, when I was working with a lot of people who weren't exactly designed for their jobs," Prince says. "I had to do a lot, and I had to have control, because a lot of them didn't know exactly what was needed."

The most often-told tale involves Prince firing the then-unknown Jimmy Jam and Terry Lewis from the Time in 1982. Jam and Lewis, all parties now agree, left a Time tour on a day off to produce their first record for the SOS Band. A freak snowstorm in Atlanta grounded them for an extra day, and the two missed a gig. When Jam and Lewis returned, they were summarily fired. Jobless, the two missed Purple Rain, so they set up as producers and went scrounging for clients. In the years since, they've produced everyone from Janet Jackson to Herb Alpert, becoming the other superpower on the Minneapolis music scene.

"I'm playing the bad guy," says Prince, "but I didn't fire Jimmy and Terry. Morris *asked* me what I would do in his situation. Remember, it was *his* band."

Despite the rap, Prince says, he harbors no ill will toward the now-famous producers working across town from Paisley Park at their Flyte Time studios. "We're friends," he says. "We know each other like brothers. Jimmy always gave me a lot of credit for getting things going in Minneapolis, and I'm hip to that. Terry's more aloof, but I know that." And their music? "Terry and Jimmy aren't into the Minneapolis sound," Prince says. "They're into making every single one of their records a hit. Not that there's anything wrong with that, we're just different."

With this, Prince cues up the Graffiti Bridge movie to the sequence in which the Time performs "Shake!" The scene looks like something Busby Berkeley would have cooked up if he had choreographed funk.

The Time, Prince says, is proof of the good that can come from a group dissolving and eventually coming back together. "They broke up because they'd run out of ideas," he says. "They went off and did their own thing, and now they're terrifying."

Prince said this formula was just what he had in mind when, in short order, he broke up the Revolution. "I felt we all needed to grow," he says. "We all needed to play a wide range of music with different types of people. Then we could come back eight times as strong.

"No band can do everything," he continues. "For instance, this band I'm with now is *funky*. With them, I can drag out 'Baby I'm a Star' all night! I just keep switching gears on them, and something else funky will happen. I couldn't do that with the Revolution. They were a different kind of funky, more electronic and cold. The Revolution could tear up 'Darling Nikki,' which was about the coldest song ever written But I wouldn't even think about playing that song with *this* band."

The breakup of the Revolution apparently didn't go down easy. Today, Prince's relationship with his onetime best friends Wendy Melvoin and Lisa Coleman is somewhere between uncomfortable and estranged. "I talk to Wendy and Lisa, but it's like this," Prince says, moving his hands in opposite directions. "I still hear a lot of hurt from them, and that bothers me. When I knew them, they were two spunky, wonderful human beings. I honestly don't know what they're hurt about."

So far, Prince says, the two women haven't listened to the few tidbits of advice he has offered. For their first video, Prince recommended that they try to announce themselves by making a splash, by "doing something like jumping off a speaker with smoke pouring out everywhere. *Something.*" When he saw the video, however, Wendy was sitting in a chair, playing her guitar. "You can't do that when you're just getting established—kids watching MTV see that and they go *click*," Prince says, miming a channel being changed. "They'd rather watch a commercial."

Still, Prince's pronouncements seem proffered more in mourning than in malice. "Wendy and Lisa are going to have to do some more serious soul-searching and decide what they want to write about," he says sadly and shakes his head. "I don't know what Wendy and Lisa are so hurt about. I wish I did, but I don't."

It's a broiling summer afternoon in nice, France and Prince is performing before an almost completely empty soccer stadium. It's a sound check, and Prince and his band have been going for over an hour, segueing from John Lee Hooker's "I'm in the Mood" to the freeform jamming in "Respect."

After the check, Prince retreats to the bowels of the stadium to wait for night. Camped out in his dressing room under a gaucho hat, Prince plugs in a tape bearing some early versions of some songs he's written on tour. Prince says the first song, called "Schoolyard," is about "the first time I got any." Funny and funky, the song is an inner city summer of '42 that tells the story of a fumbling sixteen-year-old-boy trying to seduce a girl to the strains of a Tower of Power album. "I think that's something *everybody* can relate to," he says.

Still, that probably wouldn't prevent the song from getting a parental-warning sticker. "I don't mind that," Prince says. "I think parents have a right to know what their children are listening to."

At first it seems an unlikely sentiment coming from the man who once wrote about the onanistic doings of a woman sitting with a magazine in a hotel lobby. But Prince hasn't turned into a bluenose, he insists—he's just changed his outlook on how to present his still eros-heavy creations.

The change, he says, came soon after he finished the Black Album, in 1987. The reason the album was pulled from release had nothing to do with record-company pressure, he insists, or with the quality of the songs. Rather, Prince says, he aborted the project because of one particular dark night of the soul "when a lot of things happened all in a few hours." He won't get specific, saying only that he saw the word *God*. "And when I talk about God," he says, "I don't mean some dude in a cape and beard coming down to Earth. To me, he's in everything if you look at it that way.

"I was very angry a lot of the time back then," he continues, "and that was reflected in that album. I suddenly realized that we can die at any moment, and we'd be judged by the last thing we left behind. I didn't want that angry, bitter thing to be the last thing. I learned from that album, but I don't want to go back."

By the time of the album Lovesexy, Prince says, he was a certifiably nicer human being—and a happier creator. "I feel good most of the time, and I like to express that by writing from joy," he says. "I still do write from anger sometimes, like 'Thieves in the Temple.' But I don't like to. It's not a place to live."

He's been angling for a different effect on each album he has made in the last few years. "What people were saying about Sign o' the Times was 'There are some great songs on it, and there are some experiments on it.' I hate the word *experiment*—it sounds like something you didn't finish. Well, they have to understand that's the way to have a double record and make it interesting."

Lovesexy, Prince says, was "a mind trip, like a psychedelic movie. Either you went with it and had a mind-blowing experience or you didn't. All that album cover was, was a picture. If you looked at that picture and some ill come out of your mouth, then that's what you are—it's looking right back at you in the mirror."

The Graffiti Bridge soundtrack, a couple cuts of which have been floating around for a few years, "is just a whole bunch of songs," he says. "Nobody does any experiments or anything like that. But I still want to know how it stands up to the other albums. I'm always going forward, always trying to surprise myself. It's not about hits. I knew how to make hits by my second album."

Not that Prince is above appreciating a good old Number One with a bullet—especially when he wrote it. "I love it, it's great!" he exclaims when asked about Sinead O'Connor's version of "Nothing Compares 2 U," which Prince wrote in 1985 for the Paisley Park act the Family. Is he sorry he didn't get to sing the song before O'Connor? "Nah," Prince says. "I look for cosmic meaning in everything. I think we just took that song as far as we could, then someone else was supposed to come along and pick it up."

While being so productive on his own, Prince has also found time to produce such disparate talents as Mavis Staples, George Clinton and Bonnie Raitt. "The best thing about producing is that there are so many really talented people who just never got that push over the top," he says. "Without that push, they just get lost."

Raitt was perhaps his most talked-about reclamation project. "Oh, those sessions were kicking!" Prince says. But nothing was ever released—a fact which Prince takes the blame for. "There was no particular reason it didn't come out," he says. "I was just working on a lot of things at the same time, and I didn't give myself enough time to work with her. I used to do that a lot—start five different projects and only get a couple done. That's the biggest thing I'm working on: patience and planning."

What Prince listens to on his own time is a grab bag. He likes rap: he's recently signed rappers T.C. Ellis and Robin Power to record on his Paisley Park label but denies that he'll be producing songs for M.C. Hammer.

"I like his stuff a lot," Prince says. "We've talked but not about working together." He also gives highly favorable mentions to the likes of Madonna, Michael Jackson, Patti LaBelle and Bette Midler. "I'm not real into Bruce Springsteen's music," he says, "but I have a lot of respect for his talent."

Prince and Springsteen occasionally exchange notes; in recalling a Springsteen concert he saw from backstage a few years back, Prince displays the respect of a general reviewing another man's army. "I admire the way he holds his audience—there's one man whose fans I could never take away," he says with a laugh. And how does he compare their stage tactics? "I'm not sure," says Prince. "But at one point, his band started going off somewhere. Springsteen turned around and shot the band one terrifying look. You *know* they got right back on it!"

For his own enjoyment, however, Prince just relies on himself. "I like a lot of people's music, and I'm interested in what's going on," he says, "but I don't listen to them. When I'm getting ready to go out or driving in the car, I listen to my own stuff. Never the old stuff. That's the way it's always been."

Prince walks back over to the stereo and plays with the cassette of his latest creations until he finds a number featuring Rosie Gaines, the band's unknown keyboardist and vocalist, who may be the next big star to come out of Prince's camp.

"Terrifying," says Prince, shaking his head. "Simply *terrifying*."

It's another sweltering afternoon in another soccer stadium, this time in Lucerne, Switzerland. It's as tame as a church picnic in the dressing rooms; drugs have long been a firing offense, and even cigarettes have been forbidden from the entire area.

Killing time in the hallway, the members of Prince's band seem more like the kind of winning, good-natured characters in a script for the television show Fame than jaded road warriors. Gaines is doing her imitation of Daisy Duck as a soul sister. "Be quiet, boyfriend!" she quacks. "What's happening, baby?" goes a squawk directed at fellow keyboardist Matt "Doctor" Fink.

Fink, the only member of the Revolution still playing with Prince, has just read in the USA Today of a 2 Live Crew parody made by a group called 2 Live Jews. Shticking in his own estimable Jewish-man voice, Fink begins rapping: "Oy, it's so humid!" Over in the corner, Michael Bland is poring over a purple copy of The Portable Nietzsche. A corpulent twenty-year-old drummer, Bland is probably the most fearsome-looking band member. Actually, he's a scholarly innocent who still lives with his parents in Minneapolis and still plays drums in his Pentecostal church. "Nietzsche's cool," Bland says, putting down his book. "But Schopenhauer—now there's a brother with no hope!"

Also lolling in the hall are Miko Weaver, a hunkish guitarist, and Levi Seacer, Jr., a thoughtful bass player, who has been entrusted with speaking to the European press about this roadshow. The Nude Tour is a greatest-hits production with lean arrangements and none of the Liberace-on-acid costumes and special effects of the Lovesexy tour.

Prince, hanging out behind a closed door a few feet away from his band, makes no apology for the show's programming. "Kids save a lot of money for a long time to buy tickets, and I like to give them what they want," he says. "When I was a kid, I didn't want to hear James Brown play something I never heard before. I wanted to hear him play something I knew, so I could *dance*."

For now, Prince has no plans to bring his tour to the states, The main reason, he says, is that he wants to get back to Minneapolis and the studio. Prince also says that Warner Bros. is pouring increasingly large amounts of cash into Paisley Park Records, which means he must "put in some serious time behind the desk." It was only a couple of years ago that Prince was rumored to be in financial straits. But Forbes magazine that in 1989, Prince earned $20 million in pretax profit, and the New York Times recently reported that his Paisley Park empire was quite solvent. "We're doing okay" is all that Prince will say.

He has other reasons for wanting to get back home. Prince wants to get rolling an a screenplay he has been working on with Gilbert Davison, his best friend, his chief adjutant and the owner and proprietor of the soon-to-open Minneapolis nightclub Glam Slam.

Prince has lent the club his full endorsement as well as its name, the motorcycle from Purple Rain and some of his more-historic guitars. "Glam Slam's gonna kick ass," Prince says. "It'll be one of those joints that's remembered! I've always just wanted to have a place where I knew I could just show up and my stuff would be there, so I wouldn't have to jump onstage with equipment meant for Dwight Yoakam."

The point of helping Davison, Prince says, goes far beyond nepotism. "Glam Slam will be another thing to center Minneapolis in the national eye," he says. "People talk about the Minneapolis sound or the Minneapolis scene, but they don't really know what the place looks like or means. I want it to mean something."

For Prince, the place still mostly means home. "It feels like music to me there," he says. "You don't feel prejudice there. I know it exists, but you don't feel it as much. I can just drive around the lakes or go into stores without bodyguards or just hand out."

Nursing a cold and chewing on Sudafed, Prince excuses himself to rest up for the show. The next time he appears in the doorway, his intimidating game face is on. The band comes in for a last-minute huddle; Paisley Park costume designer Helen Hiatt fixes a crucifix necklace big enough to scare off Nosferatu.

"It's raining," Davison says to Prince. "It's raining" is Prince's mumbled reply, accompanied by a thousand-yard stare. Moments later, an army of damp and screaming Swiss teenagers hear the first beats of "1999."

The oldies come, as do some nifty hommages beyond the requisite James Brown footwork. Prince sings "Nothing Compares 2 U" with a Wilson Pickett wail, the song ending with him crucified on a heart. "Blues," sung with Rosie Gaines, hearkens to Otis Redding and Carla Thomas doing "Tramp." "Baby I'm a Star" last twenty-four minutes, and after two encores, Prince is whisked to a backstage BMW that is gone well before the fans stop screaming for more.

Soon after, the band bus is being rocked in the parking lot by highly non-neutral Swiss. "We're the Beatles!" says Michael Bland, giggling and waving to the fans.

"Oy, it's so humid," raps Dr. Fink.

At four in the morning, flying into their third country in the past twenty-four hours, the band and the entire entourage of about thirty are sacked out in what looks like the sleep of the dead. Everybody's unconscious on this charter, including one of the flight attendants.

There's movement, however, up in row 1. Prince's headphoned head is bopping against the back of his seat, his arms pounding the armrests. From the back, it looks like a prisoner is being executed in an upholstered electric chair.

Earlier in the day, Prince had refused to make any predictions about his future. "I don't want to say anything than can be held against me later," he'd said with a laugh. "Mick Jagger said he hoped he wouldn't be singing 'Satisfaction' at thirty, and he's still singing it. Pete Townshend wrote, 'Hope I die before I get old.' Well, now he is old, and I do hope he is happy to be around."

And himself? "When I pray to God, I say, 'It's your call—when it's time to go, it's time to go.'" Prince had said. "But as long as you're going to leave me here"—he slapped his hands—"then I'm going to cause much ruckus!"

Now, while his band mates and support staff snooze around him, Prince keeps air-jamming beneath the glare of his seat's tiny spotlight. Listening to a tape of his own performance that day, Prince stays up all night, all the way to London.

Chapter Twenty-Two

PRINCE IN THE NEWS
PRINCE PREVIEWS EUROPEAN SHOW
BY DAVID FRICKE JUNE 14, 1990

THIS WAS THE kind of Prince gig you don't get to see much anymore: no props or heavy sacred-sexual shtick, just hit songs, dirty dancing, whiplash funk and blowtorch guitar. On April 30th, at Minneapolis's yuppie watering hole Rupert's Nightclub, the paisley potentate of Eighties crossover pop played his first live show of the Nineties, stripping down to pre-Purple Rain essentials in a torrid ninety-minute club preview of his European summer road show, appropriately titled Nude.

Fronting a five-piece band augmented by three male dancers, Prince didn't actually take his clothes off for the sellout crowd (he did start the evening shirtless). But he let his R&B soul hang out all over the place, giving "Housequake" the hyper-James Brown treatment and transforming his latest "hit" (via Sinead O'Connor), "Nothing Compares 2 U," into a steamy Stax-Volt prayer. He even whipped into a quick version of "Respect" during the encore, with new singer-keyboardist Rosie Gaines wailing like a brassy young Aretha Franklin.

It was actually a sober occasion, a $100-a-ticket benefit concert for the family of Prince's former bodyguard, Charles "Big Chick" Huntsberry, who died April 2nd of heart failure at age forty-nine. After leaving Prince's employ in 1985, Huntsberry—who died without life insurance—kicked a serious cocaine habit and became an evangelist, setting up Big Chick's Ministries and speaking in schools and prisons. The show raised about $60,000 for Huntsberry's widow, Linda, and their six children.

Prince, however, conducted the whole affair like an Irish wake. He opened with a brief eulogy and an eerie reading of "The Future" (one of four songs he performed from Batman), performed entirely in dusky silhouette. Then he went into funkadelic overdrive with a lengthy bump-and-grind suite that featured "1999," "Housequake," "Kiss" and a short, saucy dose of "Sexy Dancer" from his 1979 LP Prince. Fueled by the muscular whomp of new drummer Michael Bland, the corpulent sticksman from the "Partyman" video, this was a leaner, meaner act than Prince's recent stage productions—no jazz brass, no Cat, no mating-ritual playlets. Instead, Prince and his Revolution-style lineup of guitar, bass and twin keyboards, including the veteran Prince sideman Matt Fink, concentrated on vocal sass and snappy propulsion, turning "Alphabet St." into a rap & roll mini-epic, complete with a quick snip of "It Takes Two," by Rob Base and D.J. E-Z Rock.

The show found Prince more celebratory than sentimental. He dedicated "Purple Rain" to Huntsberry and paid his final respects with several hallelujah choruses of incendiary Hendrixian guitar. The only new song in the set, "The Question of U," from Prince's upcoming film Graffiti Bridge, was a complex, compelling number that began as a bluesy piano romance, accelerated into a stirring Latin-flavored guitar sequence and climaxed as a funky raveup.

Alas, the Big Chick benefit was the only scheduled American performance of Prince's Nude revue. He will tour the U.S. this fall with a revamped production featuring music from the double-album soundtrack of Graffiti Bridge, which is scheduled for release August 10th. But if Prince's return to full-tilt sex boogie and mischievous good humor at Rupert's is any indication (he finished the set with the Joker's classic bon mot from "Batdance": "This town needs an enema!"), he still plans to keep his promise to "party till it's 1999."

Chapter Twenty-Three

ACT I—SAN FRANCISCO
APRIL 10, 1993

"CAN YOU KEEP a secret?"

These—I kid you not—are Prince's first words to me. (And since the answer is yes, all I can tell you is that you really wouldn't be all that interested.) This is back when things were simple, when Prince was still Prince, blasting through a lengthy international tour.

I receive a call in New York on Friday saying that Prince has read something I wrote about the tour's opening shows. He wants to meet me in San Francisco on Saturday.

The driver who picks me up in San Francisco shows me the erotic valentine his girlfriend made for him, then tells me about the work he and his wife are doing for the Dalai Lama. It's time to wonder, is this whole thing a put-on? But no, I get to the arena and there is Prince, sitting alone in the house, watching his band, the New Power Generation, start sound check. He is fighting a cold, so we speak quietly back and forth for a while, and then he leads me onstage to continue the conversation while he straps on his guitar and rehearses the band.

Mostly, Prince talks about music—about Sly Stone and Earth, Wind & Fire. He leads me over to Tommy Barbarella's keyboards to demonstrate how he's utilizing samples onstage now (such as the female yelp in the new song "Peach," which came courtesy of Kim Basinger, though she doesn't know it yet). He sits down at the piano to play a new, unfinished song called "Dark"—a bitter, beautiful ballad.

The band sounds ferocious and will sound even better at the evening's show. Prince works them unbelievably hard: A standard day on tour includes an hour-and-a-half sound check, a two-hour show, and an after-show at a club most nights. "The after-shows are where you get loose," he says. "It's that high-diving that gets you going."

The NPG have gotten noticeably tighter from all this old-fashioned stage sweat, funkier than any of his previous groups. Watching him cue them, stop on a dime, introduce a new groove, veer off by triggering another sample, you can only think of James Brown burnishing his bands to razor-precision, fining them for missing a single note. "I love this band," says Prince. "I just wish they were all girls."

He is talkative, with that surprisingly low voice that loses its slightly robotic edge when he's offstage. He is indeed tiny—what's most striking isn't his height but the delicate bones and fragile frame. He is also pretty cocky, whether out of shyness with a new person or the swagger needed to keep going through a tour. "You see how hard it is when you can play anything you want, anything you hear?" he asks underneath the onstage roar of the NPG. They play "I'll Take You There" at sound check, and Prince and I talk about the Staple Singers and Mavis Staples, whose new album he is just completing.

He leads the way to his dressing room—a blur of hair products and Evian water, with off-white mats on the floor and paintings stuck on the walls—and plays some of the Mavis album, singing along with her roof-raising voice. "Jimmy Jam is going to hear this and throw all those computers away," he says. "This is what we need now—these old kind of soul songs to just chill people out. The computers are as cold as the people are.

"That's what I went through with the Black Album. All this gangsta rap, I did that years ago. 'Cause if you're gonna do something, go all the way in. But there's no place to go past the samples. You can only, y'know, unplug them!"

There's a knock on the door, and a bodyguard says that someone named Motormouth wants to see Prince. He laughs and waves the visitor in—turns out to be an old Minneapolis DJ, a neighbor for whom Prince used to baby-sit. The gentleman lives up to his name; Prince listens politely and giggles softly, as Motormouth talks about his ex-stripper wife and his daughter and the days back in Minnesota.

Prince desperately wants to play a club show after the San Francisco gig, but his throat is too sore. Instead, there's a party at the DV8 club. He arrives with a phalanx of bodyguards, clears out half the room, and sits alone on a sofa. One of the security guys grabs me and sits me on the couch.

Prince hands me a banana-flavored lollipop. "I would have brought you a cigar, but I didn't think you smoked," he says. He pours us each a glass of port ("I learned about this from Arsenio"). Occasionally, acquaintances manage to make their way through the wall of security, but he is wary of touching them. "I don't like shaking hands," he says. "Brothers always feel like they got to give you that real firm handshake. Then you can't play the piano the next day."

We chat about the new contract he signed with Warner Bros., which was reported to be worth as much as $100 million. He says the deal is nothing like it is being reported, and though he wants most of the conversation to remain "just between us—I just wanted to talk about some of these things," he makes a few mysterious comments that will prove crucial to the next stage of his continual metamorphosis.

"We have a new album finished," he says conspiratorially, "but Warner Bros. doesn't know it. From now on, Warner's only gets old songs out of the vault. New songs we'll play at shows. Music should be free, anyway."

Before he heads off into the night, Prince lifts his glass of port and offers a toast.

Leaning closer, he whispers, "To Oz."

Chapter Twenty-Four

ACT II—CHANHASSEN, MINNESOTA
JULY 12, 1993

PAST THE CHANHASSEN Dinner Theatre, past the American Legion post where a Little League game is in progress, after miles of fields and open spaces lies the gleaming, towering Paisley Park, the studio and office complex that houses Paisley Park Enterprises. There are dozens of people on the Paisley staff—an entire industry built around one man in heels—working to keep the studio and the songs and, mostly, the person at the center of it all humming and creating at their maximum potential. There's a lot that seems like star-tripping inside Prince's world, lots that can make you impatient—and multiple costume changes, even on off days, don't help matters—but over time it becomes clear that the whole structure exists so that absolutely nothing gets in the way of the music, nothing touches Princethat he doesn't choose to address.

Tonight Prince will go through his final rehearsal for a greatest hits tour of Europe. Several hundred tickets have been sold to benefit local radio station KMOJ, and the mixed-race, well-to-do crowd mills around the Paisley Park soundstage in flowery prints and orange suits, waiting for Minneapolis's favorite son.

The NPG and gospel singers the Steeles play brief opening sets. Prince makes no reference to the name-change or the retirement when he ambles onstage to the opening chord of "Let's Go Crazy." In fact, he hardly talks at all through a loose 90-minute set. He closes the show with two new songs: a sexy shuffle called "Come" that he occasionally dropped into the U.S. concerts, and "Endorphinmachine," a metallic rave-up that kicks and stomps like the Purple Rain hits that made him a household name exactly 10 years ago.

But as always, what it really seems to come down to is the music. Prince decided that it was time to close the book on one stage of his musical development and find a way to move on to the next. "Prince did retire," says Prince emphatically in the Cote Jardin, waving away the pastry delivered with his tea. "He stopped making records because he didn't need to anymore." Later, at the Sporting Club, he'll add that "it's fun to draw a line in the sand and say, 'Things change here.' I don't mind if people are cynical or make jokes—that's part of it, but this is what I choose to be called. You find out quickly who respects and who disrespects you. It took Muhammad Ali years before people stopped calling him Cassius Clay."

He is, quite simply, fixated on one thing: He has too much music sitting around, and he wants people to hear it. As Prince explains it, Warner Bros. says it can handle only one album per year from him, while he's recording the equivalent of at least three or four every year. By the time an album makes its way through the corporate machine for release, he's finished another one. By the time he goes on tour to promote the first album, he's done with a third.

So what's a Prince to do? The plan he is devising works like this: He will fulfill his Warner's contract—he still owes them five albums—with Prince material from the vaults at whatever rate they want (and, he adds, "the best Prince music still hasn't been released"). Meanwhile, Prince will work with a smaller label to put out new music under his new name.

From almost anyone else, the whole thing would seem like a scam; from someone with a legitimate claim to having wrested the Hardest-Working-Man-in-Show-Business title from James Brown, it starts to sound a little more reasonable. Reasonable, that is, to everyone but his bosses at Warner's. "I knew there would come a phase in my life when I would want to get all this music out," he says. "I just wish I had some magic words I could say to Warner's so it would work out."

Prince emphasizes that he has no beef with Warner Bros. or chairman Mo Ostin, that he understands their concerns about this proposed plan and respects them for allowing him to try out this arrangement with Bellmark for "Beautiful Girl." "I really think they would find a way to let me do this," he says, "but they're afraid of the ripple effect, that everybody would want to do it." His problem, ultimately, is with the structure of the music industry.

"Did you see The Firm?" he asks. "I feel like the music business is like that—that they just won't let you out once you're in it. There's just a few people with all the power. Like, I didn't play the MTV Music Awards; suddenly, I can't get a video on MTV, and you can't get a hit without that. I've come to respect deeds and actions more than music—like Pearl Jam not making videos."

What is seeking is the opportunity to get more involved in the presentation of the music, which is why an indie label like Bellmark appeals to him. He's shot a video for a song called "Love Sign," directed by Ice Cube, and he's looking into possible outlets for its release. He wants to be able to sell records at concerts and in clubs—a logical move, especially for someone like George Clinton, best known for his tireless touring—but Warner Bros. feels, according to Prince, that such a move would cause problems with retailers. He wants to use his music to raise money for charities, but "they don't want to hear about giving music away."

"Shouldn't it be up to the artist how the music comes out?" he asks, shaking his head and staring at the floor of the spartan Sporting Club dressing room. Several times, he points to George Michael's lawsuit with Sony Music U.K. over "restraint of trade" as an example of how twisted things have gotten in the biz. "They're just songs, just our thoughts. Nobody has a mortgage on your thoughts. We've got it all wrong, discouraging our artists. In America, we're just not as free as we think. Look at George Clinton. They should be giving that man a government grant for being that funky!

"People think this is all some scheme. This isn't a scheme, some master plan. I don't have a master plan; maybe somebody does." He shakes his head again. "I just wish I had some magic words," he repeats. "It's in God's hands now."

He has asked me to fly out for this show, but we never speak. After the performance, his publicist says that Prince wants to know what I thought of the NPG's set and how I liked the new songs.

What really happened tonight, though, was Prince's final appearance in this country as part of what is now a farewell tour. Which means that if he keeps to his word, this is the last time he will ever play such songs as "Purple Rain," "Kiss," and "Sign O' the Times" in America.

Chapter Twenty-Five

PRINCE IN THE NEWS
THE ELUSIVE PRINCE RETURNS TRIUMPHANT
ROLLING STONE MAGAZINE
BY ALAN LIGHT—1993

"Y'ALL MAKE ME sorry I stayed away so long!" So crowed a jubilant Prince near the end of a powerhouse two-and-a-half-hour concert at the Sunrise Musical Theater, outside Fort Lauderdale, Florida, which opened his first American tour in more than five years. And judging from the first two nights, this twelve-city theatre tour features the most accessible and freewheeling version of Prince since 1999 catapulted him to superstardom a decade ago.

At the Sunrise shows, the new up-close-and-personal Prince worked the crowd, joked with his musicians, played guitar in the aisles and even executed a glorious stage dive at the end of the first night, reducing the sold-out audience of 4000 Floridians and spring breakers (much older and whiter than Prince fans of yesteryear) to a sweaty mess. Perhaps most impressive, though, the shows marked the coming of age of his band, the New Power Generation, as a first-rate ensemble, fluid, versatile and whip-crack tight.

This tour is the centerpiece of a multimedia Prince blitz that began when he signed his highly publicized six-album contract with Warner Bros. last September. Though his fourteenth album, Prince, continues to hover in the middle regions of the charts five months after its release, it is sneaking up on sales of 2 million in the U.S. It seems likely the album will sell the 5 million worldwide necessary for Prince to receive a $10 million for his next album, as his new contract reportedly specifies.

While the emergence of the newly media-friendly Michael Jackson may render Prince the word's most famous recluse, Minneapolis's favorite son is also making moves to get closer to his fans. These first concerts and his selection of smaller venues for this tour exhibited this new intimacy despite some excessive staging. Unlike the elaborate sex-versus-God metaphors of the Lovesexy tour, this time the themes were simple and straightforward: sex, partying, more sex and showing off the smoking funk of the New Power Generation. "Can't nobody fuck with my band!" Prince exclaims repeatedly while putting the players through stop-on-a-dime turnarounds worthy of James Brown. Prince has also finally found a rap style with which he seems comfortable, a slower, more leisurely than the clipped barks he has grappled with in the past.

The first half of the show focused exclusively on his newest material. Starting with a pounding "My Name Is Prince," he played eleven of the sixteen songs of Prince's "love opera," in which he struggles to win the heart of Mayte (the belly dancer who Prince describes as his latest "inspiration") from her family of Arabian royalty.

Though the lights and costumes were appropriately dramatic, the most notable element of the setting was something resembling Saran Wrap growing like kudzu on the keyboards. Some silly between-song skits—including a "reporter" and film crew chasing Prince for an interview—added up to a plot that made as little sense onstage as it does on the record, but it was most unobtrusive. (Prince did get a laugh the second night when the reporter asked, "Where have you been the last five years?" and he shot back, "Your mom's house.")

The album, while Prince's strongest in years, ultimately can't bear the weight of such close focus, but as drummer Michael Bland put it, "being on tour is like being a traveling salesman; you got to show off what you got." Even locked into a set list, Prince found new ways to enliven his material. The crunching groove of "The Continental" turned into a smooth, Philly-soul-style jam resembling Archie Bell and the Drells' party classic "Tighten Up." ("We'd never done it that way before," said guitarist Levi Seacer Jr. before the second show, "and it may never happen again.") Prince also premiered a new song at Sunrise, much to the band's surprise: a chugging, crowd-pleasing rocker titled "Peach."

A bombastic medley of "And God Created Woman" and "3 Chains o' Gold" made for an unsatisfying narrative conclusion to the set. But a stunning coda of the recent hit "7," featuring a lengthy, Middle Eastern-flavored multiple-guitar introduction, was one of the night's peaks.

The second half of the show was neither a simple greatest-hits collection nor a survey of the other three albums Prince has released since the Lovesexy tour of 1988. Instead, such Prince smashes as "Let's Go Crazy" and "1999" were juxtaposed with the obscure B side "Irresistible Bitch" and a blistering "She's Always in My Hair."

The second night's show, identical in song selection minus encores of "Cream," "1999" and "Baby I'm a Star," didn't have the steamrolling force of the opener. Its highlights, however, were even higher, including a majestic, ferocious "Purple Rain" and a show-stopping medley of the bedroom ballads "Insatiable" and "Scandalous" that had every woman in the place on her feet, screaming. (Said audience member Luther Campbell of 2 Live Crew, "I model myself on Prince—I thought I got women at my shows, but not like this motherf—er!")

As for offstage Prince projects, the Joffrey Ballet debuted Billboards, a full-length work set to Prince songs, including an extended version of "Thunder," from Diamonds and Pearls, written specially for the company. Billboards, which present four noted choreographers' interpretations of such Prince gems as "Sometimes It Snows in April" and "Computer Blue," opened in Iowa to rave reviews in January and went on to Chicago in March. (It will play in Washington, D.C. in June, Los Angeles in July and New York in November, among other stops.) In addition, Prince is producing several tracks for an upcoming Earth, Wind and Fire reunion album; ironically, fifteen years ago EWF leader Maurice White was approached to produce Prince's first album—which White turned down. In the most extensive off the new efforts, before starting the tour Prince wrote ten songs for I'll Do Anything, a new James L. Brooks musical-comedy film starring Nick Nolte and Tracey Ullman due out in the fall.

The new high-profile Prince sang four songs from 0{+> in a rare television stop on The Arsenio Hall Show on February 25th. More surprisingly, he did an in-store performance and record signing at Atlanta's Turtle's Rhythm and Views, drawing more than 1000 fans (his signature of choice was the album-title symbol rather than a name). And on top of the usual onslaught of surprise club appearances that always accompanies a Prince tour, an invitation-only benefit show by Prince at the historic Apollo Theater for various underprivileged-children's groups in Harlem was slated for March 27th.

But all it really takes for people to remember why Prince is a superstar is for him to get back onstage. At Sunrise, he sang at peak form, danced up a storm, led chants, jumped from guitar to piano and from booty-shaking funk to skull-crushing rock with equal ease. After five years away from most of America, he reasserted himself as the hardest working man in show business today and the baddest motherf—er in the atmosphere. (RS 655)

Chapter Twenty-Six

PRINCE RETIRES—MAYBE
ROLLING STONE MAGAZINE
BY MICHAEL GOLDBERG—1993

PRINCE TO RETIRE from studio recording! That was the headline of a press release faxed to the media on the evening of April 27th. Earlier that day, less than a year after Prince signed a recording and publishing deal with Warner Bros. Records potentially worth an estimated $100 million, Warner Bros. chairman Mo Ostin and company president Lenny Waronker were informed by Gilbert Davison, president of Paisley Park Enterprises, that Prince would not be delivering any more studio albums to the company.

Instead, the press release said, Prince would fulfill the remainder of the six-album deal—for which he receives a per-album advance of $10 million—with old songs from his immense library of "500 unreleased recordings." In that way, new Prince albums can be released "well into the twenty-first century." The statement, which was ent out by Prince's New York-based publicist Michael Pagnotta, also said that "after releasing fifteen albums in fifteen years, [Prince] is turning his creative talents to alternative media—including live theater, interactive media, nightclubs and motion pictures."

The announcement was greeted with skepticism at Warner Bros., throughout the record business and even among some of Prince's associates. "Prince is a very mercurial fellow," said Eric Leeds, a saxophonist who has toured and recorded with Prince and who currently records solo albums for Prince's label, Paisley Park. "He could change his mind tomorrow. I just kind of chuckle when I hear those things. I say, 'Okay, here he goes again.'"

At Warner Bros., there was no official comment, but executives are apparently taking a low-key, somewhat amused approach to the news. "People were laughing," said a source at the company.

"Anything he says you have to take with a grain of salt," says Danny Goldberg, a senior vice-president at the Time Warner-owned Atlantic Records.

No official explanation from wither Prince or his employees was forthcoming. Those who know Prince have a few theories about the announcement. Some feel this could be Prince's way of expressing his disappointment with U.S. sales of his latest album, 0{+>, which are in the neighborhood of 2 million copies. The Warner Bros. source said that a week before the announcement, Prince had been in the office meeting with Ostin and Waronker "expressing his dissatisfactions and frustrations."

Eric Leeds thinks Prince may want to renegotiate some part of his deal. "Maybe there's a point in the new deal that he's not particularly thrilled with and he's saying, 'Well, let me play hardball with them for a minute,'" said Leeds.

Or it could be, as some current and former Prince business associates believe, that Prince is fed up with the rock-star treadmill. Alan Leeds, who was vice-president of Paisley Park Records until about eight months ago, and is Eric Leeds' older brother, said, "This is a guy who is simply uncomfortable with the confines of the 1990s music industry and the constraints it puts on a prolific artist.

"The idea that you're dictated to: 'Okay, you make a record this month, you release it that month, you sit on your ass for three months, you tour for three months, you sit on your ass for another three months'—that's not the kind of guy Prince is," continued Leeds. "He's a guy who lives on the edge, who likes spontaneity above all else. And all of those things about his lifestyle are discouraged by the structure of the music industry. It's an enormously frustrating existence for him." This is not the first time Prince has made a dramatic public announcement. In April of 1985, just a few days before the conclusion of the *Purple Rain* tour, Prince announced he was going to stop touring for "two to three years." Prince's explanation at the time, as relayed via his then manager Steve Fargnoli: "Sometimes it snows in April."

"Five months after that we were in rehearsals for the next tour," said Eric Leeds. "And we were out playing gigs within a year."

Chances are that the retirement will be short-lived. In fact, a source who works with Prince says that the day after the press release was issued, the star was in an L.A. studio producing an album for his current band, the

New Power Generation. "I can guarantee that if he comes up with another 'When Doves Cry,' the first thing he's going to do is go to Warner Bros. and say: 'Release this. Tomorrow!'" said Eric Leeds.

"There's only three things for sure in this life," said Alan Leeds. "We're all born, we all die, and Prince will make another record on of these days."

Chapter Twenty-Seven

VIBE MAGAZINE INTERVIEW
PRINCE MONTE CARLO
MAY 2, 1994

"SO HOW CAN we do an interview that's not like an interview?" asks Prince as he spoons a dollop of jam into his tea. We're sitting in the Cote Jardin restaurant in Monte Carlo's historic Hotel de Paris, overlooking a small garden that overlooks the Mediterranean Sea. He is here to accept an award for Outstanding Contribution to the Pop Industry at the 1994 World Music Awards. I am here at his request, the final step in a full year of putting together his first lengthy conversation with a journalist since 1990.

Those 12 months have been an especially remarkable time for Prince whom some call "the artist formerly known as Prince," or any number of variations on that theme; others, of course, will always call him Prince, much to his dismay. The year has included—in addition to the controversial name-change that signaled the "retirement" of one of this era's biggest pop stars and the songs that made him famous—a sales slump and the closing of his Paisley Park Records label. He went through four publicity firms in nine months. But this run of hard times was quickly followed by a triumphant rise with the single "The Most Beautiful Girl in the World," his biggest hit in several years. And at the end of this particular peculiar period, Prince has emerged with some of the best music he's ever made—though whether the world will ever be able to hear it is another question, in the hands of managers and lawyers and Warner Bros. Records as they negotiate how or if all this music will be released.

Which, perhaps, is why he feels that now is the time to talk after a long silence. It seems to be part of a campaign to generally increase his visibility by appearing at events like the World Music Awards, for instance—exactly the kind of thing the reclusive Prince of old would have avoided like the plague. Or to introduce three new songs on Soul Train or publish a book—titled The Sacrifice of Victor—of photos from his last European tour that presents him much more up close and personal than he has been shown in the past.

Meanwhile, he continues to move forward, exploring new, alternative outlets for his music, like an innovative CD-ROM extravaganza, Prince Interactive, that incorporates dozens of songs into a kind of video game/video jukebox—or the Joffrey Ballet's wildly successful Billboards, set to his music, which may lead to his writing a full-length ballet score soon. And through it all, he has kept writing and recording new songs—or "experiences," as he now likes to call them—and struggling to find a way to get as many of them as possible released to the public.

"I just want to be all that I can be," Prince says in his dressing room at the Monte Carlo Sporting Club, site of the World Music Awards. "Bo Jackson can play baseball and football—can you imagine what I would do if I could do all I can? If they let me loose, I can wreck shit."

ACT III—Monte Carlo—May 2, 1994

SCENE I

So how do you pronounce it?
"You don't."
And is that ever a problem when people around you want to address you?
"No." A very final, definite no.
But what becomes clear is that there are reasons for the name-change, and after sitting with Prince for several hours, it even starts to make some kind of sense. "I followed the advice of my spirit," is the short answer. But it is, first of all, about age-old questions of naming and identity.

The man born Prince Rogers Nelson goes on to explain, "I'm not the son of Nell. I don't know who that is, 'Nell's son,' and that's my last name. I asked Gilbert Davison, Prince's manager and closest friend, and president of NPG Records] if he knew who David was, and he didn't even know what I was talking about. I started thinking about that, and I would wake up nights thinking, Who am I? What am I?"

SCENE II

There are three DO NOT DISTURB signs on the door. A desk and a white upright Yamaha piano face the floor-to-ceiling windows with a breathtaking view of the Mediterranean Sea. A bowl of Tootsie Pops and assorted sweets sits on a coffee table. Tostitos, Sun Chips, and newspapers lie scattered in the corners. 7Up fills the bar, and various colored cloths are draped over all the furniture in the room.

Prince's room in the Hotel de Paris is fancy, if not exactly elegant. It is here that he wants me to check out two albums that may or may not see the light of day: the next Prince album, Come, scheduled for an August release, and the first Prince collection, titled The Gold Album, both pressed on CDs with hand-drawn cover art. This time I'm the one fighting a cold, and he expresses concern, keeping the tea flowing, pouring for us both when it arrives.

First comes the Prince album, which includes "Endorphinmachine" and "Come" and a fleshed-out version of "Dark," complete with a slinky horn arrangement that completes the sketch I heard a year before. Prince skips back and forth between tracks. It all sounds strong—first-rate, even—but he seems impatient with it, like it's old news.

The Gold Album is another matter. He lets the songs run, playing air guitar or noodling along at the piano. The songs are stripped-down, taut, funky as hell, full of sex and bite. "Days of Wild" is a dense, "Atomic Dog"-style jam with multiple, interlocking bass lines. "Now" (which he debuted on Soul Train this same week) is a bouncing party romp; "319" is rocking, roaring, and dirty; and "Ripopgodazippa" is just dirty. This album is more experimental, more surprising structurally and sonically. Hearing the two albums back-to-back, it's clear that the album may be more commercial than Prince's, but it's also more conventional—as conventional as he gets, anyway.

Prince says that since the name-change, he's writing more about freedom and the lack thereof, and that's it exactly: The Prince songs sound freer than he has in years. He sounds energized, excited, and also humbler and more focused than he did a year ago in San Francisco. His album covers used to include the phrase "May U live to see the dawn." This album opens with the words "Welcome 2 the dawn."

That night, the songs take on even more life at a late gig at a Monte Carlo "American blues and sports bar" called Star's n Bars. The occasion is a private party for Monaco's Prince Albert. Earlier in the evening, 0{+> committed a faux pas that received international coverage when, dressed in see-through gold brocade and toting one of those lollipops, he left a royal reception before Albert did. To make up for his breach of protocol, 0{+> is on especially good behavior at the show.

"Much props to Prince Albert for having us in his beautiful country!" are his first words onstage, and he later refers to Albert as "the funkiest man in show business." After the show, he autographs a tambourine for our host, inscribing inside, "You're the real Prince!"

The NPG are lean and in prime fighting shape, trimmed down to just Tommy Barbarella and newcomer Morris Hayes on keyboards, Sonny Thompson on bass, monster drummer Michael Bland, and dancer/visual foil Mayte. No more rappers, extra dancers, or percussionists. "This band is just beginning to play to its strength," 0{+> said earlier. "The Lovesexy band was about musicality, a willingness to take risks. Since then I've been thinking too much. This band is about funk, so I've learned to get out of the way and let that be the sound, the look, the style, everything. They've never played together like this before."

They storm through 11 new songs, winding things up at 3 a.m., a pretty early night by 0{+> standards. The next night, they're back at Star's n Bars, and even at sound check this time he's really ready to rip. We talked earlier about the title track to The Gold Album, which members of his entourage were raving about but he didn't play for me. He said then that he's worried about playing some of the new songs because the bootleggers will have them out on the market before he will. Here in sound check, though, he lets it go, and it's a stunner—a soaring anthem of "Purple Rain" scale, a gorgeous warning that "all that glitters ain't gold." (He recently quoted these lyrics as part of his speech at the Celebrate the Soul of American Music show, directing his comments toward the music industry.)

0{+> bounds off the club's stage and strides over, greeting me with a big smile and even a handshake. He's excited for tonight's show because "tonight we're playing for real people."

Well, as real as people get in Monaco, anyway. Before the band starts, at around 1:30, talk of international finance and the restaurant business fills the air. You could choke on the Chanel in here, and the number of coats and ties makes it feel like a boardroom instead of a barroom. But let me tell you: People in Monaco are ready to party.

Soon they're dancing three and four to a tabletop, screaming along chants, soul-clapping straight outta Uptown. "Days of Wild" goes on for 20 minutes, and an obviously impressed 0{+> says from the stage, "I didn't know I had to come all the way over here to get a crowd this funky!"

They don't respond as much to the slower songs, though, not even to a drop-dead knockout version of "Dark," a reminder that this man not only has the most emotionally complex falsetto since Al Green but plays the baddest guitar this side of Eddie Van Halen. But when he takes the tempo up, they can't get enough. "Don't you got to go to work tomorrow?" he asks. "Oh, I see. I'm in Monte Carlo—everybody just chills."

Finally, at 3:30, he closes with "Peach" ("an old song"), and everyone puts their heels and sweat-stained blazers back on and calls it a night. He has played 14 songs, and—other than snippets of John Lee Hooker's "I'm in the Mood" (a longtime jamming favorite) and Sly Stone's "Babies Makin' Babies"—no one had heard a note of them before. No one was calling out for "Little Red Corvette." No one seemed to mind.

Earlier, I asked if the idea of never playing all those Prince songs again made him sad at all.

"I would be sad," he replied, "if I didn't know that I had such great shit to come with."

SCENE III

At the Monte Carlo Sporting Club, Prince is checking out the set for his performance at the Awards. The backdrop is a big, silver, fuzzy Prince symbol. "They got my name looking like a float," he whispers, more amused than annoyed.

But then, if your tolerance for tackiness is low, the World Music Awards is no place to be. The nominal point here is to honor the world's best-selling artists by country or region, plus some lifetime-achievement types. The presenters and hosts—the most random aggregate of celebrities imaginable—seem to have been chosen based on who would accept a free trip to Monaco. Ursula Andress? Kylie Minogue? And in clear violation of some Geneva convention limit on cheesiness, Fabio and David Copperfield are both here to present awards.

Honorees include Ace of Base, smooth-sounding Japanese R&B crooners Chage & Aska, Kenny G (who annoys everyone backstage by wandering around tootling on that damn sax), and six-year-old French sensation Jordy (who runs offstage and kisses Prince Albert in mid-performance, which somehow does not create an international scandal). Whitney Houston wins her usual barrelful of trophies, and the whole thing is almost worth it to hear Ray Charles sit alone at the piano and sing "Till There Was You." Prince sits patiently through it all, not something he usually does (but again, this is royalty, you know). Before receiving his award from Placido Domingo (!), he puts as much as he can into "Beautiful Girl," though the show is making him do something he hates: lip-synch.

"It's cheating!" he says backstage, adding slyly, "Lip-synchers, you know who you are. See, if I would lip-synch, I'd be doing backflips, hanging from the rafters, but to cheat and be tiredä" I ask if he thinks people feel too much pressure to live up to the production quality of their videos. "Concerts are concerts and videos are videos. But I'm guilty of it myself, so that's going to change.

"Concerts, that whole thing is old, anyway. To go and wait and the lights go down and then you scream, that's played. Sound check is for lazy people; I want to open the doors earlier, let people hang out. Make it more like a fair." In his room, he has a videotape of the stage set he's having built for the next tour—a huge, sprawling thing, something like an arena-size tree house.

But still, the first thing Prince does when he finishes "Beautiful Girl" at the Awards is ask for a videotape, wondering how one dance step looked, concerned that he has reversed two words and rendered the lip-synch imperfect. Even here, he is simply incapable of just walking through it.

And that's what it always comes back to. There is only the music. Look at him, putting more into a sound check than most performers put into their biggest shows. Laugh at his ideas, his clothes, his name. But look at what he is doing: He's 15 years into this career, a time when most stars are kicking back, going through the motions. But he is still rethinking the rules of performance, the idea of how music is released, the basic concepts about how we consume and listen to music, still challenging himself and his audience like an avant-garde artist, not a platinum-selling pop star. And we still haven't talked about his plans for simulcasts and listening booths in his Glam Slam clubs in Minneapolis, L.A., and Miami, or about the 1-800-NEW-FUNK collection of other artists he's working with for NPG Records, or his thoughts on music and on-line and CD-ROM systems, or the two new magazines he's started . . . .

Of course, from where it stands, Warner Bros.' objections to his ambitious (some would say foolish) plans make conventional business sense: Would the increase in new music, coming from so many media, create a glut and cut into the sales of all the releases? Is it financially feasible? But these kinds of questions seem to be the furthest thing from Prince's mind. And okay, maybe the unpronounceable name is a little silly, and let's not forget—he retired from performances once before, back in 1985, and how long did that last? But there's no arguing with the effort, the seriousness, the intensity with which he is approaching this new era in his life.

"There's no reason for me to be playing around now," says Prince, laughing. "Now we're just doing things for the funk of it."

Chapter Twenty-Eight

**TIME OUT INTERVIEW PRINCE
BY PETER PAPHIDES
MARCH 1995**

NO FOOTBALL. THERE'S no football allowed in here. 'Can we switch it off?' The Wembley catering staff is looking decidedly agitated. It's not clear whether or not the directive concerning the backstage TV has come from higher up, but you can sense the relief when the offending footy fans switch back to Bugs Bunny. Royalty is in the vicinity. Consequently, even though The Artist Formerly Known As Prince's minders are taking it easy over some lunch and a coffee, there's a palpable tension about the place.

Minder One: 'Did you see what she called him?' He's referring to 'Sunday Show', BBC2's new youth magazine show hosted by Donna McPhail and Katie Puckrik. Prince performed an as-yet-unreleased song live from Wembley Arena.

Minder Two: 'She didn't call him Prince, did she?'

Minder One: 'She did, you know! She was in the studio and she said, "And now we're going to Wembley for Prince!" She said it!'

Minder Three shakes his head, incredulous. Staring at his pizza for inspiration, he reflects on it for a moment and inhales sharply: 'Heads will roll.' Before anyone has time to work out whether or not he's joking, the door opens. A voluptuous young woman in cycling shorts strolls in. Clearly, this is some kind of sign. Six minders grab their radios and jump to attention just as Prince follows behind her, heading for the canteen. However, by the time they've come to their senses, he's gone again, evidently not peckish. Then the summons. 'He's ready,' shouts his publicist, avoiding at all times the dilemma of having to address Prince by his new name.

More minders line the walls as I pass through another layer of security blokes, until finally I'm faced with a small subcontinent in trousers. I offer a joke following a somewhat erotic body search, but it seems this is no time for funnies. The point, of course, isn't that I might be an assassin, more that Prince is one of the most famous pop stars in the world. And along with 15 albums, an entire Minneapolis studio complex, several other solo careers launched on the back of his patronage and an untouchable respect within and beyond the music industry such is the paraphernalia of that fame.

As you may have heard, Prince wants to wrestle ownership of his songs from Warner Bros Music. At this point I ought to explain that the concept of ownership in music is kind of an odd one. When you sign to a label, you basically sell them your songs. Consequently, any time one of your songs is covered or used by another artist, on film or in an advert, the record company receives a large percentage of the royalties. For example, since Paul McCartney was outbidded by Michael Jackson in the battle to buy The Beatles' songs, even he would need Jacko's permission to sample or use Beatles songs in any unorthodox way.

Warners, then, has responded to Prince 's dissent by refusing to release his new album, 'The Gold Experience'. So he's taken to writing 'SLAVE' on his face, changed his name and refrained from performing any 'Prince' songs at his current shows, opting instead for songs from 'The Gold Experience'. As long as Warners owns his songs, it is claimed, you won't get to hear the album on record. Terrible shame, really, as it's his finest album since 1987's 'Sign O' The Times'. If you've seen Prince's first run of Wembley dates, then you will probably know all this. Prince 's set comprises almost entirely unreleased material, yet it's only upon going home that you realise he didn't play 'Alphabet Street', 'Gett Off', '1999', 'The Most Beautiful Girl In The World' and 'Kiss'.

The new songs suggest a man in the throes of some kind of creative rebirth: 'Gold', which closes the set in a slo-mo tornado of stardust and iridescence, lies at the core of this rebirth evoking the grandeur of 'Purple Rain' albeit in a more languorous setting, 'Endorphinmachine' is also remarkable, especially the way Prince squeals 'Prince is done with!' over all manner of bustling funk syncopations. Mercifully, it's much less clumsy than the eponymous stage set—a big blobby climbing frame representing a colossal hybrid of the male and female genitalia, in fact most of 'The Gold Experience' bulges ripely with a life-affirming spontaneity more common to mid-'80s gems like 'Mountains' and 'If I Was Your Girlfriend', rather than last year's flaccid 'Come' effort.

So: Prince wants to talk. About 'The Gold Experience' and about his 'enslavement', and he wants to talk about these things to me. The last time I saw Prince speaking was his acceptance speech at last month's Brit Awards. This is what he said: 'Prince? Best? "Gold Experience", better. Get Wild. In concert, perfectly free. On record, slave. Peace.' Can you see why I'm nervous?

'Sorry about the glasses. We were up kind of late last night,' smiles Prince, pointing to his Bono-style 'Fly' shades. In terms of fame, he may be even bigger than Minneapolis, but right now he's smaller than my mum. His dressing room is tiny, rendered claustrophobic by the sheer volume of patterned drapes and velour hangings that frame the dim light. Sifting through the awe, I remind myself that I've been summoned here for a reason. Prince is using Time Out to tell everyone how oppressive his record company is. When I suggest to Prince that he's only decided to talk to the press because he has a vested interest in doing so, he snaps, 'Well, Prince never used to do interviews. You'd have to ask Prince why he never used to do interviews, but you're not talking to Prince now. You're talking to me.'

Okay then. So why are you doing interviews at the moment? 'We have to free the music,' explains the pantalooned sex dwarf opposite me. 'I don't own my music at the moment. That's why I'm in dispute with the record company.'

Apparently, Prince's record company thought he was releasing too much material. This is why it claimed to be putting off the release of 'The Gold Experience'. According to Warners, if it released Prince's albums as often as he wants they'd swamp the market and everyone would lose interest in Prince. Aesthetically too, it might make more sense for Prince to release fewer records: many critics have commented that if he was more selective and released fewer albums, they would be stupendous rather than merely very good. Prince, unsurprisingly, has little time for either line of thinking.

'There's a lot of things that critics don't understand,' he responds conspiratorially, as if I'm not one of those critics. 'Like the second song in our set is a track called "Jam", and what people don't realise is that in America that's the number one track at house parties. Now, the audience knows that, they've respect that! But that's not something that most critics are down with, you know what I'm saying? So when people say I make too many records, I just show them the Aretha Franklin catalogue in the '60s, when she made a new record every four months.'

That's the kind of work ethic you aspire to then, is it?

'That's right. I work hard with the best musicians in the world. We work all day; you know what I'm saying? But those people at the record company who own my music, they go home at 6pm! And they're the people that control my music. Can you see how there's no room for debate between myself and them?' Prince 's eyes peer up from beneath the shades as if to punctuate the assertion: 'You know, they still call me Prince!'

Is that so surprising?

'No! That's my point! They have to! It's the name that's written down in the contract. If they acknowledge that I'm not Prince, that Prince is different to Prince, then they can't hold me to the conditions of their contract.'

One's initial reaction to Prince 's tale of semantic crosswits is to laugh in disbelief, but the point beneath his almost whimsical reasoning is a serious one: 'The concept of ownership of music by record companies is senseless. Like, you know the singer Seal? He's a wonderful talent, but how do I go about telling him and all the other brothers about the battle that we have to fight, when I don't own my music?'

The more you talk to Prince, the more you begin to feel that he's been planning this whole stunt for a long time, just waiting to reach a position of sufficient power from which he could pull it off. Look at the sleeve to Prince's 'Purple Rain' album, made 11 years ago. You'll see a primitive version of the 0{+> sign clearly emblazoned on the side. It's been appearing since then with increasing regularity. Presumably, that was the point of the Paisley Park studios and pressing plant, to create the beginnings of a separate infrastructure in the music industry. One that doesn't have to go through the exist in white multinationals, and ultimately exists an alternative to them.

Prince sits upright in affirmation: 'That's what the live show is about. I've done it! And if you look around at the fans, so many of them are waving signs with the new symbol. It's such beautiful sight.' You can see why Warners is worried. For commitment to the promotion of a separate infrastructure is no longer a distant dream. Far from the patronising jests of certain broad sheet writers who see endless comedy mileage in referring to Prince as Squiggle Man, the motivations behind the name change are, to a degree political. Sure, Prince doesn't need the extra money, but if he's making you question the ownership of intangibles like music (and the political implications thereof) then Prince deserves much respect. The idea of record companies actually owning the songs you write is outrageous. It s like demarcating a piece of the pavement and charging people 'Pavement Tax' to walk on it.

'That's exactly what it is,' smiles Prince. 'Do you see how suddenly, writing "Slave" on my face suddenly doesn't seem as strange? It's a gesture that communicates my position very well. It's like this is what my record company has reduced Prince to. So now, Prince is dead. They've killed him. Prince, on the other hand, is beyond contracts. They can talk about contracts till they drop, but they're Prince's contracts, not mine. The record company can't afford to accept that though.' Now the relish on his face is palpable . . . 'They're still expecting me to do "Purple Rain", a cabaret set.'

Of course, there are other ways of getting 'The Gold Experience' out. How about the Internet, for instance? 'We're currently looking into that one,' says Prince, 'The important thing is that my fans hear this music, whether it be through duplicating cassettes, or if we press up 10,000 CDs after the show and charge $5 each, just to cover costs you know? Even if we do what Pearl Jam do—just turn up at radio stations and play the people our music. That's what these shows are about, communing with the fans. I go to a club and I see fans dancing to my records. They wave to me, I wave back, and I realise that this is why I make music. Not for record companies.'

Prince is always quick to mention how his fans 'understand'. While I don't doubt he's genuinely moved by the adulation he receives, it also strikes me as a pretty basic ploy of testing the commitment of the diehards while bringing the waverers closer to you. It's what any cult from Morrissey to Michael Jackson to the Reverend Moon, does in the face of adversity, and implicitly calls the love of The Fans into question by appealing to their loyalty. Still, as long as the majority of your fans are prepared to, ahem, die 4 U, there's never too much need to worry about what critics say. So when I start asking Prince anything more probing than 'Why are you so wonderful?' he clams up visibly.

Anyone with a passing familiarity with Prince's canon will already know the three main themes of his music: shagging, humping and fucking. An elementary knowledge of psychology tells me that anyone so eager to impress on the world his sack prowess ('you jerk your body like a horny pony would' and 'there's a lion in my pocket and baby it's ready to roar' are my personal faves) must be motivated, in part, by a deep—rooted misogyny. It's also worth bearing in mind that early in his childhood the young Prince Rogers Nelson ran away from his mother in order to be with his father, a musician. For the first time in our little meeting, Prince stumbles on his words: 'Aah . . . oh well, that's a whole concept that, aah . . . you know, I could say something about that, and you could take a line out of context that might change the meaning entirely. It's all in the songs anyway.'

Yes, but you do see, don't you, that the sheer volume of fucking that goes on in your songs, is frankly bizarre. Don't you?

'Um, I believe that sometimes hate can be love and love can be hate.'

'Gett Off' boasts your, sorry, Prince's ability to assume '22 positions in a one-night stand'. Any chance of passing a few tips on to a mere novice like myself?

'Oh . . .' Prince is now visibly buckling beneath the ignominy of having to entertain a question this moronic. 'That's not what all this is about . . . That's not something I, aaah . . .'

All what?

'Aaaah.' Big pause. He looks away. All right then. What about marriage, then? Any plans to singlehandedly put Durex out of business by having lots of little Princes?

'Not really,' smirks the compact sex symbol. 'I decided that things like family don't have a big part to play in my future. I'm dedicated to music, to the point that I see all of life through it.'

What would seem like a flippant, sentimental declaration from any other pop star becomes a fierce declaration of humanism from the mouth of Prince. The past two weeks have seen him deliver night after night of rambunctious boilerhouse funk while the psychedelic harems of his mind are recreated on stage around him. 'A couple of years ago perhaps,' he concludes, 'I had a spiritual, uh . . . rebirth. I was lacking direction for a very long time. But I saw a light which I realised I had to follow. At that point I became . . .' Prince points to a drape bearing his hieroglyphic name . . .

By the way, how do you pronounce that? 'It isn't pronounced. It just is.' 0{+>, aka The Artist Formerly Known As Prince plays two more dates at Wembley Arena on Tuesday and Wednesday.

Chapter Twenty-Nine

PRINCE IN THE NEWS
STORIES FROM SAINT PAUL PIONEER PRESS
BY BRUCE ORWALL—1995

Story One:

WITH A NAME that can't be pronounced and the word "slave" scrawled on his cheek, Prince has put his faithful through a mighty test of patience in the past year.

Fans may be put off by Prince's oddball star turns, but one group is a little testier than others: his creditors.

Paisley Park Enterprises, the company that oversees most of Prince's business interests, is not paying its bills on time or at all. From the Twin Cities to Los Angeles, businesses that have done work for Prince say they must hound the pop star for payment and even take him to court.

Some Twin Cities companies have stopped working with Paisley Park. Others now demand payment upfront for services. One Minneapolis film producer declared bankruptcy last year after Paisley refused to pay a $400,000 debt, then settled the bill 10 months late for 70 cents on the dollar.

"People haven't gotten paid, it's absolutely true," says Randy Adamsick, president of the Minnesota Film Board.

Since soaring to multimillion-dollar fame with the "Purple Rain" film and soundtrack in 1984, Prince has operated as if money is no object, according to interviews with nearly 30 former employees and business associates. Despite earnings that easily top $150 million since then, the 36-year-old Minneapolis native has twice found himself in severe financial disarray—first in 1989, and again today.

His associates blame Prince's habit of spending lavishly on his creative projects, with a cavalier disregard for budgets and professional advice.

"He'll say, 'We do this, this and this, and pretty soon . . . Jurassic Park!'" said Jenifer Carr, former chief financial officer of Paisley Park Enterprises. "He always thinks every project he works on is a home run, and the reality is it isn't."

Creditors say they don't even know who to badger for payment anymore because Paisley Park is in such chaos. Every key company executive has quit or been fired by Prince in recent months, as have a slew of lower-level workers.

Meanwhile, Prince is locked in a cryptic sparring match with his label of 17 years, Warner Bros. Records, rooted in his desire to release new material more frequently. That battle prompted his much-ridiculed name change to 0{+> and his declarations that "Prince is dead" and that his Warner Bros. contract amounts to "institutionalized slavery."

Despite lagging record sales, Prince's exalted place in the pantheon of contemporary music is not in question. Few who have worked with Prince question the artistic direction of a man who ranks more with Miles Davis and John Coltrane than with the Michael Boltons and Jon Secadas with whom he shares chart space.

But even hard-core fans are starting to wonder where his career is headed.

"He's losing a lot of his fans," said Nathan Wright of Minneapolis, who operates a 900 line that trades in Prince information. "A lot of his fans are tired of it. It's like a gigantic game that only he seems to know the rules to."

Prince declined to discuss Paisley's troubles. Through a Los Angeles publicist, the company issues a one-sentence statement: "There were management changes in 1993 and 1994, and we look forward to a happy and prosperous 1995."

Story Two:

A late night phone call has typically meant one thing for Paisley Park employees: Prince wants something done.

"He'd call on Friday night and want a set for Saturday morning," said Blaine Marcou, who owned a company that did Prince's set design for several years. "We'd work all night. Then he'd come in a 4 a.m., look at it and say, 'I'm too tired. Go home.'"

But the money was already spent. Prince's snap decisions might cost $20,000 or more, but many associates say he doesn't seem to care. In Los Angeles, he often pays to have a crew of recording engineers on hand around the clock while he is in town, whether he plans to show up or not.

"Where other guys go out and buy cars and buy drugs and buy jets," said Steve Fargnoli, the manager who guided Prince to stratospheric success from 1978 to 1988, "this kid is not interested in that. He's interested in things that satisfy his creative urge. They may not be intelligent business decisions."

Prince strikes the same risk-taking profile in business as in art. His style is hit and run; try something fast, and if it doesn't work, move on to something else.

In a meeting, Prince will often listen impassively while advisers tell him why something can't be done. When they finish, says Rob Borm, the Minneapolis filmmaker whose company went bankrupt, Prince will remind them whose ideas got them all there in the first place, then say: "I'll bet the house on this one."

When one project doesn't pan out, Prince makes the same bet on the next one. That willingness to spin the wheel and create a kaleidoscopic musical vision is part of Prince's appeal as an artist. But it has proved a costly way to do business.

"Part of Prince's creative energy is fueled by walking the edge," said Craig Rice, former director of operations for Paisley Park Studios. "I don't have a problem with walking the edge. The problem is, you've got to win occasionally."

Prince's associates point to his penchant for investing large sums of little or no commercial value: an erotic stage version of "Ulysses" that cost several hundred thousand dollars in 1993; the recent introduction of a cheaply packaged "poly-gender fragrance" called "Get Wild"; expensive stage sets and band rehearsals for tours that never occur.

And while he has taken to saying that "music should be free," he clearly wants to be paid for the use of his image. Shown how much his activities are discussed on the Internet, Prince talked about trying to start his own on-line service, Carr said.

More expensive still is Prince's non-stop production of music videos. Record companies consider music videos promotional tools whose sole purpose is to get MTV airplay and sell records. They are usually made only for the singles the artist releases.

But Prince makes videos for an entire albums that never see a second of MTV time and are not financed by his record company. He makes videos for songs he has recorded but will never release. And he shoots footage that is of no apparent value to anyone but himself: Prince driving around Los Angeles in his new gold Mustang, or playing on the beach with dancer Mayte from his band, the New Power Generation.

"I call it his home movies," said Bill Felker, a former Paisley Park production manager.

Most associates recognize it as plain wasteful. "It's like Vietnam," said Rice. "They just shoot and shoot. They don't even know who the enemy is anymore."

The people hired to do the work normally wouldn't care what Prince intends to do with the products, as long as they get paid. But Prince's recent antics with Warner Bros. have struck a raw nerve when employees and vendors are being stiffed.

"He talks about himself being a slave to Warners," said Heidi Presnail, former Paisley Park wardrobe director. "Hello? Let me knock on your door. We don't work for free."

Story Three:

Prince's problem isn't a lack of earnings. Even though his commercial fortunes aren't what they once were, he may still earn $10 to $20 million in a given year from record advances, publishing royalties and fees for producing other artists.

That money goes to Paisley Park Enterprises, the company that owns the $10 million Paisley Park Studios in Chanhassen and acts as an umbrella for most of Prince's activities.

Some companies working with Paisley report slow but regular payments. "They've fulfilled all obligations to us on every level," said Gerry Wenner, vice president of the Los Angeles production company Planet.

But Paisley's freewheeling spending and subsequent inability to manage it have taken their toll on a growing list of people who do business with the company.

People like Gary and Suzy Zahradka, a St. Paul couple who made the ornate canes that Prince toted to French fashion shows and Monte Carlo parties last year. Their $4500 bill was nearly half a year late when they filed suit against Paisley Park in Carver County District Court in November. Paisley settled the case in late December.

While some have gone to court, others have simmered in silence when Paisley Park snubbed their bills or arbitrarily cut in half the fees for a makeup artist or hairstylist.

"There's a lot of little guys out there," said Julie Hartley, a former Paisley Park production manager. "I have a friend who used to borrow money from his mom to pay his mortgage" because of Paisley's nonpayment.

The big guys have not had much better luck. Northwest Teleproductions in Edina has worked on Prince-related projects for several years. Paisley Park has always been a slow payer, said Northwest President Bob Mitchell, but a few months ago the payments on a months-old debt in the tens of thousands of dollars simply stopped. When the company called to collect, it finds confused employees trying to piece things together.

"Mostly, we just meet with the frustration of employees over there," Mitchell says. "There's often continual replacement of middle-management-type people over there . . . . The people that created the work simply aren't there anymore."

Broken promises extend beyond the Twin Cities. In Los Angeles, Prince spends about $500,000 a year to have a crew ready for him at The Record Plant, a recording studio where he works when away from Paisley Park Studios.

Until last year, Prince's representatives have always paid the bill on time. But last summer, said a source close to the situation, a $150,000 bill went five months without payment. The debt was not paid until Paisley Park called asking for a master tape Prince had recorded there. The studio owners struck a deal: Pay the debt and you can have your tape. The bill was paid the same afternoon.

Smaller vendors usually do not have Princely valuables to take hostage.

Jim Mulligan, owner of the Minneapolis company Videoworks, did one project for Paisley Park last spring. His $1,400 bill languished for months before he waged a time-consuming collection campaign.

Each morning, Mulligan faxed Paisley an invoice detailing his work. Then he called the accounting department, where he was thwarted each day by voice mail. Then he began faxing his invoice twice a day. For six weeks, there was no response.

One morning late last summer, Mulligan simply announced to the Paisley Park voice mail that he expected the check to be waiting for him at the front desk that afternoon. His strategy worked—the check was there.

"I never talked to an actual human being," he said.

Story Four:

Rob Borm's pitch to Prince was: "Hire me. I'm young. I'm hungry. I can make you some money."

Three years later, Borm's association with Paisley led to the end of his business.

Borm says the story of his association with Paisley Park is a rags-to-riches-to-rags story. He had just launched his film production company, Point of

View Films, in 1991 when Prince gave him a break, hiring him to produce a video for the hit song "Gett Off."

The instructions from Paisley Park Enterprises President Gilbert Davison were vague: "Prince wants his yellow suit in it, and he wants his yellow car in it, and he wants it to look a little like 'Caligula,'" a reference to the 1980 film that oozed Roman decadence.

Borm crunched a careful budget that would bring in the two-day shoot well within the $220,000 allocated by Warner Bros. for the project. According to Borm, Davison barely looked at it, saying: "Oh, by the way, there's probably going to be quite a few changes to the concept."

By the time it was completed, the "Gett Off" video had cost $1.3 million over seven days—the overruns owing to Prince's desire to keep shooting on the surreal fall-of-Rome set Borm created, stocked at Prince's request with erotic imagery and women recruited from a local strip club.

When Paisley was slow to pay the million-dollar overrun, Borm began a two-year high-wire act with his own creditors, as he produced 47 more music videos without the aid of a budget.

The fast and loose spending caught up with him two years later. In summer 1993, Borm was preparing to film shows in London for Prince. But back home, Paisley was $450,000 behind on its payments to him, and Borm's creditors were getting antsy.

He said he asked Prince about it before a London concert and got a mild scolding: "You should know better than to talk to me about money, especially before a gig." Subsequent lectures were delivered by Prince's attorney and business manager. But the payment was never made.

That's when Borm pulled his crew off the tour and returned to the United States on the advice of an attorney. It took 10 months of rugged negotiations and threatened lawsuits before Borm reached a settlement of $315,000.

But the money wasn't enough to satisfy Borm's creditors. Since Paisley represented 90 percent of his work, his company was essentially doomed: Live by Prince, die by Prince. Point of View Films declared bankruptcy with about $5,900 in assets and $135,000 in debts.

Story Five:

Certain that his judgment is on the mark, Prince sometimes grows exasperated when people say "no" to him.

"I don't need a mother," Prince once said to Rice when a business manager tried to reign in his spending.

Several generations of attorneys, managers and accountants have been put through the same wringer. One of the first was Steve Fargnoli, who hooked up with Prince in 1978 and took him to the top.

Prince was exuberant but more impressionable in those days. Fargnoli manages to bottle the magic and parcel it out in marketable bursts.

"He's a pure musician and artist who is so much more prolific than your average rock star," Fargnoli said in his first interview about Prince since being fired in 1989. "He's constantly frustrated by the environment he's in He's constantly trying to grasp at new ideas because it's not moving fast enough."

Because Prince liked to work so much, Fargnoli tried to keep him focused on revenue-generating projects such as writing and producing records for protégés' acts, including The Time.

"There were years when he wrote and recorded four albums," Fargnoli said. "It added up, all that stuff."

But Fargnoli's ability to control Prince's wandering ideas faded with the rocker's ascension to post-"Purple Rain" superstardom.

For example, Prince wanted his second movie, "Under the Cherry Moon," to be black and white; Fargnoli predicted, accurately, that it was a commercial misstep. Fargnoli wanted him to buy an existing studio in Los Angeles; Prince wanted to build Paisley Park Studios in the Twin Cities. (There were minor victories: "He wanted blue mosque domes on it," Fargnoli recalled, "which we, uh, didn't get to.")

Their relationship ended in 1988, when Prince tried to back out of a Japanese tour so he could get to work on his fourth film, "Graffiti Bridge." The shows were already booked and the tickets sold.

"He could have been sued to $10 to $20 million," Fargnoli said. "If you don't show up, you pay for it."

Prince responded by firing him at the start of 1989, at the same time he fired his attorney and business manager. The two traded lawsuits for a few years, with Prince claiming mismanagement and Fargnoli saying he had been libeled in a Prince song. The suits were either dismissed or settled out of court. Fargnoli has written to Prince several times, but there has been no response.

"He looks at it as, 'These guys are old now. We'll get somebody younger,'" Fargnoli said. "It's always, 'They're the new heroes and the old guys are the bad guys.'"

Story Six:

When prince's deposition was taken for a lawsuit two years ago, he was asked to provide a small description of what he has done since graduating from Minneapolis Central High School in 1976.

"Gotten a job as a songwriter and performer," he lowballed. "I have done some movies, and a lot of concerts."

Of his work at Paisley Park Studios, Prince added: "I basically come in the back entrance and just pretty much use the studios . . . . I basically work here. I don't run it."

Although he is the sole shareholder in Paisley Park Enterprises, Prince didn't get into the music business to be a corporate executive. The concept at Paisley Park was intended to keep the artist in the process of creating, while professionals ran the recording studios and 12,000-square-foot sound stage. Prince would book his time like anyone else.

Paisley Park's opening seemed to be the culmination of a sweet success story: a local man, from a poor family in North Minneapolis, who willed himself to the top, then chose to give something back to his hometown. Work at Paisley Park helped the Twin Cities film and music communities grow and flourish.

But Paisley needed professional management. After a decade in which he had known only tremendous commercial success, Prince was several million dollars in debt as the '80s drew to a close.

"There was a serious debt level," Rice said. "It was boggling. But there was a way to dig out from beneath it. It was cost cutting."

The financial struggle is confirmed in a deposition by Nancy Chapman, an entertainment industry CPA in Los Angeles who was Prince's business manager from 1989 until last year.

"When we became involved with Prince in his corporate activities, he was in financial trouble," said Chapman, detailing how she and others completely overhauled the company. ". . . During the first 1 1/2 years of our involvement in his life, this was a search-and-rescue mission."

Sound operation of the studio and new management helped dig Prince out of the hole. Paisley played host to such international superstars as R.E.M. and Madonna, and its sound stage was usually booked solid with commercial and film work. "It was a concentrated effort by a group of people to alleviate the debt and bring it back to a good, solid financial ground," Rice said.

Because Prince is a sharp thinker who devours newspapers and magazines, most people figured the financial crisis would never be repeated. But they say Prince is proving otherwise.

"I don't think he ever did reform his practices," said David Rivkin, a record producer whose association with Prince dates back to the 1970s. "It happened so fast in the beginning for him that it's always been 'easy come, easy go.'"

Story Seven:

The Paisley Park of the '90s has been a roller coaster ride, as company employees attempted to keep up with both the highs and the trials of a workaholic genius.

A bodyguard, Gilbert Davison, was elevated to company president in 1990. Former employees say Davison let Prince do as he pleased, attempting to do damage control when possible. Sometimes he would scurry around behind his boss's back, telling vendors not to heed Prince's expensive requests. "They say, usually after the fact: 'You can't listen to what he says,'" said Marcou, the set designer.

When Prince would learn that his request had been dismissed, Carr said, he would just write a check himself, on an account to which only had access, and get what he wanted.

In interviews with former employees and vendors, Prince's associates said that the business began to stray in new, expensive and unprofitable directions. Prince provided most of the $2 million to launch the Minneapolis Glam Slam nightclub, which was technically owned by Davison. Vanity projects such as a Prince comic book took a lot of time but generated little revenue.

Paisley also ran a 10-person wardrobe department, which made all of Prince's clothing as well as costumes for his band and street clothes for his girlfriends.

Prince's record label, Paisley Park Records, also struggled for financial success. Where Prince had once launched new stars like The Time ad Sheila E., his more recent protégés produced a log string of bombs.

Most notable were Prince's efforts to manufacture hit records for his girlfriends, among them a dancer named Tara Patrick, a k a Carmen Electra, whose aptly titles "Go Go Dancer" album came out in 1993.

The record received a top-drawer promotional campaign worth about $2 million, according to industry sources, about half of which came straight out of Paisley Park's pocket. But the record still died a quick death.

"If it's a personal relationship," said Carr, "he's going to spend money on it."

Some projects have found success. A CD-ROM game featuring Prince has sold more than 60,000 copies and won praise for a pioneering concept that was developed by a California software company. In 1994, the renamed Prince released a single, "The Most Beautiful Girl in the World," which enjoyed a lengthy Top 10 run—but was also very expensive for Paisley Park to produce.

Price has also done some high-profile charity work in recent time, performing benefit concerts for the National Kidney Foundation in Minneapolis and the Dance Theater of Harlem in New York.

If Prince noticed the failures, he didn't show it. He told employees he did not want to be involved in business discussions but found himself drawn into them anyway.

Chapman said in her deposition: "I may go to him to run something by him, and his response to me is: 'Why do I have to get involved in this? That is what I pay you for. If I have to make these decisions, why do I have you'"

Story Eight:

Prince cleaned house at Paisley Park in 1994. He appointed his older brother, Duane Nelson, to head a five-member committee that would downsize the company, and pink slips started to fly. Even as the company has continued mounting expensive projects, vendors say that Paisley, and sometimes Prince himself, have asked vendors to take less for their work.

What they told me is that I was being fired on a cutback, and they were eliminating my position," said former wardrobe director Heidi Presnail. The committee disseminated no information explaining the need for cuts.

Longtime employees and confidants left or were fired. Davison left in a dispute related to the ownership of Glam Slam. Sound stage manager Mark "Red" White, who had been with Prince for a decade, left. Chief financial officer Carr was fired. Publicist Karen Lee quit in November. Levi Seacer Jr., a former band member who was running Prince's new NPG Records label, departed at the same time.

Several of those people hired attorneys to collect their money when their severance payments stopped last fall. By year's end, most had negotiated a final settlement with Paisley Park.

Duane Nelson's committee started to resemble a "cage match" in professional wrestling—last one in the cage wins. Today, Nelson is the only one left from the original downsizing committee.

The studio, meanwhile, has operated less as a business available for rent and more as Prince's private work space. Twin Cities film producers say the sound stage has not been reliably available for some time because of Prince's perpetual video production.

According to the film board's Adamsick, Warner Bros. had to intervene with Prince himself to get the star to clear enough time to shoot the movie "Grumpy Old Men" there in 1993.

Prince has also been asserting himself in the recording studio. Record producer Rivkin said Prince once put up the money to move a Rivkin recording project to Los Angeles because Prince wanted to work at Paisley.

Rivkin, who used Paisley Park so frequently that he rented an office in the building, moved out last summer. The loss of a reliable client didn't stir much interest in the studio, though.

"They didn't seem to give a s—if I was leaving or not," said Rivkin, who produced the demo tape that got Prince signed to Warner Bros. in 1977. "They just said, 'If you're not going to use this office, can we use it?'"

Despite the financial problems—and the declining use of the studio by insiders—Paisley Park invested several hundred thousand dollars in new recording technology last year.

The experience of working at Paisley Park has left some people disillusioned or angry. But some—even those who have lost jobs—say they would love to work with the company again and see it prosper.

Julie Hartley was fired as a production assistant last year when Prince accused her of lying about how much it would cost to build "The Endorphinmachine," a new stage set he dreamed up. She remembers with exasperation how Prince ordered all but two members of a film crew off the sound stage, then ordered: "Now here's the shot. I want the bed to get up and fly over me to there."

But the frenetic pace of Paisley was addictive, and she would do it again—if Paisley Park pulls out of its tailspin.

"I like the allure that that place brings here," she said. "I hope it stays, and I'm sad that it's tarnished."

Story Nine: Saint Paul Pioneer Press—1995—Story by, not listed

At an awards ceremony last year, Prince read from a legal pad to explain his side of the war he has waged against his label of 17 years, Warner Bros. Records:

"Perhaps one day, all the powers that are will realize that it is better to let a man be all that he can be than to limit his output to just what they can handle," Prince said at the Soul of American Music awards.

In Los Angeles Monday, Prince will get another chance to explain himself when he meets with Warners chairman Danny Goldberg. The topic: the relationship between Prince and the company, which Prince has described as "institutionalized slavery."

After seeing Prince's strange performance on "The Late Show With David Letterman" Dec. 13th—in which he sang, "If I came back as a dolphin, would you listen to me then?" before performing a mock suicide—many fans were more perplexed than ever about Prince's contract struggles.

In a nutshell: Prince has been frustrated that the company won't release his records more regularly. He produces the equivalent of three or four albums a year; the record company would rather have just one and milk it.

Hoping to squirm through a contract loophole, Prince changed his name to 0{+> and said he would fulfill the remainder of his Warners contract with selection from his 500-song vault of unreleased material. New songs he records, though, would be released on another label as 0{+>.

While Prince's stand does not seem to hold much promise as a legal theory—he currently owes Warner Bros. four more albums—he has won praise from artists. Last month's Musician magazine declared him one of several industry "revolutionaries" who are challenging the status quo that exists between artists and corporations.

At stake in this week's meeting with Goldberg is an album recorded last year called "The Gold Experience," which contains some of Prince's most commercially viable and adventuresome music in years. The lead track, "Gold," has a grandeur that has been compared to "Purple Rain."

Prince representatives have regularly tweaked the company publicly for the past year. "'The Gold Experience' likely will never be released," publicist Mitch Schneider said last week.

The company says that isn't true. "Yes, we would like to put out the next Prince or symbol-person album," said Bob Merlis, vice president for communications at Warner Bros. "And we will, once he delivers the masters." That delivery hasn't taken place.

Warner Bros. executives, who will not speak for the record, say that Prince has at least three times negotiated a deal to release "The Gold Experience," then backed out of it. Once regarded as a reliable, if sometimes hard to handle asset, Prince, they say, has been a different, less reliable person since he changed his name to a symbol in 1993.

Adding to the tension was Prince's 1992 announcement that he had signed a $100 million deal with Warners, when the reality was much more modest. The deal did call for Warner Bros. to become a partner in the operation of Paisley Park Enterprises, but that partnership was curtailed about a year ago. Warners spent about $5 million on the partnership.

Chapter Thirty

ESQUIRE GENTLEMAN INTERVIEW PRINCE
BY JULIE BAUMGOLD FALL, 1995

THE DARK CAR slid into the well-guarded alley. On the day after his second birthday as Prince, he got out of the car and walked quickly into the Glam Slam in South Beach, Miami. For twenty years, Prince has had a life of rear entrances, underground passages, announced and plotted arrivals, usually when night is well tipped into day.

He owns the Glam Slam and two other clubs like it and was here to perform on his birthday, make a video, and straighten out a little business problem. He stared straight-ahead, the master of the place, with debutante posture and, as is usual, "Slave" written artistically with marker on his right cheek.

His white silk shirt floated back from his frail body, a white Borsalino rode high on his hair, which glowed with glitter like stardust. He wore a mask of absolute expressionless stillness. His vacant face is his armor. It allows him to think without being bothered. It is convenient for creation, and it keeps the mystique.

Living in mystery is a stage of stardom, a reaction to early fame. Sometimes it is risky because silence can be misconstrued, but this is how 0{+> wants it. No interviews—or if he does agree to one, he cripples the writer by removing his pen.

The big disco room had become a movie set since he left it after performing until five that morning, his wet body wrapped in a robe. As he had reminded the Glam Slam audience many times, "Prince is dead." He was feeling good, for each day was bringing him closer to the end of the contract with Warner Bros. Records that he feels enslaves him.

No one approached him. Those who did not know him well quickly averted their eyes when they passed, as though even to look on him were forbidden. He is the perfect combination of tininess and threat: Though he is thirty-seven in his past life as Prince Rogers Nelson, with a deep voice and a hairy chest—this is still a boy-man. With his long, slender fingers, slightly pointed ears, and large beautiful eyes, the effect is elfin. He is very small and so dainty in his visible proportions that it is hard to imagine his childhood in a rough part of Minneapolis.

Here, as he sits with Carolyn Baker, a vice president of artist development for Warner Bros. Records, and two members of the band, the NPG, he is completely accepted as the genius, the boss, the coddled star, and the reason everyone is in this room. They are used to his ways—the fabled sleepless energy that leads him to do aftershows in clubs following is performances. They know his talents as songwriter, performer, star of four movies, producer, autodidact on sixteen instruments, miniature sex machine. They know he is so prolific he could put out four albums a year if the record business worked that way. They know him in the many reincarnations as he redefines himself with the times. They know the things that make him an artist: the fact that he changes and gives himself the possibility to fail, that he moves through different mediums, that his life is the stuff of his work and the reverse. They accept—it goes with the job.

"He's a genius . . . like a Miles Davis, who sounds like no one else heard. They hear, see, feel something we don't, and their job is to interpret for us," Baker says a few days later. "His whole world is colored differently from mine. People used to say, 'Will you tell him to do something?' And I'd say, 'No, you need to work around it.' He has a vision. He has got to be able to do it his way . . . . It's kind of like being an alien."

The large, heavily fringed Prince eyes are sneaking a peek at me, checking me out although I have been preapproved or I would not be in this room. One does not approach. One waits as the big white hat swivels slowly, the outlined eyes blink and consider. A little pencil line of hair surrounds his mouth. When he is ready, he comes over sucking a cherry Tootsie Pop, smiling redly. Juli Knapp, his director of operations, privately refers to and introduces him as "The Artist Formerly Known as Prince." Everyone is very scrupulous about this name thing.

Prince and I go up into the balcony to talk. His bodyguard sits down in the row behind us, but Prince sends him away. "I'm a terrible interview," he says. His speaking voice is very low, like his low-register singing voice. I think he is afraid of not being as interesting as this whole edifice he has created, happier to hide behind his scarves and costumes and characters. With the press, as with his record company, he has trusted people and been burned. Actually, he is the perfect star in this era for which, as someone said, the best way to get attention is to shun attention. At least until the next album.

The stage Prince, historically dirty with his sex talk, is obviously showbiz. He is very well spoken; intense, funny, dipping into funk speech when he wants to, and very smart. He leans forward to tell me he feels angry at himself. When he signed the Warner deal he didn't know what he knows now, and sold what he feels is his birthright. He sold his master tapes. And now his future children won't have them. This is why he turned in disgust from "Prince"—taken as a seventeen-year-old boy, his image controlled—and the work that was Prince. This is why he became 0{+> and does not sing Prince songs: If I can't have me, they can't.

Of course he took the money, a deal worth a variously reported $30 million to $100 million. But they are not releasing or promoting his work the way he wants. Warner Bros. Records refuses to put out albums at the fast rate he writes songs, preferring to promote one album and one tour a year, as more might overwhelm the market.

All of this is involved in the name change. It was both a spiritual conversion and a business move. Just when he had been around long enough to have generations of fans, he became someone else and was reborn, artistically recast. He has his slave self, which is issuing a new album, The Gold Experience, and his semifree self, which contributed to Exodus, by the NPG. And there is a third self, a big hidden album.

For some time, he has been working on Emancipation, which will be his first album when he is free—maybe fifty new songs. Then, he says, he will reemerge. He will speak to the press. His face has changed now, as though the plastic boss face was to keep everyone else calm. He tells me that his heart and perhaps his best work are in Emancipation. This album is a big surprise to people to people at Warner. No one seems to know about it.

"He's been here since the '70s," says Baker. "He was very young. Sometimes you love your parents but want to leave home. None of us wants to see it happen."

Prince is a businessman. He has a $10 million studio, Paisley Park, where he produces other recording artists; he has these clubs throbbing until dawn, Prince stores in London and Minneapolis, where the symbol and the face take on iconic dimensions, his own love scent, and so forth. In 1992-93, Forbes ranked him the fifth most highly paid entertainer in the world. But a part of the Warner deal was a restructuring. Right now he is a businessman who made a bad deal. He doesn't want it to happen to others. He says he want to take care of other artists. His ambition is nothing less than to form an alternative recording industry where artists own their own work and have creative freedom. The NPG, the New Power Generation, the people of the sun, are part of this new quasi-hippie world. When he performs with them he is "Tora Tora," his head and face wrapped in a chiffon scarf, yet another self. He is hidden, as he was in the "My Name is Prince" video when he wore a curtain of chains over his face.

O{+> Is in an artistic conundrum—art versus what is "commercial." When he hears that word, he almost leaps from his seat in the balcony. When they let him handle the single "The Most Beautiful Girl in the World," he says he had his most commercial hit of the decade. ("It would have been spooky if it was the whole album," he says later.) It is every artist's devil—his vision and the world's may not always mesh. His best stuff may be beyond them, but he knows how good or bad it is. Though sometimes he can fool himself, inside the artist always knows. The record company sometimes knows. The dilemma was there as early as his movie Purple Rain. People kept warning The Kid (Prince's role): "Nobody digs your music but yourself." Of course, central to artistic freedom is the freedom to fail on your own terms.

He talks about people who don't own their parent's work—Nona Gaye doesn't own Marvin. Does Lisa Marie Presley own Elvis's masters?

He talks of the creative accounting of the record business, how black stores don't always have the digital scanners and miscount, so say, for instance, a big rap artist, who is said to have sold four million copies, might really have sold twenty million. He totally sympathized with George Michael, whom he considers a great talent, in his fight with Sony, which he says is an "even worse" company than Warner. Warner goes ahead and promotes what they want from the NPG album, which isn't always the right song, though the one he likes is nine-and-a-half minutes long. "Everyone gets to play on it. I have the best drummer in the world," he says.

According to his people, his deal is this: He gets an advance that might cover his living expenses while making an album. Once the work is delivered, Warner can decide how or if to promote and market it. The final decisions are not his. Thus, he is a "slave" to the system. Warner, I'm sure, has a different interpretation. I do not say to him that perhaps it trivializes the African-American experience for a millionaire rock star—who travels with aides, bodyguards, a chef, a hairdresser, valet, backup security, wardrobe, band, technical people, a personal dancing muse, and a man who sits behind him in the Concorde handing him freshly sharpened pencils—to write "Slave" on his face. This—glittery chains on the face versus chains on the ankles—is his version of slavery. Though he is half white, he identifies completely as a black man and talks about the lack of images for black children in movies and television.

"And who is at the head of those companies?" he says.

Mayte wafts into the balcony. She is his current inspiration after a long line of protégés including Apollonia and Vanity. Prince tells her what to wear for the video. Mayte has been with him for four years, since she was a famously virginal seventeen. Mayte, who is also of mixed parentage, grew up on army bases and studied ballet and belly dancing from the age of three. She fulfilled her mother's own balked ambition in the way Prince fulfilled his father's. Mayte is his Tinkerbell, his Linda McCartney. She bumps and grinds and tosses her black hair and cheerleads his songs. She shakes her ass and belly dances with a sword on her head. She punches the air and stalks the stage in hot pants, not shy about showing the cheeks of her tush, her dancer's thighs flexing. Her poster sells next to his in the lobby. She is always next to him.

Together they look like they live on sweets and air, two ethereal beings who inflate, take on power, persona, and sexiness onstage. Offstage they look like they should be wrapped in bathrobes, fed warm starches, and kept safe till it is time to step out again into the pink smoke.

They reappear—she in her gold costume and he with his face wrapped in a chiffon scarf beneath a Mad Hatter hat with a rose and wearing a floor-length black gospel robe with the NPG insignia. When I tell him that he looks like Thing in the Addams family, he starts to shuffle and make squeaking Thing noises.

Glam Slam's lights are flashing, rebounding off the mirrored disco ball in the ceiling, and a member of the crew falls to the floor in an epileptic seizure. Prince looks at him with his blank expression and, standing rigid, alienated from the situation, makes no move to help. There are other people helping the man. Prince is disconnected. When things go wrong in the world he controls, he does not scream. He walks away. He and Mayte stand there in their funny show clothes with Marcello Mastroianni in La Dolce Vita on the monitors because the songs they will be doing is "The Good Life." The man is carried out on a stretcher and the video goes on.

It is Prince's birthday night. He is onstage in a burnt-cherry-red jumpsuit cut open in the back all the way to the cleavage of his tiny behind. A fabulous dresser, masculine in his feminine clothes, he has always dressed out of his times and just like a prince in his frock coats, rampantly ruffled shirts with fingertip-dragging cuffs, tight high-waisted pants with matching French-heeled boots, royal medallions, arrogant walking sticks, tiny boleros with high Beau Brummel collars. He has borrowed from both masculine and feminine figures: the toreador, the languid Byronic poet coughing in his cuffs, the dandy, the fop, Prince Charming, Coco Chanel.

It's 2 A.M. or so in the Glam Slam and he is playing the music he wants to play. The place, which has been in a bit of a slump, is now filled with bobbing, heaving fans, their arms waving in the dark like undersea fronds blown back and forth by the currents. Mayte is strutting in her black boots, punching the air with a tambourine, keening, sweating alongside him, her ambition intertwined with his. The monitors are going, as are the video cams, in this big throb of video love. Prince pounds out the show—all rocking, all beat, jamming and funk. He is the complete mid-career 0{+>. This is his night in his club with his symbol over the bar, on the waitresses' chests, on his boots, on his 0{+>-shaped guitar "Prince is dead," he keeps saying, enjoying it, shucking the old self, as Mayte flips her hair down and back. He asks to hear the crowd; he wants to hear feedback from the void.

He says the obligatory "motherf—er" to prove he has not crossed the line to Lite Rock. Reminiscent of his old dirty days, he gets into a whole "pussy control" rant: "How many ladies got pussy control?" "I got a headache tonight," says Mayte. "I got something for your headache," he says—kind of like a dirty Captain and Tenille. He is no longer feeling "The Kid" when he says to them, "I am your mom's favorite freak." Mayte carries out a cake but he waves it away. "I hate that Happy Birthday song."

The next night he plays even longer—three hours instead of two—and is even hotter, released from his video chores, having imparted his bit to me. He has a chiffon scarf over his face, a white suit with fringe, another Elvisoid chest-baring white suit with gold trim. Up in the balcony, at 4:30 A.M., his three aides in black dresses are dancing away—his accountant, one of his lawyers, his director of operations, all reminded of why they work for this man.

"This is your captain," he says onstage in the colored cone of streaming light, his rhinestone necklace shining on his slender throat. He is at his best in the hour of the owl with the creatures of the moon. Now, over these bodies, he has the power. When he is free, emancipated from his demon Warner, if it all works out, he will be laughing in the purple rain. And maybe it will be the last laugh.

Chapter Thirty-One

FORBES MAGAZINE INTERVIEW PRINCE
BY JOSHUA LEVINE—1996

SITTING ON THE floor of his pastel-colored recording studio near Minneapolis, the pop singer formerly known as Prince—he now wants to be known simply as The Artist—spins a newly minted demo track from an upcoming album. It's a thick fog of organ chords, electronic drums, the singer's own moaning falsetto and, recorded in utero, the heartbeat of the baby his new wife will deliver in November.

Love it, ignore it or hate it, the elfin rock star has sold close to 100 million records for the Warner Bros. label in the past 20 years. Come November, his Warner Bros. contract settled, he will be out on his own—no link-up with any big label. It's something no pop star of his stature has done on this scale.

Late last month the musician-turned-business-mogul outlined for Forbes his recording and marketing plans. They are nothing if not ambitious. He wants to flood the market with his work. That's something Warner would never let him do, and it was this issue that helped trigger the split. The disagreements got pretty bitter. While carrying out his last few remaining obligations to Warner, he always has the word "slave" scrawled on his cheek. Says an ex-Warner executive: "Despite his brilliance, one record after another causes burnout."

If so, then it's burn, baby, burn, the singer retorts. "My music wants to do what it wants to do, and I just want to get out of its way," he says. "I want the biggest shelf in the record store—the most titles. I know they're not all going to sell, but I know somebody's going to buy at least one of each." With the marketing shackles off, his fans can expect what the poet Shelley called "profuse strains of unpremeditated art."

Already stored in his studio vaults are literally tens of thousands of hours of music, including an unreleased album he made with legendary jazz trumpeter Miles Davis. The first independent release will be a 3-CD, 36-song set called *Emancipation*. It will probably sell for between $36 and $40. Pretty stiff? He's not modest. "I polled kids on the Internet, and no one said they would pay less than $50 for a new 3-CD set," he says.

When the musician talks about being independent, he means independent. He plays all the instruments—except horns and tambourine—on *Emancipation*. He's also considering pressing his own records and handling his own distribution. With no percentages to pay distributors, he figures he could net as much as $21 on the 3-CD set—a 45% margin on retail price. Why let the middlemen make so much money?

Londell McMillan is a lawyer with the firm of Gold, Farrell & Marks, who represented the musician in the breakup with Warner Bros. "You see what's going on in the industry," says the New York City-based showbiz attorney, "and you have to ask yourself, is this artist the kind of mercurial crazy some people say, or is he the wise one who understands where he fits at the start of a new century?"

By this time next year the answer may be in. Plans are for a worldwide tour to support *Emancipation* in 1997, worth as much as $45 million in ticket sales—and, of course, he'll sell albums at his concerts. "Maybe we could put a sampler on every seat," he says with a sly grin. "Or give them the whole thing, and build it into the ticket price."

Then there's the 1-800-New Funk direct-selling hotline, which gets some 7,000 calls a month, for clothing and related merchandise. Will *Emancipation* also be sold direct via phone? "You bet," he says.

The go-it-alone strategy got a test-run in 1994 with a single called "The Most Beautiful Girl in the World" and an accompanying seven-song sampler released independently. The single sold a million units just in the U.S., but the economics of selling a $1.85 (wholesale) single virtually insured that it couldn't make money. Still, the man who branded himself a slave liked his first taste of freedom. He figured that with a bigger-ticket item he could pull it off. "I was number one in countries like Spain and the U.K. where I never had a number one single before," he says of his earlier marketing effort.

Al Bell, who used to own Stax Records, now owns Bellmark Records, which distributed "The Most Beautiful Girl." But there's a difference. At a full three hours, there's a heaping helping of music. "I don't recall seeing anything like this before, but I would not bet against it," says Bell. "All bets are off on normalcy here."

Big-label insiders naturally take a more skeptical view. "He's got a real strong ego, but if he takes all this on himself, it's going to be difficult," says a former Warner Bros. executive. "Too many hats to wear. Something has to give." They hope.

Chapter Thirty-Two

USA TODAY INTERVIEW PRINCE
BY EDNA GUNDERSEN NOVEMBER 12, 1996

CHANHASSEN, MINN.—AS the slamming R&B of "Somebody's Somebody" cranks out of his office CD player, the former Prince cocks his head and smiles.

"This is what freedom sounds like," he says, sinking into a pillow on the floor. The track is one of 36 songs recorded in the past year for the three-disc *Emancipation*, due Nov. 19. The set heralds a divorce from Warner Bros., his label since 1978. Seeking total control of his career, he negotiated out of a contract that had granted him advances of $10 million per album.

"When I saw light at the end of the tunnel, I made a beeline for it," says The Artist, as he's known to the camp at Paisley Park Enterprises, his studio west of hometown Minneapolis. "This is the most exciting time of my life. There was nothing in the way when I recorded (*Emancipation*). Nobody looked over my shoulder. Nothing was remixed, censored, chopped down or edited."

He's so proud of Emancipation, issued by his own NPG label, that the famously reclusive star, 38, is promoting his creative rebirth with a high-profile promo blitz, including a Nov. 21 appearance on The Oprah Winfrey Show. Tuesday night, he'll perform four songs live during a half-hour global radio, TV and Internet broadcast (midnight ET/9 p.m. PT on VH1, MTV, BET and at http://www.thedawn.com; check local radio schedules). It kicks off with the debut of his self-directed video for "Betcha By Golly Wow!" featuring 50 dancers and the gymnastic feats of Olympic gold medalist Dominique Dawes.

He'll crop up on The Rosie O'Donnell Show, on an episode of Muppets Tonight and in several radio ads. "I'm doing my own commercials, like a used car salesman," he jokes.

The Artist, sporting short hair, a goatee and a bright tangerine suit, hopes his efforts eclipse what he calls the "chaotic and disorderly" promotion of *Chaos and Disorder*, his last Warner effort. It sank off the charts after five weeks.

Though personal animosities subsided, the funk wizard clearly loathes music industry practices. His relationship with Warner deteriorated after the label balked at releasing a glut of Prince product. He responded by scrawling "slave" on his cheek.

"I was a slave to the process," he says. "I don't think it's their place to talk me into or out of things. Nobody should run our creative flowers out of the business or break their spirit or tell them how to create. "Artists don't like business. We like being successful and sharing an experience with an audience. In Mozart's time, word of mouth built an audience. People found him and heard him play. Then someone came along and said, 'We can sell this experience.' Right there, you got trouble. Music comes from the spirit, but where does the guy selling music come from?"

He's reminded of a scene in Amadeus where Emperor Joseph II complains that a Mozart composition contains "too many notes." The Artist was similarly insulted when a record exec heard the lush, 7-minute The Holy River and asked, "Got a radio version?"

"I thank God every day that I never have to talk to that guy again," he says. "They don't even realize what they're saying. It's all habit now. In the end, I was disappointed to see the things that mattered to Warner. When we got down to the wire, people started saying what they meant. They think of artists as children, not men and women capable of running their own affairs."

"The label wanted him to adhere to his contract," says Warner exec Bob Merlis. "Our dispute was not the content but the quantity. He had artistic control. We didn't want to stifle his creative spirit."

The Artist insisted on releasing more records than his contract stipulated, each entailing a hefty advance. "He made a habit of it, and we accommodated him to the best of our ability," Merlis says. "It was better for everyone that it ended . . . . He's happier, and we don't have to fuss and fume with him anymore."

After leaving Warner, The Artist struck an alliance with EMI to globally distribute and market his work. He has unrestricted output, keeps his master tapes and is free to market and price his albums. *Emancipation* will sell for about $25, the cost of a double album. "A lot of bang for your buck," he says, grinning.

"I could have stayed longer and negotiated to get my masters back," he says. "I don't own any Prince masters, but Warner gave me gold records. Ha! What's that worth? Ask a pawn shop. Do the math."

Moments after he describes Warner's function as "putting plastic around a cassette, not brain surgery," the bitterness evaporates and ex-Prince says, "I sat across the table and realized, that's just another dude. All he can do is sue me!"

He laughs loudly. It's water under the Graffiti Bridge. *Emancipation* marks a new dawn. "This is my debut. My name represents this body of work, not what came before."

His new name, the curlicued male-female glyph, evolved over years of doodling. Unfazed by constant ribbing or the problem it poses to anyone addressing him, he insists it's permanent and proper.

"My name is the eye of me. It doesn't have a sound. It looks beautiful and makes me feel beautiful. Prince had too much baggage."

Such as? "A massive ego," he says. "All that goes away when you commit to someone."

Mayte Garcia, the 23-year-old dancer he married Feb. 14, represents his heart's emancipation. She recently gave birth to their first child. That's all the father will divulge on the topic. No name, gender or birth date. Tabloids claim the couple's baby boy was born prematurely Oct. 16 with severe birth defects.

"Mayte and I decided it's cool to talk about ourselves but not about our children," he says wearily. "There is a rumor out that my baby died. My skin is so thick now. I care much more about my child than about what anyone says or writes."

He gazes at a huge photo of Mayte on his wall. She inhabits his music and conversation and inspired Paisley Park's conversion from corporate austerity to a kaleidoscopic fun house with cloud-mottled blue walls. No wonder he's ditched Prince, the rake whose salty tunes celebrated promiscuity. The Artist is plum bewitched and happily monogamous. "There's always been a dichotomy in my music: I'm searching for a higher plane, but I want the most out of being on earth," he says. "When I met Mayte, I looked at my situation and wondered what I was running from. Am I lonely? Is that why I surround myself with so many friends? "I don't think I knew the answer until I got married and made the commitment: 'I will take care of you forever.' When she walked down the aisle, and I looked into the eyes of this woman-child, I could see our future and the eyes of our child. At moments like that, you are floating. There is no ego."

He was not instantly smitten when Mayte joined his troupe as a teen.

"She was my friend and my sister for years, the one person who never showed any malice toward anyone." Gradually, he recognized their destiny. He rattles off a list of coincidences that rival the JFK-Lincoln parallels: He was christened Prince. Her childhood nickname was Princess. Their fathers are both named John. His mother is Mattie, oddly similar to Mayte. Her mom is Nelle, akin to his surname, Nelson.

Though The Artist rails against the record industry in songs like "White Mansion" and "Slave," most tunes wax romantic. Mayte inspired "Let's Have a Baby," "Sex in the Summer" and "Friend, Lover, Sister, Mother/Wife." On "Saviour," he coos, "We're like two petals from the same flower."

"There's an overall tone of joy and exhilaration," he says. "In the angry songs, I found a sense of closure. I don't mind going into that dark corner (for) answers, but you got to get out before spider webs grow on you." *Emancipation* may be the last we hear from The Artist for a while ("I emptied the gun on it"), but he's plotting a long future.

"Not to sound cosmic, but I've made plans for the next 3,000 years," he says. "Before, it was only three days at a time."

Chapter Thirty-Three

**NEW YORK TIMES INTERVIEW PRINCE
BY JON PARELES
November 17, 1996**

CHANHASSEN, MINNESOTA—PAISLEY Park, the studio complex Prince built in this Minneapolis suburb, is abuzz. On a 10,000-square-footsound stage, workmen are rolling white paint onto a huge runway of a set, preparing it for a video shoot later in the day. In a mirrored studio down the hall, two dozen dancers are rehearsing. Upstairs, an Olympic gymnast, Dominique Dawes, is trying on a wispy lavender costume. A sound engineer is editing a promotional CD; a graphics artist is putting the final touches on a logo. Through it all strolls the man in charge, attentive to every detail. A hole in the gymnast's leotard? A bit of choreography that needs broadening? As songwriter, video director and record-company head, he takes responsibility for everything, makes all the final decisions and couldn't be happier about it.

The 38-year-old musician who now writes his name as 0{+> is gearing up for the release on Tuesday of *Emancipation,* a three-CD, 36-song, three-hour album intended to return him to superstardom. Over a recording career that stretches nearly two decades, the musician who was born Prince Rogers Nelson earned a reputation for unorthodox behavior long before he dropped his name. Just in time for the music-video explosion, he invented himself as a larger-than-life figure: a doe-eyed all-purpose seducer for whom the erotic and the sacred were never far apart. Outlandish clothes, sculptured hair and see-through pants made Prince a vivid presence, but behind the costumes was one of the most influential songwriters of the 1980s.

He toyed with every duality he could think of: masculine and feminine, black and white, straight and gay. While he made albums virtually by himself, like an introvert, his concerts were in the grand extroverted tradition of rhythm-and-blues showmen like James Brown. His music pulled together rock and funk, gospel and jazz, pop ballads and 12-bar blues. His most distinctive rhythm—a choppy, keyboard-driven funk—has permeated pop, hip-hop and dance music, while his ballad style echoes in hits like TLC's "Waterfalls."

His only guide seemed to be a musicianship that drew admiration from many camps. Peter Sellars, the revisionist opera director, once compared Prince to Mozart for his abundant creativity. Yet for much of the 1990s, the quality of his output has sagged—a result, he says, of his deteriorating relationship with his longtime record company, Warner Brothers.

"He's one of the greatest ones," says George Clinton, himself an architect of modern funk. "He's a hell of a musician; he has really studied everything. And he's working all the time. Even when he's jamming he's recording that. He gets to party; he listens to everything on the radio; he goes out to clubs, and then he goes to the studio and stays up the rest of the night working. He has more stuff recorded than anybody gets to hear.

"Sometimes I think he puts too much effort into trying to take what's out now and put his own thing on it. To me, ain't none of the pop stuff happening that's half as good as what he can do."

Emancipation is a make-or-break album. It will inaugurate a new recording deal with a gambit that may turn out to be bold and innovative or utterly foolhardy; will the 3-CD set be received as an act of generosity or a glut of material? For a major performer in the 1990s, releasing a three-CD set of new material is unprecedented; even double albums are rare and commercially risky. And *Emancipation* is financed and marketed by the songwriter himself. "All the stakes are higher," he says as he picks a few berries from a plate of zabaglione in the Paisley Park kitchen. "But I'm in a situation where I can do anything I want."

His day's project is to direct the video for the first single from Emancipation, a remake of the Stylistics' 1972 hit "Betcha by Golly, Wow." At the same time, he's making last minute marketing decisions and doing a rare interview. Ever the clotheshorse, he's wearing a long, nubby gray-and-black sweater and a shirt with lace tights. A chevron is shaved into his hair next to one ear, with glitter applied to it. Clear-eyed and serious, he speaks in a low voice, in a conversation that veers between hardheaded practicality, flashes of eccentricity and professions of faith in God. He is businesslike one moment; the next, he invokes his self-made spirituality, in which musical inspiration and carnality are both links to divine creativity.

For all the music he has put out since the first Prince album in 1978, he has remained private. The songs on *Emancipation* take up his usual topics—sex, salvation, partying all night long—along with new ones like cruising the Internet. But a few have hints of the personal. On Valentine's Day he married Mayte Garcia, who had been a backup singer and dancer in his band. A few months ago, he announced that she was pregnant and that the child was due in November. Since then he has refused further comment. "I'm never going to release details about children," he says. "They'll probably name themselves."

On the album, he proposes marriage in "The Holy River," a rolling midtempo song akin to Bruce Springsteen's quieter side. Later, a sparse, tender piano ballad begs, "Let's Have a Baby". Asked about that song, he talks about the couple's wedding night. "I carried her across the threshold and gave her many presents," he says. "The last one was a crib. And we both cried. She got down on her knees in that gown, and I did next to her, and we thanked God that we could be alive for this moment."

Marrying Mayte, he says, seemed inevitable. Her middle name is Jannelle; his father is John L. Her mother's name was Nell; he was born Prince Rogers Nelson: "Nell's son," he says. "Am I going to argue with all these coincidences?" he asks, at least half seriously. Like a man in love, he adds: "She really makes my soul feel complete. I feel powerful with her around. And she makes it easier to talk to God."

Emancipation includes shimmering ballads and fuzz-edged rockers, bump-and-grind bass grooves and a big band two-beat, Latin-jazz jams, and dissonant electronic dance tracks. "People will say it's sprawling and it's all over the place," he says. "That's fine. I play a lot of styles. This is not arrogance; this is the truth. Because anything you do all day long, you're going to master after a while."

On the new album, keys change and rhythms metamorphose at whim. One tour de force, "Joint 2 Joint," moves through five different grooves and ends with all its riffs fitting together. The seeming spontaneity is more remarkable because nearly all the instruments are played by the songwriter himself. The toil of constructing songs track by track is worth it, he says, for the unanimity it brings. "Because I do all the instruments, I'm injecting the joy I feel into all those 'players.' The same exuberant soul speaks through all the instruments."

"I always wanted to make a three-record set," he adds. "*Sign O' The Times* was originally supposed to be a triple album, but it ended up as a double. For this one, I started with the blueprint of three CD's, one hour each, with peaks and valleys in the right places. I just filled in the blueprint."

While most songwriters are hard-pressed to come up with enough worthwhile material for an album a year, he has never had that problem. He can't stop writing music; his backlog includes at least a thousand unreleased songs and compositions, and new ones are constantly pouring out, all mapped in his head.

"You hear it done," he says. "You see the dancing; you hear the singing. When you hear it, you either argue with that voice or you don't. That's when you seek God. Sometimes ideas are coming so fast that I have to stop doing one song to get another. But I don't forget the first one. If it works, it will always be there. It's like the truth: it will find you and lift you up. And if it ain't right, it will dissolve like sand on the beach."

Commercially, *Emancipation* hedges its bets. There are straightforward groove songs and lush slow-dance tunes alongside the more idiosyncratic cuts, and there are remakes of other people's hits, including "One of Us" from Joan Osborne and "La, La (Means I Love You)" from the Delfonics. An associate producer, Kirk A. Johnson, punched up the rhythm tracks, giving some of them the crunch of hip-hop.

The album is priced under $30, like a two-CD set.

Emancipation, produced by the performer's own label, NPG Records, is his first album to be distributed by EMI.

The album title is a pointed reference to the end of the reported six-album deal, potentially worth $100 million, that he made in 1992 with Warner Brothers. He had been making albums for the label since 1978 and sold millions of copies in the 1980s; the soundtrack for his 1984 movie, *Purple Rain,* sold more than 10 million copies. He continued to release No. 1 singles as late as 1991, with "Cream."

But once Warner Brothers had committed such a large investment, the label wanted to apply proven hit-making strategies: putting out just one album a year, packing it with potential singles, issuing various trendy remixes of songs and following the advice of in-house experts on promotion and marketing. Rationing and editing his work grated on Prince, and he began wrangling with Warner Brothers over control of his career.

"The music, for me, doesn't come on a schedule," he says. "I don't know when it's going to come, and when it does, I want it out. Music was created to uplift the soul and to help people make the best of a bad situation. When you sit down to write something, there should be no guidelines. The main idea is not supposed to be, 'How many different ways can we sell it?' That's so far away from the true spirit of what music is. Music starts free, with just a spark of inspiration. When limits are set by another party that walks into the ball game afterward, that's fighting inspiration.

"The big deal we had made together wasn't working," he says of Warner Brothers. "They are what they are, and I am what I am, and eventually I realized that those two systems aren't going to work together. The deeper you get into that well, the darker it becomes." In 1993, he adopted an unpronounceable 0{+> as his name, ignoring warnings that he was jettisoning the equivalent of a well-known trademark.

His associates now refer to him as The Artist, a merciful shortening of The Artist Formerly Known As Prince. He knows the name change caused confusion and amusement, and he doesn't care. "When the lights go down and the microphone goes on," he says, "it doesn't matter what your name is."

As an experiment, Warner Brothers gave him permission in 1994 to release a single, "The Most Beautiful Girl in the World," through NPG Records on the independent Bellmark label. It was an international hit, further straining his relations with Warner Brothers. He began performing with the word "slave" written on his cheek.

"We never were angry; we were puzzled," says Bob Merlis, senior vice president of Warner Brothers Records. "He evinced great unhappiness at being here. He wanted to release more albums than his contract called for; he wanted a different contract, which ran contrary to good business practices. Eventually, we agreed that his vision and ours didn't coincide on how to release his output."

People familiar with the Warners contract say that it called for Warner Brothers to pay an advance for each album submitted and that speeding up the schedule and submitting more albums meant more payments in a shorter time.

There were rumors of bankruptcy in Paisley Park, that the entertainment empire (which for a short time also included a Minneapolis nightclub, Glam Slam) was too expensive to maintain.

Eventually, Warner Brothers agreed to end the contract. Warner Brothers still has rights to one album of previously unreleased material, and it owns the master recordings of the Prince back catalogue, a situation that rankles the performer. "If you don't own your masters," he says, "your master owns you."

Under the new arrangement, he finances all his albums and videos and puts them out when he wishes. He pays EMI to manufacture the albums, and the company provides its distribution system and overseas marketing clout. He describes EMI as "hired hands, like calling a florist to deliver some flowers to my wife." (Other NPG albums, including his ballet score, *Kamasutra,* and Mayte's debut album are for sale through a Web site: http://thedawn.com/.)

Once he explains his business arrangements, he shows a visitor through Paisley Park, which is the size of a small shopping mall. In the recording studio, a half-dozen guitars are lined up, each with specific qualities: the leopard-patterned one is "good for funk"; the 0{+>-shaped one is "the most passionate." Paisley Park was once painted all white, inside and out, but after he got married he decided that the place needed some color. Now there are carpets with inset zodiac signs, a mural of a tropical waterfall behind the water fountain, walls of purple, gold and red and a smiley face in Mayte's office.

Past a birdcage holding two white doves named Divinity and Majesty is his office. A photograph of Miles Davis and Charlie Parker is by his desk. He shows the visitor an inch-thick worldwide marketing plan, with sales targets and promotion strategies, just like an executive. But as he plays the album, he gets caught up in the music.

"Sometimes I stand in awe of what I do myself," he says. "I feel like a regular person, but I listen to this and wonder, where did it come from? I believe definitely in the higher power that gave me this talent. If you could go in the studio alone and come out with that, you'd do it every day, wouldn't you?"

"It's a curse," he concludes. "And it's a blessing."

Chapter Thirty-Four

MSN MUSIC CENTERAL INTERVIEW PRINCE BY EDNA GUNDERSON—1996

"WHAT DO I call you now?" I asked him during a recent interview at his Park empire in Chanhassen, Minnesota, just west of his hometown Minneapolis.

He flashes a beatific (or is it diabolical?) smile. "Whatever you like," says what's-his-name, sporting a spiffy tangerine suit, high-heeled boots, and a goatee.

"Just not the P-word, right?" I venture.

"Right," he says curtly. "Prince no longer exists."

Taking Prince's place is the newly liberated, highly visible TAFKAP, whose three-CD Emancipation contains some of the most dazzling and stylistically diverse material of his prolific career: from the swing of "Courtin' Time" and the Spanish rhythms of "Damned If I Do" to the rap of "Mr. Happy" and the techno of "Slave."

The set marks The Artist's long-sought liberation from Warner Bros., his home from 1978 until last summer's release of the overlooked Chaos And Disorder, an album that he says suffered from "chaotic and disorderly" promotion.

Though he re-upped with Warner in a much-hyped and lucrative 1992 deal, The Artist soon realized that he and the label were not in synch. Specifically, Warner did not warm to Prince's boundless productivity. In 1993, Prince abruptly changed his name to the unutterable male-female glyph and grew even more alienated from Warner.

A couple years ago, he and Lenny Kravitz mulled the idea of making a record together and distributing it with zero label assistance. The notion stayed with The Artist, and he resolved to escape his contract and have full creative control over his career.

His split with Warner was only one high note in 1996. The other was his marriage to muse and former belly dancer Mayte. He married the 22-year-old Puerto Rican beauty on Valentine's Day, then happily awaited the birth of their first child. That event proved tragic, though The Artist, 38, never confirmed any details of his baby boy's widely reported death from severe birth defects.

Earlier, he had poured much of his newfound domestic joy into Emancipation's 36 tunes.

"We worked nonstop," says co-producer Kirk Johnson, whose first role at the kingdom was as a dancer during the Purple Rain tour. He evolved into Prince's remixer and, a year ago, best man in his wedding and chief sounding board in the fevered Emancipation sessions.

"We'd cut three or four songs in one day," Johnson recalls. "He'd come in with a new song or a new idea every day. In the studio, he was confident and relaxed, but so excited about the music he was making. We vibed off each other."

So, how does Johnson, a fellow alumnus of Central High School, address his longtime pal and employer? He doesn't.

"His name is not a problem," Johnson says. "I agree with what he's doing and I respect the fact that the name Prince is somebody else and is owned by somebody else."

Of late, the notoriously press-shy ex-Prince has repeatedly subjected himself to the media spotlight, appearing on The Today Show, Rosie O'Donnell, and Oprah. He remains mum on the topic of his firstborn, but expounds freely on matters of music and freedom.

For someone who spent years ducking the press, you're certainly keeping a high profile these days.

That's because the music is so important. There was nothing in the way when I recorded it. This is the most exciting time of my life.

But you've made great music before now. Why didn't you speak up?

I hate to do interviews because I can sound arrogant. I'm trying to speak the truth as I see it. Now I feel like doing a speaking tour. When I met with journalists and industry people in Japan, they talked to me with utmost respect.

You seem very eager to promote Emancipation.

I'm even doing my own commercials, like a used-car salesman.

In the song "Emancipation," you say you'd "rather sing with a bit more harmony." I presume you're referring to your contract with Warner Bros. If it was so oppressive, why did you sign with Warner again in 1992?

It was fine for awhile, then it didn't work. When I first got into it, there was tour support; (label executives) came to the studio. That stopped. I was a slave to their process, and it's not a good process to put artists in. Artists are our creative flowers. You don't run them out of the business or break their spirit or tell them how to create.

You lost a lot of money getting out of that contract, didn't you?

Yeah, about $10 million up front for each album. But I had to get out.

Warner balked at your intention to release records frequently and argued that too much product creates a glut and hampers its efforts to promote your music and sustain a public interest in it. Why couldn't you agree to stagger the releases further apart?

It's hard to hear this music played complete in my head and not be able to get it out. If I don't get it out, it won't exist on earth. I can't ignore what I hear in my head. They were like the king in Amadeus, telling Mozart his music has too many notes. Please. You can't say or do much in just 10 songs, especially when you're talking about someone who can play a lot of styles. *Emancipation* is what *Sign O' The Times* was supposed to be. I delivered three CDs for *Sign O' The Times*. Because the people at Warner were tired, they came up with reasons why I should be tired too. I don't know if it's their place to talk me into or out of things.

You don't agree in principle that there's too much music out there?

There's not too much music. That's censorship. But a lot of the so-called great new innovators are deconstructing music.

Were you ever frustrated to the point of wanting to quit?

I asked myself if I could stay in this business. I couldn't stay and play by their rules, because I've always been honest in my music. But I never lost hope. I was disappointed to see the things that mattered to people in the end. When we got down to the wire, people started saying what they meant. They think of artists as children, not men and women capable of running affairs.

You scrawled the word "SLAVE" on your cheek, and it was apparent you were angry and bitter for a time.

I wrote "slave" on my face to remind them in meetings that I know what time it is. They put ceilings on us so we can only go so far in our experiences. If we let them stop us, we ARE slaves. A lot of artists are manufactured but that doesn't work for me.

You seem more mellow on the issue now. How did you get past the resentment?

When I could see clearer, I became less bitter. I didn't have anyone to be angry at. I started to look at Warner Bros. as my ally. I started to care about them as human beings.

So ultimately, the struggle was a positive experience.

Yes, once I just started focusing on the way out of the box. I designed that box to teach myself something.

Most musicians crave success and acceptance, yet they uniformly despise, or pretend to despise, the machinery that helps them get there.

Artists don't like business. We like being successful and sharing an experience with an audience. In Mozart's time, word of mouth built an audience. People found him and heard him play. Then someone came along and said, "We can sell this experience." Right there, you got trouble. Music comes from the spirit, but where does the guy selling music come from?

In hindsight, do you see any drawbacks in leaving Warner?

I could have stayed longer and negotiated to get my masters back. That became less important than being here today. *Emancipation* is my first record. My name will mean this body of work, not what came before.

Didn't you benefit from the label's expertise in nonmusical areas, like advertising, marketing, radio promotion?

The audience is going to be my record company. And the deejays and the retailers.

And what about your arrangement with EMI (which will distribute and market 's output on his NPG label)?

It's not an "arrangement." I'm not signed up with anybody. Why would I hook up with the monolith I emancipated myself from?

So how does this nonarrangement differ from conventional contracts?

I own my masters. I can do my own marketing. I can price records. That's important. Emancipation will sell for the price of a double CD, a lot of bang for your buck. Artists can stay in the system if they want, but there's an alternative.

Despite your protracted battle with Warner, Emancipation has a celebratory feel to it.

There's an overall tone of joy and exhilaration. In the angry songs, I found a sense of closure. I don't mind going into that dark corner to seek answers, but you gotta get out before the spiderwebs grow on you.

Like earlier albums, there's an intriguing mingling of sex and spirituality. You seem simultaneously drawn to the carnal and the sacred. Can you explain that?

If there were no shadows, we wouldn't know where the light was. We all want to be spiritually light, to walk on water. It's just a metaphor. Jesus could do it because he was free of sin. On the other hand, we have too much cholesterol. (Laughs)

So, why does the name Prince no longer fit you?

My name's been dragged through a lot of stuff, true and untrue. And I don't own Prince's master tapes. Besides, Prince was never a name I chose. My father gave me that name because he wanted his son to be greater than himself.

This entire building seems much more festive and friendly than when I first saw it eight years ago. There are white clouds on blue walls, astrological symbols in the carpet, a huge photo of your wife. Is this the result of Mayte's influence?

Yes. When I met her, I started examining everything around me. Who do I want to be and what do I want to represent? When I opened Paisley Park, I was so excited to have my own studio that I just started recording and didn't come out for 20 years. After I got married, I finally looked at the place.

Until recently, you never really seemed inclined toward monogamy. What happened?

Mayte changed everything. She was my friend and my sister for years. She's the one person who never showed any malice toward anyone. Commitment is a complex thing. If you can't completely love one other person, how can you learn to love everyone? I believe we're here to get along and love each other. Everyone has a higher self they aspire to be. We want to be better, braver, stronger. You find that in love and commitment. I hear about these self-help programs people go into. It's all about feeding their ego. All that goes away when you commit to someone.

Everyone is talking about your baby except you. Why not?

Mayte and I decided it's cool to talk about ourselves. My child hasn't told me it's all right to talk. I care much more about my child than about what anyone says about me.

Do you want more kids?

Yes! The more the merrier. My child will have so much fun, all the fun I never had as a child.
How would you sum up your experiences in 1996?

I don't regret anything. I can't be lied to anymore.

Chapter Thirty-Five

**HELLO MAGAZINE INTERVIEW PRINCE (UK)
BY SOLANGE PLAMONDON
DECEMBER 1996 ISSUE**

FAMED FOR GUARDING his privacy and seldom granting interviews, the enigmatic Artist Formerly Known as Prince broke his strict code of silence recently and spoke candidly about life, love and work. The diminutive 38 year old singer, songwriter, one of the world's top-selling recording artists, first found stardom in the early 1980s with his definitive party hit 1999. In the years since, he has built a huge music complex, Paisley Park, in Minneapolis; been through a legal battle with his former recording label Warner Bros. (during which he appeared in public with the word slave written across his cheek); swapped the name Prince for an obscure symbol; and, on Valentine's Day last year, married Mayte, one of his backing singers and dancers.

The couple were delighted when Mayte, 23, fell pregnant and they planned to celebrate the birth by recording 8 children's songs and developing children's fiction. But tragedy struck in October when their baby boy was born badly brain damaged, a month premature. Characteristically, the singer refuses to confirm or deny reports that the baby died a week after birth. But his commitment to work remains firm as he continues to promote his new triple CD and cassette *Emancipation*.

Dressed typically flamboyantly in black lace trousers and shirt, he insisted on the usual restrictions for an interview in the Montreal hotel where he was staying during a week long promotional trip: No tape recorder, no photos during the interview and certainly no video cameras.

How long did it take you to record Emancipation?

I worked on it for a year and I must admit I'm amazed by the results. I think Emancipation is, without a doubt, the best album of my whole career. I thank God for the gift.

Are you pleased with the response it received?

Yes, as people seem to like it. The critics haven't always been kind in the past, but reviews for this have been better. Some have said that it's too long or that certain songs were too long—but what should I have taken out? It's a question of balance and harmony. Harmony is important and I don't like people who criticize music when they're not musicians.

You seem to have decided to get on better with the press.

To be honest, I've never wanted to talk about anything apart from my music. I wasn't confident enough and I had nothing to say. But now I know exactly who I am and what I want—although some people accuse me of arrogance because I have such a clear vision about things.

Do you have a favourite song?

Not really, but I like the second CD best. I could say "The Holy River"—right in the middle after 5 romantic numbers—is my favourite, but then I also like "Let's have a baby." Just before our wedding, Mayte spent a few days away from our home so I made a lot of changes to our house—especially in our bedroom, where I placed a crib. It was beautiful. Then, on our wedding night, Mayte was still wearing her long white dress when I brought her into the room and played her "Let's have a baby" for the first time. She couldn't stop crying—it was an unforgettable moment.

Do you think your wife has had a positive influence on your life?

Yes, certainly. She is the woman of my life, my best friend. We were made to be together and all the ingredients were there to unite us. Our fathers have the same name and our mother's names are similar. My family's name was Nelson and hers was Nells. We're definitely made for each other. With her, I've learnt what faith is and I no longer worry.

Why have you decided to spend next Valentine's Day in Hawaii?

We'll be celebrating our first wedding anniversary. Last year we were on our honeymoon in Hawaii and put on a show where Mayte danced for the last time. To celebrate this year, I'll sing but Mayte won't be dancing.

Do you believe in God?

Yes. With time, I've learnt how to be confident in God and to become whatever he wanted me to be. I'm also a vegetarian—I only eat fruit and vegetables.

How do you feel about your 20th recording anniversary next year?

20 years isn't that long really. I prefer to think about eternity—that's how I got myself out of the trap I was in. When I changed my name and wrote Slave on my cheek, it was because I felt like a prisoner trapped in a system. People thought I was crazy, but I didn't make the decision lightly—I did it out of pure conviction. I could not open up and do what I wanted to do in the way I wanted. All decisions were made for me.

What has been your best experience?

My evolution. Now, I feel free, I can see eternity. I know that everything was planned for me. I might not know where I'll be tomorrow, but I know where I'll be in 3,000 years time. Since I accepted God, I have faith in life.

Is it a coincidence that you're staying in the same hotel as Celine Dion?

Prince: Yes, I had no idea that she was here! I like her a lot and even wrote a song, "With This Tear," for her once. It's on one of her albums and is really beautiful. I'd love to play and sing with her in a show one day.

How come you've included two guitarists from Montreal—Rhonda Smith and Kathleen Dyson—in your band?

Sheila E. introduced me to them and they're unbelievable. They came in just at the moment in my evolution when I decided to eliminate negative music and be more joyous and uplifting. I wanted a more optimistic attitude and they're not only exceptionally talented but in perfect harmony with the rest of my life.

Is music a way of life for you?

Yes. Music is a gift from God and I would be very ungrateful to say that it is work. Life is a gift.

Chapter Thirty-Six

MINNEAPOLIS ASSOCIATED PRESS STORIES—MARCH 1997

Story One:

AUTHORITIES ARE REVIEWING the case of a boy who died a week after he was born to the artist formerly known as Prince and his wife. The Hennepin County Medical Examiner, prosecutors and police confirmed the inquiry Monday, but would not provide details. Erlene and Arlene Mojica, described as personal assistants close to the musician's wife, have contacted authorities about the case, said their attorney, Larry Altman. Altman said the twin sisters were fired Dec. 23 by Paisley Park Enterprises, Prince's company, but declined further comment. The 38-year-old musician, who uses a symbol for a name, acknowledged in December that the child was born with a problem. The death certificate for the boy, who was born Oct. 16 and apparently died Oct. 23, lists his cause of death as complications caused by a rare skull deformity. Neither the birth nor the death certificate lists a father, and the death certificate does not clearly identify the child's mother. Dr. John Fangman, listed as the baby's doctor on the death certificate, said the cause of death was natural.

Story Two:

Prince is reportedly trying to prevent two former employees from talking to the media about the death of his son. Larry Altman, an attorney for twin sisters Erlene and Arlene Mojica, told the Star Tribune newspaper he expected the musician, who prefers to be known as an unpronounceable symbol, to seek a temporary restraining order barring the women from talking to reporters. The sisters were personal assistants to Mayte Garcia-Nelson, Prince's wife. Altman and Prince's attorney, Bob Weinstine, both told The Associated Press on Thursday that they could not comment. Prince acknowledged last December that the baby was born with a problem but has said little else. A birth certificate said that a boy was born to Garcia-Nelson Oct. 16, but said the "mother refused information" about the father. It lists the child's cause of death Oct. 23 to be complications of Pfieffer's syndrome Type 2, a rare skull deformity.

Story Three:

The artist formerly known as Prince wants to keep a lawsuit about his private life away from the public. The Purple Rain star asked a judge to keep proceedings closed in his lawsuit against two former employees who went public with their story about the death of his newborn son. The rock star has sued Erlene and Arlene Mojica for going to a London tabloid last October, claiming they violated a confidentiality agreement. His lawyers asked Carver County District Judge Jean Davies on Thursday to make sure nothing more comes out publicly. Davies gave lawyers for both sides until Monday to file papers on the request. The Mojica sisters have claimed that Prince decided prematurely to shut off life support for his baby, who was born with a deformed skull that often causes retardation or early death. The artist and his wife have not publicly acknowledged the baby's death, and the child's birth and death records do not clearly document his parentage.

Chapter Thirty-Seven

SPIKE LEE INTERVIEW PRINCE THE ARTIST—1997

THOUGH THE BUZZING of the talk around him threatened to drown out the music that made him a cultural landmark, the Artist Formerly Known as Prince is once again writing and performing his trademark sexually potent pop. His newest album, *Emancipation* (NPG Records), marks an important turning point in a career peppered with (as he once sang) controversy. Most recently, his battle to break free of his former record label, Warner Bros., led to speculation that he was withholding Grade A material until he had a more satisfactory deal elsewhere. Whether or not that was the case, the double platinum and counting *Emancipation* is a three-disc dish of classic funk, pearly ballads, pastel-hued jams, and even a creamy cover of the Joan Osborne hit, "One of Us." It is a romantic, emotional record, and one that is also powered by the Artist's (as he is now called) faith in God and love for his wife, Mayte Garcia. Here he sits down in New York with writer and director Spike Lee, whose 1996 film *Girl 6* featured on its soundtrack songs by the man record sellers now "file under Prince."

Spike Lee (SL): It is February 7, in the year of our Lord 1997, St. Moritz Hotel, New York, and I am here with the Artist Formerly Known as Prince. To start, there's something that we need to get out of the way. I really feel awkward asking you this, but I just have to. Will you say anything about your child [who, it has been widely reported, died shortly after his birth last fall]?

The Artist (Prince): I have written a song that says: If you ever lose someone dear to you, never say the words, "They're gone," and they'll come back.

SL: That will be a highly anticipated song. Before we drove down to The Chris Rock Show, where you were taping a segment, I asked you about the title of your multi-platinum album *Emancipation*. I said, "Do you feel free?" and you gave a great response.

Prince: There is something that happens when you get emancipated. You approach life differently. You eat differently. You respect yourself more. You respect the gift you have been given. Everything has changed for me since I changed my name. It's one thing to be called Prince but it's another thing to actually be one. I have such a reverence for life now. And I have stopped eating all animal products.

SL: So, when you look back, do you see periods in your life when you did not like your Prince persona?

Prince: Toward the end I was a little ashamed of what Prince had become. I really felt like a product, and then I started turning in work that reflected that. I had no problem with people saying I was repeating myself. I knew where I was headed and I just needed direction. I looked up and L. Londell McMillan was there.

SL: You mean your new lawyer?

Prince: Yes. He also has a reverence for life. He seems to be a righteous soul and is focused as to what he is on earth for. Those are some of the things we talked about—what we as black people are supposed to represent during this time period.

SL: Six or seven years ago I had the audacity to write you a letter about your choice of women used in music and music videos. Do you remember that?

Prince: Yes.

SL: Let's talk about it. I think it was very rude on my part. I'll be forty on March 20th and in a lot of ways back then I was too righteous about that type of stuff. Tell the audience what was in the letter I wrote you.

Prince: I don't remember exactly. It's really vague to me.

SL: I wrote, are there going to be any women of dark complexion in your music videos and your films? You had only white women in your stuff. Do you recall what you wrote back to me? You set me straight there?

Prince: I probably said, One had to look at everything I had done, not just the most successful pieces. But I have to be honest, I know you as a different person now, too. We met under different circumstances back then, and I have grown and so have you.

SL: Do you remember the first time we met?

Prince: *Graffiti Bridge* [the Artist's 1990 dramatic film]?

SL: Yes, you invited me and my producer Monty Ross up to the shoot. Now I'd like to ask you, how has marriage changed you?

Prince: It is ever-evolving every day. It is not a subject I like discussing, but my wife's pregnancy made me an adult four times over. Kids will do that. Just dealing with every circumstance is an emotional roller coaster, but nevertheless I have grown so much as a soul. I can see the light at the end of the tunnel a lot better now.

SL: Let's talk about your last couple of years at [your former label] Warner Bros. records. Would it be safe to say that the music you were putting out was just fulfilling a contract, or were you giving the best you had to offer at that time?

Prince: I was doing my best to fulfill my contract. You can now hear that my soul has been in love with [my wife] Mayte for thousands of years. I believe that I was just trying to express it in a simple record. I wanted to say friend, lover, sister, mother, wife back then, but it wasn't the time. If you check the video for the song "Seven," you will see Mayte and I walking through the doors hand-in-hand and the dove exploding. That was when I spiritually checked out of the situation; but I did what I had to do.

SL: Right now I have a copy of your *Emancipation* CD and my wife wanted to kill me because I had "Soul Sanctuary" on repeat. I played that song for two hours straight. It's four minutes long. Divide that into two hours. She was about to go upside my head. But tell me about that song. I love it!

Prince: Sandra St. Victor helped with that one. The melody is basically mine, but the lyrics were inspired by verses that Sandra wrote. I love the idea of an ex-lover leaving her reflection in the mirror after she's gone. You know, I just hope to see the day when all artists, no matter what color they are, own their masters [tapes].

SL: Let me ask you this: Why don't African-American artists own their own masters? Is it because we don't have the right lawyers?

Prince: I think we *can* get the right lawyers, but I think we all need to change our mind-set and go in specifically after that [ownership of master recordings] and not just take the pink Cadillac. Then you will see change. It *is* befuddling how other people own their masters. I guess it's who you know and what deal you make.

SL: It's about ownership, isn't it?

Prince: Ownership, that's what you give your kids. That's your legacy. Every one of those songs!

SL: And what about your name?

PRINCE: You know, black people still call me Prince. Sometimes I ask them, "Why do you call me Prince?" And people say, "Because you are a prince to us." Usually when they say that, you know my heart goes out and I say, "I don't mind your calling me that." If there is a pronunciation to my name in the future, I hope it will be "Prince." That's my dream. But until that day, I'll just go by this. *[Holds up a necklace with his symbol on it]* This is my "X."

SL: You said that a lot of people were confused when you wrote "slave" on your face. People said they didn't know what to call you, but you got it all worked out now?

Prince: We got it all worked out! My worth went down a little bit during that period. *[laughs]* I'm sure there will be a few doors closed to me now because of my emancipation.

SL: Yeah, well that's the mentality of a runaway slave. You're no longer a house-negro. The millennium is coming up. Everybody knows what song is going to be played on New Year's Eve 1999. *[laughs]* Can you talk about any of your plans? When will we see another album?

Prince: To be honest, I thought I had emptied the gun with this one *[Emancipation]* and I wouldn't have to record for awhile, but some new things came up that are all acoustic.

SL: Acoustic?

Prince: Yeah, just me and a guitar in a room. One song is called "The Truth" and one is called "Don't Play Me." There is a line about ebonics in it but I won't get into that. *[both laugh]*

SL: No, let's get into that. What do you think about ebonics? I think it's a plot! And there's black people behind that plot.

Prince: Comedian Chris Rock said it best: There is language that will get you a job and there is language that won't. Make that choice as an American. This is where you live now.

SL: Tell me honestly, and you can answer this any way you want: How did you like the way we used your songs in *Girl 6*? Talk about that process, because the way we did it I had already cut the film before adding your songs. You were also generous enough to give us three *new* songs. Tell me which songs worked for you in the movie and which ones didn't?

Prince: Some worked stronger than others, but overall, musically, I didn't know what to expect. I was pleasantly surprised and I like the film for the style in which you did it. I'd never seen that done before. The scene at Coney Island, where you used "How Come U Don't Call Me Any More" is my favorite scene. In fact it forced me to put that song back into our set. I said I would never play it again because I used to think I couldn't do it better than I did with my band, the Revolution. But your film gave me newfound respect for the music.

SL: When you came up with that song, "Sexy Mother Fucker," I said, "My man is losing his mind." But I liked it.

Prince: The chorus was a little "different" for you, huh? *[SL in background singing, "shakin' that ass, shakin' that ass"]* I was talking to Chris Rock and he said the same thing. "Every time you put out an album, I think you've lost your mind!" The music I make a lot of the time is reflective of the life I am leading, and "Sexy MF" came during the period I had the Glam Slam disco [in Minneapolis] and I was hanging out there a lot. There was a dance troupe there, and the sexier the dancers, the bigger the revenues and the noisier the crowd. It's funny, but you have to remember that was during the time when the biggest club song was "Bitch Betta Have My Money." When you hear something constantly, you can get swayed by the current. I was swayed by hip-hop at the time.

SL: Do you feel that you successfully incorporated rap into your music. Sometimes it felt like it was just stuck on.

Prince: I've gotten some criticism for the rap I've chosen to put in my past work. But there again, it came during my friction years. If you notice, not a lot of that stuff is incorporated into my sets now. I think you'll be pleasantly surprised when you hear the new remixes we are working on. On the rap tip though, it is an old style and I have always done it kind of differently—half sung, you know, like "Irresistible Bitch" and some of the other things I use to do.

SL: Do you ever think that you have been cursed? That you can't stop the music in your head?

Prince: Sometimes it is a curse, but it's also a blessing. It's a gift that I am completely grateful for. That's why I keep [making music], because I don't want to be ungrateful for the gift.

SL: I know you guys like to keep it all mysterious, but I know there is a creative process to how you write a song. It might now be the same thing all the time, though.

Prince: Yes, it is different all the time. The main way that something comes is fully completed. And the fun part is just listening. When I'm writing, sometimes the pen just goes. I'm not in charge and I'm almost listening outside of it. That's when I realize that we all have to start looking at life as a gift. It's like listening to a color and believing that these colors have soulmates and once you get them all together the painting is complete.

SL: What is Cat [a former dancer with the Artist] doing now?

Prince: Last time I spoke with her she walked up to Mayte and me and said to us, "I like you two dancing together, but she'll never be what I was with you." The *very* last time we spoke. *[laughs]*

SL: And Apollonia?

Prince: To be honest, I haven't really spoken to anybody. Once I got married, the phone stopped ringing.

SL: You said earlier that you have been in love with Mayte for one thousand years. Can you elaborate on that?

Prince: I am a firm believer in reincarnation for people who either have more work to do or have so much debt to pay back that they have to be here. I hope for me it is the former, and my work was finding Mayte and having a child, which we will continue on until there are several here.

SL: Would you like to comment on how the media attempted to make a circus out of that particular episode?

Prince: What people have to realize is that if one has a firm belief in God and the spirit, then one does not make statements that are negative and untrue. I would have been lying to myself and the spirit of the child. I have a very thick skin. I take everything that comes and let it bounce right off of me because I know the time will come when nobody will be able to speak falsely. Mankind doesn't understand the whole process yet; that we have to ask for ownership of our masters, instead of taking the Cadillac, so to speak.

SL: Quick music question: Why did you decide to make "Betcha By Golly Wow!" the first single from *Emancipation*? Why did you want to do a cover?

Prince: I don't believe in singles. The singles market has changed. I am trying to get to the old days of releasing albums at will, like *Star Wars* coming out again.

SL: I want to ask you about how you pick your bands. You've had several. Can you tell me about the whole process? Is it the same way a general manager would pick a team?

Prince: I have been blessed with having these people come to me. I don't want to sound cosmic or anything, but it really seems magical because in this case I was looking for a group of four vegetarians.

SL: Was that actually a criterion that they have to be totally vegetarian? Do you think that meat and stuff clogs up your brain?

Prince: Our people have the worst diet of anybody. I'm ready to put a farmer on my payroll. We've got to get back to growing our own food. You are what you eat!

SL: For our audience, I want to present this question to you: How is it that Geffen, Spielberg, and Katzenberg got together? How was it that these three giants put aside their egos and came together for the whole? What would stop African-American artists like me, yourself, Michael Jordan, Bill Cosby . . .

Prince: My hat goes off to anyone who can sit down and put their heads together. I am ready for something like that because I am free and I am happy and I have time. There were a lot of things in the way before. I have nothing put time now, and I love getting older.

SL: We've got to do a musical together.

Prince: We have to do several. Some will hit and some won't, but hey, we have the time.

Chapter Thirty-Eight

ABOUT SPIKE LEE

SHELTON JACKSON LEE was born March 20, 1957, in Atlanta, Georgia to William "Bill" Lee, a jazz composer and bassist, and Jacqueline Shelton Lee, an art teacher. His mother, who died in 1977 of cancer, nicknamed him "Spike" as toddler, evidently alluding to his toughness. Spike grew up the oldest three brothers, David, Cinque, and Chris, and one sister, Joie. The family moved from Atlanta shortly after Lee's birth and lived briefly in Chicago. In 1959 they moved to Brooklyn's predominantly black Fort Greene section. Jacqueline Lee provided a rich cultural upbringing that included plays, galleries, museums, and movies. Bill Lee saw that the family experienced music, occasionally taking them to his performances at the Blue Note and to other Manhattan jazz clubs.

After graduating from John Dewey High School in Brooklyn, Lee majored in mass communications at his father and grandfather's alma mater, Morehouse College in Atlanta. At Morehouse Lee took an interest in filmmaking, and upon graduation in 1979, was awarded a summer internship with Columbia Pictures in Burbank, California. In the fall, he returned to New York to attend New York University's Institute of Film and Television, Tisch School of the Arts. One of the few blacks in the school, Lee's first year at NYU was not without controversy. For his first year project he submitted a ten-minute film, The Answer that told of a young black screenwriter who remade D. W. Griffith's The Birth of a Nation. A pointed critique of the racism in Griffith's silent film, the faculty was displeased with his work, saying that he had not yet mastered "film grammar." Lee suspected, however, that they took offence to his digs at the legendary director's stereotypical portrayals of black characters. An assistantship in his second year provided full tuition in exchange for working in the school's equipment room.

Lee earned his master's in filmmaking from NYU in 1982, and as his final film project, he wrote, produced, and directed Joe's Bed-Stuy Barbershop: We Cut Heads. His father composed the original jazz score, the first of several he created for his son's films. The film was set at a barbershop in Brooklyn's Bedford-Stuyvesant neighborhood that serves as a front for a numbers running operation. The Academy of Motion Picture Arts and Sciences awarded Lee the 1983 Student Academy Award for best director. The Lincoln Center's New Directors and New Films series selected the film as its first student production.

Upon graduation two major talent agencies signed Lee, but when nothing materialized, he was not surprised. In a New York Times interview, Lee said that it "cemented in my mind what I always thought all along: that I would have to go out and do it alone, not rely on anyone else." Even though the honors enhanced his credibility, they did not pay the bills. In order to survive, Lee worked at a movie distribution house cleaning and shipping film.

At the same time, he tried to raise funds to finance a film entitled Messenger, a drama about a young New York City bicycle messenger. However, in the summer of 1984, a dispute between Lee and the Screen Actor's Guild forced a halt in the production of his first film. The Guild felt the film was too commercial to qualify for the waiver granted to low-budget independent films that permitted the use of nonunion actors. Lee felt that the refusal to grant him the waiver was a definite case of racism. Unable to recast the film with union actors, he terminated the project for lack of funds. Lee told Vanity Fair that he had learned his lesson: I saw I made the classic mistakes of a young filmmaker; to be overly ambitious, do something beyond my means and capabilities. Going through the fire just made me hungrier, more determined that I couldn't fail again.

With the disappointment of Messenger behind him, Lee needed a film with commercial appeal that could be filmed on a small budget. His script for She's Gotta Have It (1986) seemed to fill the bill. The $175,000 film was shot in 12 days at one location and edited in Lee's apartment. The plot follows an attractive black Brooklyn woman, Nola Darling, and her romantic encounters with three men. Lee played one of the three suitors, Mars Blackmon. In the comedy Lee poked fun at the double standard faced by a woman is who involved with several men. After the film's successful opening at the San Francisco Film Festival, Island Pictures agreed to distribute She's Gotta Have It, beating out several other film companies. At the Cannes Film Festival it won the Prix de Jeuness for the best new film by a newcomer. A success in the United States, it eventually grossed over $7 million.

Lee based his next film, School Daze (1988), on his four years at Morehouse College. Set on a college campus during homecoming weekend, it explores the conflict between light-skinned and dark-skinned blacks. Those with light skin have money, expensive cars, and "good hair." The ones with darker skin are "less cool" and had "bad hair." Lee aimed to expose what he saw as a caste system existing within the black community. Lee began filming at Morehouse, but after three weeks the administration asked him to leave citing his negative portrayal of black colleges. Lee finished filming at Atlanta University. School Daze opened to mixed reviews but was a box office success, ultimately grossing $15 million. However, Lee's efforts to explore a complex social problem offended some, while others applauded.

Do the Right Thing (1989) opened with even more controversy. It portrays simmering racial tensions between Italians and African Americans in Brooklyn's Bedford-Stuyvesant section that erupt when a white police officer kills a black man. Some critics said Lee was endorsing violence and would hold him partly responsible if audiences rioted upon seeing the film. Lee stated that he did not advocate violence, but intended to provoke discussion. The Cannes International Film Festival included a screening of the film and the Los Angeles Film Critics gave it an award for best picture. Do the Right Thing received Golden Globe nominations for best picture, best director, best screenplay, and best supporting actor, but failed to win in any category. It was also nominated for an Academy Award for best original screenplay and for best supporting actor. It lacked a nomination for best picture despite its high acclaim. According to Lee, in Jet magazine, "the oversight reflects the discomfort of the motion picture industry with explosive think pieces." It cost $6.5 million to produce and grossed $28 million.

Lee's father inspired the main character and wrote the score for Mo' Better Blues (1990). A jazz trumpeter—who might be based on Lee's father, Bill Lee—tries to balance his love of music with his love of two women. However, Lee said the film was about relationships in general and not just the relationship between a man and a woman. He wanted to portray black musicians not dependent on drugs or alcohol.

Jungle Fever (1991) had another provocative theme, that of interracial sex. It also explores color, class, drugs, romance and family. A black married architect and an Italian American secretary are attracted to each other through the sexual mythology that surrounds interracial romance. At the end of their affair, they admit that they were just "curious," but not before both are at odds with their families. Color, class, drugs, romance, and family are all dealt with in this movie. Lee noted that whether the movie endorses or rejects interracial romance is not the point.

Next Lee directed a film on the life of Malcolm X. He knew from the start that it would be controversial. Warner Brothers originally chose Norman Jewison to direct the film. When Lee announced publicly that he had a problem with a white man directing the film, Jewison agreed to step down. Lee problems began early on with a group called the United Front to Preserve the Memory of Malcolm X and the Cultural Revolution. Their objections were based on their analysis of Lee's "exploitative" films. Others doubted that Lee would present a true picture of Malcolm X. After reworking the script, Lee battled with Warner Brothers over the budget. He requested $40 million to produce a film of epic proportions. Warner offered only $20 million. By selling the foreign rights for $8.5 million and kicking in part of his $3 million salary, Lee made up the difference by getting backing from black celebrities such as Bill Cosby, Oprah Winfrey, and Michael Jordan, much to Warner's embarrassment. Under Lee's direction, Malcolm X was released in 1992, grossing $48 million. It played a major role in elevating the black leader to mythic status, portraying him as a symbol for the extremes of black rage as well as for racial reconciliation.

Lee wrote Crooklyn (1994) with his sister, Joie, and brother, Cinque. Originally a short story by Joie, Cinque encouraged her to turn it into a screenplay. Joie and Cinque had planned for their own company to make the film, but after reading it, Spike was interested in producing it. The black family in Brooklyn during the 1970s sounds a lot like the Lees, but Joie Lee warned not to assume it is autobiographical. It is an unusual film, lacking a dysfunctional family, violence, gangs, and drugs. Instead, it follows the struggles and strengths of a family despite odds and obstacles.

In direct contrast to Crooklyn is Clockers (1995), Lee's intimate but violent look at the inner-city drug trade. Adapted from Richard

Price's novel, initially the film was to be directed by Martin Scorcese and focus on the story's police murder investigation. However, Scorcese had other commitments, and Lee took over. He shifted the emphasis to the relationship between two brothers. One is on the "up and up" and the other is a clocker (a street level worker in the drug trade, always ready at any hour to provide crack.) Lee concentrated more on the bonds that connect black men rather than making another "gangsta" movie.

Lee released two films in 1996. The first, Girl 6 (1996) had a cast and crew made up mostly of women. It follows a struggling actress who takes a job for a phone-sex line. Her sense of reality deteriorates when the calls begin to matter to her, and she eventually hits rock bottom. Reviews were not favorable, one critic wrote that this was the worst film Lee had made. Lee's tenth film in as many years was an investigation of the Million Man March of 1995. Get on the Bus (1996) details the voyage of 12 men from Los Angeles to Washington, D.C., to take part in the march. They represent the diversity of male African Americans, and Lee contrasted the men's speeches and debates so that the differences and tensions between them are intensified. Made in 18 days, Get on the Bus cost $2.4 million. Its entire budget came from black male investors who were inspired by the march's message.

Lee's earlier films courted controversy that helped maximize profits, but critics have said that since Malcolm X Lee has been less discerning, and his films have not done as well at the box office. However, his willingness to tackle sensitive issues of relevance to the black community has made his films profitable, awakening the industry to an untapped market. In 1997 Lee released 4 Little Girls, about a 1963 church bombing in Birmingham, Alabama, which killed four young girls. He then moved into what Maclean's Brian D. Johnson called "nervy satire" with a 2000 release, called Bamboozled. In that film, Lee delves into the delicate emotions associated with blackface minstrel shows as entertainment. In 2001 Lee released a television miniseries about the controversial Black Panthers cofounder, Huey P. Newton. Lee seems to be misquoted often, and finds it a nuisance to explain things he did not say. He would rather be out of the papers than see false claims. He told American Film, "All I want to do is tell a story. When writing a script I'm not saying, 'Uh-Oh,' I'd better leave that out because I might get into trouble. I don't operate like that." His goal is to prove that an all-black film directed by a black person can be of universal appeal.

In keeping with his interest in encouraging others who want to enter filmmaking, Lee established a minority scholarship at New York University's Tisch School of the Arts in 1989, and he also supports the College Fund/UNCF.

Lee is about five-feet six-inches tall and has a mustache and small beard. He wears glasses. Lee is a dedicated New York Knicks fan and has been known to plan film projects around the Knicks' basketball schedule. Associates describe him as possessing a fierce determination and unshakable self-confidence. Philip Dusenberry of New York advertising agency BBDO said of Lee in Business Week, "You get the impression that Spike is a devil-may-care kind of guy, but he's also a shrewd self-promoter." Other long-time associates told Ebony that Lee, "is an obsessive workaholic who seems intent on cramming a lifetime of work into a few short years." Lee is unusual in the filmmaking business in that he not only writes, directs, and produces, but also acts in all his films—although most of his roles are marginal. He does not consider himself an actor, but feels it creates box office appeal.

Lee makes no apology for his success and defends himself against charges of commercialism. His motivation for business investments comes from Malcolm X's philosophy that blacks need to build their own economic base. Lee was recognized as a marketing phenomenon and multimedia star only four years after his surprise hit, She's Gotta Have It. His first enterprise, Forty Acres and a Mule Filmworks, moved from his apartment to a remodeled Brooklyn firehouse in 1987. With tongue in cheek, Lee says the name reflects the arduous struggle he went through to make She's Gotta Have It.

In addition to his films, he has written several books that recount his experiences as a director. He has also produced music videos for Anita Baker, Miles Davis, Michael Jackson, and Branford Marsalis, among others. In 1988 he produced and directed a television commercial for Jesse Jackson's presidential campaign.

Lee also has his own collection of promotional movie merchandise, such as baseball caps, t-shirts, posters. Beginning with a rapidly expanding mail-order operation, Lee opened his retail store, Spike's Joint, in 1990.

Lee directed commercials for Levi's $20 million campaign for its 501 Jeans, as well as for Nike, The Gap, Barney's of New York, Philips Electronics, Quaker Oat's Snapple, and Ben & Jerry's ice cream. Appearing in Nike commercials with Michael Jordan, Lee was criticized for making Nike's expensive Air Jordans such a status symbol that many young people reportedly were stealing from each other. According to Business Week, Lee dismissed the charges as "thinly veiled racism." He also appeared in television commercials for Taco Bell and Apple Computer, and in print ads, "Milk. Where's your mustache?" for the National Fluid Milk Processors. He recorded the voiceover for a television ad for Topps Stadium Club basketball cards; a special set of "Spike Says" insert cards feature Lee's commentary on ten of the National Basketball Association's biggest stars.

Lee served as executive producer for several films, marketed his own comic book line, and directed short films for Saturday Night Live and MTV. His Forty Acres and a Mule Musicworks, which joined MCA Records in 1994, has been responsible for his movie soundtracks. In 1994, the TNT cable network signed Lee to be executive producer of the documentary Hoop Dreams. In 1995 Columbia Pictures TV signed him as one of several filmmakers in a series of one-hour documentaries, "American Portraits" for the Disney Channel.

In late 1996, Lee joined DDB Needham Advertising to form a new ad agency, Spike/DDB. Their agreement called for Lee to direct urban-oriented commercials for a variety of clients. He previously worked with DDB on an educational spot for the College Fund/United Negro College Fund.

Lee married attorney Tonya Linnette Lewis, in October of 1993. They met in September of 1992 during the Congressional Black Caucus weekend in Washington D.C. Their daughter, Satchel Lewis Lee, was born in December of 1994. She was named after legendary black baseball star Satchel Paige. In May of 1997 their son, Jackson Lee, was born.

Known as one of the most original and innovative filmmakers in the world, Lee presents the different facets of black culture. He is quick to admit, however, that there are those in the black community among his detractors. Lee says that he is neither a spokesman for 35 million African Americans nor tries to present himself that way. He will probably continue to court controversy, but with his savvy and salesmanship skills, Spike Lee will remain a significant influence in the entertainment world.

July 7, 2003: Lee and Viacom reach a settlement over the rights to the name "Spike." The terms of the deal were not disclosed, but Viacom will begin using the name as soon as possible. Source: E! Online, www.eonline.com, July 8, 2003.

July 28, 2004: Lee's film She Hate Me was released by Sony Pictures Classics. Source: New York Times, www.nytimes.com, July 28, 2004.

October 2004: Lee joined the advisory board of the inaugural National Geographic All Roads Film Festival. Source: USA Today, www.usatoday.com/life/digest.htm, October 18, 2004. *Source: The African American Almanac, 7th ed., Gale, 1999.*

Chapter Thirty-Nine

HARPER'S BAZAAR BY EVE MACSWEENEY MAY 1997

IT'S MIDNIGHT AT SmashBox studios, in L.A.'s desolate Culver City. The team—photographer (now napping), his two assistants, two stylists, hair, makeup, two record-company reps, and me—has assembled for the night ahead. The clothes—Helmut Lang, Gucci, Galliano (for him and her, and they share a shoe size)—have been hung on the racks, the jewelry laid out on the bench. We chit, we chat, we stroll back and forth for another canapé or Coca-Cola, but there's suspense in the air. Everyone's attention is subliminally fixed on the door at the far end of the studio, to which out eyes flicker repeatedly, as if expecting a hot wind to blow through.

With the Artist Formerly Known as Prince, who now goes by the slightly less chewy title of the Artist, there are more variables than with most. The man who scrawled slave on his cheek during the final stages of disentanglement from his recording contract with Warner Bros. is clearly his own master now: Earlier in the day, he rescheduled a sedate Sunday afternoon session to this late hour, right after the Image Awards at the Pasadena Civic, where he was receiving a Key of Life special achievement award from Stevie Wonder. Besides, there's no absolute guarantee that he will show, or for how long; that he will talk, or for how long. A couple of days before, he had posed for a photographer, then left after the first roll of film had been shot, not digging the vibe. He's a night owl, his people tell us, and tonight he'll be on a high. For the rest of us, it's caffeine all the way.

Finally it happens. And it's less a whirlwind than a light breeze as the Artist, his wife, Mayte, and one bodyguard walk quietly through the door and introduce themselves. The Artist is wearing a long feminine rollneck sweater and bell-bottoms, a pendant with a rendering of his name, 0{+>, an elaborate silver sickle-moon cuff on top of one ear, and pink Cuban-heeled boots. Mayte, sleek and sexy, wears a one-shoulder Versace dress, a ponytail, an ankle bracelet, and a large rock on her fourth finger. Aaron, the bodyguard, who looks like a deflated version of a James Brown thug—young, shaved-headed, and Eastern European-looking, with an earpiece and the obligatory facial scar—gets straight on the phone. The Artist's luggage was lost between Minneapolis and Los Angeles, and he's trying to track it—I think I hear the word *purple*. A message has been discreetly conveyed, and the Sam Cooke that has been playing on the sound system is replaced with the Artist's current triple CD, Emancipation, which at three hours long almost lasts us through the session. Mayte settles in for makeup, and I sit down with the Artist to talk.

After all the ripples that surround him, being one-on-one with the Artist is a bit like finding yourself in the eye of the storm. In conversation, he's low-key and polite—not charming, exactly, but with flashes of warmth. Signs of the showmanship he displays onstage—his is the tightest, the most humorous and entertaining live act I've ever seen—occasionally break through his offstage wariness.

At first his eyes are on the wall, then he gets more animated and turns the kohl-rimmed beauties on me. (This, I gather, is a fairly recent breakthrough in the Artist's interview etiquette.) Part of his relative openness these days is no doubt because these are happier times for him: He married Mayte, a 23-year-old Puerto Rican dancer, just over a year ago, and he's signed a new record deal, on his terms, with EMI. (What's particularly rankled him about his Warner Bros. contract was that he doesn't own his own master recordings, and that the company rationed his musical output.) *Emancipation,* which he released at his own financial risk, has just gone double-platinum—"Not bad for someone whose career was supposed to be in the gutter," he says, with a trace of bitterness. There's a sense that he has come through an early midlife crisis—he has, after all, been a professional musician for half of his 38 years—in which he's wrestled with success, ego, religion, and control, and struggled to come to some sort of resolution.

We start with this, and with what the word emancipation means to him.

"You have to emancipate people first from themselves," he says. "Your ego want to have the biggest and best for yourself. But you have to think what path that would lead you down. You find nothing that satisfies you. You're continually given things you've seen before—money, gold records, sold-out shows. You forget that you should be thankful." Just when you're gasping at this humility rap, he comes through with some humor. "Do you have to have a big ego to be an artist?" I ask. "If you do it right," he says, and smiles.

The business with his name is in part a negation of ego, but the slave/emancipation riff is also more political than the Artist's publicity machinery would have us believe. He talks about slave names. "Nel-son," he enunciates. "I've been looking for the Nel in my family tree, and I don't see one. You really do belong to something or someone, and until you get out from under that, you're not free." (Obviously the bank doesn't tolerate these complexities: A check he later sends the magazine for ownership of these photos, which he insists on, is stamped with a no-nonsense P.R. Nelson.) He likes to roam the Internet, he tells me, under a name we'll never know.

God has helped him, and so has Mayte. The Artist is very serious about God, and he's very serious about sex. He expresses his amazement that anyone could accept an award and now find the time to thank God. "That's how you can *really* tell what time it is," he says. (And judging by the recent Grammys, God is at the top of a lot of artists' lists these days.) As for sex, when I ask him how it feels to finally be free of his Warner Bros. deal, he tells me, "It's like eighteen orgasms at once." I laugh, but he's not trying to be funny. Later we talk about Kamasutra, the ballet he is currently creating for Mayte. It is, he says, "perfect music to make love to." And he means it.

"Mayte grounds me," he says. "She doesn't try to change me, but she makes me more aware of certain things. She's given me respect for life. She's brought in animals to the house—two dogs, two cats, two doves." Together they've been working on a charity, Love 4 One Another, for underprivileged children and people in need.

The couple are very clean and green. Mayte, he says, has a vision of the future where kids will go to nightclubs not to drink or take drugs but just to chill and get into the music. And she's converted her husband to a "complete vegetarian kick"—he talks of wanting to get a farmer on the payroll at Paisley Park.

The sadder element of their marriage—the fact that they apparently had a physically impaired son who died soon after birth—is off-limits, and is something that you sense the Artist has again made an effort of will and spirit too come to terms with. "When you have faith in God, you don't have bad days," he says at one point. When I ask if I can talk to Mayte, he demurs, saying that she's had a lot to deal with lately.

The famous eyes are beginning to stray toward the door, so I wind up the questions. Then the fun begins in front of the camera. The Artist and Mayte try on clothes, falling about in hysterics at the sight of him in a red-and-white-leather biker-style Galliano jumpsuit. "You look like Eval Knievel," she says. "They got some pretty weird clothes back there," he tells me with a camp roll of the eyes, before getting back onto safer ground by pulling out his own array of trilbies and fedoras.

Visually they make and interesting couple: he so delicate, she with a dancer's body, womanly curves, and a broad-planed, beautiful face. Physically, she's relaxed and confident, at ease with herself. Posing together, she and the Artist throw shapes like a practiced double act, as though they do this every day in the mirror—and they probably do.

After three costume changes and a hundred variations of the embrace, the Artist sends the hairdresser out from under the lights to announce that they're about to call it a night. He takes one more trip across the floor in those Cuban heels and, without looking at Aaron, holds a finger out toward him for his pendant. And they're off.

Three weeks later, the Artist throws a private party at Manhattan's Life club to celebrate *Emancipation*'s sales. It's a cool scene, with black royalty gracing the small subterranean room, into which a Minneapolis DJ has been imported to spin the decks. Quincy Jones is here, and Spike Lee, Tony Rich, L.L. Cool J, and Savion Glover; industry big-wheels Guy Oseary, Dallas Austin, Motown's Andre Harrell, and Def Jam's Russell Simmons; and a smattering of white rock stars, such as Billy Corgan, Marilyn Manson, and Joan Osborne, whose song about God, "One of Us," is covered on Emancipation. Lenny Kravitz arrives with much ado in an enormous hat and shades. The Artist, dressed in red, moves through the crowd, with Aaron in discreet attendance, taking in the jazzed-up, low-key vibe until 6 A.M.

Everywhere he goes, he is smiling, smiling.

Chapter Forty

AOL LIVE INTERVIEW PRINCE JULY 22, 1997

Online Host (AOL The Artist (Prince)

The Artst:	The artist is here . . . where are you?
The Artst:	Prince is dead
Online Host:	Welcome Prince
Online Host:	We are so happy to "see" you: D
The Artst:	Thank u all
Online Host:	Well, we are a little behind, so let's get started . . . .
Online Host:	OK?
The Artst:	OK

Online Host:	Your first question of the evening:
Question:	Love four one another charities . . . . How does it fit in your plan? . . . . Who does it involve?
The Artst:	Hopefully everyone online . . .
The Artst:	The idea is to make it . . .
The Artst:	A webwide effort
Question:	Where are you planning to perform next?
The Artst:	Jones beach . . .new york
The Artst:	Is the next gig
Online Host:	Who are you listening to now for inspiration in your music?
The Artst:	My wife
The Artst:	. . .
The Artst:	And the friends online
The Artst:	Webheads inspire greatly
Question:	What is the Truth? What is CB Set?
The Artst:	Crystall ball was inspired by the sites that dig r music
The Artst:	The truth will be given away free to the friends who . . .
The Artst:	Donate database to the love4oneanother site
Question:	Are you planning a party for 1999?
The Artst:	Of course . . .
The Artst:	Foo fighters are going
Question:	Whats next for the man of 1,000+ sounds?
The Artst:	Now that i am free . . . i let the wind blow me
Question:	Are you coming out with any love songs
The Artst:	There is a song on the truth album . . .
The Artst:	Entitled—comeback . . .
The Artst:	Which was written for a lost friend
Question:	How do you feel about copyright infringement and musicans . . . . Sampling your music? How are you different?
The Artst:	It was cool at 1st but now it has gotten out of hand . . .
The Artst:	I have never seen so many bad musicians in my life
Question:	If you could change one thing about the music business what . . . . would you change?
The Artst:	Too many things wrong,I could not settle for one

Question:	Why are you doing this?
The Artst:	Love for one another
Question:	How did you first get into music?
The Artst:	Head1st
Question:	Do you really eat Capt. Crunch cereal?
The Artst:	Yes
Question:	What's your musical goal?
The Artst:	I want to one write the grand progression . . .
The Artst:	The perfect song that makes me never want 2 sing again
Question:	What's your opinion on scalpers?
The Artst:	Get a real job!
Question:	Do you still keep in touch with any members of The Revolution?
The Artst:	Not really no . . .I wish . . . sometimes they call . . . usually when they . . . . want to confirm a rumor
The Artst:	Oops
Question:	What's different about your music now vs when you were with . . . . Warner?
The Artst:	listen to crystal ball and the truth u will hear what freedom . . . . sounds like . . .
The Artst:	There is a track called baconskin that thumps for fifteen . . . . minutes . . . SICK
Question:	What material are you planning to perform on your current . . . . tour?
The Artst:	This tour is very interesting inasmuch as it will constantly b . . . . changing . . .
The Artst:	Lenny Kravitz . . .
The Artst:	Will
The Artst:	B
The Artst:	Joining some of the . . .
The Artst:	Concerts . . .
The Artst:	As
The Artst:	Well
The Artst:	As

The Artst:	Carlos Santana
The Artst:	This will affect r playlist
The Artst:	We play many songs . . .
The Artst:	That i have not . . .
The Artst:	Played in years . . .
The Artst:	Like when doves cry
Question:	If you had the chance to play with any artist who is no longer . . . . with us, whom would you choose?
The Artst:	probably jimi
Question:	Will The Artist Formerly known as Prince ever make another . . . . movie??
The Artst:	Secret
Question:	Prince are you going to put together another group someday?
The Artst:	I love the band I have now
The Artst:	They stomp much booty
Question:	You seem to write songs extremely well. Do you write your songs . . . . at the spur of the moment or do you wait untill you start on a . . . . new project or album?
The Artst:	I write and record constantly . . .
The Artst:	There are many songs that were never bootlegged that will come out soon
Question:	First of all you are fabulous!!!!! Second I have a copy of purple . . . . rain on purple vinyl . . . is this a rare copy or were there alot of . . . . them printed?
The Artst:	It is very rare . . . during the time when my comrades and I got . . . . along
Question:	My wife and I think that you are a great musician and we were . . . . really psyched to see you get a lifetime achievement award. . . . . We've noticed that your music is taking a turn to being a little . . . . more rebellious and shocking, what has caused you to go in this . . . . dire
Online Host:	I think that mean direction
The Artst:	This "dire" direction with my music . . .

The Artst:	Is in response to the ever pressing . . .
The Artst:	Fact that most musicians especially of tha darker persuasion . . .
The Artst:	Usually leave this business with nada . . .
The Artst:	Broke
The Artst:	Such a shame
Question:	What all instruments can you play?
The Artst:	I can play any instrument . . .
The Artst:	Only 27 good
Question:	Your song. "319" Where did you come up with the idea?
The Artst:	Elizabeth Berkley
Question:	What is 1800NewFunk?
The Artst:	Call and find out . . . .
The Artst:	I believe when it is organized . . .
The Artst:	It will become the future of distribution . . .
The Artst:	At least as far as my music . . .
The Artst:	Is concerned
The Artst:	I am hungry
Question:	Do you really ride a motorcycle? And if so, what kind?
The Artst:	I do not ride anymore . . . .
The Artst:	cuz I get followed . . .
The Artst:	And not every intention is welcome
Question:	What some advice you can give to an up coming artist?
The Artst:	First of all, don't eat anything that has parents . . .
The Artst:	Because you will inherit their dreams . . .
The Artst:	And second and for most give praise unto your creator . . .
The Artst:	Because soon only the truth will remain
Question:	Sir, did the Beatles influence directly any of your music, they . . . . seem to peek their heads out every once and a while with your . . . . older music.—Angie in Indy
The Artst:	I cannot lie . . .
The Artst:	When you were mine was written . . .
The Artst:	in a hotel room in Birmingham . . .
The Artst:	After listenin to John sing

Question:	Could you see yourself going in a more jazzier forum of music in . . . . the near future, not madhouse type, but a purer miles type . . . . improve jazz.
The Artst:	I am working on a free for them record with Jacob armen . . .
The Artst:	The most frightening drummer I have ever heard
Question:	Your videos have a stylish look. Do you use specific directors and . . . . cinematographers to acheive this look?
The Artst:	I hate videos . . . . they are for kids
Question:	How does one order tshirts if you don't go to a concert of yours?
The Artst:	1800newfunk
Question:	Hey I live a stones throw away from Paisley. How do you like . . . . the rain?? Do you think you show more of your outstanding . . . . guitar on any of your future records??
The Artst:	I am growing my own food now . . .
The Artst:	So I love the rain . . .
The Artst:	I understand better now
The Artst:	4444
The Artst:	Oops
Question:	What do you want to acomplish most in life?
The Artst:	I can only pray that i am doing my God's will at this stage . . .
The Artst:	I worked very hard 4 what i have so i feel deserving . . .
The Artst:	Of things accomplished . . .
The Artst:	But when it is all said and done . . . . one must please God first and . . . . last
Question:	When does the tour officially start?
The Artst:	Yesterday
The Artst:	It pounded
The Artst:	You should have been there
Question:	We have read that David Bowie admires your work, have you or . . . . would you work with him?
The Artst:	I would love to work with almost anyone who is + and owns their . . . . masters

Question:	How old were you when you wrote your first song?
The Artst:	My first song was written at 7 and it was called FunkMachine
The Artst:	These are cool ?'s
Question:	What inspired your storyline in your film "Under the Cherry.... Moon"? My wife and I consider it our favorite.
The Artst:	that film went thru many drafts...much was lost in the shuffle
The Artst:	But I must admit...
The Artst:	There are some very funny scenes...
The Artst:	It was inspired by the comedies...
The Artst:	Of the forties
Question:	What inspired the release of a 3 song CD set "Emancipation"
TheArtst:	The breaking of the chains.... clik, click
Question:	You are so intense now were you like that when you were.... younger?... Did you always know what you wanted to do?
The Artst:	I was as intense... yes I used to play act my whole future...
The Artst:	I willed this whole trip...
The Artst:	l do not want to wake up to the universe that way...
The Artst:	But I did
The Artst:	So what...big deal...
The Artst:	Want something then wish for it
Question:	What was your inspiration for the song Forever In My Life?
The Artst:	Susannah
The Artst:	She knows
Question:	Planning on ever releasing a live cd
The Artst:	Yes... Lenny and George and i talk abiut that all the time
The Artst:	About
Question:	You seem ageless... does your music keep you young?
The Artst:	Yes... but most of all...

The Artst:	Trusting the present . . . "the present" . . . the gift
The Artst:	Yes
Question:	Do you have an official website?
The Artst:	www.love4oneanother.com
The Artst:	The $
Question:	Do you ever hang out in an IRC chat room on your website?
The Artst:	No
Question:	Are you interested in doing any duets, & if any, who?
The Artst:	I want to sing with anyone at the Ali concert in October
Question:	You were one of the first artists to make a fashion statement. . . . Who are your designers?
The Artst:	Myself and a strange and gifted woman named-debbie mcguan
Question:	What is the best gift a fan has ever given you? What is the best . . . . gift a fan can give you?
The Artst:	First of all to not be a fan . . . it is short for fanatic
The Artst:	. . . love is all we need . . .
The Artst:	Sounds cliche but it makes me feel good
Question:	Do you choose the people you perform on stage with and how are . . . . they chosen?
The Artst:	Oddly enuff they come to me through other musicians
The Artst:	Some I steal
The Artst:	Hee hee
Question:	What is your preconcert preparation like
The Artst:	Laughing . . . lots of that and then prayer
Question:	Tell us somethingabout you that we would not expect
The Artst:	I hate massages . . .
The Artst:	Despise them Question: do you worry about negative influence . . . . on young people?
The Artst:	Yes . . . .
The Artst:	I do not regret anything i have done
The Artst:	But

The Artst:	The industry seems to only promote the absurd
The Artst:	Nowadays
Question:	Any accoustic songs in the future?
TheArtst:	The truth album is almost completely acoustic
Question:	Have you written any music for other artists lately?
The Artst:	Question?
The Artst:	Uh oh
Question:	So, Prince, are you still hungry?
The Artst:	Yes
The Artst:	Come see me on tour .... like a dog in heat, I will not disappoint
The Artst:	!
The Artst:	!
The Artst:	!
Online Host:	We want to first of all, thank our special guest: O(+>
The Artst:	Peace and b wild
Online Host:	And we want to thank all of you in the audience for hanging in there and
Online Host:	Sending in all these
Online Host:	Great questions.
The Artst:	Yes

Chapter Forty-One

VEGETARIAN TIMES INTERVIEW PRINCE
OCTOBER 1997

Vegetarian Times (VT): How, when and why did you and Mayte become vegetarians?

The Artist (Prince): I've not eaten red meat for about 10 years now. Mayte for a lot longer. I've always had a preference for all things vegetarian but not until recently did I find out how good they were for you (in a physical sense)

VT: How far have you taken your vegetarianism? The lyrics on *Emancipation*'s "Joint to Joint" suggest you like soymilk on your cereal. Have you given up dairy and eggs as well as flesh foods?

PRINCE: We don't eat anything with parents. Complete vegans—both of us! The opening lyrics to "Animal Kingdom" (on the forthcoming album *The Truth*) refer to a conversation between Spike and me about the benefits of cow's milk over human. I believe they are few.

VT: Many people become vegetarian out of concern for their health, but I know that's not what motivated you and Mayte. Can you tell us how your beliefs affected this decision?

PRINCE: Thou shalt not kill means just that! We don't have to kill things to survive. In fact, the complete opposite happens: If you kill, you will die.

VT: That sounds pretty dire. Speaking of dire: Some people think vegetarianism is all about denying yourself pleasure. Have you found this to be true? You don't strike me as the kind of guy who thinks sensual pleasure is negative.

PRINCE: Mayte and I get no pleasure from playing Russian Roulette with food. Eating anything ridden with bacteria raises your chances for disease. Being sick is not pleasurable.

VT: I gather that Mayte is the driving force behind your interest in vegetarianism. Would you have gotten there without her influence?

PRINCE: Mayte showed me how many different vegetarian dishes one could have and never miss the things you would imagine. I never was a big milk drinker anyway, but I really like vanilla soy milk. Being without my wife's influence is not a reality to me, so I don't speculate on life without her.

VT: What changes have the two of you noticed since becoming vegetarians?

PRINCE: I actually enjoy eating more. I have more energy and most of all, my aura is stronger. One can actually feel one's karmic debt decrease with every meal. Mayte enjoys preparing meals for the two of us. It strengthens our bond.

VT: Your practical, as well as philosophical experience, is of interest to us. Now that you're eating vegetarian meals, are you learning to cook differently? Do you have a chef who cooks for you? Do you have a favorite style of cuisine or a favorite meal?

PRINCE: Mayte cooks for us. She's always trying new things. The wonderful thing about vegetarianism is there is no favorite dish because there is no addiction. Non-vegetarians always speak about their favorite because it usually involves something artificial or something that doesn't belong in them. Ah, the universe keeps expanding!

VT: I noticed that a major theme in your recent music is freedom. It's on tracks like "Animal Kingdom" and "Joint 2 Joint" Is this a new area of exploration for you or has your freedom always been a central theme of even your early work? Has vegetarianism expanded the horizon of this concept?

PRINCE: Freedom has always been a theme in my work. Vegetarianism is a natural step for anyone seeking oneness with the spirit. The conscience is powerful (in a good way) when clear and weak when not.

VT: Life can be pretty brutal. There's a lot of senseless pain and suffering in the world, and some people say "Why waste your time worrying about animals when so many people are suffering?" Are vegetarians wasting their compassion? Distracting themselves from human pain?

PRINCE: Compassion is an action word with no boundaries. It is never wasted. To eat a tomato and then replant it for your nutrition as opposed to killing a cow or a pig for your meal is reducing the amount of suffering in the world. Besides, pigs are too cute to die.

VT: Do you worry that fans of your music might be put off by the message of songs like "Animal Kingdom" or by the public declaration of your vegetarianism?

PRINCE: Fan is short for "fanatic." I call my supporters "friends." My friends are very forward-thinking individuals. I'm not sure how many are meat eaters but soon all will know the consequences of a barbarian lifestyle. It's called karma! My music is dictated by the spirit. Not worrying about people's reaction is what has sustained me. I believe.

VT: Speaking of worrying about the public: There are lots of people who think vegetarianism is weird. You're already the subject of lots of public speculation and gossip. Will declaring yourself vegetarian add fuel to that fire?

PRINCE: We'd rather be looked over than overlooked. In all seriousness, it's obvious that the world has problems, but doing nothing about it is foolish. We have holidays for dead presidents who stood for everything but freedom of the soul. We need an Animal Rights day when all the slaughterhouses shut down, and people don't eat anything they can't replace. Yeah!

VT: Much has been made of your name change. Does that signify a reinvention of self? A rebirth? What has fallen away with the old name?

PRINCE: My name change is a complex issue not really suited for this discussion but what I can say is that it is much easier to separate the ego from the personality now. And I'm much happier since my name change.

VT: Tell us about the new album and your latest projects. What can we look forward to next?

PRINCE: Emancipation is a tour de force and what's best is that I finally own the master tape—so if you have any of my work and you like it, please support this project because it's the closest to my soul. Thank you for a chance to speak to the enlightened vegans of your magazine. We like being one of you!

Chapter Forty-Two

YAHOO INTERNET LIFE INTERVIEW PRINCE BY BEN GREENMAN OCTOBER 1997

IN HIS EARLY days, Prince was dismissed as a sensualist. Later on, when he started writing scriptural pop like *Lovesexy* and changed his name to an unpronounceable symbol, he was ridiculed as a spiritualist. All along the way, the Minneapolis multi-instrumentalist has been at once an avid consumer and a sharp critic of technology. The title song of *1999* fretted about nuclear weaponry, while the title song of *Sign O' the Times* mused on the folly of space travel in the wake of the Challenger disaster.

In recent years, the Artist has turned his attention toward interactive technologies, particularly the Internet. Last year's triple album *Emancipation* included two songs about cyberspace—"Emale" and "My Computer," the latter of which sampled America Online's "Welcome," "You've got mail," and "Good-bye" sounds. The Love 4 One Another Web site launched this summer. And on the eve of his Jam of the Year tour, in mid-July, the Artist even drew more than 300,000 participants on an AOL chat. Because of his interest in the online medium, the Artist agreed to talk to Yahoo! Internet Life about his music, his fans, the future of the Internet, and even cybersex.

Yahoo Internet Life (YIL)

The Artist (Prince)

YIL: When did you first go online?

The Artist: I first went online alone 7 months ago, 2 the best of my recollection.

YIL: How often do you go online?

PRINCE: When I am not on the road, maybe 3 or 4 times a week.

YIL: Are there any sites that you think are especially good?

PRINCE: Love 4 One Another. I also like the news section on AOL.

YIL: Are there any sites that you think are especially bad?

PRINCE: Bad is not a word I use unless I am describing a fine girl.

YIL: Do you visit the alt.music.prince newsgroup? If so, what do you think about it?

PRINCE: I have seen it once or twice. It seems 2 just be a place 4 trading bootlegs.

YIL: Do you visit the fan Web sites devoted to your music? If so, what do you think about them?

PRINCE: There are many I really dig. I'm really interested in getting all my friends 2gether on one site.

YIL: How do you feel about tape-trading and bootleg CDs? Have you ever bought a bootleg of one of your own performances?

PRINCE: I understand their existence. But I don't agree with buying and selling stolen property. Trading isn't so despicable.

YIL: What about all the rumors, speculation, and criticism about you that circulates online? Is it amusing or annoying? For example, someone wrote to the newsgroup to complain that you always release the weakest songs from albums as singles.

PRINCE: Opinion is how the world changes. That's cool, but lies and rumors don't deserve response. Also consider that any release of a single is only an advertisement 4 the album. And guess which 1 costs more?

YIL: On your newsgroup, some people have worried that the charity aspect of the Love 4 One Another site will be overwhelmed by the fandom aspect. Are you concerned about this?

PRINCE: Not in the least bit. Negative souls are bored by things like charity. They obviously think the world revolves because of something other than love.

YIL: Why did you close your previous official site, The Dawn?

PRINCE: Because without my involvement, the message was getting blurred. In my humble opinion, the dawn occurs when spiritual enlightenment takes place. When 1 learns of his or her relationship 2 everything on Earth and the universe. The new Web site will mirror the positive aspects of the dawn. In my rush 2 enlighten myself and others, I tried 2 "buffalo the vibe thru" when it was not ready. Love 4 One Another is the dawn.

YIL: Since you broke with Warner Bros., you've explored alternatives to traditional distribution. Do you have any plans to sell your music directly to consumers via the Net?

PRINCE: Yes. NPG Records will sell as well as give away a lot of new and old music over the Internet in the not-too-distant future.

YIL: Will record labels eventually disappear?

PRINCE: The writing is on the wall. Other souls were successful in their divide-and-conquer approach 4 a while. But now that we communicate with each other on a worldwide basis, the need 4 an "in4mation censor" is no longer a reality. The process of manufacturing and delivering music 2 a "friend" is not brain surgery.

YIL: On *Emancipation,* you wrote two songs about the Internet—"Emale" and "My Computer." What was the inspiration for those songs?

PRINCE: A man who unsuccessfully tried 2 "play me" was the catalyst 4 "Emale." I imagined his woman looking at her computer and being seduced by her "emale." "My Computer" was inspired by some of the insightful talks I have had with many positive people on the Net.

YIL: "Emale" is about cybersex. What do you think about cybersex? Have you ever done it?

PRINCE: Ain't nothin' like the real thang.

YIL: In *Graffiti Bridge*, you use a Macintosh. Do you still use a Mac?

PRINCE: My art department does. My wife owns an IBM. That's what I use.

YIL: Does "Computer Blue" have anything at all to do with computers?

PRINCE: It may. That hasn't revealed itself yet.

YIL: What is the place of computer technology in composing new music?

PRINCE: I try 2 let the song dictate its own direction. If one makes music with a computer, one has 2 be satisfied with the computer's limitations (and there are many, especially when it comes 2 music), though some songs only "sing" when programmed on a computer.

YIL: On the *Interactive* enhanced CD and *The Gold Experience* LP, there's a lot of talk about interactivity—"over 500 experiences to choose from," etc. Have you ever thought about creating new types of music especially for the Internet-interactive environments, personalized songs, and so on?

PRINCE: Yes. We are in discussion now 2 design a computer that can be a member of my band as well as interact with the audience. I have always been intrigued by the notion of being inside a computer.

YIL: OK, now for some final questions. If you were to write a theme song for the Internet, what would it be called, and what would it sound like?

PRINCE: "New World."

YIL: The Net seems to attract lots of studio-obsessed musicians. Is surfing the Net at all like being in the studio?

PRINCE: No, no, no, no, no, no, no, no!

YIL: Do you think "Shockadelica" is your best song? If not, why not?

PRINCE: "Shockadelica" is about a witch. "The Holy River" is about redemption. I am no judge.

YIL: What do you think about the Warner Bros. site?

PRINCE: I never visit their site.

YIL: Most of the online search engines still have you listed as "Prince," rather than the androgyny symbol, "The Artist Formerly Known as Prince," or "The Artist." How do you feel about that?

PRINCE: 2 each his own. I am a progressor. Some like the past. I don't mind.

YIL: This may sound nuts, but does the Camille alter ego, which you used on *Sign O' the Times*, have anything to do with the famous nineteenth-century hermaphrodite Herculine Barbin, who was nicknamed Camille? If so, my younger brother will be very, very happy, since he has spent roughly a decade trying to convince me of this.

PRINCE: Your brother is very wise.

YIL: And finally, will you be online in 1999?

PRINCE: In some form, yes.

Chapter Forty-Three

E EL PAIS SPAIN INTERVIEW PRINCE BY BRUNO GALINDO DECEMBER 15, 1997

Prince: When I am on stage I realize that this is why I write music. The most important thing a musician can experience is to be able to share that magic, to exchange that energy. Look at Warner: I gave them my music for years and they gave me a lot of golden albums. Look what I do with them: I just hang them in a wall. They don't make me happy. We, as musicians, need love: That's the only thing that makes us happy. I don't regret my relationship with them; in any case, they helped me build this place where I have been doing music for 15 years. But contracts don't interest me anymore; I just care about my family, my friends and music.

B.G.: Do you think someday the artists will be able to split up with their record companies and freely distribute their creations to the public?

Prince: It would be fantastic. But that is a very delicate question, because many artists are too weak and frightened to just go outside. The most important thing for us is to follow spiritual impulses.

B.G.: Now that you are, at last, free from any contracts, why don't you go back to the name your parents gave you?

Prince: I didn't change my name to escape from my Warners contract. That can not be done: it is illegal. I did it because my spirit told me so. At that moment I stopped being the person I was to become someone more complete. But, anyway, right at that moment they stopped wanting Prince's albums. Interesting, isn't it?

B.G.: It seems that, while you are one of the biggest names in pop music, you are one of the most misunderstood as well. You don't do too much to clarify your situation. Doesn't it bother you?

Prince: Of course it bothers me. The name change liberated me, it allowed me to become the person I wanted to be, and leave behind the one I had become. In front of you you have a person who is searching for peace and who is much more focused than before. The time of truth has come, this must be known at last, and I would like you to tell people. However, I believe a lot of people realized this change when they heard "The most beautiful girl in the world".

B.G.: Do you believe in any particular religion?

Prince: I only believe in looking inside yourself. You always need to do that in order to realize that there are two different beings inside you: The one who thinks and the one who talks. When you can see this . . . (While saying this Prince looks down in his very own, well-known fashion) . . . that's when you've reached your personal Dawn.

B.G.: What exactly does "the Dawn" represent to you? There are references to it in many of your songs; even your Internet site bears this name.

Prince: The Dawn means looking inside yourself. Everybody is capable of visualizing Love inside of themselves. I had ever thought it was difficult to love someone that hurts you. Until one day when I began to see that the one that hates you the most and the one that loves you the most are the same person.

B.G.: What? Can you explain this?

Prince: When someone hates you, what they really want is to be you, and that's a sign of love. Anybody who can see the Dawn will be able to see it for the next 3000 years.

B.G.: All that spirituality isn't it shocking with the ostentation of this place? I hope I am not offending you, but you seem to be Captain Nemo onboard the Nautilus. What would you save from this place if it was destroyed by, for example, fire?

Prince: This will never happen (says Prince with an angry voice, but he quickly regains control of himself). If you leave a piece of bread on a table, someday it will become moss, and this will become medicine. Tupac Shakur isn't here anymore, but this loss has mitigated the aggressiveness of lots of people. In the same way, Paisley Park will never be destroyed; it will just become something else.

B.G.: Excuse me if I insist, but it's hard to believe, when one sees you living in this palace, that you have no interest in material things . . . .

Prince: I'm not scared of poverty. I grew up being poor. Between 17 and 19 years, I didn't have a dollar in my pocket. But money finally comes, and friends help. And these times are positive, because they force you to decide if you're interested in living on this planet or not. I'm not here for money, because that doesn't make me happy. Musicians don't reach the top for money, and if they do, they have chosen the wrong way. Money is the source of every bad thing, and I have never let it destroy me. I am not even used to having it in my pockets. What I do is change it for positive energy. Everyone and everything is nothing but energy. And we need positive electricity to convert that energy into something good.

B.G.: Your new work, Emancipation, seems to be inspired by the pyramids of Egypt: they are three discs of the same duration. What keeps you fascinated with the subject?

Prince: The way Egyptians were helped by the stars, their faith and mental power when they built the pyramids. To move these stones they had to make a tremendous collective mental effort. Nowadays we wouldn't be able to do it. We are too divided to be able to concentrate on that kind of concern. Very often I wonder about the human nature: Were we, at the beginning, more intelligent and are now becoming idiots, or is it the opposite? I prefer to think that every time we are becoming a little bit more brilliant. We have to create something together.

B.G.: Recommend me a book.

Prince: "Embraced by the Light", by Betty Eadie. It is about experiences after physical death.

B.G.: Have you experienced something like that?

Prince: No.

B.G.: Do you believe in life after death?

Prince: Believing in it gives faith to a human being and makes him or her lead a better life. When I meet someone who doesn't believe in God, what he or she says acquires the cadence of a preacher. I wonder how can he or she live without wondering about the subject. That attitude terrifies me, because I think that if you don't believe, after life you won't go anywhere. I'm not scared by death; I know there is something after. I am more scared about life (joking). You have to choose between positive and negative. Faith is positive because it fights the fear.

B.G.: Do you have dreams?

Prince: Many of them. Yesterday I dreamt about Mayte. She was running. She was chasing me. Then the game changed and she made me chase her.

B.G.: What is your worst nightmare?

Prince: I do not remember . . . (Prince pauses and thinks for a while.) Now that you mention it, I realize that in fact I have stopped having nightmares. I haven't had a nightmare since I decided to get married. That's extraordinary!

B.G.: When did you make that decision?
Prince: Six months before the wedding.

B.G.: Is true Mayte and you met the first time in Spain?

Prince: Yes . . . (Prince pauses . . .) No! The first time she saw me was at a concert in Madrid, but our first encounter was in Frankfurt. On another occasion we went together to Barcelona.

B.G.: What do you remember of Spain?

Prince: Spain! You Spanish people love life, man! You don't know how lucky you are living here. I remember some incredible concerts and never-ending parties.

B.G.: Tell me about one.

Prince: I can't, I am a married man (Prince says with a smile while playing with his neck tie).

B.G.: Twelve years ago a first version of your name-logo appeared on "Purple Rain". This fact makes me think you have been thinking about your name change for a while.

Prince: All my life is included on my albums.

B.G.: As you made it known, this is the first time that you have been editing an album without being preparing another at the same time. Are you afraid of losing your interest in music someday?

Prince: No, sir. As long as my spirit is alive my music will be too. Let me tell you something. The other day I was on a TV show with Mayte when, suddenly, in the middle of the interview, she said something that made me all emotional: "We are returning together." In that moment I knew that words came straight from her spirit and I felt her love. When you hear true words, soon you know it's the spirit of the person, which pronounces them because they are not adulterated. My spirit expresses itself in other ways: through music. When I write a song it's my spirit that talks. If I weren't here talking with you I would run to write a song for her right now.

B.G.: Where could you take Mayte?

Prince: Far away from this planet.

B.G.: Are you afraid of getting older?

Prince: I love getting older. That means more music, more children, more experiences . . . more everything! I want to live so many, many years . . . .

B.G.: Don't tell me: Three thousand years.

Prince: Exactly! You have hit the nail, man!

B.G.: Do you sign autographs?

Prince: No. I can't sign anymore. I signed the last one when I was still Prince.

B.G.: You've denied him, but you're still playing his songs . . .

Prince: I am not the owner of the masters, but I know how to play them. (The secretary opens the door and says that the interview is over. I am just about to say goodbye to Prince when he says:)

Prince: Wait a minute ! Aren't you going to ask anything about the business?

I almost forgot: Prince has decided to do interviews because he has an album to sell.

Prince: This is the most important time of my life. At last I am going to be the owner of my own career. And I have created a foundation, Love For One Another, that is going to help children and whoever needs medical care.
Prince: I have lived in many places in my life, but I always return here. The grass and lakes calm me down. This is the place where I want to die.

Chapter Forty-Four

ABC GOOD MORNING AMERICA INTERVIEW PRINCE BY KEVIN NEWMAN

INTRODUCTION: WELL, WHEN it comes to pushing the envelope, few people can rival our next guest. Throughout his career, The Artist has fused pop, rock and soul music and created a sound that is very much his own. The Artist's newest release, *Newpower Soul*, is no exception, but it seems The Artist's enormous success has gone hand in hand with his struggle for creative independence.

He was called simply Prince in 1982 when he exploded onto the scene with the new millennium's first anthem, "1999." Two years later he starred in the film *Purple Rain* about a troubled rock star. The movie score won an Oscar and Prince's soundtrack sold 10 million copies around the world. Prince became known as a prolific artist, playing guitar, piano, keyboards, but he was also controversial. He battled with Warner Bros., his CD label of 18 years, culminating with his renouncement in 1993 of his own name: he changed it to a symbol to represent the The Artist and his freedom from the power of the music industry. In 1996, he severed ties with Warners and celebrated with the release of *Emancipation*, a 3-disc set that went double platinum. On Valentine's Day that same year, he married his 23-year-old backup singer, Mayte.

Clip from "The One" video

And it is interesting, the single "The One" is on The Artist's newest CD, and the video for "The One" was produced by The Artist's wife, Mayte—that's her there, a beautiful woman, a wonderful dancer, and we are honored to have The Artist with us this morning.

Kevin Newman: Good morning.

Prince: Good morning.

Prince is wearing a black sequined jumpsuit with matching black heeled boots and a plain gray silk jacket with stand-up collar. He also carries his lucite cane and wears ear wraps.

Kevin: I love the notion of "The One," because in my life I think I've found my "one."

Prince: Congratulations.

Kevin: . . . and it is a wonderful feeling. What to you makes it different, to feel when you've found "the one"?

Prince pauses so long that he asks the question again.

Kevin: How is it different feeling?

Prince: So many different things happen 2 u when u finally connect with your soul mate. U eat better . . .

Kevin: She cooks meals?

Prince: Oh, yeah. U sleep more, u want 2 stay in the house a little more. I don't record as much as I used 2. *Crystal Ball* was just released, that's all old material, it's a 5-record set that's available through a 1-800 line, 1-800-NEW-FUNK, and you can also pick it up, a four-CD set, in local stores.

Kevin: Alright. But you know you're quite romantic and I think that might surprise people who were familiar with your early music. I mean you're almost reverential, in fact I think you are reverential towards women. You have a line in "The One": "If U're looking' 4 a man who will make U feel like time has just begun/A man that'll make U feel like U're the only thing that ever mattered underneath the sun/I'm the one." Is that the way you feel about women now? In some ways you put "the one" on a pedestal.

Prince: "The One" video is very special 2 Mayte and I. We tried 2 go back 2 the notion of The Garden of Eden, when there was one idea, instead of having ten women and thinking that that is equivalent to wealth, we wanted 2 just focus on the one idea and see if that would bring us our personal heaven. She did a wonderful job with the video. I'm so proud I finally found a director that I don't have 2 scream at.

Kevin: Can she direct you? I would think it would be hard to work with your wife.

Prince: No, no, no—I completely trust her. She edits with "the one" in mind. "The one" being the choreography, the music, she makes her edits and all her shot selection based upon what it is she's trying 2 convey. That's what the song is about, it's about respecting "the one" idea, whatever that genesis is, so that u reach your revelation.

Kevin: You said a minute ago that you've been writing a little bit less because of more time obviously for your family life and for romance. Has that been hard for Mayte or either yourself to sort of figure out because you're somebody who's had a creative surge in your life and to share that surge and to find a place for the love in your heart with that music, has that been an interesting process to come together?

Prince: She represents music 2 me. She's a dancer by trade and she's inspired so much of my work. The whole second side of *Emancipation* is dedicated 2 her.

Kevin: She brings the color to your life?

Prince: Yeah, she brings the glint in my eye, so 2 speak.

Kevin: In "Newpower Soul," which is the title track here, there's another line I wanted to ask you about: "Every while in a great once/there comes 2 town a show/Lives up 2 all your Funkspectations/no matter how high or low." When you were growing up, what act, what band came to town that inspired you?

Prince: Hmm, Sly and the Family Stone.

Kevin: Was it?

Prince: Yeah . . . [munching on a cracker he took from his pocket] I didn't have breakfast, sorry.

Kevin: No, you're more than welcome. We can do better than a cracker, too, if you'd like. It was Sly and the Family Stone, which must make the fact that you've just signed Larry Graham, Sly's bassist, to your new label, that must be a special thing for you.

Prince: Yeah, Larry's a special individual. Not only has he shown me so much spiritually about the truth, he's given me a lot of bass licks I can steal.

Kevin: That you can use? (laughs) Sometimes in your life you get to work with mentors. I mean, is that what it's like having Larry on your label, is it a special feeling for you?

Prince: Yeah, u know Larry had a lot of trouble with the music industry, as I did. A lot has 2 do with just owning your master tapes. For example, David Bowie recently just signed away the rights 2 use his master tapes for $90 million. I don't own "Purple Rain" and I don't own "When Doves Cry" or "Little Red Corvette" and things like that and if I had the ownership rights 2 these particular masters, I can do the same.

Kevin: Right.

Prince: Cheddar like that makes u a player and u know, when u have money like that u can regenerate the careers of people like Chaka Khan and Mavis Staples, Doug E. Fresh and Larry Graham, that's what it's about.

Kevin: One of the reasons you left Warner, and the big reason, was you didn't have that kind of creative control. Now that you have your own artists on your own label, what are you not gonna do?

Prince: Well u know, I have no contract with Larry. We have a joke, u know, he says 2 me, "Contract? Let's see, what would we put on it? The prefix on contract is 'con'. I'm not trying 2 con him, I trust him and he trusts me and if we sign a contract between each other, that becomes the genesis of our relationship. Based upon love and truth . . .

Kevin: So you just have an understand with your people then?

Prince: . . . that's unecessary.

Kevin: All right. Your new CD, a lot of people are listening to it saying it's kind of a return to funk. Do you view it that way?

Prince: Uh, yeah, um, speaking about "the ones" and "genesis" and things like that, this particular album, I allowed the band and different players in it and their ideas 2 be the genesis of the creation of a lot of the songs. Kirk Johnson was very prominent in the production of this, as was Rhonda Smith—she's playing fretless bass on "The One." U know, there was just a drum computer and her bass when the song started, and then when u hear the way she plays, it's very . . .

Kevin: Really? It's organic.

Prince: . . . very central, the choreography and all that, we got a good crew now.

Kevin: We're gonna take just a break for a commercial break because we still have to do that and then come back and have a couple more questions and we'll bring some cheese for The Artist [Prince nibbling on a cracker again]. We'll be back in a moment.

Kevin: "The One," part of the *Newpower Soul* CD The Artist has come out with. I was saying earlier, there's a nice degree of sentimentality I think to some of the lyrics in this CD, but do you ever worry that as you age, and I think a many of us become more sentimental, that you lose edge?

Prince: Edge? Let's see, um, let's see. Matching socks? No. [Prince crosses his legs and pulls up his pants leg.]

Kevin: (laughs) We'd expect nothing less, of course.

Prince: No, never lose that.

Kevin: You don't necessarily have to lose edge when you become more sentimental.

Prince: Yeah, u know I'm more concerned with breaking the cycle of births and deaths than I am with just celebrating birthdays and things like that. I did the Today Show recently—sorry!

Kevin: That's OK. We like them, too.

Prince: All right. And I saw a sign that said, "Happy 40th," u know. I looked at that and it seemed like my dad's age, it didn't seem like me.

Kevin: No, I know. That's a tough one, I gotta say.

Prince: As long as I'm jumpin' off pianos, I'm cool with it.

Kevin: We have a piano—no, never mind. Are you gonna be touring again? A lot of people hoping for that.

Prince: Yeah, we're thinking about going to Europe and doing a hit-and-run tour where they never know where we're gonna show up and we had a lot of success . . .

Kevin: Kind of like The Stones when they just show up in a nightclub and whoever pays the $5 gets the best . . .

Prince: It's gonna be a little different than the Stones [leaning forward for emphasis] . . .

Kevin: Well you can bet on that!

Prince: U know why? 'Cause it's gonna be funky [pointing his finger for the funk], funky!

Kevin: You define that. Anyway, The Artist, thank you very much for being with us this morning.

Prince: Thank u.

Kevin: It was a pleasure to meet you.

Prince: Aww, it's appreciated.

Kevin: **All right. His new CD,** *NewPower Soul* **. . . it's a lot of fun. We'll be back**

Chapter Forty-Five

**GUITAR WORLD INTERVIEW PRINCE
BY SERGE SIMONART
OCTOBER 1998**

Guitar World: You won't allow your interviews with the press to be tape-recorded. Why? Presumably, you'd like to be able to guarantee more accurate representation of our conversation with a recorder.

Prince: To me, a tape recorder is like having a contract. And I don't want to have a contract with you. I don't want this to be business. I want this to be a normal conversation about something that we're hopefully both passionate about: music. And when there is no tape recorder, our relationship is based on trust. So if you write lies, you're the one betraying that trust, and you'd be the one soaking up all that negative energy. But I trust you, so we don't need a tape recorder. And I can talk now, because I'm free. A lot of my music has to do with being free. I'm not chained anymore. And being married to Mayte has made me feel more comfortable with speaking in public.

GW: Earlier this year you released *Crystal Ball,* a mammoth five-CD set. It contains some incredible outtakes and a number of unreleased tracks, but still no live music. You're hailed as being one of our best live performers. You've been doing incredible shows for years. Why have you avoided releasing live material?
Prince:: I have everything on tape, man, including all the informal jams. I record everything I do, just like Jimi Hendrix did. And eventually a lot of it will be released. To me, *Crystal Ball* was a test case. I was testing the water to see if people would buy music over the internet, and whether they would be receptive to a five-CD set.

Since the album was a success, it leads me to believe that the whole interactive thing offers great possibilities. I mean, why not make a five-CD live album, with people on the internet choosing their favorite tracks? Why not poll the fans on our web site and let them compile it? All this will happen. Soon.

For example, I just performed and recorded a 45-minute jam with Larry Graham called "The War," which I edited down to 26 minutes. It's a fantastic track. In the past, my old record company would never allow me to release something like that. Now that I have my own label, I can think about releasing that kind of stuff.

GW: What were some of your most memorable jam sessions?

Prince: God, there have been so many. I've actually recorded some indescribable music with Miles Davis—long improvisations that I will release at some point. But again, I want to wait until the spirit moves me, you know. Bring those recordings to the public when it feels right. Like release it on his birthday or his death day, when Miles was released from the circle of life and death.

GW: In addition to bringing attention to bassist Larry Graham, you've also resurrected Chaka Khan's career. For years, she seemed to be lost, yet she's one of the best soul voices of all time.

Prince: Chaka is another artist who was temporarily choked by restrictions, contracts and bad business deals. She's free now, free to release as many new songs as she likes. And man, what a voice. One of the pleasures of my life is being able to work with some of my musical heroes, asnd in doing so pay back some dues and have a great time. It was an honor to release Chaka's *Come 2 My House* and Larry's *GCS2000* on my label.

I realize I'm part of a musical history and I revere the legacy of my predecessors, so, for instance, when playing live I'll do some of their bombs, like when we do a song like "Cream," we'll segue a snippet of Aretha Franklin's "Chain of Fools" into it. Or we played "Jailhouse Rock" as a tribute to Elvis.

GW: It's interesting to hear you cite Elvis Presley, a white artist, as an influence.

Prince: I was brought up in a black and white world. I dig black and white; night and day, rich and poor, man and woman. I listen to all kinds of music and I want to be judged on the quality of my work, not on what I say, nor on what people claim I am, nor on the color of my skin.

But you have to have a certain empathy in order to understand a situation. Like when people made fun of my name change. It was mostly white people, because black people empathize with wanting to change a situation. My last name, Nelson, is really a slave name. A hundred years ago it meant "son of Nell," and it was white slave owners who gave it to their slaves, so why should I go by that name now? Why not do what Muhammad Ali and Malcolm X did?

GW: The last time you performed in Brussels, you played a cover version of Creedence Clearwater Revival's "Proud Mary," but you changed the lyrics around to: "I left a good job in the city, workin' for a man of a record company, a creep earning a living on a nigger's black butt." That was presumably aimed at Warner Bros. Records. Now, you no longer write "slave" on your face. You've renegotiated your contracts and started your own independent record company. Would you care to explain briefly what all that was about, as I'm sure it seemed very confusing to anybody outside of the music business.

Prince: Okay. Suppose you're a young musician and you want to make a record because you have something to say musically. Well, the record company usually makes you sign away the rights to your songs. In other words, you become a slave to them in the sense that they own the rights to the master recordings of your music for all time, and you're merely an employee. So if you don't own your master, your master owns you. And what we've been trying to do with the NPG label, what it stands for, is trying to create more freedom, including financial freedom, so that artists control their own genesis and can reach a much brighter revelation.

GW: On *Newpower Soul* you seem less preoccupied with producing hit singles than you have in the past. Cynics would say you're unable to write them anymore.

Prince: Well, that's what they said before "The Most Beautiful Girl in the World," too. And that's what they said after *Purple Rain*, and I had 10 hits after that. And *Lovesexy* was supposed to be a failure. But I've heard people say that record saved their lives, so I don't care what the media says. I know how I am and what really counts. I just want it more to be like the old days, you know: it's about the book, not the quote. In the old days, you used to buy an album, not a single. I want my records to work as a whole, not a collection of unconnected little bits.

GW: Have any lyrics of yours acquired new meaning to you with the passage of time?

Prince: Yes, my current single, "The One." That went from a love song to a song about respect for the Creator—God. The lyrics' meaning changed for me after reading the New World translation of the Bible [the Jehovah's Witness translation]. It has to be the New World translation because that's the original one; later translations have been tampered with in order to protect the guilty. There's a Garden-of-Eden feel to "The One." It's about following the highest ideal, and about living up to the goals of the apex, the Creator, "the One."

GW: You usually avoid talking about your direct influences, but since you've cited Miles, Chaka and Larry Graham, I'd like to ask you what impact James Brown had on you.

Prince: James Brown was an inspiration. Was and is. We play JB riffs all the time. I saw James Brown live early in my life, and he inspired me because of the control he had over his band . . . and because of the beautiful dancing girls he had. I wanted both. [laughs]

GW: Did you ever fine your musicians when they played bum notes, like James Brown used to do?

Prince: No, I don't have to.

GW: With digital editing, it is now possible to create a situation where you could jam with any artist from the past. Would you ever consider doing something like that?

Prince: Certainly not. That's the most demonic thing imaginable. Everything is as it is, and it should be. If I was meant to jam with Duke Ellington, we would have lived in the same age. That whole virtual reality thing . . . it really is demonic. And I am not a demon. Also, what they did with that Beatles song ["Free As a Bird"], manipulating John Lennon's voice to have him singing from across the grave . . . that'll never happen to me. To prevent that kind of thing from happening is another reason why I want artistic control.

GW: Has it ever occurred that something happened while you were recording, a mistake or coincidence, perhaps that changed the whole song around?

Prince: I don't believe in coincidence. But one thing leads to another. Playing "Head" live led to "It's Gonna Be a Beautiful Night," in a way.

GW: One thing I find fabulous about your songs is that you pay such attention to details. Especially in the ballads, like the siren and the background noise in "Wasted Kisses," on your new album, or the sexy and funny court interlude in the extended version of "I Hate U" on The Gold Experience.

Prince: I always spend a lot of time and energy thinking about and seeking out those little touches. Attention to detail makes the difference between a good song and a great song. And I meticulously try to put the right sound in the right place, even sounds that you would only notice if I left them out. Sometimes I hear a melody in my head, and it seems like the first color in a painting. And then you can build the rest of the song with other added sounds. You just have to try to be with that first color, like a baby yearns to come to its parents. That's why creating music is really like giving birth. Music is like the universe: The sounds are like the planets, the air and the light fitting together. When I write an arrangement, I always picture a blind person listening to the song. And I choose chords and sounds and percussion instruments which would help clarify the feel of the song to a blind person. For instance, a fat chord can conjure up a fat person, or a particular kind of color, or a particular kind of fabric or setting that I'm singing about. Also, some chords suggest a male, others a female, and some ambient sounds suggest togetherness while others suggest loneliness.

But with everything I do, I try to keep that blind person in mind. And I make my musicians pay attention to that, too. Like my bassist, Sonny T., can really play a girl's measurements on his instrument and make you see them. I love the idea of visual sounds.

GW: Have you ever composed a particular song because you never heard that kind of song on the radio?

Prince: Yeah. Absolutely. That happens all the time, I guess. What you've just said is one of the prime reasons why I make music.
GW: Some people use your ballads and more sensual songs as a form of aural foreplay.

Prince: So do I.

GW: I was going to ask: What kind of music do you play at home, at night, to get in the mood?

Prince: The same.

GW: You mean you play your own music as foreplay?

Prince: Yeah. I make music for all occasions. Including ambient music. I composed *Kamasutra,*which is on *Crystal Ball.*That's pretty ambient, and great for sex. Hence the title.

GW: You've always sung about sex. But then on *Emancipation* you sang: "You can't call nobody 'cause they'll tell you straight up, come and make love, when you really hate them." So all the time we envied you for great casual sex while you privately didn't like it?

Prince: Well, obviously now I'm married, so I've found that the spiritual peace that genuine love and passion brings makes anything less than that irrelevant. When I still wrestled with demons, I had moods when I couldn't figure something out and so I ran to vice to sort myself out, like women or too much drink, or working in order to avoid dealing with the problem.

GW: Now that you're married, do you still spend as much time in the studio?

Prince: Yeah, but my wife, Mayte, has me on "studio rehab." People call me a workaholic, but I've always considered that a compliment. John Coltrane played the saxophone 12 hours a day. That's not a maniac, that's a dedicated musician whose spirit drives his body to work so hard. I think that's something to aspire to. People say that I take myself too seriously. I consider that a compliment, too.

Chapter Forty-Six

**BASS PLAYER INTERVIEW PRINCE
BY KARL CORYAT
NOVEMBER 1999**

IT STARTED OUT simply enough. The Artist was coming out with a new record, *Rave Un2 the Joy Fantastic,* his people told us. Did we want to come to Minneapolis and do a story on him?

The Artist? Is he BASS PLAYER material? Yes, he is. The man can play every instrument sickeningly well, bass certainly being no exception. A listen to any of his early-'80s LPs, on which he played nearly all the parts, bears this out. Being an old Prince fan myself—who still can't quite cop the vibe of his disarmingly simple "Let's Work" [*Controversy*]—I jumped at the chance.

There was a small catch: The Artist doesn't allow his interviews to be tape recorded. Perhaps something about losing domain over the sounds he creates. Would he allow me to bring along a stenographer? Apparently, no problem.

Several months later I'm in the foyer of Paisley Park, The Artist's decade-old recording/performance complex just outside the Twin Cities. Accurately described by one journalist as a "musician's *Alice in Wonderland*," the plain-exterior place is an eye-feast inside—painted with countless bright colors, adorned by scores of platinum records and other awards, and outfitted with such necessities as a fitting room (for the two on-staff clothes designers), a faux diner (complete with menus), and a covey of unseen doves, cooing somewhere from 20-plus feet above.

While waiting for the Great and Powerful Oz to arrive, I chat with our hired stenographer—who, like many, was once a Prince fan but hasn't followed his career since the late '80s. "Are there names or technical terms I should be familiar with?" Not really—Larry Graham and "bass" are all that come to mind with the scary moment fast approaching. After reading numerous accounts of The Artist's often combative demeanor toward journalists, I was still unsure how to keep the conversation steered toward music specifics and away from his usual fashion-mag spiel: God, the millennium, and record-label wars.

Finally The Artist appears—and seems a bit surprised to be meeting a stenographer. "Okay," he hesitates with a slight smile, "but that hasn't worked out too well in the past." In a flash he commands her to stay put and whisks me off to a studio control room. Before I can even orient myself, the door slams behind me with an airtight thud.

Even the Cowardly Lion had Dorothy and friends to quiver with. And a place to run.

"I like to start by feeling out a person through conversation," says His Hisness as I begin to scrawl whatever I can in my notebook. "When we talk in here, it's your word against mine. These walls are completely soundproof. I prefer it this way." Still hoping the real interview had yet to begin, I manage a few general questions about the nature of funk, causing The Artist to wax spiritual in his rich but slightly nasal timbre. Finally he bursts forth with a delighted cackle and then pauses to think. "See that? Would words on a page capture my laugh, or the irony in what I just said? I'd much rather you write about the vibe of our conversation, rather than trying to get my exact words so people can analyze them to death. Why do you need to know exactly what I'm saying? How would that make for a better article?"

Do It All Night

The Artist cues up a *Rave Un2 the Joy Fantastic* tune. Hands flying over the board, he solos the drums and bass, which he played on Graham's Moon 4-string (see below). "Hear that? That's the bass sound. I just turn it up full," he says, pantomiming diming all the knobs at once with the edge of a hand. The old Prince bass feel is right there, ghost-notes and vibrato laden with greasy funk. "There's bass all over this record, and it's seriously funky," he adds as he hits stop after only a few bars. "One of the funkiest records of recent years. There's no good funk happening these days. I'm still waiting for George Clinton to do something."

The Artist first picked up bass years after he began playing guitar in 1975—which, in turn, was years after he started playing the family piano. "Bass was a necessity," he confesses. "I needed it to make my first album." Already a solid drummer, he translated his rhythmic chops to the bass, and everything fell into place fairly quickly. "That's the thing about playing both bass and drums—the parts just lock together. Lenny Kravitz is the same way. If you solo his drum part on 'Are You Gonna Go My Way,' it sounds like, hey—he ain't that good. But put everything on top and it comes together. He just gets high on the funk."

So how can a bassist achieve that kind of lock with a live drummer? "I'll tell you how Larry Graham does it: through his relationship with God. Bootsy plays a little behind the beat—the way Mavis Staples sings—but Larry makes the drummer get with him. If he wants to, he can stand up there and go [mimics 16th-note slap line] all night long and never break a sweat." Like the whirling dervishes of Sufi tradition? Exactly. But isn't it possible to create music as deep as Graham's without drawing inspiration from a higher power? "No, it isn't. All things come from God and return to God. I wouldn't say it necessarily needs to come from a higher place—but it does need to come from another place."

Release It

Of course, The Artist is less known for bass than for the controversial eroticism of such early songs as "Head," "Do Me Baby," and "Darling Nikki." Yet it seems many of his more lurid lyrics are backed by bass-heavy arrangements. Is there a connection between the two? "I've never thought about that," he muses with a smile. "But no, there isn't. Bass is primal, and it reminds me of a large posterior—but both spirituality and sexuality originate higher up in the body. I see them as angelic."

The Artist's all-time biggest hit, "When Doves Cry" [*Purple Rain*], is most distinctive because of its lack of a bass line. The song had one but it was pulled at the last minute. "They were almost done editing the movie," he explains, referring to his big-screen debut in *Purple Rain*. "'When Doves Cry' was the last song to be mixed, and it just wasn't sounding right." Prince was sitting with his head on the console listening to a rough mix when one of his singers, Jill Jones, walked in and asked what was wrong. "It was just sounding too conventional, like every other song with drums and bass and keyboards. So I said, 'If I could have it my way it would sound like this,' and I pulled the bass out of the mix. She said, 'Why don't you have it your way?'" From the beginning Prince had an inkling the tune would be better bass-free, even though he hated to see the part go. "Sometimes your brain kind of splits in two—your ego tells you one thing, and the rest of you says something else. You have to go with what you know is right."

So bass can work against a song then? "Not necessarily. 'When Doves Cry' does have bass in it—the bass is in the kick drum. It's the same with 'Kiss' [*Parade*]: The bass is in the tone of the reverb on the kick. Bass is a lot more than that instrument over there. Bass to me means B-A-S-E. B-A-S-S is a fish."

My Name Is Prince

Prince's first four albums were basically one-man efforts, with a few guest spots (though he kept all bass duties to himself). One of the most prolific artists in rock history, he also wrote, produced, and recorded for others—most notably fellow Minneapolis band The Time. In fact he performed nearly all the instrumental parts on the Time's first two records, choosing to take only a production credit under the pseudonym Jamie Starr (which he also used for credits on two of his own records). "I was just getting tired of seeing my name," he explains. "If you give away an idea, you still own that idea. In fact, giving it away strengthens it. Why do people feel they have to take credit for everything they do? Ego—that's the only reason."

He adopted yet another pre-symbol nom de plume, Camille, for "female" sped-up vocal parts. Ever the gender bender, Prince had begun performing in women's undergarments as early as 1979. His opening slot on a Rolling Stones tour, where he was pelted with garbage by disco-hating hooligans, is now part of rock legend. "Don't say that was because of me," he admonishes, wagging a finger. "That was the audience doing that. I'm sure wearing underwear and a trench coat didn't help matters—but if you throw trash at anybody, it's because you weren't trained right at home."

Starting with 1982's *1999*, Prince began crediting a band, the Revolution, on his recordings. Though he still played many of the parts, over the next few albums the Revolution played an increasingly important role. "I wanted community more than anything else. These days if I have Rhonda [S., formerly The Artist's primary live bassist] play on something, she'll bring in her Jaco influence, which is something I wouldn't add if I played it myself. I did listen to Jaco—I love his Joni Mitchell stuff—but I never wanted to play like him." The Artist still raves about the original Revolution bassist, Brown Mark (who took over for Andre Simone), calling him the tightest bass player next to Graham himself.

The latest version of New Power Generation is The Artist's most skilled band to date; in addition to Graham, the group's Mill City Music Festival performance included James Brown saxophonist Maceo Parker, who also has free rein over the Paisley Park facilities for his own projects. Of course, Graham fits seamlessly into New Power Generation—and you can be sure The Artist never needs to tell him to play less and listen more.

The Beautiful Ones

The interview is winding down. With most of my questions answered (or at least chewed up and spit out), I pose another: Of all the bass lines you've created and played over the years, which stands out the most? As if he's answered the query in every interview, he instantly volleys back, "777-9311" (the Time's *What Time Is It?*). Why? "Because nobody can play that line like I can. It's like 'Hair' [1973's *Graham Central Station*, Warner Bros.], or 'Lopsy Lu' [*Stanley Clarke*, Epic]—nobody can play those parts better than Larry and Stanley." I mention I was glad to hear him dig up "Let's Work" for the previous night's show. "Hmmm—that might be a tie with '777.'" The Artist gets up and heads over to the bass sitting in the corner but then waves a hand at it. "Oh, 5-string—a mutant animal." I start to scribble down the quote. "Don't print that! People will say I don't like the 5-string because I can't play it. We do have to keep an open mind to things. We need to be open to evolution."

The Artist picks up a phone receiver and—without dialing—summons Hans-Martin Buff, his engineer, who fetches Graham's white Moon bass. "Now imagine me teaching Larry Graham how to play this," he scoffs as he plugs into the board and lays into the "Let's Work" line. With no rhythm track, his feel isn't quite as slinky as on record, but all the elements are there—subtle ghost-notes, vibrato, funky push-and-pull.

Suddenly he stops and hands me the bass. What? "Let's see what you can do," he says. (Sure am glad I'm not a spy.) As I grab the neck he snatches my notebook and crosses his legs. "Now I'm gonna ask you some questions," he toys. Stalling, I inquire about the xlr jack on the upper horn. "For his mike," he says, as if I needed to ask. I tentatively try out a generic finger-funk groove in A. (I am not going to slap in front of the "Let's Work" guy.) "That's the sound, isn't it?," asks The Artist. The tone is indeed perfect, but aside from the very low action and super-zingy strings, there's nothing terribly magical about the instrument's feel. And of course it sounds like me coming out of the monitors, not Graham. "Do you ever practice?" I ask, handing back the bass. "Do you get rusty when you don't play for a while?" "No," he sighs, almost bored. "Playing is like breathing now."

We get up and start to move to the door. "I was a little worried there at the beginning," he says. "But it wasn't that bad, was it?" And I'm out of there—but not before one last awkward moment as I shake his hand, unsure how to address him. "It was very interesting. Thank you. Um, yeah—thanks." Hoo-boy.

Beginning to sweat, I try to explain I had planned a Q&A in which I'd ask very specific, technical questions that would interest only other musicians—in a context where bassists would want to absorb every word. "Then ask me something," he replies. "Ask me any question on that list of yours, and we'll see what happens."

Skipping my planned opening query, I quick-search the page for the most technical question I can find. "Okay. Do you have a tone recipe for great funk bass?"

Without a pause: "Larry Graham. Larry Graham is my teacher." The Artist continues, veering quickly away from funk tone to God, to all of us being connected by the Spirit—but just as suddenly he claps his hands sharply, jumps up from his seat, and bellows a joyful noise. "Why do you need a stenographer to type out 'Larry Graham'? That's my answer to your question—it is all you need to know. Just write down 'Larry Graham' in your notebook!"

Time to find that man behind the curtain.

The Artist's gaze shifts slightly sidelong. "Why do you want a witness, anyway? This isn't a deposition." A pause. "Are you a spy?" he asks with a sly smile. "Who sent you here? What did you do before you worked for this magazine? Are you working for someone else? Did somebody put something in your ear?"

Resisting an urge to flee, I try to think of something—anything—to settle myself and keep the interview intact. "Okay. No stenographer then. But the least I can do is go out there and tell her she's free to leave."

"Fine," says The Artist with a flick of his hand, turning toward the massive console. "I'll be right here."

When I return less than a minute later, he's singing into a mike poised over the board.

"There," he purrs as I sit back down, hoping some color is returning to my face. "Now we can have a conversation."

Nothing Compares 2 U

Things went much smoother once I had been paisley-whipped into shape. Yet it seemed no matter what I asked, the conversation turned to either God, Larry Graham, or both—The Artist freely admitting he modeled his bass style after Graham's. Prince first briefly met the slap pioneer at a Warner Bros. company picnic in 1978, by which time Larry had moved on from Sly & the Family Stone and was a star in his own right fronting Graham Central Station. The two met again a few years later, this time at a Nashville jam. "Larry's wife came up to him and pulled an effects box and cord out of her purse," The Artist remembers warmly. "Now that's love." But Graham and the man he calls "Little Brother" didn't develop a real relationship until the '90s—"relationship" perhaps being an inadequate description. "Here's a guy who has a brother hug for you every day," says The Artist. "And once Larry taught me The Truth, everything changed. My agoraphobia went away. I used to have nightmares about going to the mall, with everyone looking at me strange. No more." The couple forged an ocean-deep spiritual connection—The Artist is a Seventh Day Adventist, Graham a Jehovah's Witness. "I mean, Larry still goes around knocking on doors telling people The Truth. You don't see me doing that!"

The Artist invited his "older brother" to Minneapolis, set him up with a house of his own, and welcomed him into the Paisley Park family, "signing" him to a handshake-based deal with NPG Records. Before long Graham was playing with The Artist's band New Power Generation and feasting Graham Central Station on Paisley's incredible rehearsal and studio facilities. And ever since, after years of always picking up the bass for at least a few numbers per set, The Artist has hardly touched the instrument onstage. "I can't even physically reach for it anymore," he laughs. Why? "I don't know. I hope it's out of respect for Larry, and not because I feel inadequate compared to him."

Baby I'm A Star

The night before our interview, New Power Generation and GCS co-headlined the last night of the Mill City Music Festival, a kind of Woodstock-in-a-parking-lot in Minneapolis's warehouse district. The Artist's performance was as energetic as any '80s Prince show, the only down moments coming with his between-song proselytizing and boasting. "People say to me, 'Congratulations on your new [record] deal' But they ought to go find the president of the record company and congratulate him!" Years ago that would have been a sure cheer line—but on this night the mostly 30-something crowd stood reserved, waiting for the next "Let's Go Crazy" or "U Got the Look" sprinkled among the newer, unfamiliar tunes. Later The Artist reclined on a riser and pouted, "You might love Larry Graham, and you might love Morris Day—but you don't love me!"

Yet The Artist has plenty to say about the dangers of ego in a musical context. "My first bass player was Andre Cymone," he remembers, "and Andre's ego always got in the way of his playing. He always played on top of the beat, and I'm convinced that was just because he wanted to be heard. Andre and I would fight every night, because I was always trying to get him to sound like Larry Graham. Larry's happy just going [mimics thumping open-string quarter-notes]—he's not interested in showing off. When you're showing off it means you aren't listening." The Artist shifts gears to describe a present-day rehearsal and grows excited again. "Space!" he bellows. "Space is what it's all about. I'm always telling people in rehearsal you've got to shut up once in a while. Solo spotlights are fun and everything, but if you make music people want to hear, they'll keep that tape. You can listen to one groove all night, but if everyone's playing all over the place all night and not hearing each other—not respecting the music—ain't nobody gonna want to listen."

Housequakin'

The Artist currently owns eight basses, according to his tech, Takumi (who also works for Larry Graham). When he picks up a bass onstage, he favors his white Warwick Thumb "Eye Bass" (so named because of the eye painted on the front), a white fretless Warwick Thumb, or his custom Lakland with a fist-shaped headstock. Other basses include an old Guild Pilot and a gold-colored Ibanez Soundgear. And even though he's not likely to need it, The Artist has Takumi set up his bass rig at every show, just in case the spirit moves him to strap on a 4-string. Takumi covers up the rig onstage and doesn't reveal any further details about it, since The Artist doesn't endorse equipment.

The Artist plays bass on nearly all of the *Rave Un2 the Joy Fantastic* tracks. (Rhonda S. appears on two songs.) For most of his parts The Artist used Graham's Moon bass with Bartolini pickups; when the Moon was unavailable he used the Warwick Eye Bass. Engineer Hans-Martin Buff ran the signal into an Avalon U5 active DI, either a Demidio or Neve mike preamp, a Summit Audio compressor, and sometimes an API 550 EQ. The Artist rarely mikes a bass amp in the studio. The only bass effects on the record are a Zoom 9030 (usually on its "slap wah" setting) and a Danelectro Fab Tone pedal for fuzz.

Chapter Forty-Seven

NEW YORK TIMES INTERVIEW PRINCE BY ANTHONY DE CURTIS—1999

NEW YORK—THE artist formerly known as Prince leaned forward, pointed to my notebook and raised his voice. "I'm not going to be on 'Behind the Music,'" he asserted. "Will you please say that?" It's a demand in the guise of a question. And he was laughing, but he was also dead serious.

It's not that the Artist—the tag by which he's come to be known, for convenience as much as metaphoric resonance—doesn't watch the popular VH1 series himself. As he sat in a lounge at Electric Lady Sound Studios in Greenwich Village, he cited chapter and verse of shows about Hammer, TLC and Lenny Kravitz—all, significantly, African-American artists who, like him, have had run-ins with the music industry. It's just that he has no patience for the show's inevitable 12-step-derived emotional arc: Performer enjoys huge success and gets ego-crazy; performer makes, then ruefully acknowledges, enormous personal and professional mistakes; performer makes amends and, chastened, moves on.

The Artist, who is now 41, views his life in nothing remotely like those terms. He may have spent much of this decade engaged in an excruciatingly public battle to free himself from Warner Brothers Records, the label that in 1992 negotiated a deal with him that was reported to be worth as much as $100 million. He may have disowned all the albums he made as Prince—including such masterpieces as "Dirty Mind," "Purple Rain" and "Sign 'O' the Times"—and sworn that he will re-record his entire catalog to deprive Warner Brothers of royalties. He may have painted the word "slave" on his face and changed his name to an unpronounceable symbol. And, despite having once been one of pop music's biggest stars, he may have spent the last three years releasing music exclusively—and extensively—on his own independent label, NPG Records, and through his Web site. "I don't even know how many albums I've made now," he said coolly.

Yes, all that may be true, but the Artist is absolutely unrepentant. On Nov. 2 he will release a new album, "Rave Un2 the Joy Fantastic," through an arrangement with Arista Records. It is his first association with a major label since he put out the three-CD set "Emancipation" (1996) through a similar agreement with EMI Records, which subsequently went out of business. (Warner Brothers, which dissolved its contract with the Artist in 1996, has also just released an album of Prince outtakes titled "The Vault . . . Old Friends 4 Sale." The CD's notes include a disclaimer that the "enclosed material . . . was originally intended 4 private use only.") "Rave" will be introduced at a listening party in New York for the international media—and the Arista sales force—on Saturday. The first single, a powerful ballad called "The Greatest Romance Ever Sold," will be released on Sept. 22, and the Artist will make a video to accompany it. "I will be touring to promote this album—definitely," he said, and the tour will be extensive and international. He tapped Gwen Stefani of No Doubt and the rapper Chuck D. for cameos on the album. He has even announced that while he remains the Artist Formerly Known as Prince, "Rave," surprisingly enough, was produced by none other than Prince.

Asked if these developments signal a comeback of sorts, the Artist shot back, "A comeback from what?" As far as he is concerned, his way of going about things has not changed at all since his chart-dominating days of the mid-80's. "'We want you to do this. We want you to do that'—I've had people talk to me like that. And loud," he said. "'Everybody has to answer to someone,' they'd tell me." His sense of insult—and, again, his voice—rose. "I'd say, 'I answer to God, fool.'"

Clive Davis, the renowned founder and chief executive of Arista and a no-nonsense industry veteran, is betting that "Rave" will please Mammon as well as God.

While he has supported outsiders like the Grateful Dead and Patti Smith, Davis is best known as a hit maker, a man with sharp commercial instincts and ambitions. Most recently, he signed the guitarist Carlos Santana—one of the Artist's idols—to Arista, helped produce his new album, "Supernatural," and guided him to the Top 10 for the first time in decades.

Typically, the Artist professes no awareness of Davis' relationship with Santana or anything else about Davis' career. "I knew nothing about him," he said simply, explaining that their meeting came about at the suggestion of L. Londell McMillan, the Artist's business partner. "But he knows me. We agreed that the album is full of hits. It was just a question of whether or not we would agree on how it should be put out."

And, the Artist added, Davis "agreed that I own the master tapes"—a crucial issue in the Artist's war with Warner Brothers.

For his part, Davis has long wanted to work with the Artist, and he is determined to make "Rave" a success. Indeed, when Davis speaks about the Artist, "rave" is the operative word. "This is a poet, a renaissance man, an iconoclast," Davis said. "This is someone who is bringing the state of music further and further along. I don't want to get involved in whether this is hype or not—the man is at the top of his form. He's coming back peak. I don't think it's an accident that the album is produced by Prince. That says it right there."

But that says what, exactly? Davis comes gently down to earth.

"Look, you're never going to pin him down on something like that," he said with a laugh. "He said with a twinkle in his eye that Prince has always been his favorite producer, and he was the right person for this project. There certainly have been hits associated with Prince. But whether it's the Artist Formerly Known as or the production of Prince, it works."

It would be easy to be skeptical about Davis' enthusiasm, but the undeniable fact is that, regardless of his commercial fortunes, the Artist still holds a great degree of allure among both executives and performers in the music industry. Label honchos often take their ability to work successfully with eccentric artists as a point of pride, and the Artist has no equal in that regard. Performers, meanwhile, view him as the epitome of an artist's Artist, a man who creates whenever and however the mood strikes him and who plays by nobody else's rules.

That the Artist carries himself, both on stage and off, with instinctive rock-star hauteur doesn't hurt either. "He's splendid, he's sumptuous, oh my God, he's so striking," said Ani DiFranco, another rebel artist, who plays guitar on one track on "Rave." "Being someone who also lives in her own world and makes a ridiculous amount of records, just to watch him work was fascinating. Any instrument he picks up, he speaks through. He's an example of the ability to keep being inspired by your life. Also, he's sexy. I certainly haven't been immune!"

Sheryl Crow also appears on the new album, singing and playing harmonica on a ballad titled "Baby Knows." "It's not only his ability to play so many instruments, it's the level at which he plays them," said Ms. Crow of the Artist, who plays virtually all the instruments on "Rave." "I've heard him play piano like Chick Corea or Herbie Hancock, move over to bass and play like Larry Graham, then play guitar like Jimi Hendrix or Buddy Guy. He's written some of the most amazing songs ever. And the main impression I was left with is that he really loves what he does."

Dressed entirely in black save for his yellow, ankle-length, high-heeled boots, the matching gold trim on his beret and the gold pendant with the symbol that is his name hanging around his neck, the Artist was putting the final touches on his album at Electric Lady, which was built by Jimi Hendrix, another of his heroes. His wife, Mayte, sat nearby. The Artist's distrust of contracts extends to their marriage bonds, which they have mutually dissolved, though they remain a couple. "We read them over, and there were a lot things in there we didn't like," the Artist casually explained, referring to the marriage documents they signed in 1996. Any further consequences of that decision remain unspecified. Mayte currently lives in Spain, while he continues to live in his hometown, Minneapolis.

At first the Artist was reluctant to let me hear any of the album or even to reveal the titles of the songs. "I'm tripping on that; when I listen, I prefer not knowing what the titles are," he said.

Then, as I was about to leave a couple of hours later, he asked, almost shyly: "Would you like to hear some of it? I'd hate to have you go without hitting you with something." In the studio's control room, he played sections of four songs at such crushing volume that a rubber fish sitting on top of a speaker fell off because of the shaking. The Artist can't be still while the music is playing, so every few seconds he came over and shouted commentary into my ear. He was speaking as loudly as he could, but I could barely hear him.

One sentence came through loud and clear, however. "Tell me that's not a hit," he insisted as the swelling choruses and Arabic scales of "The Greatest Romance Ever Sold" washed over us. I turned to look at him. His chest was puffed out and he was smiling. His hips and shoulders were moving. But in his dark eyes, beneath the bravado, there was a vulnerability he refused to acknowledge, as well as a hope that the answer would be what he needed to hear.

Chapter Forty-Eight

MINNEAPOLIS STAR TRIBUNE INTERVIEW PRINCE BY VICKIE GILMER—1999

AT HIS PAISLEY Park studio, Prince is a gracious tour guide. He escorts a visitor through his wardrobe room, his rehearsal space, his studio, making introductions to his musicians and wife, Mayte, and pausing to pet bassist Larry Graham's Maltese dog, who nips at his heels.

But when it comes to talking about his music, he pauses. He talks about records he likes—James Brown and the old-school sound of certain hip-hop recordings—and his desire to sell software of samples of his music. But it seems he'd rather just shut up and play.

"It's been a great year for me," he says. He has a new record, "Rave Un2 the Joy Fantastic," to be released in November on Arista Records. And he's preparing to take the stage Monday at the Mill City Music Festival—his first-ever outdoor performance in his hometown.

"There will be special guests—very interesting people—and a lot of surprises," he promised Wednesday. We'll play one song from the new album and we'll probably do a Sheryl Crow cover. 'Pretty Man' is the new song that I originally wrote for the Time [who also are playing Monday], but it was so good I kept it. In fact, I wish I had kept some other songs I gave them. I wish I had kept 'Cool' or at least still had one like it," he adds, laughing.

The new album features Crow—with whom Prince jammed recently in Toronto—Chuck D of Public Enemy, saxophonist Maceo Parker, Gwen

Stefani of No Doubt, and indie singer/song writer Ani DiFranco. Prince long has been an admirer of DiFranco, a pioneer in setting up her own record company.

"I wanted to meet Ani DiFranco and, lo and behold, she's everything I expected," he says. "We jammed for four hours and she danced the whole time. We had to quit because she wore us out. After being with her, it dawned on me why she's like that—she's never had a ceiling over her. People want to put ceilings on you or people think they have ceilings over them. We don't come here [Paisley] to be put in a box."

Querying him about the motives behind his art seems to demean the funky, butt-shaking synergy inherent in it. It's all about sound and feeling, not definitions of why or how. And as the Artist—a name he says he adopted out of necessity to distance himself from the media hype that depersonalized his given name—he wants to talk of "the Truth."

It's a Truth with a capital "T" because it's tied to his spirituality; it's what he lives day in and day out. It's also a Truth that he doesn't think a lot of people understand, and he tried to explain why he wants to look forward rather than back.

"I know that people want to talk about the past," he says. "But we're not at 'Purple Rain' anymore. We don't look like that, we don't dress like that, we're different people now. If you talk about that, the next thing you know, people start writing things like the Revolution is going to reunite!

"I can't really tell you why I decided to do things or play Mill City, because they're decisions in the past and to go back and try to remember why I agreed to things before is difficult. I am living in today and looking forward," he said.

A degree of separation

He's not ready to let outsiders listen to the new record, but the Artist talked about his decision to enlist an outside producer: someone by the name of Prince.

Making that distinction was a way to draw a line between the performer standing in front of the control booth and the person sitting inside it.

"You do have to mentally divorce yourself. And when you do allow yourself to have a 'different' producer on an album, I allowed him to have the final say. As strange as that may sound, it's really not strange. Look at it this way: Malcolm X thinks differently than Malcolm Little [Malcolm's birth name]. When you're trying to change, you have to divorce yourself from the past."

Because Arista will distribute "Rave Un2 the Joy Fantastic," it's been trumpeted as his return to a major label after his much-publicized departure from Warner Bros. Records and his recent effort to sell CDs via the Internet. But Prince makes it clear that this is not the kind of traditional relationship between musicians and labels with a lengthy contract that sets boundaries as to what each party will or won't do.

"People are looking for drama in it. It's for one album. There could be a second. The contract is [only] this thick," he said, holding his forefinger and thumb millimeters apart.

"When I was at Warner Bros., I always heard from a third party," he said. But Prince met directly with Arista's president, Clive Davis. "Record companies want to own their creations, but no one owns the creation but the creator. It's an actual ideology and Clive agrees you should own your masters. He also told me, 'I have free will, too.' Which was good that he said that to me."

Prince's belabored battles with Warner Bros. have made him a staunch advocate for artists' rights. And he holds the same ideal for all artists.

He's helped release albums by Chaka Khan and Graham—best known as bassist for Sly and the Family Stone—allowing them use of his studios and distribution through his NPG Records without all the restrictions involved in most recording contracts.

He says all artists should have the same right to own their master recordings that he now does. He laments the "mental and emotional" abuse that musicians such as Phoebe Snow have suffered at the hands of an industry that's made them captives by not releasing their work. He applauds the work of Jimmy Jam and Terry Lewis and gripes about the low "points" (percentage of record sales) that most musicians receive.

He and Mayte have founded a charitable organization that has donated money to various organizations, including the Rhythm & Blues Foundation, which provides help to musicians, and he's donated instruments through Mill City's Music Cares program to the Minneapolis school district.

He's also gotten inspiration from some of his new collaborators. "Chuck D. and I talked about hip-hop and how we have to knock down what they value, and the dollar bill is nothing to put a value on . . . . What I would like to see is the spiritual aspect come back in to the inner city. It's very important that people realize that we're in a situation that only God can fix at this point."

His beliefs—spiritually, musically and professionally—make him animated. He jumps up to make a point, cites biblical references that drive home his spiritual beliefs and exalts the positive influence of those around him.

Clearly, there's a lot of Truth to be told, and he wants to know that you "feel" what he's saying, because it's not just words, he says—it's a way of life.

"I implore you to realize that I'm perfectly healthy and happy. My wife and I, you can see nobody's kicked her out. We decided to do this whole thing together. The main course is spiritual well-being. My protection comes from my faith in God. I know I'm going to be all right."

He stands and offers an invitation to sit in on his rehearsal. In the room, it's obvious he's happy, as are those around him. He smiles as the group runs through "Let's Go Crazy," breaks out laughing when one of his back-up singers comes in too early on the chorus for "Kiss" and drills home the groovy rhythm of "U Got the Look" and other songs he'll play in concert.

After a quick 20-minute drill, he walks his guest to the door. As Mayte showed him a magazine article on their new home in Spain that she's working on, you don't need to be persuaded that Prince is healthy, happy and, above all, all right.

Chapter Forty-Nine

USA TODAY INTERVIEW PRINCE
BY STEVE JONES
APRIL 13, 1999

NEW YORK—TWO years after severing ties to the record industry, The Artist is considering dipping a toe back into it—but only on a limited basis and only if it's on his terms.

Since leaving Warner Bros. in 1995 and ending a distribution deal with now-defunct EMI Records in 1997, The Artist has successfully marketed a constant stream of music via the Internet and other avenues.

But he's hoping to put out his next album—*Rave Un2 the Joy Fantastic*—on a major label as long as he retains ownership of the master tapes.

"The title track is one I did 12 years ago, but it sounded so much like *Kiss* that I wanted to put it in the vault and let it marinate for a while," he says, holding court in a suite in the Trump International hotel.

He hasn't decided on a release date but says the album will include some surprising collaborations—and, for the first time in his 21-year career, he'll let somebody else produce him, although he won't say who.

"This business is really structured and rigid, and I had to get outside of it to see things differently and to see the effect it has on your psyche," he says of possibly working again with the companies he fought so hard to get away from.

"Now it's like going back to school and knowing that you don't have to stay."

Not that he's about to get himself back into the situation that had him writing "slave" on his face during his battle to get out of his contract with Warner Bros.

"This is the best time of my life," he says. "It's like the awakening you get when you are at the top of the mountain looking down instead of being on the side or at the bottom and not seeing everything. Record companies expect artists to lose their voice, their hair and their energy, and I'm not doing any of that."

The 40-year-old vegan, whose Web site (love4oneanother.com) mixes commentary on the industry, race relations, spiritualism and a wide range of other topics, is a crusader for artists' rights.

Though his albums sell only a fraction of the multiplatinum numbers he once did with the likes of *1999*, *Purple Rain* and *Sign 'O' the Times*, his direct-marketing approach through his NPG Records gives him a much fatter profit margin.

He sold 250,000 copies (at $50 a pop) of the five-CD vault-scouring collection *Crystal Ball* without the benefit of video or radio play but didn't have to share the profit with a record company or have to wait months to get royalty payments.

"It only costs $2 to press a CD, and then people will go to the store and pay $13," he says. "Our only additional cost is the shipping. And then most of my money goes into helping other artists."

Good friends and R&B legends Larry Graham (*GCS 2000*) and Chaka Khan (*Come 2 My House*), who were featured on his *New Power Soul* album last year, put out some of their best work in years on NPG, and The Artist gave them free use of his studios and full ownership of the albums. He says recording contracts aren't even necessary.

"If we did have one, what would it say? That I agree to pay you on time?"

He says he tried unsuccessfully to buy the rights to his 26 Warner Bros. albums, but he's doing everything he can to cash in on his previous work.

"Once Warners refused to sell me my masters, I was faced with a problem," he says. "But 'pro' is the prefix of problem, so I decided to do something about it."

The first step was February's *1999—The New Master*, seven re-creations to compete with the classic version of his 1983 song, which will obviously be getting an inordinate amount of attention this year. This fall, he's releasing a seven-CD collection of samples of his vintage songs that DJs and recording artists can use without paying clearance fees.

He says he never liked the fact that people who had nothing to do with his music profited whenever it was sampled.

"I had former managers coming to me, wanting money, when Hammer did *Pray* because he sampled *When Doves Cry*. They said it was in the contract I'd had with them."

He says other artists can follow his lead in using the Internet and other technology to create an alternative system that will put more money in their pockets and keep them from paying the "slew of managers, executives, radio DJs and promotion people that they have to go through now."

But even with that freedom, he still has to stay vigilant.

In February, he sued nine Web sites for copyright and trademark infringements, saying they were offering bootleg records and unauthorized downloads. He also sued Swedish publisher Uptown Productions, charging it with unauthorized use of photographs and the unpronounceable symbol to which he changed his name from Prince in 1993, as well as the unauthorized sale of biographies and a CD-ROM.

"Telling people where to buy and sell bootlegs and using my symbols is diminishing our own sales," he says. "We are not seeking damages so much as we just want them to stop. A fanzine is one thing, but when they are actually trying to sell your work, that is something else."

Chapter Fifty

ENTERTAINMENT WEEKLY INTERVIEW PRINCE
BY TOM SINCLAIR
MAY 28, 1999

EW Online: How did rock & roll change the world?

The Artist: Any time truth is recognized, whether it's in art, music, media, it changes consciousness. When people hear freedom in the music that we record, that's change. But few people had the creative control that I've had right from the beginning, to produce myself and to put out double, triple, even five-record sets.

Is rock finally dead?

Real music—God-given music—won't fade. Look at Lauryn Hill. I wore her record out. And Jonny Lang—that's a kid who takes pride in what he does. It has to do with vibrations and God. If you get into God, if you love and respect all things equally, what comes out of you musically will emulate that. A kid with a spiritual foundation can figure out the truth.

Talk about your influences.

Carlos Santana. Jimi Hendrix. James Brown, of course. On piano, I was influenced by my father, who was influenced by Duke Ellington and Thelonius Monk. I like to say I took from the best.

What would you say was *Purple Rain*'s overall impact?

In some ways, it was more detrimental than good. That's a very complex question. People's perception of me changed after that, and it pigeonholed me. I saw kids coming to concerts who screamed just because that's where the audience screamed in the movie. That's why I did "Around the World in a Day," to totally change that. I wanted not to be pigeonholed.

What do you think about the prefabricated-teen-pop phenomenon?

Prefabricated—that's exactly it. You've got to look at who's in control. Don't talk bad about Britney Spears, because somebody is doing this [he makes puppeteer gestures] with her. It's all about the money.

Who best exemplifies the spirit of rock & roll?

Patti LaBelle. I played a show with her, and her keyboard player had just died of cancer. She was wrecked, but she came out and gave her all. A lot of people around her have died of cancer in the past few years, but she keeps on keepin' on. *That's* rock & roll. All this other stuff—pppsheww.

What was the moment when you most hated being a rock & roll performer?

Never. I've loved making music and touring from the get-go. It's kind of what I was made for.

Chapter Fifty-One

REVIEWS OF 3121

Rolling Stone Magazine Review
By Robert Christgau
Subject: Prince 3121 (Universal)

THE RADDEST SONG on the second consecutive album to reassert Prince's funk bona fides is arresting in part because it's so unassuming. Spare bass and drums, then an acoustic-sounding guitar, catchier synth and a conversational vocal with a devilishly hooky street-chant shape—not futuristic, but definitely not trad. The rad part is a lyric that explicitly invites us to "get saved." Christ is never mentioned, but Prince's talk of "new exaltation" and "streets of gold" can't be rationalized away as sex talk. More than any Kirk Franklin or Stevie Wonder number, "The Word" makes religiosity sound hip.

Doing his best to reassure fans who think their souls are fine, thank you, Prince doesn't abjure sex talk on *3121*. But the famed Lothario turns down the ID-needing "Lolita": "What do you want?" "Whatever you want," she saucily replies. "Then come on, let's dance." She's shocked: "Dance???" The greasy organ R&B of "Satisfied" "ain't talking about nothing physical." And "Incense and Candles" turns on an unusual entreaty: "I know you want to take off all your clothes/But please don't do it."

As Prince well knows, however, these songs are erotic regardless—more recognizably than those on 2004's *Musicology*, where he turned down yet another hottie in "What Do U Want Me 2 Do?" That's because lyrics always come second for the most gifted popular musician of our era—amid the keepers are bad poetry you ignore on tracks you can't get enough of. As on *Musicology*, the beats get pretty wicked here—wildly canted, eccentric, exciting. But while *3121* is no funkier than *Musicology*, it does emphasize speedier tempos and, two nods to Zapp aside, more conventional sonics. Guitars and synths tend toward the middle registers: "Fury" is a slightly grander rewrite of the indelible "U Got the Look." This is all reassuringly normal for fans put off by the artist's recent forays into jazz and such. Anyway, Prince leaves no doubt that he's still interested in sex. He can resist temptation, if that's what gets him through the night. We don't have to. And we can still dance together. Right?

BILLBOARD Review
By Clover Hope

Prince is one of those rare artists who can remain relevant without compromising his eccentric style. Though his last few albums have been less than stellar, "3121" is a testament to the singer's versatility and musicianship. The 12-track set runs the gamut from uptempo pop ("Fury") to steamy R&B ("Incense and Candles"). It also finds Prince revisiting racier themes, as on the bluesy bedroom ballad "Satisfied" and the guitar-driven "Lolita," a potential pop hit about affection for a younger woman. While "Black Sweat" is too erratic, live instrumentation is celebrated as usual (saxman Maceo Parker graces "Get on the Boat"). Despite several lukewarm tracks, "3121" proves that Prince has not lost his luster and could very well return him to the top of the charts

Entertainment Weekly Review
Raymond Fiore
March 24, 2006
Subject: PRINCE *3121* (Universal)

When Prince staged a colorful 2004 resurrection (*Musicology* "sold" over 2 million copies, thanks to an ingenious ploy of bundling a CD with every ticket purchased for that year's top-grossing concert tour), he achieved something resembling renewed cultural relevance. Playing mostly smashes from his prolific career and impressing a new generation with his enviable instrumental chops, the tour made a convincing case for why the art of showmanship sans pricey effects and grotesque production numbers should be preserved. And two decades past his commercial peak, Prince also proved that there's still no other artist who can simultaneously captivate and baffle an arena with such an arresting arsenal of humor, charisma, weirdness, and undeniable talent.

But lest there be any confusion, the masses were actually celebrating a peerless stage performer and combustible musical force, not the return to form of an ex-hitmaker. *Musicology* hardly constituted a bona fide comeback disc; its derivative, retro-tinged tunes barely made a squeak at radio, and simply buckled in concert when sandwiched between classics like "Kiss" and "Let's Go Crazy." Apologies, O Purple One—having once raised the pop-music bar means you get away with less than the rest.

And so comes his umpteenth disappointment—*3121*, a messier, more self-indulgent affair than its predecessor. At least *Musicology* had a coherent point to prove: that Prince could make real music with real instruments as the old-soul masters—and he—used to. Sonically, this new disc feels like a random sampling of 12 tracks from his unedited unconscious. Zigzagging from a distorted synth-funk groove on the title track to the abominably boring slow-dance "Te Amo Corazón" to the Muscle Shoals-style gospel-blues of "Satisfied," it finds Prince striking his familiarly cocky I-Can-Do-It-All pose.

Only he can't do it all anymore, at least not on record. While his electro-soul stylings are regularly referenced by the likes of OutKast and the Neptunes, Prince hasn't figured out how to reach back into his '80s bag of tricks and create something that feels contemporary in the way those disciples have. Instead, tracks that might have rocked in 1986, like the guitar-heavy romp "Fury," feel perilously caught in a time warp somewhere between cool-dated and wack-modern. Only the new single "Black Sweat" does a laudable job of referencing O.G. Prince while still reminding the industry's young 'uns that he's got more mojo in just one of his meticulously plucked eyebrows than all of them combined.

But that's not to imply said young 'uns couldn't help him make something truly great. Maybe let Andre 3000 and the Roots' ?uestlove put some sizzle on those used-to-be-fresh, middle-aged-man beats. Because when left alone with his own limitless potential, Prince can't resist getting in his own way, as evidenced by "The Dance," an overblown

Latin-shuffle melodrama loaded with every superfluous bell, whistle, clap, and string sound at his disposal. And while the song climaxes in some passionate, cord-shredding screams that recall *Purple Rain*'s orgasmic symphony "The Beautiful Ones," it's a contrived moment. One that epitomizes why *3121*'s tired tracks aren't worthy of Prince's prodigious gifts. C+

The Times UK
By Pete Paphides
4 stars (out of 5)

In the Sixties, when record companies thought nothing of squeezing two albums a year from their artists, the music industry benefited rampantly productive artists. As such, it didn't seem incredible that, during a period in 1967, the Beatles released the *Strawberry Fields Forever/Penny Lane* double A-side, *Sgt Pepper* and *All You Need is Love*.

Back in those days, no one dreamed of likening major record labels to slave-drivers. When Prince made the analogy, writing "slave" on his face at the 1995 Brits, it was hard not to smile at the irony. Interviewed at the time, the singer criticised a record company that refused to put out his records when he wanted them released, citing "market saturation" in their defence. They wanted him to slow down, but Prince's work-rate defied the notion. By the end of the decade he was hawking CDs over the web to a dwindling fan base.

With hindsight, it's easier to see both sides. When supply outstrips demand—whether it be Crazy Frog merchandise, solo projects by ex-members of Blue or noodly treatises on cosmic sexuality by once-great Minneapolis monoliths—people's interest inevitably wanes. Perhaps it's something that he has belatedly come around to realising. Two years after the patchy *Escapology* he sounds like a man set on arresting his commercial decline.

At last month's Brits performance he adhered to the first rule of commercial rehabilitation: the best way to get people interested in your new stuff is to mix it with the old. So along with a honey-dripping *Purple Rain* and a rousing *Let's Go Crazy*, we got a balmy, Santana-esque newie, *Te Amo Corazón*, and *Fury*. If the latter sounded familiar, that's because its synth riff first appeared as the chorus of *Boys and Girls* in 1986.

It's not the only time you suspect that Prince has been perusing his back pages for inspiration. Black Sweat, more of an erotic mood piece than a song, sees its creator deploy a trick its creator first used to thrilling effect on *When Doves Cry*: forgoing bass for space, in which his priapic falsetto gets busy over a primitive robot groove.

The levity that seems to permeate almost every track here is unmistakable. On the title track he's cast as a pygmy pied piper of funk, supplying helium harmonies over a moreishly sluggish rhythm: "You can come if you want/But you can never leave."

He also wants us to know that he may be dirty but he still has standards. In *Lolita* he ventures into the same treacherous terrain as Björn from Abba when he wrote the belief-beggaringly bad *Does Your Mother Know*. The 48-year-old singer rebuffs the advances of his teenage muse, but where the Swede came a cropper Prince prevails with prizewinning couplets such as: "You're much too young to peep my stash/ You're trying to write cheques your body can't cash."

Better still is *The Word*, a lithe, locomotive call to arms against unspecific satanic forces, in which Prince intones: "Get up, come on, Let's do something" over a sinuous acoustic loop.

He's still practically peerless when he's funky; less so when he's soppy. As such, it's no coincidence that the two skippable songs on *3121* merge to form one sloppy suite. *Beautiful Loved and Blessed*—a ploddingly generic duet with his current purple protégé Tamar—is just the kind of joyless soul ballad that made Prince such hard work through most of the Nineties.

And while you have to admire his insistence on playing everything himself, Prince's Claydermanesque plinking on *The Dance* does little to stop the song resembling the incidental music you might hear when a postcoital James Bond pours himself a cognac.

But, of course, there's no telling a control freak. He has to learn his own lessons. And Prince's 25th album portrays an artist learning to make peace with his past without turning into his own tribute act. If the generous proliferation of tunes on here is anything to go by, Prince has freed himself from a more pernicious form of self-inflicted slavery. Which can only be good news for all of us.

New York Times
By Jon Pareles
Subject: Prince "3121" (Universal)

Prince doesn't sing any complicated messages on his new album, "3121." He has his perennial topics in mind: love, partying and sex (monogamous now that he has declared himself a Jehovah's Witness), with some salvation on the side. It's a friendly, happy, concise album, clocking in under 54 minutes and just about always putting the funk in the foreground. But within the grooves, Prince enjoys some sly musical games. It's not what he says, but what he plays, that gives the songs their snap.

When Prince went fully independent in 1996, his first impulse was to pour out all the music he made: triple and quadruple albums, cover versions, Internet-only songs, instrumentals. But since 1999 he also has been making deals with the major conglomerates, one album at a time, and giving them some of what they want: songs that reaffirm his gift for pop hooks and that also deliberately stir memories of his 1980's hits. With any luck the new songs could sound familiar enough to reach a generation raised on sampled 1970's and 80's R&B. He reaches back to "1999," for instance, in "Fury," a tale of pop ambition and parted lovers.

Yet he's experimenting too, perhaps goaded by atonal liberties of hip-hop. Working alone in the studio, Prince becomes the opposite of his onstage self. Instead of working in real time with live instruments, he goes for a dizzying mix of the handmade and the surreal. "Black Sweat" is an electronic maze of claps and bass thrusts with a whistling, sliding synthesizer high above, while the murky P-Funk vamp of the song "3121" carries dissonant distorted guitars and voices that have been sped up and slowed down. When Prince proselytizes in "The Word," the track is a shifty mixture of staccato acoustic guitar, washes of string sound, a lone saxophone, simmering electronic sounds and clipped percussion.

Meanwhile, when he's not being futuristic, his music holds a history of soul. "Satisfied" is an old-fashioned falsetto ballad, complete with horn section, "Get on the Boat" mixes James Brown funk with salsa, and "The Dance" builds up to an orchestral supper-club bolero.

Prince has done some careful ethical balancing to square his old lascivious self with his openly devout one, and on "3121" he shows his sense of humor about it. He's still a seducer, but one with boundaries. In "Lolita," he's tempted by a young girl, yet insists, "you'll never make a cheater out of me"; then he starts a call and response, asking, "What you wanna do?" She responds, teasingly, "Whatever you want," but when he says, "Then come on, let's dance," she says, with disdain and disbelief, "Dance?" Still, Prince understands what made him a star, and he's not giving it up. "I'm hot and I don't care who knows it," he declares in "Black Sweat," then immediately gets pragmatic: "I got a job to do."

Star Tribune Review
By Jon Bream
Subject: Prince, "3121" (Universal)

"3121," like Prince's last album with a four-digit title ("1999"), is a party record. Like that 1983 project, this one is fun, although not as groundbreakingly fresh or as consistently exciting.

We knew what the song "1999" was all about. It's not clear what the significance of "3121" is. (I hear it's the address of his Los Angeles home.) The title song, which opens the disc, is a dense dance jam inviting you to a party: "U can come if U want to/But U can never leave." Sounds like shades of "Hotel California."

Prince is clearly in a different head space for "3121" than he was on "Musicology," 2004's strikingly mature celebration of marriage and monogamy. He seems less focused and less happy this time. In fact, he sounds a little horny, but, despite his R-rated thoughts, his lyrics are strictly PG.

"Lolita," the playful second track, is a little suggestive but no more so than any similar come-on by the Time. The album's best numbers, "Black Sweat" and "Satisfied," are sexy but hardly risqué by Purple standards.

"Black Sweat," the current single, is slinky synth funk, a spare electronic workout oozing with Prince's most emotional vocals. His "oohs" on this number provide some of the most thrilling moments on the album.

"Satisfied," a bedroom ballad, is all seductive bravado, made sumptuous by the slow, gospelly organ.

There's definitely a throwback vibe to "3121," a mostly one-man-band effort that favors the musical minimalism and reliance on synthesizers of early '80s Prince.

He also echoes some of his personal favorites: "Beautiful, Loved and Blessed," a duet with new protégé Tamar, suggests the sweet soul of Minnie Riperton; "Te Amo Corazón" evokes the slow-dance Latin romance of an acoustic Carlos Santana; "Fury" salutes '70s synth-and-guitar rock; "Get on the Boat" merges the horn-fueled funk of James Brown and Earth, Wind & Fire. Featuring saxophonist Maceo Parker, "Boat" is one of the standouts here, a terrific party jam not just for Al & Alma's but for any celebration.

Still, despite the dance-floor fun and boudoir ballads, "3121" ultimately leaves you wanting. Prince clearly has some intriguing concepts (especially rhythmically) here, but it is time that he hooked up with a younger musical genius, such as the Neptunes, OutKast's Andre 3000, Black Eyed Peas' will. i.am or the Roots' ?uestlove, who have demonstrated that they know how to take old Princely ideas and make them sound fresh. In other words, the Master should rework "3121" into, say, "Prince 3000."

Chapter Fifty-Two

**THE Y-LIFE INTERVIEW PRINCE
YAHOO! INTERNET LIFE—JUNE 2001
BY BILGE EBIRI**

BACK IN AUGUST of 1997, well before the world was talking about music on the Internet, Prince—then known as the Artist Formerly Known as Prince—made an odd announcement. Recently released from his recording contract with Warner Bros., he declared that he was going to sell Crystal Ball, his upcoming five-CD set (it shrank to four CDs in stores), over the Web. At the time, it was easy to see the move as yet another eccentric twist in the career of a musical maverick. This, after all, was a man who in 1993 had changed his name to an unpronounceable symbol.

Today Prince seems like a visionary, not simply because he was the first major pop star to sell an entire album on the Web, but also because he has devoted so much of his career to fighting the recording companies' stranglehold on the distribution of music. The name change, for example, wasn't some kind of bizarre social experiment—it was an effort to outmaneuver Warner Bros., which still retained the rights to recordings made in his name, even after he'd been freed from certain of his contracts. (He also famously scrawled the word *slave* across his face.) It's possible now to see these actions for what they were: some of the first shots fired in the war against the recording industry, a war that continues to rage among fans, executives, and artists, with controversies over copyright, Napster, and CD price fixing.

Prince reverted to his original name in May 2000, after his final contract with Warner expired. Now, looking back on his time inside the record-industry juggernaut, he is by turns indignant and reflective. But more important, as the patron saint of wired artists, he continues to push the boundaries of technology and art. At the beginning of the year, he released two free downloadable songs on his site, NPG Online Ltd. In February, he launched a fee-based subscription service called the NPG Music Club, offering fans three new downloadable singles every month. And in April, he announced that he would release a new track, "The Work—Part 1," on Napster.

Naturally, it also helps to be as prolific as Prince. Rumors still circulate that he has hundreds upon hundreds of unreleased songs in his private vaults. That all adds up to an unlimited supply of content—"the fuel," as he called it during his conversation with *Y-Life* at his Paisley Park studios in the outskirts of Minneapolis. And content, as a Prince would know, is king.

Y-Life: You've been very outspoken against the music industry, going so far as to change your name and write slave on your face in protest.

Prince: I don't have any hate for these people. Ultimately, what people don't know is what they end up focusing on and misunderstanding. If I'm changing my name and writing on my face, they assume I'm crazy. And then they'll say that I'm not capable of distributing my own materials.

My first Warner Bros. contract was huge—full of terms, restrictions, that sort of thing. We need to stay out of the way of that. If it's the music business, then the musician should get the lion's share. And when artists figure that out, there'll be an uprising. Right now, if you resist their kind of thinking, what do they do? They'll kick you out to the curb.

Y-Life: Aren't all industries like that, to a certain extent?

Prince: At least in the movies, a successful actor can get $20 million. It's not like that in the music business. Destiny's Child brought in $93 million last year. How much do you think they themselves actually got? It's totally unequal. Record executives will say, "Destiny's Child made $93 million last year." You ask them, "Why did Destiny's Child themselves only get $4 million of that money?" I mean, have you heard Beyoncé sing? Puh-leeze! She ain't even 20, and she's got a voice like that! Let's kick it up to $30 million. Is that fair? They won't answer. They'll say, "You don't understand . . . ." When you talk to record executives, you'll hear an arrogance that's astounding.

They're under the assumption that artists don't know the way the industry works. Sheryl Crow has this saying; she refers to people as having "no Midwestern common sense." So they'll say something like, "We have 85 percent failure expectations on new acts," meaning they expect the vast majority of them to fail. You've got 85 percent failure expectations, and you're signing them to long-term agreements? "Well, they might not fail." What does that mean? This system makes $40 billion a year. And it's all based on this type of logic.

Y-Life: Why don't more artists resist the record industry, then?

Prince: You saw *The Matrix*, right? The person in that predicament doesn't know where he is. It's a collective hallucination. The key is if you put people in a financial bind, and spread it around, they won't be able to resist. This whole country was based on division. All the way back in [the album] Controversy, I was trying to break from the hallucination. People said, "This is what's hittin' now, Prince." But I wasn't paying attention to that. Duke Ellington never changed. Miles Davis never changed. Their work is intact. The companies are great at distributing, but they're not creators. They shouldn't be the ones to take my work into the 22nd century.

Y-Life: When one looks at musicians who have truly embraced the Net, it's the veterans, people who have been around for a while: you, David Bowie, Pete Townshend. What's that all about?

Prince: Because when you're a new, young act and start getting a buzz, you get approached by people with a pen and an agenda. They start right away taking pieces of you. All I can say to young artists is know that you're the genesis of what comes from you. You have to keep your masters [recordings]. The record executives say, "We own the masters." I ask them, "Where are they?" And I'll just look right at them. You know, the way Norm MacDonald will tell a joke and then just look at you? I love that! (Laughs) Steven Wright, too, does that. But imagine—this is the kind of standoff I'll have with a grown man.

It'll be interesting to see what happens with Lenny Kravitz. His deal's about up. And he's going to get a big carrot dangled in front of him any day now. They'll give you a choice: "You can own all the recordings, or you can be a star." But are you a star if you're broke? Let's watch what happens with Lenny. If I want to speak out against that collective hallucination, I'm not a part of it. I did one record on my own, and that's all it took. Let Lenny Kravitz do one record on his own, and see if he ever goes back.

Y-Life: Why, exactly, do you think the recording industry is so corrupt?

Prince: Let's look at it. I mean, really look at it. It's in the Bible, which I've started reading recently. Why does a person go against his Creator? In the beginning, we have a very simple story in the garden. God tells Adam and Eve, "You have everything you need." And they begin to think they can create as well. Examine that story. Now, there's somebody else in that garden, isn't there?

In every situation, you have one person who initiates, one who benefits, and one who resists all of it. And some people are happy being in every one of those categories.

Y-Life: What's your position on Napster?

Prince: I always ask people, "Are you pro—or anti-Napster?" Now, the record companies see Napster as troublesome. Napster is a mirror. How you see Napster says more about you than it does about Napster. The fans visiting Napster, they would want everything the artist puts out. They wouldn't want to pay for it. What's up with that?

But the same goes for the recording industry. How you see the recording industry says more about you and your priorities than it does about the recording industry. Napster was inevitable—a file-sharing program that allowed the user to be a part of the process—especially given the general arrogance of the music industry as a whole. I mean, $18 a CD. Where are they getting that? The production costs aren't going up, that's for sure. People are getting hip to that. This is a wonderful time, because everything is shifting. Everybody can be an artist—and there are good and bad consequences to that. But people who control their own work will succeed. Look at Bill Gates. The man is unstoppable. He never sold out. He never sold the rights to his software.

Y-Life: Have you ever used Napster?

Prince: No. Of course, I've had people go on to see if they've got our stuff, and they definitely did. Now, NPG Music Club is a subscription club. If the songs we put up on the club end up on Napster, is that copyright infringement?

Y-Life: You asked your fans that same question on the site. What do you think?

Prince: I'm asking you. The record industry said that Napster caused them to flat-line. Are you pro—or anti-Napster?

Y-Life: Personally, I'm pro.

Prince: Now, why is that? That's interesting.

Y-Life: I discovered more new music through Napster last year, and I bought the CDs. I've paid for more music last year than I've ever done, thanks to Napster. And I think people will still buy CDs; we like objects.

Prince: Do you think individuals who spend all day on the computer will care about CDs? I'm trying to see if I can sway your opinion. How many users does Napster have—60 million? Do you think all those people are buying their CDs?

Y-Life: Probably not.

Prince: See, there you go! Now we're coming to some kind of agreement. I'm not pro—or anti-anything. I just sit back and watch the whole thing. We've got an institution here at Paisley that cares for the artist. And that's the way it should be.

I've spoken to Shawn Fanning. He's just a kid. It's a real shame what has happened to him. He's in a lot of tough water. He's scared. When Fanning got up onstage at the MTV awards, the audience started cheering and booing. First they were booing Metallica; now they were booing him. And he's thinking, "Why did this happen to me?" If I was worried about booing, I'd think I had to change. So you sign up with one side or the other. And Napster, BMG—these people aren't musicians. Shawn knows the deal. [A month after this interview was conducted, Prince reached an agreement with Napster to release a new track from an upcoming album on the file-sharing service.—Ed.]

Y-Life: Can the Napster-BMG deal eventually work?

Prince: Probably. Why not? The recording industry works. That doesn't mean it's just, or right, or fair. But it's not up to me to damn somebody or something. It's in the nature of their actions to damn themselves. When was the last time the recording industry gave anything back to the community? It's a pity that there actually has to be such a thing as the Rhythm & Blues Foundation [a not-for-profit group dedicated to fostering recognition of and support for R&B music]. This industry makes $40 billion a year—$40 billion! Can we have $1 billion? Just $1 billion, to put back into our communities and help rebuild them?

Y-Life: But some would say that running a business is a lot different from making music.

Prince: I care for artists. I care for where Bonnie Raitt gets her heart from. You want to improve the production of tennis programs on TV? Let's ask Serena and Venus Williams what they think. I'm sure they're full of ideas. I know—I've asked them. When Kobe Bryant does a 360 and dunks it, that's creation. Let's let that dictate.

Y-Life: In February, you started the NPG Music Club on your site, a paid subscription service that allows fans to receive new songs from you every month. Was the club an alternative, or a response, to the Napster controversy?

Prince: Napster had nothing to do with the NPG Music Club. Anybody who has followed my career knows how much technology has meant to me. When it was three o'clock in the morning, and I'd try to get [Revolution drummer] Bobby Z to come out to the studio, sometimes he'd come, sometimes he wouldn't. But I've had this Roger Linn drum machine since 1981. It's one of the first drum machines ever created. It takes me five seconds to put together a beat on this thing. So from the very start, technology gave me a direct result for my efforts. I'm a very simple person. If somebody wants my music, I'll give it to them.

Y-Life: Don't you worry that if your music is distributed only on the NPG Music Club, you'll lose potential new listeners?

Prince: Why would a 13-year-old be at my concerts? There're tons of them there. One night I asked them, "How many of y'all have seen me before?" Half of them cheered. "How many have never seen me before?" The other half cheered. So I see how this is going. Somebody old brings somebody new. Things get passed down—it's like oral history, the way it's supposed to be. Like you and me talking right now. I've wanted to have a direct one-on-one with people for a long time. If you see the Net as a tool to eliminate the middleman, you define it. And that reflects your personality. You get in and say, "I want to use it to get to more people"—that says something about you as well. NPG audio gives you something new. We've called the NPGMC "the experience for those who know better." Because right now, if you listen to the radio, all you'll hear is packaged pop stars. Sometimes I want to ask those people, "Do you even know a D-minor chord? Come here, play one. Good. Now step away, please. There's nothing to see here." (Laughs)

Y-Life: Earlier this year, you released two songs through your site as free downloads, calling it an "Xperiment in honor" and asking fans who profited from it to kick back some of those profits to you. How has the experiment worked?

Prince: (Laughs) It worked just like we thought it would. And that's all I'm saying about that! One of the reasons why we thought a club would be necessary is because we wanted to see how fast the music would replicate itself. And it's just incredible. It's ultimately a question of what music should be. Who should it benefit? It should benefit the creator. Ani DiFranco owns all her music.

My friend Larry Graham likes to say, "If you've got a cake pan that's dented, and you keep cooking cakes in it, then you're going to keep getting cakes with dents in them." When I do deals with record companies now, they're with people. And they're small. "I've got some music. You want it? You make some copies and give me my tapes back."

Y-Life: Will you still release albums from now on, or stay digital?

Prince: I'll probably release albums, but what's cool about the club is that the shows and the tracks change every month. So if you go in every month, you'll get to storehouse all these tracks, and by the end of the year you'll have enough for maybe three albums. I could probably release five to seven albums every year if I wanted to-polished stuff that I'm really happy with. But the market can't deal with that. So this seemed like a natural alternative.

Y-Life: How did you first get online?

Prince: Instantly, the thing that attracted me to the Net was the idea that I could reach a lot of people without going through a matrix. Unfortunately, the Net is a reflection of what's going on in the world. School shootings, things like that. It reflects that kind of violence. That's why I don't live there. Here in Paisley, it's a very isolated environment. You can't just see all that pornography and deceit and mendacity all the time. That's what the world has become. There are pockets of beauty out there still, though.
Y-Life: Where are those pockets of beauty on the Net?

Prince: That's a tough one. I'm not one to judge what is beautiful. I do know what isn't beautiful. Everybody's a critic. People are flaming each other without any knowledge of the effect it has on others—the kind of physical, psychological effect it has on them.

Y-Life: Have you been in chatrooms devoted to your work?

Prince: A couple of times—not much. When I first started, I tried one time to unify a group splintered by whether I was still "funky" or not. That question still goes on, obviously. But what ended up happening was that I got a webmaster out of it—Sam Jennings, who runs the NPG site out of Chicago. But I guess what I find beautiful on the Internet is wherever I find agreement. That's beautiful even to people who are full of hate.

Y-Life: Don't we need disagreement before we can have agreement?

Prince: I believe people of like mind will agree. This'll sound like a cliché, but people need to be under a creator. Clive Davis doesn't want to take any direction from me. Should he? You tell me. Is this the music industry? All the musicians, please stand up. Miles Davis and Duke Ellington went to school for music. They learned how to create; they became seasoned performers. Now they pop these kids out like it's nothing. And the record executives say, "We love music." You love music? You can't even tap your foot on the two and the four.

Y-Life: There was a quote on your site recently, saying "Beyoncé can sang!" Was that from you?

Prince: The tidbits of information on the site don't come from me. Sometimes people will ask me a question, and I'll give them a quote. My end is shipping out the music. But it's evident that Destiny's Child is an industry act. We want to keep the focus on why they're successful. And that's because of the people in the group, not because of the label and the marketing. That's why you'll see tidbits like that, about Beyoncé and other performers. The people that are here at Paisley with me—we're all like-minded. They stay free—and free means free. And that's what the club is about. It's a haven for anybody who's got their music and is free. We're all very down-to-earth. No matter what the press likes to write about me.

Y-Life: So what kind of Web sites do you like to visit?

Prince: I go to the educational ones. I like to study history—especially Egyptian history. I don't want to start endorsing any sites right now, but I like the ones that go back the furthest. 'Cause I'm interested in how we got in this predicament in the first place. You can talk about symptoms all day long. But I like to talk about solutions.

Chapter Fifty-Three

ROLLING STONE INTERVIEW PRINCE BY ANTHONY DECURTIS—2004

"HAMMERING! THAT'S THE word. That's it!" Prince folds over in laughter and stamps his high-heel boots on the floor. Those heels, as it happens, are clear plastic, and lights twinkle within them. It's a perfect metaphor for the electricity that seems to be coursing through the singer at the moment.

Prince is responding to a description of the torrid version of "D.M.S.R."—a jam from 1999 touting the virtues of "dance, music, sex, romance"—that he and his backing band, the New Power Generation, unleashed earlier that evening at the sold-out Gund Arena in Cleveland. It was a full-on funk stomp that got the house up and shaking. Hammering only begins to convey the performance's pulverizing rhythmic assault. "Pulverizing! That's good, too," Prince says, laughing again. "What you see is people responding to what this band is—and what we're doing."

It's just twenty minutes after the show, and, at a time when most performers would be just beginning to cool down, Prince is utterly composed. He's crisply dressed in a purple tunic and black pants and looks as if he has spent the evening relaxing in his living room rather than burning down a 20,000-seat house. But that's how effortless things seem to be of late for the forty-five-year-old musician. Everybody in the Prince camp—most definitely beginning with Prince himself—bristles when anyone suggests that the current wave of Princemania constitutes a "comeback." The official line is that he never went away. From a strictly literal standpoint, of course, that's true. He's been as busy as ever, using his own label and his Web site, the New Power Generation Music Club, to release CDs such as *The Rainbow Children* (2001) and *N.E.W.S.* (2003), as well as the DVD *Prince: Live at the Aladdin Las Vegas*.

But whether or not you buy the message that Prince never left, it's clear that many of his millions of fans had gone somewhere in recent years, and now many of them are staging a comeback of their own. Suddenly, liking Prince doesn't feel like such a chore; in fact, it's fun. His stripped-down, pleasingly straightforward new album, *Musicology*, delivers on the promise of his spellbinding performances earlier this year on the Grammy Awards broadcast and at his induction into the Rock & Roll Hall of Fame. His live shows have become ecstatic parties, sweaty, two-hour romps through the likes of "Controversy," "U Got the Look," "Take Me With U" and a sizzling version of Sam and Dave's classic "Soul Man." Nearly a recluse before, Prince is now all over the media, chatting on talk shows, posing for photographers, being interviewed by reporters.

It's like an old friend has returned. Indeed, the spring of 2004 is beginning to feel like the summer of 1984, when Purple Rain made Prince one of the biggest rock stars in the world. When he sings, "Don't you miss the feeling that music gave you back in the day?" in "Musicology," he might as well be speaking about his own music. After abandoning his name for an unpronounceable symbol, after painting the word "slave" on his face as part of a battle with his record label, after disowning decades of his own work, Prince is enjoying himself again. And, as always, his enthusiasm is irresistible. I had an epiphany last night," Prince says about his appearance in Columbus, Ohio. He's sitting on a couch in his dressing room, shortly before taking the stage in Cleveland. The room is warm and humid, to keep his throat and nasal passages clear and his vocal cords supple. Candles burn on every available surface.

"I was offstage, listening to Michael Phillips take his solo," he continues, alluding to the instrumental portion of the show in which the saxophonist takes a long, atmospheric excursion during "God" while Prince changes clothes and takes a break. "I was thinking, 'Wow, listen to those people responding, and all he's doing is playing a saxophone.' They can feel that what he's doing is real. So many shows now, they have pyrotechnics, pre-taped vocals and musical parts, and it's so dead. But here's one man breathing into an instrument, and the whole room feels alive. It made me want to rise up to that level when I came back onstage."

Part of the goal of the *Musicology* album and tour is to connect audiences once again to the power of live music. "Take your pick—turntable or a band?" Prince challenges on the album, and his concerts are like a clinic in inciting the sort of pandemonium that only a band can create. That's true even for the players themselves. "This is school for me," says Phillips, 27. "Every night I watch how he connects his gift to the crowd. I've spoken to him about it. He told me that playing a solo is like making love. You have to pay attention to the things that make your partner respond—and space them out so they come at exactly the right time. It's one big, long orgasm."

Prince's deal with Columbia: Because "Musicology" is so listener-friendly, Prince overcame his near pathological wariness about record companies and agreed to allow his lawyer to work out a deal with Columbia Records. Columbia, which is part of Sony Music, will distribute and help the market the album domestically (and be reimbursed for the costs of doing so) and license it for sale in the rest of the world. It's an arrangement that essentially requires no upfront costs on the label's part, while providing a strong profit incentive for the company to sell as many copies as possible. On his end, Prince gets the enormous reach of an international corporate powerhouse.

According to Sony's president, Don Ienner, the label has filled orders for upward of a million copies of the album worldwide. "And with the first copy shipped, we started making money," he adds. "We have really high expectations for this, and, though there are no guarantees, we hope to remain in business with Prince for a long time. How often does an artist of his stature become available on any terms?"

Prince receives no payment from the label. But retains complete ownership of the album. He also gets a much higher percentage of sales than he would under a more traditional arrangement. "One advantage of writing "slave' on my face back then was that when I meet with a label now, they already know they're not going to be owning anything", Prince says wryly. "Maybe at one time they could get Little Richard for a new car and a bucket of chicken. We don't roll like that no more.

Being at Peace: "I feel at peace. I knew it would take time, and I had to deal with a lot of ridicule. But this feels like peace right now. Spiritually I feel very different from the way I used to, but physically? Not at all. I don't look at time that way, and I don't believe in age. When you wake up, each days looks the same, so each day should be a new beginning. I don't have an expiration date."

About Tom Petty: "It was an honor to play with Tom Petty (at the Rock N Roll Hall of Fame ceremony). "Free Fallin'" is one of my favorite songs. I used to love whenever he would come on MTV, because you knew you were going to get a great tune. MTV isn't like that anymore."

"Kiss" Highlight: For a tumultous run of songs at the end of the Cleveland show, Prince invites perhaps two dozen women in the audience onto the stage to dance. One willowy girl wears a purple two-piece bathing suit

festooned with the gylph that had become the singer's name for a time. Prince struts over to her, and she becomes his dance partner during "Kiss". After the line "Act your age, not your shoe size", he holds the mike out for her, and right in tune, she sings, "And maybe we can do the twirl!" Prince's eyes widen and he yowls, "Wooo!"

"The security guard wasn't going to let her get onstage", Prince says backstage after the show. "I said, "You can't send that girl home dressed like that!"

Chapter Fifty-Four

CBS INTERVIEW PRINCE
BY CO-ANCHOR RENE SYLER NEW YORK—JULY 20, 2004

IN A WIDE-RANGING interview with *The Early Show* co-anchor Rene Syler, Prince spoke about the war in Iraq, politics and, of course, his music, which includes his latest project, "Musicology."

If you're a fan, you know "Musicology" when you hear it—the funk, the mix, the melody is pure Prince. Some of the songs on "Musicology" make one want to groove like the dancers on the video, but there's another layer here.

After 25 years of making music, this album, in particular one song, "Cinnamon Girl," looks at exploitation. In the lyrics Prince says: "Cinnamon Girl, mixed heritage. Never knew the meaning of color lines. 9/11 turned that around when she got accused of this crime. Terror alibi. What's the use when the god of confusion keeps on telling the same lie?"

Why is it important for Prince to address some of the issues that we're facing today? "Well," Prince says, "It seems to be the age old problem of prejudice and misunderstanding between so-called races. You know, I wrote a song once about a large ball, black on one side, white on the other. And the other person, about this big, only seeing that one side. That's the way they think the world is.

"Unfortunately, in war there are children dying on both sides," he continues. "So sooner or later, I think, as a people we're going to have to discuss some of these issues. So I just wanted to put my little two cents in."

Prince started making music in a pre—Sept. 11 world. And he continues on in a post—Sept. 11 world. So the questions are: Is it important to him to use his music to educate? And is that why he draws on current events for some of his music?

Prince replies, "Well, I think music, not only should it be entertaining, but it should try to uplift you in some form or fashion. I mean, I think that's the purpose of music. It's to make light of otherwise dire situations. You take music out of the world it's going to be pretty dark. I think, of course, I would say that, I'm a musician."

How much of his own experience as an African-American is embedded in the lyrics of his music?

"I almost think that we were taught race," Prince says. "It wasn't something that we were just born with. We all look different, and we are all varied in our complexions and sizes. And all that's wonderful. That's good, you know? That reflects the way the universe is built. But when we are—put in boxes, I've always railed against that. So this isn't a new topic for me."

He's 46 now, but doesn't look anywhere near that. And he exhibits a deepening understanding of what he says, does, and sings about and its influence on society as a whole.

"The simple fact that I'm not alone on the planet." he says. "There are others around me, just by virtue of the children that come to our concerts and things like that. I have a responsibility to them to perform in a manner that I would like my children to be performed in front of. So, that said, I just want to be the best human being I can be so that my faith is going to try to lead me in that direction in all aspects of my life, on stage and off."

The Prince of 2004 is quite a bit different from the Prince 1979, who was singing songs with some pretty explicit lyrics. About this, Prince says, "I always challenge people to play one of my so-called explicit songs up against an explicit song of today.

"If you take some of the music off these songs of today you've got straight pornography. And one thing, I always tried to keep raw sensuality in my music. It was never done in a spirit of misogyny or meanness."

It is evident he is not a misogynist because he tends to employ female musicians in his band. Asked why, he answers with laughter, "That's a good question. They're the better sex? Watch it now. Watch it."

Seriously, he says, "Female musicians, I think, tend to listen better. And they don't let their ego get in the way of music."

Prince wraps of the East Coast part of his sold-out U.S. tour Tuesday night with a stop at Nassau Colisseum. The tour continues through September. *Source: CBSnews.com*

Chapter Fifty-Five

**EBONY INTERVIEW PRINCE
BY LYNN NORMENT SEPTEMBER 2004**

PRINCE HAS RECLAIMED his throne. After years of self-imposed semi-exile from the constant glare of cameras, the artist formerly and currently known as Prince is enjoying a resurgence in popularity and attracting an enormous amount of media and fan attention. His *Musicology* CD has sold millions of copies, and he is a constant on radio and music video channels, He's also reclaimed his perch in higher echelons on Billboard's music charts, and his Musicology tour is selling out arenas around the country.

Yes, the Prince has returned, much to the delight of his fans and music lovers in general who long for *real* music and *real* concerts without the lip-syncing and salacious lyrics and antics, His resurgence, along with his model of successful insurrection and independence, undoubtedly stirs discomfort in music's corporate suites, where this versatile, multitalented and visionary artist is viewed as the wave of the future, and perhaps the beginning of the end of the way things are done in the music industry.

Since he burst onto the music scene 25 years ago, Prince has marveled the world as a creative dynamo who writes, sings, composes and plays all the instruments on most of his recordings. It was clear then as it is now that this creative genius loves music, and he loves making music. At times he's been called salacious and lascivious, and early in his career he created sensation with his suggestive lyrics and moves. He's also been described as eccentric, mercurial, mysterious, even bizarre.

That was then. "I call myself a musician and a child of God," the new Prince says in a calm, serene manner when asked how he'd describe himself. "Others call me what they want to call me."

He smiles warmly as he settles comfortably before an SSL 8000 G+ film-ready console in Studio A at his famed Paisley Park Studios outside Minneapolis. Dressed in a white Chinese silk shirt over a red t-shirt emblazoned with NPGMC and white pants with buttons lining the side seams, he projects an everyday casualness. Four years ago, he became a Jehovah's Witness and consequently a changed man.

As he talks about his music, renovations at Paisley Park and his spiritually enhanced life, Prince appears to be at peace with himself and the world. No longer is slave scrawled across his handsome face, as it was years ago during his pro-test against music industry royalty rules. And no longer is he distant and elusive, as he was in earlier years when he was probably trying to find himself. Today, Prince is at peace with himself and the world. He has evolved into a caring, informed, well-read, history-conscious and spiritually enriched artist and businessman who is determined to keep making music and directing his career as he sees fit.

During an hour visit that lasts almost three hours, he is animated and often leaps from his chair and dances around the studio to make his point. At times he leans in close and whispers as he shares a bit of knowledge from experience, He does not dwell on his controversial exit from the contract he had with Warner Brothers, the company front which he launched his career in 1978 and achieved fame and riches during the 1980s. He fulfilled his contract by releasing music on Warner Brothers under the name Prince; but during this same period in the 1990s the prolific music maker also released music under his New Power Generation label. He referred to himself as an unpronounceable glyph. Most just called hint The Artist.

Once he satisfied his legal obligations to Warner Brothers, he reclaimed his moniker Prince (his given name is Prince Rogers Nelson) and continued to release music through his NPG label and music club Web site. Occasionally he would do live performances, and in 1999 he teamed with Arista Records to release *Rave Un2 the Joy Fantastic.* For the most part, Prince stayed below media radar though he was ever present to his ardent fans who staved in touch via his Web site.

And he was very industrious. For a one-time $25 fee, subscribers to his NPG Music Club (npgmusicclub.com) have access to music downloads and advance notice and discounts on concert tickets. He has sold millions of records through the club. At Paisley Park, he creates and records his music; he contracts out the pressing of the discs, then oversees distribution.

Consequently he retains ownership—and the profits—of his music. It is a model for independence he encourages other artists to consider.

"When I went back to the name Prince and independently released *Rainbow Children* in 2001, that was the beginning of where I am now," he says. "But you have to do the work . . . That's what independence is. It's my catalog, my dynasty. I'm selling hundreds of thousands of records. I'm the Record Company now." (And he makes $7 on a $10 CD, rather than pennies he received in traditional record contract.)

This is a subject about which the new Prince, as was the old Prince, is passionate. He is an advocate for artists' rights and feels that the powerful "corporations" should not own aim artist's music. He talks about the compulsory license law, "where anybody can take my song and sing it, against my will. I'm a writer. Stephen King is a writer. Can I take a page out of his book and call it *Prince's Shining*? Can I take a scene out of a movie and call it my own? They say the law, helps the writers. I don't need help; I don't need your money. Let us steward our own music.

"Sister Lynn, look at all this!" He jumps up and bounces in a 360-degree turn as he points to various pieces of equipment and musical instruments in the studio. "We don't own any of this. We can buy it, but we don't make it. We want to start making our own instruments."

Prince made waves in the music industry when he launched his Musicology tour in March without attaching an end date. He can perform under the banner of the Musicology tour over the next several years, and Billboard is required to attribute the sales to this one tour. Another point of contention is the fact that Prince's concert ticket price includes a *Musicology* CD, and those sales must be counted for Billboard's chart rankings. Record sales will increase as long as the tour continues. "We have sold more than 3 million CDs worldwide, and it will continue," he says. (In response to Prince's innovation, Billboard and SoundScan, which compiles the charts, quickly changed the method for counting album sales, but it does not affect *Musicology*.)

"We do this out of necessity;" Prince says. "We are not trying to one-up anybody else. We are not mad at anybody. God expects us to work for ourselves. We can't sit back and wait for reparations. We've been waiting for 400 years. Are the politicians going to repeal these laws? Are they going to put music back in the schools?"

Prince also is disturbed by what he calls "processed music, corporate produced music" that proliferates the airwaves. "Machines calm do about anything to music," he says. "Corporations are trying to turn music into media, into bits and numbers, into binary codes so it can be controlled like they control the media. Before long, we won't have real music," he says, picking up one of the several guitars nearby. "This is real music." He plays a melody. "I control it. It's not a machine . . . That's why artists like Alicia Keys are so loved. People feel her, and she doesn't have to take her clothes off."

The days of taking his clothes off onstage are in the past for Prince. So are the raunchy lyrics and antics, and the parade of women through his life. There are songs he will no longer perform. Prince has changed, and his audiences have changed. ("You get the audience you deserve. When I played freaky music, I got freaky audiences. I finally straightened it out"). He always has expressed a spiritual side, and he says he's always felt that sexuality and spirituality were intertwined. Now he says that he practices monogamy, and he encourages others to do the same. In December 2001, Prince married Manuela Testolini, who formerly worked at Paisley Park.

On this visit to Paisley Park, Manny (as Prince refers to her) serves her husband, a long-time vegetarian, and their guest roasted pepper soup she made that morning. ("I've been roasting peppers all day," she says.) He agrees that the soup, heavy with garlic and other healing spices, is delicious. In the dining area of the studio, Manny shows their guest a sampling of the home products, including fragrant and beautifully packaged incense, they plan to market under the NPG Home brand. Later, when Prince gives a tour, he points out more of Manny's tasteful decorative art.

"We plan to have interns in here working and learning every aspect of the music business," he says during the tour of the 65,000-square-foot Paisley Park. In addition to the reception and atrium seating area, there are four recording studios (two new, two upgraded) that are technological marvels. They are outfitted with Bryston high-performance amplifiers and custom-made BMDI monitoring systems. By updating to the newest digital technology, combined with high-speed connectivity and efficient workflow, Prince says Paisley Park Studios is in a position to offer musicians an ideal environment in which to make music.

There is also a huge soundstage that has been used to make movies and music videos; in the past it has been the scene of memorable parties. (It now some times hosts community and religious meetings.) There are also several dance and rehearsal rooms, one in particular with granite walls and floor that houses an expansive drum set on which Prince demonstrates the "loudness" of the sound. In a room nearby is a grand piano, and again he sits (if only for a moment) and tickles the ivory keys melodically.

Prince bemoans the fact that super producers Jimmy (Jam) Harris and Terry Lewis have relocated their Flyte Time Studios to California, leaving Paisley Park as the sole major recording studio in the area.

The times are changing, the music industry continues to go through upheavals, and Prince is a changed man, though one who is still devoted to making good music. "I was always different," he says. "I continued to grow continued to evolve, thank God."

To young people and other artists in the music business, he advises revolution and independence. "Stay out of the music industry stay out of the system," he advises. "Be revolutionary. Some of these young kids say they want to follow me. Well, if you do, then get your spiritual life together if you want your relationships to go right, and it will happen."

Chapter Fifty-Six

ENTERTAINMENT WEEKLY INTERVIEW PRINCE
BY JEFF JENSEN APRIL 23, 2004

PRINCE, IN AN unusually revealing interview, talks about his wild and wicked past, holding hands with Stevie Wonder, and why the music biz deserves William Hung.

They've been rocked. They've been funked. They've been wooed. Now it's time to show him the love. It's a manic Monday night in late March, and 19,000 men, women and even children—the largest crowd ever to see a concert at Los Angeles' Staples Center—are giving it up for Prince. He has plied them with hits—from "Let's Go Crazy" to "Kiss" to "U Got The Look"—but one song in particular has brought them thunderously to their feet: an unplugged, stripped-down rendition of "Little Red Corvette." It is the centerpiece of a solo acoustic set by turns warm, funny, and riveting, and it earns him a standing ovation that goes on and on and on . . .

Prince beams. He covers his me-so-pretty face with his hands, and the applause only gets louder. It's a big, messy, wet kiss and it clearly means a whole lot to him. More than his fans might have considered possible. More, perhaps, than he's willing to admit.

The last time we paid attention to Prince, it was as much for his increasingly bizarre behavior as for the brilliant rock/funk/R&B fusion that made him one of the greatest artists of modern pop. Changing his name to an unpronounceable symbol. Scrawling the word *slave* on his cheek. Releasing half-assed albums like *Come* to burn off his contract with Warner Bros. His most notable cultural contribution of the past decade? *Carmen Electra*. Thanks, Prince. Thanks a lot.

Yet through it all, there still existed the hope that a talent called "genius" time and again could return to form. That moment finally seems to have arrived. In February, his electrifying Grammy duet with Beyoncé opened the show, and stole it. That was followed by Prince's induction into the Rock and Roll Hall of Fame; his guitar heroics were the highlight of the ceremony. His current tour—on which he's allegedly playing his hits for the last time—is selling out across the country. Critics are calling his new CD, *Musicology* (in stores April 20), his best in years. It's the kind of thing we media types like to call a comeback, though according to Prince, we media types, as usual, are mistaken.

Two nights after playing to an ecstatic L.A. crowd, Prince is backstage before a sound check at the Glendale Arena outside Phoenix, a city named, appropriately enough, after the fiery, feathered avatar of resurrection. Clad in a black sleeveless tunic and cranberry pants, Prince takes a plate from his bodyguard and loads it up with fruit, pasta slathered in cream sauce, and salad. Yes, Prince eats. He also goes to the multiplex. Last night, after his show in Bakersfield, Calif., he and his band unwound by checking out Kevin Smith's latest flick, *Jersey Girl*, a so-so departure from his usual lewd-and-crude comedies. Prince was unimpressed. Not that the 45-year-old, happily married, devout Jehovah's Witness can't appreciate a cleaner act; he himself has scrubbed from his set list staples like "Head" and "Jack U Off." It's just that according to Prince, Smith didn't replace it with nothing interesting. "We walked out after an hour," he sniffs. "Guess that's what happens when the potty mouth doesn't work for you anymore."

Though 5 foot 2, Prince does not radiate "short." From his complicated poodle haircut, to his dark doe eyes and the geometrically groomed stubble along his razor-sharp features, to his toned arms and quirky, customized attire, Prince's carefully considered visage is a superconductor for his considerable charm, and it tricks the eye. He even has a scent, though an elusive one. Not a perfume but a powder, like he's been dusted with incense. Prince in the flesh is pop evanescence incarnate. It's only when he opens his mouth that he resembles the rest of us mortals.

Hearing him talk about ordinary things is almost a shock. He speaks in hushed-voice gushes—megabyte downloads of wit, logic, and Christian evangelism. In one rant about the nature of democracy, how the media shape perception, and the decline of morality in America, Prince links terrorism-induced regime change in Spain, *Bowling for Columbine*, *The Matrix*, Adam and Eve and the Fall of Man, the Jayson Blair/New York Times scandal, Mariah Carey, MTV's *Jackass*, and Santa Claus. (We were discussing whether he thinks he's misunderstood.) Strangely, the whole thing makes sense.

Of course, he does have his obsessions. Or perhaps *obsession* would be more accurate. Nearly every answer to questions about *Musicology* or his career is colored by his battle with Warner Bros. over ownership of his master recordings and the pace of his output (beginning with 1978's *For You*, Warner released 20 albums in 21 years). Talking to him can be like chatting with a flashback-racked war veteran, or a heartbroken ex dumped for no good reason.

Prince's attitude about the music industry in a nutshell: He wishes it would go away. He hates how labels have exploited our warp-speed culture at the expense of nurturing long-term careers. "It took me four albums to get on the cover of *Rolling Stone*. Now it takes new artists only one. There should be rules for that kind of thing!"

His rhetoric is either deeply cynical or worldly-wise, depending on your point of view; he is convinced record labels conspire to phase out their most successful artists at their peak in order to avoid getting locked into cash-rich deals. But occasionally, some grace breaks through. His beef is with "the system," not the people who run it. "When I realized that, that's when I took the word *slave* off my face," he says. "I realized that they are as much slaves as I am."

That's why in 2001 Prince created the NPG Music Club, an online service that is now the official outlet for most of his music. He's giving *Musicology* away to everyone who attends his concerts, an experiment he's been itching to try since 1994 (the cost—about $9.99—is included in the ticket price). With its focused songcraft and shout-outs to James Brown, Earth, Wind & Fire, and Sly & the Family Stone, "Musicology" has an old-school vibe that reflects Prince's belief in old-fashioned musicianship. If today's young artists just knew their stuff, Prince suggests, they could have greater control over their careers and gain the clout to transform the industry.

"I think of the music business as a city," he says. "You tear one down, another whole city starts developing. But a city needs human beings to run it. My whole point is that if the music came first, if the city was run by musicians instead of people with MBAs, everything would flip. This is what we need today. This is what I want to be—a musical mentor. To pass on the knowledge."

He doesn't find the current system completely useless: Columbia Records is handling the traditional retail distribution of *Musicology*. "I expect people will respond to it as a 21st-century Prince record," says Sony Music U.S. president Don Ienner, who likens *Musicology* to Bruce Springsteen's *The Rising* and Bob Dylan's *Time Out of Mind*: urgent (and commercially successful) statements from supposedly dusty maestros. As for Prince's desire for music-industry regime change, Ienner says: "There are certain things we don't talk about. Obviously, he doesn't feel the same way about us as he does about [his old label]. I hear what he's saying. I don't necessarily have to agree with everything he's saying, but I hear him."

Prince does see a place in his new world order for the current power players. "You know that guy who dances funny on *American Idol*? The Asian-American kid?" He means William Hung. "That works for the record industry," he says with a laugh. "We need somebody to release those kind of records." Does his implied critique include packaged popsters like Britney Spears, too? Prince begs off, not wanting to name names. Kinda. "I mean no disrespect," he says. "But I see it as my duty to school young people coming up. Lip-synchers? What does a kid—what do other artists get out of that? I don't mind if Mariah Carey hits bad notes."

Being a role model doesn't mean Prince lacks mentors of his own, like Stevie Wonder. "His insight is priceless," says Prince. It's easy to see why he would connect with Wonder. Both are undisputed musical geniuses who fought for—and got—total creative control over their music. Prince Rogers Nelson was just 19 when he signed a multimillion-dollar, three-album deal with Warner Bros. in 1977. A wunderkind from Minneapolis who could play a dozen instruments by ear and wanted to combine James, Jimi, and Sly into a single, idiosyncratic sound, Prince used his freedom to create three albums of mounting brilliance that set the stage for his '80s reign—and, perhaps, for a profound sense of entitlement.

So what is he learning from Stevie these days? "I just learn by watching him," he says. "One day, he wanted to show me what it's like for him to experience the world, to actually feel a piece of music, so he held my hand. Here, hold my hand." Prince extends his palm, and I take it. It's warm and dry, and his nails are exquisitely manicured. "Now at first, it's like 'Whoa, I'm holding hands with a man!'" He quickly released his grip and throws his hands up. "Now, those thoughts and feelings are mine, and we all have to work those things out for ourselves. But then I started thinking what it means for Stevie to be able to hold someone's hand—anyone's hand, even a man's. He's telling me he respects me. And by extension, he's teaching me that I have to have that same respect for everybody in life."

There are two things Prince doesn't talk about. The first is his personal life, which means that we won't be chatting about his wife, Manuela Testolini, whom I meet briefly in Prince's candlelit dressing room after the sound check. She shakes my hand and tells me it's a pleasure, all without breaking stride as she leaves the room. Her husband looks longingly toward the door, then invites me to sit on a small sofa. *Musicology* is steeped in the pining of a man not only in love but in love with fidelity. Yet when I ask him about this seemingly more mature Prince—a man almost as infamous for his romantic conquests as his music—he shuts me down. "That's for all of you to decide. I don't intellectualize my music."

The second off-limits topic is Prince's past . . . which rules out almost everything else you'd want to discuss with him. "I've changed. I'm a different person. I'm about the present and moving forward. New joke, new anecdote, new lesson to be discovered," he says. "You know that old lady in *Sunset Boulevard*, trapped in her mansion and past glories? Getting ready for her close-up? I don't run with that." Even so, Prince begins concerts with a self-venerating video quoting extensively from a speech by Alicia Keys at his Hall induction.

Much of what has changed in Prince's life has occurred in the several years since he committed to the Jehovah's Witness faith. His music has always wrestled with Christian-tinged spirituality, but Prince says he didn't start reading the Bible until he'd become a Witness. His religious fervor was evident in the 2001 concept album *The Rainbow Children*, which was roundly knocked by critics. (Prince also attempted to produce an evangelical video based on the album directed by . . . Kevin Smith, whose surreal tale of working with Prince can be found on the DVD *An Evening With Kevin Smith*. "I'm cool with him not liking *Jersey Girl*," says Smith. "I f—ing hated his album *Crystal Ball*, so now we're even.")

As a result of his faith, Prince has developed an uncharacteristic modesty. In concert, he's taken to changing "I'm your messiah and you're the reason why" in "I Would Die 4 U" to "He's your messiah . . . "Still, it appears he has some kinks to work out in squaring his dogma with his golden-god persona. Asked if he feels he's alienated his fans over the years, Prince says: "No. The love has never left. I've always felt that there were people in my corner. It's a gift, that God gives us the chance to feel such love. And it's all for His glory: I don't believe in idol worship. That's why I don't sign autographs. When I get asked for my autograph, I say no and tell them why, because I'm giving them something to think about." This from a man who often prompts his concert audiences to scream his name. Ironies, contradictions, and exceptions escape Prince like doves from a cage.

There is also the predicament of his own potty-mouthed past—the one where he sang of erotic cities and a love that is soft and wet. But Prince has this problem solved as well. He doesn't perform those songs anymore. The founding father of the warning label freely concedes he's come full circle since he scandalized Tipper Gore with the word "masturbating" in "Darling Nikki." "Look at this situation with the FCC after Janet: We've gone too far now. We've pushed the envelope off the table and forgotten there was a table. You can't push the envelope any further than I pushed it. So stop! What's the point?"

But the more Prince talks about the sign of the times, the more he ends up talking about his past—and defending it. "We've all used shock value to sell things," he says. "I used shock to get attention. But back when I was doing the freaky songs in the freaky outfits, we were exploring ideas. I wanted my band to be multiracial, male and female, to reflect society. The song 'Sexuality' was about education and literacy. 'P Control' and 'Sexy MF' were about respect for women. Go and listen to the verses. All people focus on is the hooks."

Of Prince's many contradictions, perhaps the strangest is this: Here at the white-hot moment of his revival, the singer still simmers over small flash points of insult. By and large, he's flattered when told that his influence can be seen in everyone from Beck to OutKast, whose Andre 3000 describes Prince as "the total package. To me, he's the best of our generation—a total musician making almost otherworldly music."

But ask him if he's heard the Foo Fighters' version of "Darling Nikki" and Prince, who a minute earlier said he never listens to the radio ("When I want to hear new music, I go make some"), replies by describing a Hawaii DJ's response to the Foos' cover. The DJ wondered if Prince had heard it—then said he couldn't care less if he had. "Just no respect," says Prince. "I wonder if that's the kind of thing the FCC would like to clean up, too."

So . . . does he like the cover? "No! I don't like anyone covering my work. Write your own tunes!" He says he got up in R&B singer Ginuwine's face for bungling the lyrics in a 1996 version of "When Doves Cry." "I was just busting on him to bust him, but I was a little serious: Have some respect, man. If anyone tried to cover 'Respect,' by Aretha? I would shoot them myself!"

Of course, the Queen of Soul was herself covering an Otis Redding tune, but his point is clear: Young artists, respect your elder betters. Which is a savvy position for Prince to adopt in our '80s-crazed moment. It's the kind of thing a marketer might call "repositioning your brand"—as in angling for renewed relevancy while never admitting you lost it in the first place. Whatever you call Prince's resurging popularity, don't use the C-word. "People are calling this my comeback. Comeback? I never went anywhere!" Prince, in fact, denies that his Grammy appearance, his oldies-packed tour, and the nationwide movie-theater simulcast of his Staples Center concert were part of an orchestrated effort to kick-start his career. "I never stopped playing and recording. Never had a problem filling arenas. My appearance on Ellen wasn't part of some master strategy. She asked if I would perform; I said yes." Then, quoting from another man's song, Prince says, "Don't call it a comeback. I've been here for years."

When I joke that he'd better be careful or LL Cool J may come looking for him, Prince smirks: "I was about to say the same thing."

The Phoenix concert starts an hour late, due, perhaps, to a certain interview ending right at showtime. As a result, Prince has to cut the acoustic set, which means no "Little Red Corvette"—the song that brought the Staples Center crowd to its feet. But don't worry, Phoenix: You should take the whole last-time-for-the-hits thing with a grain of salt. "Well, it is called the 2004ever tour," says Prince when pressed on the subject. "And time is forever." So . . . probably not the last time? "Probably not."

Earlier, I asked Prince what the "Little Red Corvette" ovation at Staples meant to him. "What I was thinking in that moment was, without any real sacrifice, there's no reward. The affirmation of the Staples show was a blessing from God. You've read the magazines, the gossips. I'm not supposed to be here. But here I am." Guess that's what happens when the potty mouth don't work for you anymore.

Chapter Fifty-Seven

NEWSWEEK INTERVIEW PRINCE
BY LORRAINE ALI PARTY LIKE IT'S 2004

A TECHNICIAN IS sound-checking the trademark purple guitar, and the artist formerly known as The Artist Formerly Known as Prince is growing impatient. The 5-foot-2 singer adjusts the long poet sleeves of his white blouse, strokes his goatee, fidgets with his diamond-encrusted pendant and taps his platform heel on the concrete of this sports arena in Reno, Nev. Finally, he leans over to me and whispers, "I'll give you 20 bucks if you yell 'Freebird.' C'mon," he says with a nudge, "25 if you shout 'Skynyrd, dude!'"

Prince may be joking about his biggest nightmare—playing rock anthems to lighter-brandishing fiftysomethings at county fairs—but he's taking no chances. On his first nationwide arena tour in almost a decade, he'll still be performing his own anthems, such as "Purple Rain" and "Little Red Corvette." But he's using the old Prince—who busted sexual taboos on such albums as "Dirty Mind"—to introduce the new Prince, a Jehovah's Witness whose new album, "Musicology," is an enticing yet odd mix of funk, faith and fantasy. A second coming? With Prince, anything's possible.

Twenty years ago his megahit "Purple Rain," from his film and album of the same name, marked the sexy funk artist's total domination of an otherwise androgynous and angular decade. Long before the crossover success of hip-hop, Prince's intoxicating blend of dancemusicsexromance permeated the cities and the suburbs, forging a common groove between the dance floors of "American Bandstand" and "Soul Train." But the party waned in the '90s when he fought to break his contract with Warner Brothers and, in the process, alienated casual fans by dropping his name for an unpronounceable symbol, and performing with the word SLAVE scrawled across his face.

"'Prince is crazy'—I knew what people were saying," he confides in his candlelit dressing room. At 45, he's still more beautiful than Alicia Keys and Mandy Moore combined. His features are exquisite; his skin is baby-smooth; his thick hair is combed back a la Little Richard, sideburns trimmed to perfection. But yes, he's also as eccentric as ever. He wears eyeliner, even on days off, and insists that no tape recorders be used during interviews because he doesn't like the sound of his voice. "When I became a symbol, all the writers were cracking funnies, but I was the one laughing. I knew I'd be here today, feeling each new album is my first."

The rest of us, though, would never have predicted a new Prince moment 26 years—and 25 albums—after his first record was released. But here we are: there's his induction into the Rock and Roll Hall of Fame last month, his recent performance with Beyonce at the Grammys (which provided the show's biggest buzz) and the booming ticket sales for his 38-city tour, which includes three nights at Madison Square Garden. Prince even stopped his crusade against the record biz long enough to sign with Columbia for his new album (out in April), though members of his subscription-only Web site, NPGmusicclub.com (as in New Power Generation), have already downloaded "Musicology." (And everyone who buys a ticket to his show receives a copy at the door.) "See, if I sell 400,000 tickets to my shows, that would make me No. 1 on the charts before I even release a CD into record stores," he says. "You feel me? Then Norah Jones is gonna have something to worry about."

Getting one over on "the System" or "the Machine" (as he calls the record industry) is a source of pride for Prince. "I can tell you who made the System," he says. "Gangsters. Look at the jargon: hits, bullets." But when he won artistic autonomy after being released from his Warner Brothers contract on Dec. 31, 1999, his revolution was hardly televised. Instead, he churned out music on his own Web site and NPG label from his secluded compound, Paisley Park, outside Minneapolis. Now he wants more people to hear his new music—and his new message.

Prince became a Jehovah's Witness four years ago; he's been dropping references to Jehovah on his last four CDs, and he proselytizes throughout the interview about God and the Bible. Once again, he's at odds with the pop culture around him. "Now there's all these dirty videos," he says, twisting the only ring he wears—a plain silver wedding band. "We're bombarded. When I was making sexy tunes, that wasn't all I was doing. Back then, the sexiest thing on TV was 'Dynasty,' and if you watch it now, it's like 'The Brady Bunch.' My song 'Darling Nikki' was considered porn because I said the word masturbate. Tipper Gore got so mad." He laughs. "It's so funny now."

Prince clearly loves the attention but hates the scrutiny. He's uncomfortable when I write in my notebook during the practice set ("Really, don't write about the way this sounds, it's just a run-through"), but he drops my name in "Sign o' the Times" to see if I'm really listening. Does he think he's sacrificed anything by stepping out of the spotlight for more than a decade? "That notion of me losing something is a fallacy," he says, and unleashes a scriptural analogy. "There's Adam and Eve—artists—in the garden, chilling. God tells them they're supposed to have sex, and they do. Here comes a snake—the record-industry guy—and tells them the grass is greener on the other side. And when they fell for that, boy, did they fall. No, I didn't lose a thing."

But it's hard to believe Prince didn't at least miss the mass adoration. On his second tour stop last week, the sold-out 20,000-seat Staples Center in L.A., he got a standing ovation for a surprisingly moving acoustic rendition of "Little Red Corvette"—and he sat down on a stool in the middle of the stage and wept. The audience, a mix of older R&B fans, punk rockers, hip-hop kids and average-looking moms who knew every damn lyric, kept it up until he regained his composure. Even Andre 3000 of Outkast (likely taking mental notes for his next album) got to his feet for the man.

But while Prince reminded the crowd of what they'd been missing for the past decade, he also showed them who he is now. When he came out to do the long-expected "Purple Rain" for his encore, he added a line: "Say you can't make up your mind? I think you better close it and open up the Bible." The crowd may have to shrug it off, but Prince meant every word. "There's certain songs I don't play anymore, just like there's certain words I don't say anymore," he says. "It's not me anymore. Don't follow me way back there. There's no more envelope to push. I pushed it off the table. It's on the floor. Let's move forward now." His public may not go with him all the way, but nobody was hollering for "Freebird."

Chapter Fifty-Eight

THE OBSERVER INTERVIEW PRINCE
FEBRUARY 19, 2006

YES, FOLKS, WE'RE live tonight in New York City for *The Prince Show*, complete with sidekick Beyoncé Knowles and special guest Drew Barrymore. The set is a gaudy conflation of psychedelic shack and *beaux arts* boudoir, with our host kitted out in black turban and purple jacket. Except that he's barely deigning to speak, communicating his thoughts and wishes through buxom Beyoncé.

Prior to the entrance of La Barrymore there's an unscheduled appearance by a silver-haired Frenchman claiming to be Prince's chef. He says he's been preparing meals for His Royal Highness for many years 'but it's an *honneur* to finally meet you'. Prince isn't too thrilled to see the guy, complaining that he burned his tongue on his pancakes that morning. Turning away from the chef he picks up an ostrich-feathered eye-mask and contemplates himself in an ornate gold mirror. 'Prince is gazing into the mirror of reflection,' Beyoncé intones in a bored voice. Confused? You should be. Amused? Possibly not!

Beyoncé, of course, isn't Beyoncé at all. This particular night in early February, she's *Saturday Night Live*'s Maya Rudolph, just as the silver-haired chef is none other than Steve Martin, hosting SNL tonight for a record 16th time. Prince himself is being royally impersonated by Fred Armisen, another regular on the late-night show.

Like a lot of *SNL* these days, the Prince sketch isn't very funny. But it does suggest that America still believes Prince to be mildly insane. You wonder what the miniature maestro himself, sitting backstage tonight in some green room at NBC's Rockefeller Plaza studios, feels as he watches on a TV.

'Why does everyone think I'm mad?' he once asked his British press person. 'Because,' the PR replied, 'you do weird things and you don't explain them.'

Prince does do weird things, but he also performs live with a stage presence and a charisma that's unrivalled in American entertainment. Appearing on *Saturday Night Live* for the first time in 25 years, 10 days before his hotly-anticipated performance at the Brit Awards in London, he gives television debuts to two songs from his forthcoming album, 3121. One of them, 'Fury', is a decimating blast of pop-rock, complete with squealing guitar arpeggios and fabulously sexy choreography. When the number finishes, Prince lays his souped-up Stratocaster on the stage and casually upends his microphone stand before moseying towards the exit with the cockiest smirk you ever saw on a pop star's face.

The smirk says 'I killed 'em again' and it's an expression I've seen on Prince's face for a quarter of a century, ever since I watched him play in this very city in February 1981. That night, at the Ritz Theatre, I saw rock'n'soul's future: a devastatingly assured set of taut new-wave funk from a kinky genius who made Michael Jackson look like the buppie boy next door. I saw the smirk, too, when I went on the road with Prince and the Revolution two years later, accompanying the 1999 tour on several dates through the Midwest.

A decade later when I met him again in a hotel suite in London, it was more Mona Lisa than Cheshire Cat—coolly supercilious, ultimately indecipherable. Then, he took me to task for things other people had told me about him, hooting uproariously at the notion that any of them was in a position to talk about him. The fact that one, engineer Susan Rogers, had sat by his side on hundreds of occasions at his Paisley Park studio carried little weight with him.

'You think Susan Rogers knows me?' he asked. 'You think she knows anything about my music? Susan Rogers, for the record, doesn't know anything about my music. Not one thing. The only person who knows anything about my music [pause for very pointed effect] . . . is *me*.'

I see, I said.

As the conversation continued, Prince became progressively tetchier. 'All these non-singing, non-dancing, wish-I-had-me-some-clothes fools who tell me my albums suck,' he jeered. 'Why should I pay any attention to them?'

Right, I said.

At the very end, his pique at a peak, Prince declared that language was so confining that 'I might just stop talking again and not do interviews'. Everything, it seemed, had come full circle—back to his announcement in 1983 that he'd never talk to the press again.

Flash back a quarter of a century to the doldrums of the early Eighties: flouncy-haired synthkids, fading AOR veterans, flocks of seagulls and hosts of Haircut 100s. Vapid and sexless, pop was little more than a *Smash Hits* remake of *American Bandstand* three decades earlier. Who were Howard Jones and Nik Kershaw if they weren't blow-dried throwbacks to Fabian and Frankie Avalon?

'What's missing from pop music is danger,' Prince proclaimed in November 1982. 'There's no excitement and mystery—people sneaking out and going to these forbidden concerts by Elvis Presley or Jimi Hendrix.'

Danger is an overly mythologised quality in pop, but at the dawn of that decade Prince embodied something so thrilling and so category smashing that within five years he'd all but turned pop on its head. Of the four stars who bossed the Eighties—Michael Jackson, Madonna, Bruce Springsteen, Prince—the 5'2" prodigy from Minneapolis was the only true maverick in the pack.

'*Maybe I'm just like my father, too bold,*' he sang memorably in the heartrending 'When Doves Cry'. '*Maybe I'm just like my mother, she's never satisfied . . .*' He was an oddball and an introvert from his earliest days as a child prodigy, the son of jazz bandleader John Nelson and a Louisiana-born mother, Mattie Shaw. Brilliant but unhappy, he found a sanctuary in music that he couldn't find in a home where his parents often fought.

He played in covers bands but was happier working alone, overdubbing himself with primitive tape recorders in the basement of his friend Andre Anderson's house. Adopted by studio owner Chris Moon and manager Owen Husney, he began plotting his route to a record deal, cultivating a canny air of mystique while playing up to an X-rated image he'd developed after an early immersion in pornography.

If Husney was astounded by Prince's talent, he was also mildly alarmed by a teenager who seemed considerably older than his years. 'At 17 he had the vision and astuteness of a 40-year-old,' Husney told me. 'He was the kind of guy who could sit in a room with you and absorb everything in your brain and know more than you by the time you left the room. Prince might hang late, but it was all for music. He wasn't looking to get high with the guys.'

His first big hit, 1979's 'I Wanna Be Your Lover', was irresistibly catchy: black pop with a funk-lite guitar riff and a playfully androgynous falsetto vocal: '*I wanna be your lover/Wanna be your mother and your sister too . . .*'

Coming at the tail end of disco, it didn't sound like anything else on black radio. Black media approved but found him as hard to pigeonhole as white media did. Warner Brothers, which had given him unprecedented license to produce himself, understood that he was as much a mercurial, Todd Rundgren-esque rock boffin as a strutting funk god.

In 1984 he went for broke: a self-mythologising movie based on his own life and on the friendly competitiveness of the 'Uptown' scene he'd spawned in Minneapolis. Cheap but oddly charming for all its puerile sexism, *Purple Rain* was the pop sensation of the year, its soundtrack album shifting over 18 million copies and keeping 'When Doves Cry' at number one for six weeks. 'In some ways *Purple Rain* scared me,' Prince later confessed. 'It's my albatross and it'll be hanging around my neck as long as I'm making music.'

Twenty-two years later, Prince may have finally shaken off his purple albatross. In 2004 he was the highest-grossing live performer in America, netting a cool $56.5 million. His influence, moreover, could he heard in the music of everybody from Beck to Basement Jaxx via Alicia Keys (who had a huge hit with 'How Come You Don't Call Me Anymore?', one of Prince's great Eighties ballads).

A string of masterpieces followed *Purple Rain*: the Beatle-esque *Around the World in a Day* (1985), the funked-up *Parade* (1986) and 1987's *Sign O the Times*. Recorded at the new Paisley Park studio he had built in 1986 on the outskirts of Minneapolis, *Sign* was devilishly eclectic, travelling from the doom-saying title track—an unsettling mix of hypnotic electro rhythm, bluesy guitar and fragile, semi-rapped lyric—to the Philly rhapsody of 'Adore' via the frantic power pop of 'I Could Never Take the Place of Your Man'.

The follow-up, *Lovesexy* (1988), felt, however, like a disappointment, and with the dismal critical reception accorded the *Graffiti Bridge* movie (1990), Prince for the first time tasted failure.

He also began to regard his career differently. If the Nineties began with the big hits 'Cream' and 'Diamonds and Pearls', the next few years were dominated by his battle with Warner Brothers, the label that did so much to nurture his talent through the early stages of his career.

'The reasons that he felt the contract was unfair had little to do with money,' lawyer L. Londell McMillan would later claim in his defence. 'His interior life revolves around music, its creation and performance. But with Warners he didn't own his own creations, the masters of his recordings.'

The sight of Prince with the word 'SLAVE' daubed on his cheek will always be associated with the period in which he chose petulantly to be known as The Artist Formerly Known As Prince. Then on 7 June 1993, it was announced that Prince had changed his name to because he had been dispossessed 'in perpetuity' by his record company.

Three years later he finally severed his ties with the label, instead forming his own New Power Generation label for the purposes of releasing the triple CD *Emancipation*. Released as a celebration of Prince's marriage to dancer Mayte Garcia, the album was also intended to herald the arrival of the couple's baby boy. Tragically the child, Gregory, died in October 1996 from a rare skull disease called Pfieffer's Syndrome.

The baby's death marked the beginning of a profound change in Prince's worldview. Towards the end of the decade, with his marriage to Mayte over, he struck up a friendship with one of his musical heroes, the former bassist with Sly and the Family Stone. Larry Graham had recovered from a life of drugs and violence through being born again as a Jehovah's Witness.

'Larry goes door to door to tell people the truth about God,' Prince told me. 'That's why I told myself, I need to know a man like him. He calls me his baby brother.' By 2001 Prince had himself become a Jehovah's Witness, his new-found faith reflected in the arcane, for hardcore-fans-only album *The Rainbow Children*, which went some way to laying the ghosts of dire contract-fillers such as *Come* (1995) and *Chaos and Disorder* (1996). He had also remarried, to former Paisley Park assistant Manuela Testolini, and committed himself to a new life of monogamy.

Gone were the X-rated lyrics that had dominated so many of his songs from *Dirty Mind* to the *Black Album*. Instead the new record—released through NPG—pursued a narrative about 'the Wise One' and his struggle with 'the Banished Ones'.

'When I went back to the name Prince and released *Rainbow Children*, that was the beginning of where I am now,' he told Ebony magazine. 'But you have to do the work . . . That's what independence is. It's my catalogue, my dynasty.' Three days after the *Saturday Night Live* taping we are at a private party that Prince is hosting at his palatial Beverly Hills home to launch *3121*. To describe the singer's stately pleasure dome as Paisley Park West would be to undersell it: as LA pieds-a-terre go, this marbled movie-star crib takes some beating.

For the new record he has teamed up with Universal/Island, just as he signed a one-album deal with Columbia for 2004's *Musicology*. The onus is on the world's biggest major to prove it can keep the upward momentum of Prince's 'comeback' going. Asked about 'jumping aboard the biggest slavery ship of them all', he has insisted that 'I got a chance to structure the agreement the way I saw fit as opposed to it being the other way around.'

We are here to get a first listen to the album and then to watch His Nibs perform in the comfort of his own living room—sorry, make that ballroom. When the album comes on we're instantly launched into one of those patented Prince jams, dirty and grinding with deep funk bass and sped-up 'Camille' harmony voice. Moving through a smorgasbord of Prince turns, we jump from pop to rock to Latin to viciously pounding funk. The switch from the Latin croon of 'Te Amo Corazon' to the brutal industrial groove of 'Black Sweat' is typical.

That last song is an affirmation of black pride—a reminder that when Musician magazine's Pablo Guzman, in an overview of 'black rock' from Hendrix to Rick James, once asked him if he was competing with Devo or the Clash, Prince sneered: 'Maybe, but those guys can't *sing*.'

Unlike *Rainbow Children, 3121* seems pitched at the mainstream—some of it is Prince on autopilot, but there are moments that prove there's still fire in the guy's belly. 'Fury', its keyboard riffing redolent of '1999' or 'Let's Go Crazy', kicks like a mule. 'Satisfied' is smoochy soul with one foot in Sly's *There's a Riot Goin' On*.

With the playback concluded, its creator takes the makeshift stage with his band but stays off to one side as protégée Tamar and foxy twin sisters Mya and Mandy shake and shimmy their way through hooky originals and infectious covers. 'Support real musicians,' Prince mutters after Tamar has torn the heart out of 'When a Man Loves a Woman'. 'Ain't a loop on this stage.'

Tonight Prince confines himself to the role of sideman, occasionally sauntering out to fire off a splintering guitar solo. Halfway through the set, Prince's former drummer Sheila E arrives to add timbales to the sturdy beats supplied by the impressive Cora Coleman Dunham.

What remains awesome after all these years is Prince's command of pop history, that effortless ability to reach into a personal tote bag of songs and riffs from rock, soul, television. At one point he teases us with the intro to 'When You Were Mine'; at another he wittily picks out the theme to *The Beverly Hillbillies*. The guy's charisma is undiminished, his pocketsize physique unchanged in 28 years.

By 3:00 a.m. it's all over. The Prince who 20 years ago would have jammed until dawn thanks us for coming, sweeps out of the ballroom, and retires for the night.

As I exit Prince's LA Xanadu and head out into the balmy California night, I ask myself how much he actually cares about being a superstar again. Did he strike the Universal deal because he genuinely wants to compete with the Kanye Wests and Mariah Careys of the world, or is he actually quite content—and certainly wealthy enough—to have the kind of funky fun he had backing up Tamar tonight?

'A strong spirit transcends rules,' he told me back in 1999. 'As RZA of Wu-Tang said: "I ain't commercial, it's y'all who tell me whether I'm commercial or not".'

Chapter Fifty-Nine

LYRICS TO SOME OF PRINCE'S SONG

Album—1999
Prince
Released—1982

1999

Don't worry, I won't hurt U
I only want U 2 have some fun

I was dreamin' when I wrote this
Forgive me if it goes astray
But when I woke up this mornin'
Coulda sworn it was judgment day

The sky was all purple,
there were people runnin' everywhere
Tryin' 2 run from the destruction,
U know I didn't even care

'Cuz they say two thousand zero zero party over,
oops out of time
So tonight I'm gonna party like it's 1999

I was dreamin' when I wrote this
So sue me if I go 2 fast
But life is just a party, and parties weren't meant 2 last
War is all around us, my mind says prepare 2 fight
So if I gotta die I'm gonna listen 2 my body tonight

Yeah, they say two thousand zero zero party over,
oops out of time
So tonight I'm gonna party like it's 1999
Yeah

Lemme tell ya somethin'
If U didn't come 2 party,
don't bother knockin' on my door
I got a lion in my pocket,
and baby he's ready 2 roar
Yeah, everybody's got a bomb,
we could all die any day
But before I'll let that happen,
I'll dance my life away

Oh, they say two thousand zero zero party over,
oops out of time
We're runnin' outta time (Tonight I'm gonna)
So tonight we gonna (party like it's 1999)
we gonna, oww

Say it 1 more time
Two thousand zero zero party over oops,
out of time
No, no (Tonight I'm gonna)
So tonight we gonna (party like it's 1999)
we gonna, oww

Alright, it's 1999
You say it, 1999
1999
1999 don't stop, don't stop, say it 1 more time
Two thousand zero zero party over,
oops out of time
Yeah, yeah (Tonight I'm gonna)
So tonight we gonna (party like it's 1999)
we gonna, oww

Yeah, 1999 (1999)
Don'tcha wanna go (1999)
Don'tcha wanna go (1999)
We could all die any day (1999)
I don't wanna die,
I'd rather dance my life away (1999)
Listen 2 what I'm tryin' 2 say
Everybody, everybody say party
C'mon now, U say party
That's right, everybody say (Party)
Can't run from the revelation, no (Party)
Sing it 4 your nation y'all (Party)
Tell me what you're singin', baby say (Party)
Telephone's a-ringin', mama (Party)
C'mon, c'mon, U say (Party)
Everybody, [two times] (Party)
Work it down 2 the ground, say (Party)
(Party)
Come on, take my body, baby (Party)
That's right, c'mon, sing the song (Party)
(Party)
That's right (Party)
Got a lion in my pocket mama, say (Party)
Oh, and he's ready 2 roar (Party)

Mommy, why does everybody have a bomb?
Mommy, why does everybody have a bomb?

© 1982 Controversy Music—ASCAP

Little Red Corvette

I guess I shoulda known
By the way u parked your car sideways
That it wouldn't last

See you're the kinda person
That believes in makin' out once
Love 'em and leave 'em fast

I guess I must be dumb
'Cuz U had a pocket full of horses
Trojan and some of them used

But it was Saturday night
I guess that makes it all right
And U say what have I got 2 lose?
And honey I say

Little red corvette
Baby you're much 2 fast
Little red corvette
U need a love that's gonna last

I guess I shoulda closed my eyes
When U drove me 2 the place
Where your horses run free

'Cuz I felt a little ill
When I saw all the pictures
Of the jockeys that were there before me

Believe it or not
I started to worry
I wondered if I had enough class

But it was Saturday night
I guess that makes it all right
And U say, "Baby, have U got enough gas?"
Oh yeah

Little red corvette
Baby you're much 2 fast, yes U r
Little red corvette
U need 2 find a love that's gonna last

A body like yours (A body like yours)
Oughta be in jail (Oughta be in jail)
'Cuz it's on the verge of bein' obscene
('Cuz it's on the verge of bein' obscene)

Move over baby (Move over baby)
Gimme the keys (Gimme the keys)
I'm gonna try 2 tame your little red love machine
(I'm gonna try 2 tame your little red love machine)

Little red corvette
Baby you're much 2 fast
Little red corvette
U need 2 find a love that's gonna last

Little red corvette
Honey U got 2 slow down (Got 2 slow down)
Little red corvette
'Cuz if U don't u gonna run your
Little red corvette right in the ground

(Little red corvette)
Right down 2 the ground (Honey U got 2 slow down)
U, U, U got 2 slow down (Little red corvette)
You're movin' much 2 fast (2 fast)
U need 2 find a love that's gonna last

Girl, U got an ass like I never seen
And the ride . . .
I say the ride is so smooth
U must be a limousine

Baby you're much 2 fast
Little red corvette
U need a love, U need a love that's
That's gonna last

(Little red corvette)
U got 2 slow down (U got 2 slow down)
Little red corvette

'Cuz if U don't, 'cuz if U don't,
U gonna run your body right into the ground (Right into the ground)
Right into the ground (Right into the ground)
Right into the ground (Right into the ground)
Little red corvette

© 1982 Controversy Music—ASCAP

Delirious

I get delirious whenever you're near
Lose all self-control, baby just can't steer
Wheels get locked in place
Stupid look on my face

It comes 2 makin' a pass, pretty mama
I just can't win a race

'Cuz I get delirious (Delirious)
Delirious (Delirious)
Delirious (Delirious)

I get delirious when U hold my hand (Delirious)
Body gets so weak I can hardly stand
My temperature's runnin' hot
Baby U got 2 stop

'Cuz if U don't I'm gonna explode
And girl I got a lot

I get delirious (Delirious) {Yeah}
Delirious (Delirious)
Delirious (Delirious)

I get delirious whenever you're near (Delirious)
Girl U gotta take control 'cuz I just can't steer
You're just 2 much 2 take
I can't stop I ain't got no brakes

Girl U gotta take me 4 a little ride up and down
In and out and around your lake

I'm delirious (Delirious)
U, U, U get me delirious (Delirious)
Baby, lay me down
Delirious (Delirious)
The room, the room, the room is spinnin' around (Delirious)
Yeah, I'm delirio, yeah, oh I'm, oh I'm (Delirious)
Yeah, delirious, yeah (Delirious)
It's got me in repair, everybody u gotta (Delirious)
Everybody, oh Lord, oh yeah, I'm delirious (Delirious)
Yeah-yeah-yeah-yeah-yeah-yeah (Delirious)
(Delirious)
(Delirious)
(Delirious)
(Delirious)
(Delirious)
(Delirious)

© 1982 Controversy Music—ASCAP

Let's Pretend We're Married

Excuse me but I need a mouth like yours
2 help me forget the girl that just walked out my door
Funny but it seems that you're alone like me
If U r go let's come see what we can see

Ooh, little darlin' if you're
free 4 a couple of hours (Free 4 a couple of hours)
If U ain't busy 4 the next 7 years (Next 7 years)
Say, let's pretend we're married and go all night

JEL D. LEWIS (JONES)

There ain't nothin' wrong if it feels all right
I won't stop until the morning light
Let's pretend we're married and go all night, tonight

Ooh-we-sha-sha-coo-coo-yeah
All the hippies sing together

Excuse me but I need your chemistry
Don't U wanna be my fantasy?
My girl's gone and she don't care at all
And if she did—So what? C'mon baby, let's b-b-ball

Ooh little darlin' if you're
free 4 a couple of hours (Free 4 a couple of hours)
If U ain't busy 4 the next 7 years (Next 7 years)
Oh I say let's pretend we're married and go all night
There ain't nothin' wrong if it feels all right
I won't stop until the morning light
Let's pretend we're married and go all night, tonight

Ooh-we-sha-sha-coo-coo-yeah
All the hippies sing together

Let's just pretend we're married, tonight

Excuse me but I need a mouth like yours
2 help me forget the girl that just walked out my door
Let's pretend we're married and do it all night
I won't stop until the morning light

Let's pretend we're married and go all night
Ooh, little darlin' if you're
Free 4 a couple of hours (Free 4 a couple of hours)
If U ain't busy 4 the next 7 years (Next 7 years)
Oh darlin', let's preted we're married and go all night
There ain't nothin' wrong if it feels all right
I won' stop until the morning light

Let's pretend we're married and go all night, tonight
(Ooh-we-sha-sha-coo-coo-yeah)
Pretend we're married
Let's pretend we're married

Ooh-we-sha-sha-coo-coo-yeah
All the hippies sing together
Ooh-we-sha-sha-coo-coo-yeah
Oh everybody yeah
Ooh-we-sha-sha-coo-coo-yeah
All the hippies sing together
Ooh-we-sha-sha-coo-coo-yeah
Yeah, yeah
My girl's gone and she don't care at all
And if she did—So what? C'mon baby, let's ball

I wanna fuck U so bad it hurts, it hurts, it hurts
I wanna, I wanna, I wanna, I wanna, I wanna, I wanna, I wanna fuck U
Yeah, I wanna, I wanna, I wanna wanna, I wanna fuck U
Look here Marsha, I'm not sayin' this just 2 be nasty
I sincerely wanna fuck the taste out of your mouth
Can U relate?

My girl's gone and she don't care at all
And if she did—I wouldn't care. Let's ball

Whatever U heard about me is true
I change the rules and do what I wanna do
I'm in love with God, he's the only way
'Cuz U and I know we gotta die some day
If U think I'm crazy, you're probably right
But I'm gonna have fun every motherfuckin' night
If U like 2 fight, you're a double-drag fool
I'm goin' 2 another life, how 'bout U?

© 1982 Controversy Music—ASCAP

D.M.S.R.

Everybody, get on the floor
What the hell'd U come here 4?
Girl it ain't no use, U might as well get loose
Work your body like a whore
Say everybody—Get on the beat
We're gonna show U mothers how 2 scream
People everywhere, loosen up your hair
Take a deeper breath and sing along with me, yes
Are U ready?
Everybody everybody ooh (ooh), alright (alright), dance music sex romance
Oh, everybody say ooh (ooh), alright (alright), dance music sex romance

Everybody (everybody)—Loosen up
Shake it like U just don't care (Shake it like U just don't care)
Nevermind your friends, girl it ain't no sin
2 strip right down 2 your underwear
I say everybody (everybody)—Screw the masses
We only want 2 have some fun (Have some fun)
I say do whatever we want, wear lingerie 2 a restaurant
Police ain't got no gun, U don't have 2 run
Everybody ooh (ooh), alright (alright), dance music sex romance
Everybody say ooh (ooh), alright (alright), dance music sex romance, oh

Everybody clap your hands now

All the white people clap your hands on the four now
One two three, one two three, one two three, one two three, listen 2 me
I don't wanna be a poet
'Cuz I don't wanna blow it
I don't care 2 win awards
All I wanna do is dance
Play music sex romance
And try my best 2 never get bored
If U feel all right lemme hear U scream

Somebody say dance (dance), music (music),
sex (sex), romance (romance)

Somebody say dance (dance), music (music),
sex (sex), romance (romance)
Everybody say dance (dance), music (music),
sex (sex), romance (romance)
Everybody say dance (dance), music (music),
oh say sex (sex), romance (romance)
Everybody dance (dance), music (music),
everybody say sex (sex), romance (romance) ((D.M.S.R.))
Everybody dance (dance), music (music),
sex(sex), romance (romance) ((D.M.S.R.))
alright

Jamie Starr's a thief
It's time 2 fix your clock
Vanity 6 is so sweet
No U can all take a bite of my purple rock, can we stop?

Are U ready? (Hey!)
Everybody sing this song now, ooh (ooh), alright (alright),
dance music sex romance
Everybody sing it, ooh (ooh), alright (alright),
dance music sex romance
Negroes say ooh (ooh), alright (alright),
dance music sex romance
Puerto Ricans say it, ooh (ooh), alright (alright),
dance music sex romance
Everybody sing this song, ooh (ooh), alright (alright),
dance music sex romance
All the white people in the house say ooh (ooh), alright (alright),
dance music sex romance
Japanese say 1 time ooh (ooh), alright (alright),
dance music sex romance
Everybody sing together, say ooh (ooh), alright (alright),
dance music sex romance
Somebody call the police (Somebody call the police!)
say ooh, ooh, yeah (Help me! Someone please help me! Somebody help me)

© 1982 Controversy Music—ASCAP

Automatic

U ask me if I love U, it's automatic
'Cuz every time U leave me, I die, that's automatic 2
U ask me 2 forgive U, when U know, I'm just an addict
So stop the music baby, U know, You're all I wanna do
Hey
A-U-T-O-matic, just tell me what 2 do
A-U-T-O-matic, I'm so in love with U

U ask me if I'll kiss U, it's automatic
And if U cry, me cry, boo-hoo, that's automatic 2
I would never leave U, no matter what U do
Stop the music baby, U know, I'm an automatic fool
Hey
A-U-T-O-matic, just tell me what 2 do (And don't stop)
A-U-T-O-matic, oh, I'm so in love with U

I'll rub your back forever, it's automatic (A-U-T-O-matic)
I'll look 4 a needle in a haystack, that's automatic 2 (A-U-T-O-matic)
I'll go down on U all night long, it's automatic,
(I will, yes I will babe)
And even when I'm right, I'll be wrong, that's automatic 2 (A-U-T-O-matic)
Hey
(A-U-T-O-matic, just tell me what 2 do)
Tell me what 2 do babe
(A-U-T-O-matic, so in love with U)
Hey
So in love with U, yeah (A-U-T-O-matic, just tell me what 2 do)
Tell me what 2 do babe (A-U-T-O-matic, so in love with U)
Hey
So in love with U, baby, yeah (A-U-T-O-matic, just tell me what 2 do)
Alright, alright, tell me what 2 do baby (A-U-T-O-matic, so in love with U)
Yeah yeah yeah
Hey
A-U-T-O-matic
A-U-T-O-matic

C'mon baby
A-U-T-O-matic, tell me what to do
A-U-T-O-matic, so in love with U

Don't say no man has ever tasted your ice cream
Baby you're the purple star in the night supreme
You'll always be a virgin for no man deserves your love
I only pray that when U dream, I'm the 1 U dream of
I pray that when U dream, U dream of how we kissed
Not with our lips but with our souls
Stop me if I bore U
Why is it that I think we'd be so good in bed?
Can U hear me? Why do I love U so much?
It's strange, I'm more comfortable around U when I'm naked, can U hear me?
I wonder if U have any mercy, don't torture me

Stop the music baby, automatic fool

When it comes 2 U I'm automatic baby
There's no 1 else like me
I'm the best you'll ever find
No 1 else could understand U, you're 2 complex
They say nothing's perfect, but they don't know U
That's automatic 2
Can U hear me? (A-U-T-O-matic)
Yes, I'm addicted 2 your pleasure
I'm addicted 2 your pain
It's automatic (A-U-T-O-matic)
Automatically insane
Undress me (A-U-T-O-matic)
(A-U-T-O-matic)
Hey (A-U-T-O-matic)
(A-U-T-O-matic)
(A-U-T-O-matic)
(A-U-T-O-matic)
Hey
Fasten your seat belts
Prepare 4 takeoff

(I remember how U kissed me)
(Not with your lips but with your soul)
(With U I'm never bored, talk 2 me some more)
(I can hear U, I'm going 2 have 2 torture U now)

© 1982 Controversy Music—ASCAP

Something In the Water (Does not compute)

Some people tell me I got great legs
Can't figure out why U make me beg
Does not compute (Does not compute)
Don't not compute (Don't not compute)
U think you're special, well so do I
Why do special women make me cry?
Does not compute (Does not compute)
It don't not compute (Don't not compute)

Must be something in the water they drink
It's been the same with every girl I've had
Must be something in the water they drink
'Cuz why else would a woman wanna treat a man so bad?

Some people think I'm kinda cute
But that don't compute when it comes 2 Y-O-U
It don't compute (Don't not compute)
Somethin' mama don't compute (Don't not compute)
What's the hangup? What's the scam?
Guess U think I'm just another 1 . . . 1 of your fans
It don't compute (Don't not compute)
Somethin' honey don't compute (Don't not compute)

Must be something in the water they drink
It's been the same with every girl I've had
Must be something in the water U drink
'Cuz why else would a woman wanna treat a man so bad?

I've got 2 get 2 U, baby
Some people think I'm kinda smart
Why must a fella stop with U before he starts?
It don't compute, mama (Does not compute)
Somethin' don't compute (Don't not compute)
I'd buy U clothing, buy U fancy cars
But U gotta talk 2 me, baby, tell me who U really r

Must be something in the water they drink
It's been the same with every girl I've had
Must be something in the water U drink
Why else would a woman wanna treat a man so bad?

(Must be something in the water U drink)
(Does not compute)
(Don't not compute)
(Don't not compute)
(Must be something in the water U drink)
Bitch—U think you're special? (Must be something in the water U drink)
So do I
(second coming) (Must be something in the water U drink)
Why in God's name
do U wanna make me cry?
Why? Why? (Must be something in the water U drink)
I'd do anything 4 U, anything (Must be something in the water U drink)
Why don't U talk 2 me? (Must be something in the water U drink)
Tell me who u r (Must be something in the water U drink)
don't do this 2 me (Must be something in the water U drink)
please don't do this (Must be something in the water U drink)

Why? Why?
I do love U. I do.
Or else I wouldn't go through all the things I do

© 1982 Controversy Music—ASCAP

Free

Don't sleep 'til the sunrise, listen 2 the falling rain
Don't worry 'bout tomorrow, don't worry 'bout your pain
Don't cry unless you're happy, don't smile unless you're blue
Never let that lonely monster take control of U

Be glad that U r free
Free 2 change your mind
Free 2 go most anywhere, anytime
Be glad that U r free
There's many a man who's not
Be glad 4 what U had baby, what you've got
Be glad 4 what you've got

JEL D. LEWIS (JONES)

I know (my?) heart is beating, my drummer tells me so
If U take your life 4 granted, your beating heart will go
So don't sleep until you're guilty, 'cuz sinners all r we
There's others doing far worse than us, so be glad that U r free

Be glad that U r free
Free 2 change your mind
Free 2 go most anywhere, anytime
Be glad that U r free
There's many a man who's not
Be glad 4 what U had baby, what you've got
Be glad 4 what you've got

Soldiers are a marching, they're writing brand new laws
Will we all fight together 4 the most important cause?
Will we all fight 4 the right 2 be free?
Free (Be glad that U r free)
Free 2 change my mind (Free 2 change your mind)
Free 2 go most anywhere, anytime (Free 2 go most anywhere, anytime)
I'm just glad, I'm just glad I'm free, yeah (Be glad that U r free)
There's many a man who's not (There's many a man who's not)
Glad 4 what I had baby, (Be glad 4 what U had and)
Glad 4 what I got, oh yeah (for what you've got)
Oh I'm just glad, I'm just glad I'm free, yeah (Be glad that U r free)
Free 2 change my mind (Free 2 change your mind)
Free 2 go most anywhere, anytime (Free 2 go most anywhere, anytime)
(Be glad that U r free)
(There's many a man who's not)
I'm so . . . (Be glad 4 what U had and for)
(what you've got)

© 1982 Controversy Music—ASCAP

Lady Cab Driver

Taxi! Taxi!

Lady cab driver—Can U take me 4 a ride?
Don't know where I'm goin' 'cuz I don't know where I've been
So just put your foot on the gas—let's drive
Lady—don't ask questions
Promise I'll tell U no lies
Trouble winds r blowin', I'm growin' cold
Get me outta here—I feel I'm gonna die

Lady cab driver, roll up your window fast
Lately trouble winds r blowin' hard, and I don't know if I can last

Lady—I'm so lonely
I know that's not the way 2 be
Don't want isolation, but the air it makes me cold
Drive it, baby, drive it, drive this demon out of me
Take me 2 your mansion
Honey, let's go everywhere
Help me girl I'm drownin', mass confusion in my head
Will U accept my tears 2 pay the fare?

Lady cab driver, roll up your wndow fast
Lately trouble winds r blowin' hard, and I don't know if I can last

Lady cab driver—Can U take me 4 a ride?

Lady cab driver, roll up your window fast
Lately trouble winds r blowin' hard, and I don't know if I can last

This is 4 the cab U have 2 drive 4 no money at all
This is 4 why I wasn't born like my brother, handsome and tall
This is 4 politicians who r bored and believe in war
This—Yeah, that's 4 me, that's who that 1's 4
This is 4 discrimination and egotists who think supreme

And this is 4 whoever taught U how 2 kiss in designer jeans
That 1's 4—That 1's 4—4 U have 2 live
This 1's 4 the rich, not all of 'em, just the greedy—
The ones that don't know how 2 give
This 1's 4 Yosemite Sam and the tourists at Disneyland
And this 1—ooh! Yeah—That's the 1.
That's 4—that's 4 the—the creator of man
This is 4 the sun, the moon, the stars, the tourists at Disneyland
This is 4 the ocean, the sea, the shore
This is 4—and that's 4 U, and that's who that 1's 4
This is 4 the women, so beautifully complex
This 1's 4 love without sex
This is 4 the wind that blows no matter how fast or slow
Not knowing where I'm going
This galaxy's better than not having a place 2 go
And now I know (I know)

Lady cab driver

Lady cab driver
Lady cab driver
Lady cab driver
Lady cab driver
Lady cab driver
Lady cab driver

© 1982 Controversy Music—ASCAP

All The Critics Love You In New York

U can dance if U want 2—All the critics love U in New York
U don't have 2 keep the beat, they'll still think it's neat—in New York
U can wear what U want 2, it doesn't matter—in New York
U could cut off all your hair, I don't think they'd care—in New York

All the critics love U in New York

Why U can play what U want 2—All the critics love U in New York
They won't say that u're naive if U play what U believe—in New York
Purple love-amour is all u're headed 4—but don't show it

The reason that you're cool
is 'cuz you're from the old school, and they know it

All the critics love U in New York

U can dance if U want 2—All the critics love U in New York
U can dance if U want 2—All the critics love U in New York
All the critics love U, all the critics love U
All the critics love U in New York

It's time 4 a new direction
It's time 4 jazz 2 die
4th day of November
We need a purple high

Don't give up—I'll still love U

All the critics love U in New York
All the critics love U in New York
All the critics love U, all the critics love U
All the critics love U in New York

body don't wanna quit, gotta get another hit
body don't wanna quit, gotta get another hit
body don't wanna quit, gotta get another hit
body don't wanna quit, gotta get another hit

([fuck me over])

All the critics love U, all the critics love U
All the critics love U in New York

Whaddayou lookin' at, punk?
Look out all U hippies, U ain't as sharp as me
It ain't about the trippin', but the sexuality—turn it up

U can dance if U want 2

All the critics love U in New York

All the critics love U in New York

(Yes, we're certain of it, he's definitely masturbating)

All the critics love U in New York
Take a bath, hippies!
All the critics love U in New York
All the critics love U in New York
All the critics love U in New York
All the critics love U in New York
New York
New York
New York
New York
New York

© 1982 Controversy Music—ASCAP

International Lover

May I have this dance?

Darlin', it appears 2 me
That U could use a date tonight
A body that'll do U right
Tell me—Am I qualified?
[I say?] Baby, I know it's hard 2 believe
But this body here is free tonight
Your very own first class flight
My plane's parked right outside, baby
Don't U wanna go 4 a ride? (yeah)

I'm an international lover, yeah that's right
Let me take U 'round the world
I'll buy U diamonds and pearls
Only if you're good girl

Darlin', I know it's been a long time
Since you've been satisfied
I can tell by the look in your eyes

U need it real bad (real bad), U need it so bad, so bad (real bad)
Baby, maybe if you're good girl
I'll introduce U 2 my ride
Don't U wanna come inside?
C'mon baby, I won't fly 2 fast, I've got so—
(C'mon baby, I won't fly 2 fast, I've got so much class)

(International lover)
that's right baby
Let me take U 'round the world, yeahyeah
(I'll buy U diamonds and pearls)
I will buy U diamonds and pearls, baby
(Only if you're good girl)
Gotta be good, U gotta be good, yeah, yeah, please

Good evening. This is your pilot Prince speaking.
U r flying aboard the Seduction 747
And this plane is fully equipped with anything your body desires

If 4 any reason there is a loss in cabin pressure
I will automatically drop down 2 apply more
2 activate the flow of excitement
Extinguish all clothing materials and pull my body close 2 yours
Place my lips over your mouth, and kiss, kiss, normally
In the event there is overexcitement
Your seat cushion may be used as a flotation device

We ask that U please observe the "No Letting Go" sign
I anticipate a few turbulence along the way

We r now making our final approach 2 Satisfaction
Please bring your lips, your arms, your hips
Into the upright and locked position
4 landing—Can U feel it? Can U feel it?
Yeah

{ Let me take it around }
{ Let it all hang out }
yeah, yeah, yeah, yeah, yeah, yeah

Welcome 2 Satisfaction
Please remain awake until the aircraft has come 2 a complete stop
Thank U 4 flying Prince International
Remember, next time U fly, fly the International Lover

© 1982 Controversy Music—ASCAP

Album—Purple Rain
Prince and The Revolution
Released—1984

Let's Go Crazy

Dearly beloved
We are gathered here today
2 get through this thing called life

Electric word life
It means forever and that's a mighty long time
But I'm here 2 tell u
There's something else
The afterworld

A world of never ending happiness
U can always see the sun, day or night

So when u call up that shrink in Beverly Hills
U know the one—Dr Everything'll Be Alright
Instead of asking him how much of your time is left
Ask him how much of your mind, baby

'Cuz in this life
Things are much harder than in the afterworld
In this life
You're on your own

And if de-elevator tries 2 bring u down
Go crazy—punch a higher floor

If u don't like the world you're living in
Take a look around u
At least u got friends

U see I called my old lady
4 a friendly word
She picked up the phone
Dropped it on the floor
(Sex, sex) is all I heard

Are we gonna let de-elevator
Bring us down
Oh, no Let's Go!

Let's go crazy
Let's get nuts
Let's look 4 the purple banana
'Til they put us in the truck, let's go!

We're all excited
But we don't know why
Maybe it's cuz
We're all gonna die

And when we do (When we do)
What's it all 4 (What's it all 4)
U better live now
Before the grim reaper come knocking on your door

Tell me, are we gonna let de-elevator bring us down
Oh, no let's go!

Let's go crazy
Let's get nuts
Look 4 the purple banana
'Til they put us in the truck, let's go!

C'mon baby
Let's get nuts
Yeah
Crazy

Let's go crazy

Are we gonna let de-elevator bring us down
Oh, no let's go!
Go crazy

I said let's go crazy (Go crazy)
Let's go, let's go
Go
Let's go

Dr. Everything'll be alright
Will make everything go wrong
Pills and thrills and dafodills will kill
Hang tough children
He's coming
He's coming
Coming

Take me away!

© 1984 Controversy Music—ASCAP

Take Me With You

I can't disguise the pounding of my heart
It beats so strong
It's in your eyes what can I say
They turn me on

I don't care where we go
I don't care what we do
I don't care pretty baby
Just take me with u

Come on and touch the place in me
That's calling out your name
We want each other oh so much
Why must we play this game?

Don't care where we go
I don't care what we do
I don't care pretty baby
Just take me with u

I don't care if we spend the night at your mansion
I don't care if we spend the night on the town
All I want is 2 spend the night together
All I want is 2 spend the night in your arms

To be around u is so-oh right
You're sheer perfection (thank u)
Drive me crazy, drive me all night
Just don't break up the connection

I don't care where we go
I don't care what we do
I don't care pretty baby
Just take me with u

I don't care where we go
I don't care what we do
I don't care pretty baby
Just take me with u

Just take me with u
Oh won't u take me with u
Honey take me with u

© 1984 Controversy Music—ASCAP

The Beautiful Ones

Baby, baby, baby
What's it gonna be
Baby, baby, baby
Is it him or is it me?
Don't make me waste my time
Don't make me lose my mind baby

Baby, baby, baby
Can't u stay with me tonight
Oh baby, baby, baby
Don't my kisses please u right
U were so hard 2 find
The beautiful ones, they hurt u everytime

Paint a perfect picture
Bring 2 life a vision in one's mind
The beautiful ones
Always smash the picture
Always everytime

If I told u baby
That I was in love with u
Oh baby, baby, baby
If we got married
Would that be cool?

U make me so confused
The beautiful ones
U always seem 2 lose

Baby, baby,
Baby, baby,
Baby, baby,
Baby,
What's it gonna be baby?

Do u want him?
Or do u want me?
Cause I want u
Said I want u
Tell me, babe
Do u want me?
I gotta know, I gotta know
Do u want me?
Baby, baby, baby
Listen 2 me
I may not know where I'm going (babe)
I said I may not know what I need

One thing, one thing's 4 certain baby
I know what I want, yeah
and if it please u baby
please u, baby
I'm begging down on my knees
I want u
Yes I do
Baby, baby, baby, baby
I want you

Yes I do

© 1984 Controversy Music—ASCAP

Computer Blue

Wendy?
Yes Lisa
Is the water warm enough?
Yes Lisa
Shall we begin?
Yes Lisa

Where is my love life?
Where can it be?
There must be something wrong with the machinery

Where is my love life?
Tell me, tell me
Where has it gone?
Somebody please please tell me what the hell is wrong

Until I find the righteous 1
Computer blue
Until I find the righteous 1
Computer blue

© 1984 Controversy Music—ASCAP

Darling Nikki

I knew a girl named Nikki
I guess u could say she was a sex fiend
I met her in a hotel lobby
Masturbating with a magazine
She said how'd u like 2 waste some time
And I could not resist when I saw little Nikki grind

She took me 2 her castle
And I just couldn't believe my eyes
She had so many devices
Everything that money could buy
She said sign your name on the dotted line
The lights went out
And Nikki started 2 grind

Nikki

The castle started spinning
Or maybe it was my brain
I can't tell u what she did 2 me
But my body will never be the same

© 1984 Controversy Music—ASCAP

When Doves Cry

Dig if u will the picture
Of u and I engaged in a kiss
The sweat of your body covers me
Can u my darling
Can u picture this?

Dream if u can a courtyard
An ocean of violets in bloom
Animals strike curious poses
They feel the heat
The heat between me and u

How can u just leave me standing?
Alone in a world that's so cold? (So cold)
Maybe I'm just 2 demanding
Maybe I'm just like my father 2 bold
Maybe you're just like my mother
She's never satisfied (She's never satisfied)
Why do we scream at each other
This is what it sounds like
When doves cry

Touch if u will my stomach
Feel how it trembles inside
You've got the butterflies all tied up
Don't make me chase u
Even doves have pride

How can u just leave me standing?
Alone in a world so cold? (World so cold)
Maybe I'm just 2 demanding
Maybe I'm just like my father 2 bold
Maybe you're just like my mother
She's never satisfied (She's never satisfied)
Why do we scream at each other
This is what it sounds like
When doves cry

How can u just leave me standing?
Alone in a world that's so cold? (A world that's so cold)
Maybe I'm just 2 demanding (Maybe, maybe I'm like my father)
Maybe I'm just like my father 2 bold (Ya know he's 2 bold)
Maybe you're just like my mother (Maybe you're just like my mother)
She's never satisfied (She's never, never satisfied)
Why do we scream at each other (Why do we scream, why)
This is what it sounds like

When doves cry
When doves cry (Doves cry, doves cry)
When doves cry (Doves cry, doves cry)

Don't Cry (Don't Cry)

When doves cry
When doves cry
When doves cry

When Doves cry (Doves cry, doves cry, doves cry
Don't cry
Darling don't cry
Don't cry
Don't cry
Don't don't cry

© 1984 Controversy Music—ASCAP

I Would Die 4 U

I'm not a woman
I'm not a man
I am something that you'll never understand

I'll never beat u
I'll never lie
And if you're evil I'll forgive u by and by

U—I would die 4 u, yeah
Darling if u want me 2
U—I would die 4 u

I'm not your lover
I'm not your friend
I am something that you'll never comprehend

No need 2 worry
No need 2 cry
I'm your messiah and you're the reason why

'Cuz U—I would die 4 u, yeah
Darling if u want me 2
U—I would die 4 u

You're just a sinner I am told
Be your fire when you're cold
Make u happy when you're sad
Make u good when u are bad

I'm not a human
I am a dove
I'm your conscious
I am love
All I really need is 2 know that
U believe

Yeah, I would die 4 u, yeah
Darling if u want me 2
U—I would die 4 u

Yeah, say one more time

U—I would die 4 u
Darling if u want me 2
U—I would die 4 u
2 3 4 U

I would die 4 u
I would die 4 u
U—I would die 4 u
U—I would die 4 u

Baby I'm A Star

Hey, look me over
Tell me do u like what u see?
Hey, I ain't got no money
But honey I'm rich on personality
Hey, check it all out
Baby I know what it's all about
Before the night is through
U will see my point of view
Even if I have 2 scream and shout

Baby I'm a (star)
Might not know it now
Baby but I r, I'm a (star)
I don't want to stop, 'til I reach the top
Sing it (We are all a star!)

Hey, take a listen
Tell me do u like what u hear?
If it don't turn u on
Just say the word and I'm gone
But honey I know, ain't nothing
Wrong with your ears
Hey, check it all out
Better look now or it just might be 2 late (just might be 2 late)
My lucks gonna change tonight
There's gotta be a better life
Take a picture sweetie
I ain't got time 2 waste

Oh baby I'm a (star)
Might not know it now
Baby but I r, I'm a (star)
I don't want to stop, 'til I reach the top
Sing it! (We are all a star!)

Everybody say, nothing come 2 easy
But when u got it baby, nothing come 2 hard
You'll see what I'm all about (see what I'm all about)
If I gotta scream and shout (if I gotta scream and shout)
Baby baby (baby) baby (baby) baby (baby)
yeah
yeah yeah yeah yeah yeah (star)

Might not know it now
Baby but I r, I'm a (star)
I don't want to stop, 'til I reach the top
Sing it! (star)

Baby baby baby
oh baby I'm a (star)
baby baby baby
somebody
(We are all a star)

(Baby I'm a star)
We are all a star

We are all a star

Doctor!
Baby, baby, baby, baby,
baby, baby, baby, baby
We are all a star

{Backwards talking in the background}
"Like what the fuck do they know.
All their taste is in their mouth.
Really. What the fuck do they know?
Come on baby. Let's go . . . crazy"

© 1984 Controversy Music—ASCAP

Purple Rain

I never meant 2 cause u any sorrow
I never meant 2 cause u any pain
I only wanted 2 one time see u laughing
I only wanted 2 see u laughing in the purple rain

Purple rain Purple rain
Purple rain Purple rain
Purple rain Purple rain

JEL D. LEWIS (JONES)

I only wanted 2 see u bathing in the purple rain

I never wanted 2 be your weekend lover
I only wanted 2 be some kind of friend
Baby I could never steal u from another
It's such a shame our friendship had 2 end

Purple rain Purple rain
Purple rain Purple rain
Purple rain Purple rain

I only wanted 2 see u underneath the purple rain

Honey I know, I know, I know times are changing
It's time we all reach out 4 something new
That means u 2
U say u want a leader
But u can't seem 2 make up your mind
I think u better close it
And let me guide u 2 the purple rain

Purple rain Purple rain
Purple rain Purple rain

If you know what I'm singing about up here
C'mon raise your hand

Purple rain Purple rain

I only want 2 see u, only want 2 see u
In the purple rain

© 1984 Controversy Music—ASCAP

Album—Around The World In A Day
Prince and The Revolution
Released—1985

Around The World In A Day

Open your heart, open your mind
A train is leaving all day
A wonderful trip through our time
And laughter is all U pay

Around the world in a day
Around the world in a day

Now dig
Loneliness already knows U
There ain't no reason 2 stay
Come here and take my hand, I'll show U
I think I know a better way, y'all

Around the world in a day
(listen 2 me, babe)
Around the world in a day
(all the babies sing it now)

ooh-la-la
ooh-la-la-la-la-la-la
no-sha-sha
no shouting
no shouting
no—no shouting

The little 1 will escort U
2 places within your mind
The former is red, white, and blue
The ladder is purple, come on and climb

Around the world in a day
Around the world in a day
come on, sing
Around the world in a day
Say papa, I think I wanna dance

(summer she is sweet)

Around the world in a day
Around the world in a day
all the little babies, sing around the world
Around the world in a day

A government of love and music boundless in its unifying power
a nation of alms, the production, sharing ideas, a shower of flowers

© 1985 Controversy Music—ASCAP

Paisley Park

There is a park that is known
4 the face it attracts
colorful people whose hair
On 1 side is swept back
The smile on their faces
It speaks of profound inner peace
Ask where they're going
They'll tell U nowhere
They've taken a lifetime lease
On Paisley Park

chorus:
The girl on the seesaw is laughing
4 love is the color
This place imparts (Paisley Park)
Admission is easy, just say U
Believe and come 2 this
Place in your heart
Paisley Park is in your heart

There is a woman who sits
All alone by the pier
Her husband was naughty
And caused his wife so many tears
He died without knowing forgiveness
And now she is sad, so sad
Maybe she'll come 2 the park
And forgive him
And life won't be so bad
In Paisley Park

chorus
See the man cry as the city
Condemns where he lives
Memories die but taxes
He'll still have 2 give
(who) Whoever said that elephants
were stronger than mules?
Come 2 the park
And play with us
There aren't any rules
In Paisley Park

chorus repeated 2 times

your heart, your heart
Paisley Park
your heart, your heart, your heart (sing, sing it)
Paisley Park
Paisley Park
Paisley Park

© 1985 Controversy Music—ASCAP

JEL D. LEWIS (JONES)

Condition Of The Heart

There was a girl in Paris
Whom he sent a letter 2
Hoping she would answer back
Now wasn't that a fool
Hardy notion on the part of a
Sometimes lonely musician
Acting out a whim is only good
4 a condition of the heart

There was a dame from London
Who insisted that he love her
Then left him 4 a real prince
From Arabia, now isn't that
A shame that sometimes money
Buys U everything and nothing
Love, it only seems 2 buy a
Terminal condition of the heart

Thinking about U driving me crazy
My friends all say it's just a phase, but ooh-ooh
Every day is a yellow day
I'm blinded by the daisies in your yard

There was a woman from the ghetto
Who made funny faces just like
Clara Bow, how was I 2 know
That she would wear the same
Cologne as U and giggle the same
Giggle that U do?
Whenever I would act a fool, the fool
With a condition of the heart

Thinking about U driving me crazy
My friends all say it's just a phase, but ooh-ooh
Every single day is a yellow day
I'm blinded by the daisies in your yard

There was a girl (There was a girl in Paris)
whom he sent a letter to . . . (Whom he sent a letter 2)
(Hoping she would answer back)
She never answered back and now (wasn't that a foolhardy)
He's got a condition of the heart. (notion . . .)

© 1985 Controversy Music—ASCAP

Raspberry Beret

Yeah

I was working part time in a five-and-dime
My boss was Mr. McGee
He told me several times that he didn't like my kind
'Cause I was a bit 2 leisurely

Seems that I was busy doing something close 2 nothing
But different than the day before
That's when I saw her, Ooh, I saw her
She walked in through the out door, out door

She wore a
Raspberry beret
The kind U find in a second hand store
Raspberry beret
And if it was warm she wouldn't wear much more
Raspberry beret
I think I love her

Built like she was
She had the nerve 2 ask me
If I planned 2 do her any harm

So, look here
I put her on the back of my bike
And-a we went riding
Down by old man Johnson's farm

JEL D. LEWIS (JONES)

I said now, overcast days never turned me on
But something about the clouds and her mixed

She wasn't 2 bright
But I could tell when she kissed me
She knew how 2 get her kicks

She wore a
Raspberry beret
The kind U find in a second hand store
Raspberry beret
And if it was warm she wouldn't wear much more
Raspberry beret
I think I love her

The rain sounds so cool when it hits the barn roof
And the horses wonder who U are
Thunder drowns out what the lightning sees
U feel like a movie star

Listen
They say the first time ain't the greatest
But I tell ya
If I had the chance 2 do it all again

I wouldn't change a stroke
'Cause baby I'm the most
With a girl as fine as she was then

(Raspberry beret)
The kind U find (The kind U find)
The kind U find (In a second hand store)
Oh no no
(Raspberry beret)
(And if it was warm)
Where have all the raspberry women gone? (She wouldn't wear much more)
Yeah (Raspberry beret)

I think I . . . I think I . . . I think I love her

(Raspberry beret)
No No No
No No No (The kind U find)
(In a second hand store)
(Raspberry beret)
Tell me
Where have all the raspberry women gone? (And if it was warm she)
(Wouldn't wear much more)
(Raspberry beret)
I think I love . . .

© 1985 Controversy Music—ASCAP

Tamborine

Oh my God here U are
Prettiest thing in life I've ever seen
Close my eyes what's it like,
What's it like inside your tamborine?

Oh my God, there I go
Falling in love with the face in a magazine (uh oh, not again)
All alone by myself
Me and I play my tamborine

Tamborine
Tamborine
Tamborine
Tamborine
Long days, lonely nights
Tamborine
Long days, lonely nights
Tamborine

I don't care 4 1 night stands
With trolley cars
That juggle 17

I just want 2 settle down and
Play around
My baby's tamborine

Tamborine what are U
Why are U the star of
All my dreams
(Star of all my dreams, are U a good tamborine)
Are U good, are U bad
Are U just unnecessary means

Tamborine
Tamborine
Tamborine
Trolley cars

Long days, lonely nights
2 bad we're not allowed 2 scream (yeah, yeah, too bad)
Guess that I'll stay at home
All alone and play my tamborine (aww)

Tamborine
Tamborine
Tamborine
Tamborine
The tamborine

© 1985 Controversy Music—ASCAP

America

Yeah
Peace!

Aristocrats on a mountain climb
Making money, losing time
Communism is just a word
But if the government turn over
It'll be the only word that's heard

America, America
God shed his grace on thee
America, America
Keep the children free

Little sister making minimum wage
Living in a 1-room jungle-monkey cage
Can't get over, she's almost dead
She may not be in the black
But she's happy she ain't in the red

America, America
God shed his grace on thee
America, America
Keep the children free

Freedom
Love
Joy
Peace

Jimmy Nothing never went 2 school
They made him pledge allegiance
He said it wasn't cool
Nothing made Jimmy proud
Now Jimmy lives on a mushroom cloud

America, America
God shed his grace on thee
America, America
Keep the children free

America, America
God shed his grace on thee
America, America
Keep the children free

Freedom
Love
Joy
Peace

boom, boom, boom, boom
the bomb go
boom, boom, boom, boom
the bomb go boom.
Teacher, why won't Jimmy pledge allegiance?

© 1985 Controversy Music—ASCAP

Pop Life

What's the matter with your life
Is the poverty bringing U down?
Is the mailman jerking U 'round?
Did he put your million dollar check
In someone else's box?

Tell me, what's the matter with your world
Was it a boy when U wanted a girl? (Boy when u wanted a girl)
Don't U know straight hair ain't got no curl (No curl)
Life it ain't real funky
Unless it's got that pop
Dig it

Pop life
Everybody needs a thrill
Pop life
We all got a space 2 fill
Pop life
Everybody can't be on top
But life it ain't real funky
Unless it's got that pop
Dig it

Tell me, what's that underneath your hair?
Is there anybody living there? (Anybody living there)
U can't get over, if U say U just don't care (Don't care)
Show me a boy who stays in school
And I'll show U a boy aware!
Dig it

Pop life
Everybody needs a thrill
Pop life
We all got a space 2 fill
Pop life
Everybody can't be on top
But life it ain't real funky
Unless it's got that pop
Dig it

What U putting in your nose?
Is that where all your money goes (Is that where your money goes)
The river of addiction flows
U think it's hot, but there won't be no water
When the fire blows
Dig it

Pop life
Everybody needs a thrill
Pop life
We all got a space 2 fill
Pop life
Everybody wants to be on top
But life it ain't real funky
Unless it's got that pop
Dig it

Pop life
Everybody needs a thrill
Pop life
We all got a space 2 fill
Pop life
Everybody can't be on top
But life it ain't real funky
Unless it's got that pop
Dig it

© 1985 Controversy Music—ASCAP

JEL D. LEWIS (JONES)

The Ladder

Once upon a time in the land of Sinaplenty
There lived a king who didn't deserve 2 be
He knew not where he came from
Nor where he was going
He never once said thank U, never please

Now this king he had a subject named Electra
Who loved him with a passion, uncontested
4 him each day she had a smile
But it didn't matter
The king was looking 4 the ladder

Everybody's looking 4 the ladder
Everybody wants salvation of the soul
The steps U take are no easy road
But the reward is great
4 those who want 2 go

A feeling of self-worth (everybody's looking)
will caress U (for the answers)
The size of the whole wide world will decrease (how the story started)
(and how it will end)
The love of God's creation will undress U
And time spent alone my friend, will cease

Everybody's looking 4 the answers
How the story started and how it will end
What's the use in half a story, half a dream
U have 2 climb all of the steps in between (yeah, we ride)

Everybody's looking 4 the ladder
Everybody wants salvation of the soul
The steps U take are no easy road (the steps you take are no easy road)
(it's not that easy)
But the reward is great
4 those who want 2 go (I do)

everybody . . . everybody's looking (Everybody's looking 4 the answers)
for the answers
everybody wants to know how the story (How the story started)

started and how it will end (started and how it will end)
What's the use in half a story, (What's the use in half a story)
half a dream (half of a dream)
U, U gotta climb, U gotta climb (U have 2 climb all)
all of the steps in between (the steps in between)

everybody,
Everybody's looking 4 that ladder (Everybody's looking 4 the ladder)
Everybody wants salvation of the soul (Everybody wants salvation of the soul)
(salvation)
The steps U take are no easy road (the steps you take are no easy road)
(that's for sure)
But the reward is great (the reward is great)
4 those who want 2 go, (4 those who want 2 go)
those who want 2 go

everybody . . . everybody wants (Everybody's looking 4 the answers)
an answer
anyone who know how the story (How the story started)
started, how it will end (started and how it will end)
will it be lonely in the world (What's the use in half a story)
What's the use? (half of a dream)
(have 2 climb all)
(the steps in between)

© 1985 Controversy Music—ASCAP

Temptation

Sex
Temptation
Lust
Pop go mama

Everybody on this earth has got a vice
And mine, little darlin', mine is the opposite of ice
Mine is the running hot water of the daughter of morality
In other words, this little prince thinks a lot about U, see?
Baby, baby, baby
I'm guilty in the first degree

Temptation
Working my body with a hot flash of animal lust
Temptation
All my fingers in the pool go splash we must

Everybody in this room
Everybody in this room has got an urge
What's yours, baby?
Mine is temptation, it reigns at a party where lovers splurge
Pop go mama when daddy gets a little 2 much
You know what I'm talkin' 'bout?
Purplelectricity whenever our bodies touch
Ooh baby, I love it when our bodies touch

Temptation
Working my body with a hot flash of animal lust
Temptation
All my fingers in the pool go splash we must

Temptation, temptation, temptation

Wait a minute now

Temptation
Working my body with a hot flash of animal lust
Temptation
All my fingers in the pool go splash we must

Temptation
Working my body, working my body, working my body

Temptation
I'm not talkin' about just ordinary temptation, people. I'm talking about the kind of temptation that'll make U do things.
Oh, oh, temptation.
Oh, darling, I can almost taste the wetness between your . . .
temptation, temptation
I'm not talking about any ol' kind of temptation, people, I'm talkin' about, I'm talkin' about . . . sexual temptation.

A lover
I need a lover, a lover, I need a . . . right now.
U, I want U.
I want U in the worst way.
I want U.

"Oh, silly man, that's not how it works.
You have 2 want her 4 the right reasons."

I do!

"U don't, now die!"

No! No!

Let me go, let me go.

I'm sorry.
I'll be good.
This time I promise,
Love is more important than sex.
Now I understand.
I have 2 go now.
I don't know when I'll return.
Good-bye

© 1985 Controversy Music—ASCAP

Author's Note: Through out the book if the symbol 0{+> appears, it means Prince. I have attempted to change all those symbols to read Prince for simple clarification for the readers to realize when Prince is talking or being referred to. Prince changed his name in the early 90's to a symbol, but dropped the symbol in 2000. He is simply Prince once again.

Source: princetext.tripod.com

Source: Wikipedia, the free encyclopedia

Source: users.pandora.be/mapinguari/artist/albums.htm

Source: TV.com